Praise for
Beethoven: The String Quartets

'Authoritative ... [brings] the music vividly to life with colourful scenarios and often amusing turns of phrase ... a thoroughly accessible, enlightening and entertaining guide to these pinnacles of the repertoire ... insights that will enhance readers' understanding and enjoyment when listening to, or participating in, their performance.'

– *The Strad*

'Wonderful ... driven by deep love and an infectious sense of wonder ... a different kind of Beethoven book.'

– *Strings*

'[An] extraordinary and exciting book.'

– John Simpson, BBC News

'Love for this music shines through on every page – if you or someone you know is a Beethoven fan, this is the book for them.'

– Dr Leah Broad, author of *Quartet: How Four Women Changed the Musical World*

'This is a lively, intelligent and, above all, *fun* introduction to some of the greatest music ever written, and I very much hope it lures readers into listening to that music who might otherwise have been deterred by its monumental reputation.'

– MusicWeb International

'[A] fantastic book ... easy to read and follow, yet deep enough for experienced music lovers. ... Each quartet receives its own chapter, and each starts with a short journey in time to reveal the historical and cultural background of the piece. The music itself is analysed movement by movement, but these are not technical descriptions with musical jargon. Like a guide, rather, these are insightful narrations, often very funny and always properly connecting to the music.'

– *Popular Beethoven*

Praise for
Beauty and Sadness: Mahler's 11 Symphonies

'A beautiful and important book.'

– Marina Mahler

'Highly recommended.'

– Société Gustav Mahler France

'A book that sends you back to listen again to music you thought you knew, with fresh insight and understanding.'

– Tim Ashley

'Masterfully paced, just the right balance of continuous narrative and individual essays, all framed in beautiful writing. Can't recommend it highly enough!'

– Brian McCreath, WCRB Classical Radio Boston

'One does not expect a book on music to be this philosophically erudite. [The] use of language is masterful. ... It's an enormous achievement. An essential book.'

– Jeffrey A. Tucker

'An important contribution to the Mahler bibliography. ... A perceptive, insightful and thought-provoking book. Mahler devotees will find much in its pages to enhance their understanding of these ever-fascinating works ... Vernon has a deep knowledge of the symphonies – and a great enthusiasm for them. ... He can bring the music to life through vivid and enthusiastic turns of phrase.'

– MusicWeb International

Praise for
Disturbing the Universe: Wagner's Musikdrama

'David Vernon's new book is a rattling good read ... vivid, colourful ... and knowledgeably argued. ... This is a valuable addition to any Wagnerian's library. Highly recommended.'

– Paul Carey Jones

'A great and necessary addition to the Wagner literature. Clever and clear without being intellectually boring.'

– Matthew Rose

'A sensational tome. A perfect introduction to Wagner's complex world, but also completely engaging for the lifelong Wagner nut.'

– Kenneth Woods

'Engaging, wry and topical.'

– *The Wagner Journal*

BY THE SAME AUTHOR

Disturbing the Universe: Wagner's Musikdrama
Beauty and Sadness: Mahler's 11 Symphonies
Beethoven: The String Quartets
Ada to Zembla: The Novels of Vladimir Nabokov

SUN FOREST LAKE

The Symphonies & Tone Poems of Jean Sibelius

DAVID VERNON

Sun Forest Lake: The Symphonies & Tone Poems of Jean Sibelius
copyright © 2024 David Vernon

The moral rights of the author have been asserted

All rights reserved. No part of this publication may be reproduced, distributed, or transmitted in any form or by any means, including photocopying, recording, or other electronic or mechanical methods, without the prior written permission of the publisher, except in the case of brief quotations embodied in critical reviews and certain other non-commercial uses permitted by copyright law.

First edition November 2024

Interior layout: miblart.com

Cover art: *Pine Tree*, 1919, Joseph Stella
(Smithsonian American Art Museum, bequest of Caroline Keck)

ISBN:
978-1-7396599-4-3 (paperback)
978-1-7396599-5-0 (ebook)

Published by Candle Row Press
Edinburgh, Scotland

To

Stephen Johnson

– friend, guide, and a great Sibelian

*Hvad er en Digter? Et ulykkeligt Menneske, der gjemmer dybe
Qvaler i sit Hjerte, men hvis Læber ere dannede saaledes,
at idet Sukket og Skriget strømme ud over dem,
lyde de som en skjøn Musik.*

Søren Kierkegaard, *Either/Or*

Contents

Acknowledgements	15
Foreword by Sakari Oramo	19
Introduction: Wild-Eyed Prince and Granite Titan	21

PART ONE: EXPECTATION

1. Symphony Zero: *Kullervo*	43
2. Invisible Blood: *En Saga, Spring Song & The Wood Nymph*	89
3. Building Boats: *Lemminkäinen*	119
4. Russian Borders: *The First Symphony & Finlandia*	137
5. A Confession of the Soul: *The Second Symphony*	165

PART TWO: AMPLIFICATION

6. Progeny of the North: *Pohjola's Daughter,* *Nightride and Sunrise & The Dryad*	189

7. Pale Fire: *The Third Symphony*	215
8. Landscape/Mind: *The Fourth Symphony*	235
9. Metamorphosis: *The Bard, Luonnotar & The Oceanides*	277
10. The Noontide Sun: *The Fifth Symphony*	301

PART THREE: TRANSFIGURATION

11. Snow Country: *The Sixth Symphony*	335
12. Illuminated by Stars: *The Seventh Symphony*	355
13. A Swarm of Symphonies: *The Tempest*	381
14. Weaving Magic Secrets: *Tapiola*	415
15. Phantom and Oblivion: *The Eighth Symphony*	437

APPENDICES

Further Reading: Books on Sibelius	461
Further Listening 1: Sibelius on Record	467
Further Listening 2: Beyond Sibelius	483
About the Author	505

Acknowledgements

First of all, I would like to thank Sakari Oramo for his charming foreword to this book. Sakari has long been one of the most important and distinguished of all Sibelius conductors, his love for and knowledge of his countryman's scores boundless, and it is both a delight and an honour to have him associated with my work.

Thank you to the staff and custodians of Ainola, Jean and Aino Sibelius's home by Lake Tuusula in Järvenpää, which is now a magnificent museum dedicated to promoting the composer's life, works and legacy. Thank you, too, to the employees of the British Embassy in Helsinki, the Embassy of Finland in London and the Honorary Consulate of Finland in Edinburgh.

Providing kind words and her immaculate voice, my dear friend, the great – the legendary – Finnish soprano Karita Mattila has been a generous encouragement and constant inspiration during this often arduous project. Thank you, too, to my Finnish friends Tomi Andersson and Riku-Matti Kinnunen for your assistance in matters relating to the complex wonder that is the Finnish language, for your unflagging support, and for our shared love of many forms of music.

Thank you to Leah Broad – for inspiration, coffee and numerous details relating to the work of the mighty Finn we both admire so much.

Thank you to Steve Lally, Tim Ashley, James Taylor, Zhang Wei, David Ward, Harry Paterson, Aki Nishikawa, Herb Randall, Peter Kristiansen, Matthew Rose, Anke Staffeldt and Lucy Coatman for your knowledge, friendship and reassurance at all times.

My brilliant editor, Elyse Lyon, has provided her customary combination of perception, subtlety, dexterity and discernment, once again facing the onerous task of overseeing one of my manuscripts with tireless patience and sensitivity, seeing what I cannot and always knowing what I am trying to say. Any errors are, of course, my own.

My wife continues to give the best support any partner, any writer, could wish for. Thank you, darling, for your love, guidance, forbearance and serenity during the mad days of writing and revising this book. My life could not be lived without you.

Finally I would like to thank this book's dedicatee, the writer and broadcaster Stephen Johnson (as well as Kate and Teddy!). Through his astute and exciting writing on music, through his delightful, perceptive episodes of *Discovering Music* and *Building a Library* on BBC Radio 3, Stephen has long been an inspiration for me, showing me new ways to listen, to think and to write. I can't match Stephen's insight and intelligence, but I can aspire to attain his enthusiasm, which I hope has rubbed off in my own work. Thank you, Stephen, for your boundless joy in music, literature, nature and philosophy, for our friendship, and for everything you've taught me across the years – over the airwaves, in print, and in person.

*Nature and Art seem to shun one another,
but before one realizes it, they have found each other
again.*

Goethe

*I am wanting, I am thinking,
To arise and go forth singing.*

The Kalevala, opening words

Foreword by Sakari Oramo

We all know the picture: a bald man of imposing stature, with a twinkle in his eyes but somewhat solemn, immaculately dressed, roaming nature with his walking stick. Thinking blue and white thoughts, listening to the swans and cranes. Symbolizing his nation's cultural identity and strength of character.

The extraordinary position that Johan Julius Christian Sibelius, born in Hämeenlinna in 1865, ended up occupying in the hearts and minds of his countrymen and the whole musical world was shaped by the tumults of time and the awakening of the idea of nation states. Yet his story is also one of assimilation to the greater idea of a wider European culture, the symphonic tradition pioneered by Haydn and Mozart, perfected by Beethoven, subsequently developed by Brahms, Bruckner, Dvořák and countless others, whereby the composer moulds his material, wrestles with it like a titan, and brings it under control as a sort of demigod of time and space.

Considering his unusual longevity, the time span of Sibelius's active composing years at the top of his capabilities was remarkably short. Only twenty-five years from the First Symphony to *Tapiola* and *The Tempest*, with another seven added backwards, looking back to the days of *Kullervo*. Why did the Master of Ainola fall silent? We will probably never know for certain. Maybe the answer is: everything that needed to be said had been said.

In Sibelius's works, raw and unabridged depictions of ancient battles and suicidal behaviour after unadulterated sexual lust coexist with deepest introspection and a sense of cosmic unity. Professionals performing, researching and presenting music often fail to touch the essence of their subject, which must be the emotional, physical and intellectual impact the art form has. Sibelius's music is certainly widely appreciated and loved; however, its multifaceted expressivity easily evades even a keen listener.

David Vernon's book helps everyone, no matter how previously informed, to find their own way into Sibelius's extraordinary world.

Sakari Oramo is chief conductor of the BBC Symphony Orchestra in London and professor of conducting and orchestral studies at the Sibelius Academy in Helsinki. His previous posts include concertmaster of the Finnish Radio Symphony Orchestra and music director of the City of Birmingham Symphony Orchestra, in the latter role conducting a critically acclaimed cycle of Sibelius's symphonies and tone poems. Other recent engagements include the Berlin Philharmonic, Staatskapelle Dresden, Tokyo Symphony and New York Philharmonic.

Introduction

Wild-Eyed Prince and Granite Titan

'These old gentlemen with their "concepts" … The name "symphony" can be expanded in its meaning. It has always been that way. An example of infinity.'

Jean Sibelius, diary, 5 February 1918

At 60° 27′ N, 25° 06′ E, the traveller, leaving the railway platform at which she has just arrived, crosses a bridge above a hyper-modern highway and joins a slim road. Already the boisterous noise and bustle of the traffic vanish, turned to a hypnotic hum. The air, too, seems crisper, fresher, cleaner, more radiant. The colours are sharper: the sky bluer, the clouds whiter, the trees greener. After meandering for half a mile, and as the shrubs and conifers increase in number on either side, the traveller turns a corner and sees before her a building.

It is substantial but not excessive, striking but not imposing, humble without being frugal. It is slightly obscured by pine trees and made of white-painted wood, with a coral red tiled roof from which assorted chimneys – some slim and slender, others broad and stout – rise up like vigilant, protective sentinels (or termite hills). The sloping shapes of the roof, irregular triangles and a lopsided trapezium, prevail above neatly gridded white windows. It is an unusual but elegant structure: Romantic but modern; distinctive but approachable; homely and yet full of strength and power. It is a symphony of wood among the pines.

Entering the house via some short steps up to the porch, the traveller comes into a dwelling with plain timber walls and bare board floors. There is an unpretentious, even inviting, drawing room, with antique furniture and comfortable sofas; a Steinway grand surrounded by busts, portraits and pictures. Next a small library, with books, photographs, gramophone records and a big boxed radiogram. In the dining room, more canvases (a funeral cortège; a flock of swans) line the staircase while a window seat looks out onto a well-tended garden. The modest collection of tables and chairs is dwarfed by a great green fireplace, which – according to its owner's synaesthesia – sings out in F major.

At some point in the mid-1940s, probably between January 1944 and August 1945, on a stove above this enormous emerald hearth, a 'grand burning party' of dozens of musical manuscripts took place. As the flames consumed the sheets, which included an unfinished symphony, their composer looked on. It was almost an auto-da-fé, a tribunal and sentencing, as well as a ritual of penance, purgation and catharsis.

The house is Ainola. The symphony was to have been number eight. The composer is Jean Sibelius.

Born the year Wagner's *Tristan und Isolde* received its premiere, dying a few weeks before Elvis Presley's 'Jailhouse Rock' reached the top of the *Billboard* charts, Jean Sibelius (1865–1957) had a long and eventful life. A national icon who became a global figure, he not only helped put Finland on the map – culturally and politically – but also facilitated the wider development of a characteristically Nordic modernism, blending function with form, sensibility with style.

In his music, Sibelius influenced not just generations of composers – especially in his native Finland and throughout Scandinavia, as well as across the North Sea, in Britain – but creators in a wealth of other disciplines besides.[1] The work of architects, designers, poets, politicians, ecologists and conservationists has been profoundly shaped by his structures, his techniques, his meanings and his messages. To study Sibelius today is not only the exclusive domain of musicologists and cultural historians but embraces a variety of challenging, intersecting fields which enrich and enhance our interpretation of his art.[2]

He was a man not exactly of contradiction but certainly of complexity and, perhaps, enigma. As for Beethoven, Wagner and Mahler before him, the countryside, and often even wilder landscapes, mattered to Sibelius. He enjoyed, *needed*, the beauty and isolation of forests, lakes and fields. He was fascinated by great migratory birds – geese, swans, cranes – appreciating them with an almost mystical curiosity and including them and their

---

1   Though habitually grouped with Norway, Sweden and Denmark, Finland is not generally considered part of the Scandinavian subregion or Scandinavian culture; however, its north-west area does share some of the Scandinavian Peninsula.

2   In the darker music – the Fourth Symphony or *The Swan of Tuonela* – Sibelius might also be regarded as a soundtrack prophetic of 'Nordic noir', that gloomy, intelligent branch of twenty-first-century police procedural TV and crime fiction which explores the tension between ostensibly ordinary surfaces and their murky undercurrents, and which is exemplified by programmes like *The Killing* and *The Bridge*, as well as authors such as Stieg Larsson, Jo Nesbø and Camilla Läckberg.

calls in his compositions. He demanded natural surroundings and seclusion: they were part of his soul, his inner being, and his music explores the self and its relationship with landscape, atmosphere and setting like few other composers have, comprehending the intricacy of its intimacy and severity. Whether his eyes were fixed on rivers or reindeer, whether his ears heard thunder or the rustle of leaves, whether his feet trod mud or snow, Sibelius was always precariously alive to the wonder, fragility and psychological importance of our environment, and his greatest music is as penetrating in its exploration of nature and human sensibility as John Clare, Ted Hughes or *King Lear*.

Yet, especially in his youth, Sibelius also required strong human contact – with artists, intellectuals, poets, even members of high society in whose company he mingled with ease. For all that he needed to frequently withdraw into self-sequestration, he was also an outgoing, expansive (and expensive) man. Convivial and sociable, he loved a certain amount of attention and the company of his peers.

When he could afford it – and more often when he could not – he enjoyed a lavish lifestyle. The best hotels. The best cigars. The best wines. Some of his bar bills would make an archduke blush, a sultan panic. As the many photos of him attest, he adored exquisitely tailored suits, as ruthlessly well cut and constructed as one of his symphonies. Sibelius in his later years, adorned in an especially fetching white linen outfit, has become one of the iconic images of the composer, the suit giving him the air of a jaunty financier or genial diplomat.

Most of all he loved booze. Craved it. Demanded it. He needed it to settle his nerves – half a bottle of champagne inside him, he once wrote, and he conducted like a young god. He needed it to release the pressure of composition or performance.

He needed it to combat and indulge his loneliness. 'In order to survive, I must have alcohol', he confided to his diary. But he also knew when it had gone too far, and could occasionally abstain, especially when doctors or his wife pleaded (once managing sobriety for a biblical seven years).

Bénédictine was a brutal youthful favourite – especially during the hijinks and mischief years at the Hotel Kämp in Helsinki – but whisky was his truest prize, and Sibelius drank industrial quantities of the spirit to steady his hands, nerves and soul. But he had plenty of room for other intoxicants, too, and the final page of his diary, kept intermittently from 1909 to 1944, contains simply a shopping list:

Champagne.
Cognac.
Gin.

Yet, somehow, he survived, living to ninety-one and outliving, as he often had occasion to remark, all the friends and doctors who had told him to quit.

In part this was because he married a patient, loyal and fiercely intelligent partner, Aino Järnefelt (1871–1969), the daughter of a Finnish general and senator (who was one of the leading figures in promoting Finnish culture as well as the drive for independence, of which Sibelius himself would become a significant part). The marriage lasted over sixty-five years, ending only with his death, and they had six daughters together: Eva (1893–1978), Ruth (1894–1976), Kirsti (1898–1900), Katarina (1903–1984), Margareta (1908–1988) and Heidi (1911–1982). If the relationship could, at times, be turbulent and intense – not least because of his drinking – it was, like some of his similarly stormy friendships and professional alliances, based on a deep love and mutual respect, allowing it to withstand the crises and survive.

Wild oscillations between arrogance and despair, despondency and superiority, were a natural part of his being, a dangerous cycle which generated creativity but must have been hard to live with, both for the composer and his family. He could change moods with an alarming swiftness, travelling from Hades to Himalaya and back down again in frightening haste (something fuelled and exacerbated, of course, by the booze). There was a certain amount of vanity and narcissism to how he looked and the image of himself he wanted the world to see – when the time came for him to wear glasses, he refused to ever be photographed in them – though this was understandable perhaps for a man feted with fame and badgered by a sometimes intrusive public.

Criticism he took hard. He didn't shrink from reading articles and reviews of his music, but he could be bitterly stung by reproach and disapproval – or, worse, poor evaluation, when critics didn't seem to understand his intentions with a piece, misrepresenting his objectives. 'No one ever erected a statue to a critic', he once quipped, but he was his own worst fault-finder. At times, this was immensely valuable. Works like *Lemminkäinen*, the violin concerto and the Fifth Symphony were considerably improved by the revisions he made to them (though the original versions are hardly duds). As we might expect, given his penchant for luxury hotels and fine wines, he had rigorous, demanding standards for his art and sought the unholy grail of perfection wherever he could. But it also meant that some works ended up unrealized, undeveloped – even obliterated, consumed first by self-doubt and then by flames.

In appearance, he journeyed from a quixotic and romantic youth – slim, with a moustache and slightly windswept hair – to a middle age where he often has the look of an unyielding bank manager or stern schoolmaster, frowning above a stiff starched collar. By his old age, he has lost his locks, and there is something tortoise-like or reptilian to his aspect, though he is often a terrapin with a twinkle in his eye, a laugh under the big bald dome. From wild-eyed prince to granite titan, there were several Sibeliuses.

The lives of artists are unlike those of other people in that they really have two lives, which constantly overlap and interact. They have the familiar coinciding, intersecting series of love, work and play; but they also have an additional realm of creation and destruction, conception and annihilation, as ideas, people, objects, events and emotions are captured, transformed and set free into art.

So while the occurrences of an artist's life demand their everyday consideration, these happenings simultaneously become artistic springs and thence, at various degrees of immediacy, grist to the mill: experiences, material and knowledge that are metamorphosed – through complex procedures – into art (though often at a very great, even unrecognizable, distance from their creator, such as in Nabokov's *Lolita*). For painters and poets, this might seem more obvious. The lives of novelists, too, often seem more naturally linked to, and implicated in, their literary output: think of Dickens' boyhood trauma and *Oliver Twist*, Joyce's youthful Dublin and *Ulysses*, Melville's whaling adventures and *Moby-Dick*. The events which have shaped an artist become reshaped into art, which itself then becomes part of the life.

Composers' lives can often appear much less obviously connected to their creations, especially the abstract art of the classical symphony. Yet the networks are there. Beethoven's *Eroica* and *Choral* Symphonies are musical preoccupations and political treatises, but they are also personal voyages. Bruckner's essays in the medium offer both music and profoundly subjective expressions of faith. Mahler's symphonies expand the form while at the same time presenting chapters from the biography of their maker.

With Sibelius, too, his experiences of the world – be they personal or political, natural or mythical – moulded his musical art. A complex nexus of sources forged his symphonies and tone poems, and throughout this book we will meet glimpses, though naturally only glimpses, of what they were and how they helped fashion his music. The natural world and Finnish folklore and mythology, along with obvious musical influences, are the more palpable stimuli, but many others, not least the more intangible tensions of existence, will form and inform the very particular, even peculiar, works Sibelius created.

He began composing when he was still a child, though he was never an infant prodigy like Mozart or Clara Schumann, and retired in his late sixties, even if he never entirely stopped writing or revising his music. (As we will see, the infamous 'silence of Järvenpää' is both a little misleading and somewhat unfair: can composers not retire, like architects or accountants, barristers or baristas?)

A stupendous complete edition of Sibelius's music – released a few years ago on the BIS label – can give us an idea of the magnitude and range of his output: it requires seventy compact discs in total, of which the symphonies, tone poems and other orchestral works (in their various editions and versions) take up sixteen discs, as does the chamber music. The songs need five, the piano music ten. Theatre and vocal music require eighteen, while a miscellaneous five CDs complete the set. It is a lot of music to come from one person, a single soul, especially with the retirement and relative reticence of the final three decades.[3]

As a young man his career began, reasonably, in smaller forms – a wealth of chamber music flowed like syrup from his pen. Duos, trios, quartets, quintets: he wrote for a variety of combinations, learning how different instruments sounded together (and apart). Yet almost all this material was practically never heard after its first performances, if ever some of it was heard at all, outside Sibelius's own head. This treasure trove of early unpublished material, largely unknown until the last part of the twentieth century, came to light only in the 1980s, when the Sibelius family donated manuscripts kept at Ainola to the University of Helsinki.

Many of the pieces are quite slight, even trivial, carrying the air of either the schoolroom or the salon. But from the outset, Sibelius had a gift for melody, for mellifluous musical phrases that seduce and grab the ear, their cadence and shape satisfying, instinctive. In this juvenilia, sometimes the tune seems to be all

---

3   By comparison, though let's not be competitive about it, Mahler's complete oeuvre needs about fifteen CDs, Wagner's around forty. For all of Berlioz you need near thirty; Beethoven, eighty or ninety. For Bach and Mozart, considerably more time and space are required: two hundred–odd discs each.

there is, not least in the exceptional profusion of miniatures, before the burgeoning comprehension of structure and form begin to crystallize in pieces like the *Korpo* Piano Trio (1887), the violin sonata in F major (1889) and the astounding G minor piano quintet (1890), works now justly becoming significant features of the concert and recorded repertoire.[4]

In this youthful chamber music, the wild horses of Sibelius's melodic imagination would become tamed by the conventionally expected paddocks of form – before his music refused any such restrictions and, Pegasus-like, grew wings, subject and structure in total logical freedom, imposing and uninhibited like one of the composer's much-loved swans in full flight.

Songs and piano music formed a vital part of Sibelius's output over the years, not least as a useful means to earn money, and represent a fertile, absorbing archive of his developing musical mind. The composer's use of predominately Swedish texts for his songs helps reveal to us the poetry which meant so much to him – most especially the work of Ernst Josephson, Viktor Rydberg and Gustaf Fröding, as well as Finns who wrote in Swedish, including perhaps the greatest of them all, Johan Ludvig Runeberg, a perpetual Sibelian poet. Sibelius's choral music, habitually patriotic and usually setting Finnish texts, often uses the national epic, the *Kalevala*, as well as its more lyrical sibling, the *Kanteletar*; and from *Kullervo* (1892) onwards his writing for chorus is an important contribution not only to his career but to the rich vocal traditions of Nordic culture, especially in music for male voices.

Sibelius's music for the theatre is a substantial, if all too often overlooked, aspect of his compositional harvest. Combining

---

[4] In his maturity, there would not be many chamber works. The mesmerizing *Voces intimae* String Quartet (1909) is one of the magnificent exceptions.

music with drama mattered to Sibelius, and although he had an essentially unsuccessful opera career (one large-scale piece abandoned, leaving only a minor one-act work to survive), his incidental music for various plays contemporary and more distant is of particular note. As with his larger and more obviously important works, he had a flair for painting moods and sketching characters in sound. The scores for *King Christian II* (1898) and *Pelléas et Mélisande* (1905) are among his best-known and finest dramatic music, but it was a late turn to Shakespeare that would produce his greatest sonic inventions for the theatre: *The Tempest* (1925).

For all the wealth and abundance of these genres, however, it is in his music for orchestra, and especially his symphonies and tone poems, that Sibelius created his most innovative, extraordinary and enduring works. Although tonally and harmonically less adventurous than the work of many of his contemporaries, these were pieces that developed form into enthralling and sometimes dangerous new territories. Full of fire and ice, often blending abstract and programmatic music in mesmerizing hybrid ways to forge an intriguing and unique style, they found fresh new structures for keys and harmonies that challenged the status quo and demanded to be heard. Unity and logic were to be his watchwords, alluring but uncompromising: a master of architecture and quiet revolution.

Across Sibelius, it is the creative conflict between his ruthless structural designs and his intense expressive language that generates so much of the mystery, tension – and fascination. The seven numbered symphonies are works of immense evocative power: ostensibly abstract and absolute, they nevertheless display engagement with a complex nexus of meanings, suggestions and elicitations (including action, atmosphere, character, psychology and landscape). Similarly, the tone poems frequently rely on symphonic logic and the interaction of themes – telescoping and condensing material with ruthless lucidity and musical persuasion.[5]

Such porous boundaries between generic categories were not always apparent in the late nineteenth and early twentieth centuries. Although there were brilliant insubordinate undertakings to amalgamate symphony and tone poem, such as in Berlioz or Liszt, the symphony in the nineteenth century, conscious of Beethoven's gigantic legacy, was chiefly concerned with motivic unison, formal abstraction and goal orientation, often as part of an intricate system of musical keys achieving resolution. The great symphonists – Schumann, Bruckner, Brahms, Mahler – were for the most part conversationalists with tradition, dialoguing with the past via lofty, large-scale works of ambition, aspiration and intensity.

Tone poets, on the other hand, sought a break from this suffocating institution. Primarily concerned with articulating a narrative, personality or atmosphere, tone poems aimed to evoke their literary-pictorial programmes and as such could employ a much freer and more (superficially) inventive musical architecture: for Richard Strauss, leading exponent of the form,

---

5   The intersections are occasionally discernible in the designations used for certain works. The tone poem *Pohjola's Daughter* (1906) is subtitled 'symphonic fantasy', while the Seventh Symphony (1924) was originally dubbed 'fantasia sinfonica' – after the premiere, it was conferred 'official' status as a symphony by its composer. Moreover, Sibelius himself often claimed to have written nine symphonies, including *Kullervo* and *Lemminkäinen* in the tally.

structure existed only to serve the requirements of the work's expressive content. Tone poems tended to contract the four-movement classical symphony into a solo span, with vibrant harmonic and/or motivic growth often sacrificed on the more static altars of atmosphere, ambience and poetic rumination, with Strauss himself taking orchestration to a cinematic level of vivacity and detail.

Yet this painting of mood or character in sound, despite – or perhaps because of – its expressive brilliance and groundbreaking techniques, was typically regarded as inferior to the conceptual wonder of the symphony, an upstart and attention-seeking kid brother who, while sometimes dazzling, was not regarded as being on the same intellectual or theoretical level. And the greater scope and success the tone poem achieved, especially by the end of the nineteenth century and into the twentieth, the more this apparent distinction in musical rank held firm.

For Sibelius, such fixed, impermeable – and all too often snobbish – categories of genre/type were less stable, more blurred, intolerable. In his orchestral music, shifting, fluid categories alter connotation and perception as works slide, intwine and entangle within a range of classes and classifications, and convenient groupings into symphony and tone poem frequently overlap and merge. Accordingly, detecting the exact borders between the two forms can be not only a problematic but also a fruitless and disheartening task, limiting the depth and scope of each on behalf of the expediency of the catalogue.

The Sibelian symphony and tone poem often share many of the same pioneering formal techniques, as he undermined and overturned generic conventions: a personal, idiosyncratic, even hypnotic and aquatic feeling for momentum prevails; multi-movement structures are reduced, tapered, into much tauter spans; time-honoured sonata form, with its contrasting of multiple themes, is distorted, contorted, even replaced; musical subjects and harmonies are focused, organically and with intense concentration; tight tonal and motivic goals are pursued and realized within ambitious, determined systems, as endlessly evolving cells of sound. In his later works especially, there is a feeling of continuous and unbroken expansion, as works progress via subtle thematic mutations. As he memorably suggested in his diary:

> I should like to compare the symphony to a river. It is born from various rivulets that look for one another, and in this way the river proceeds strong and wide towards the sea.

For Sibelius, composition was an incessant, dynamic and supple musical enterprise of inner imbrication and connective synthesis. He strove to fuse and renovate the inconsistent, sometimes even contradictory, requirements of diverse musical genres into an innovative, superior kind of musical work, one with powerful emotional-intellectual-psychological subject matter which helped to dictate and (re)define the form itself.

Instinctive, intuitive, spontaneous – Sibelius was compelled to create music governed chiefly not by tradition or heritage, or by prearranged models of process and practice, but by organic occurrences and interior undercurrents. Moreover, it was not only the end results that corresponded: the preliminary throb, and then developing pulse, of inspiration – whether for symphony or tone poem – would often come from the same musical, natural, emotional, spiritual, mythical or fictional source.

For all this overlapping and interrelating, however, it is important to remind ourselves that Sibelius, as both innovator and composer, seemed to see his orchestral project as essentially 'one system, two forms'. His work utilized one overarching methodology but used it to craft two identifiably sovereign and distinctive genres – why else number exactly seven symphonies and suggestively label several tone poems? – even if the margins and frontiers between those genres are frequently hazy, opaque, even inconsequential.

Musical history, and especially in modernity, is always a tense balancing act between custom and development, between protection and revolution. Amid the team ranks of tradition, lone strikers seek to inspire with novel experiments and techniques – lone voices above, but also a part of, the congregation. Progression and preservation are always interacting, always engaging; they are rarely, if ever, entirely conflicting, totally contested, schemes.

Tendencies towards both upkeep and demolition have an intricate, often symbiotic, relationship, however opposed they are often presented as being. Exploiting this phenomenon of interaction is, in many ways, the manifestation of genius, an act apparent in the complicated collaboration between Sibelius's two principal forms, as he synthesized and transformed both the symphony and tone poem, taking genres on and infusing them with new life, with a new complexity, a new style.

More generally, Sibelius is in some ways the ultimate late Romantic, extending the nineteenth century well into the twentieth. As such, he is still regarded by many as an inhibitor, restricting the more obviously advanced propensities of figures like Schoenberg – especially after *Pelleas und Melisande* (1903), as the great Austrian experimented with atonality and then moved on into serialism. Unable to see the subtle innovations at work in Sibelius, the Finn's detractors, then as now, too often focused on his apparent devotion to tradition, rather than the ways his forms and techniques radically altered the existing situation.

Sibelius challenges our notions of musical development. A pioneer of idiosyncratically Nordic modernism, his music disrupts the cosy narrative of a progression from Romanticism to the avant-garde wonders of Schoenberg and Stravinsky, Bartók and Boulez. The more apparently palatable sound worlds Sibelius created, as well as their fluidity, has led many to presume his gloomy grandeur is simplistic, even naive. Although it is no longer possible to regard Sibelius with quite this degree of ignorance and lazy thinking, many such blinkered undercurrents of thought persist (as they do concerning a number of those he influenced: Bantock, Bax, Moeran and Vaughan Williams). Sibelius's personal and specific, even occasionally eccentric, artistic path, which alienated so many by its unswerving refusal to abide by shifts and trends in the musical topography, especially in Germany and France, forces us to reconsider not only linear aesthetic developments but wider issues of national identity and cultural boundaries as well as related questions of preference – and its darker sibling, prejudice.

Recent reassessments, building on the more enlightened and imaginative early critics, have sought to properly see Sibelius as what might be described as a 'classical modernist', divorced from and indifferent to the superficial restrictions of conflicting camps (especially 'progressive' versus 'reactionary'). Rather than seeing him as purely a category unto himself, however, it will also be significant, and beneficial, to examine the communication of Sibelius's scores with those around him – both fore and aft – as well as their internal dynamics.

For all its logic and coherence, its classical style, there is an inherent opacity and volatility to Sibelius's music, an uncertainty and flux, which confers the modernist element. Indeed, it is the synthesis between these components – between lucidity and perplexity, constancy and mutability – which assigns Sibelius's symphonies and tone poems so much of their tension and strength. They are works of order and turmoil, expansion and contraction, sun and steel.

Sibelius asks his symphonies and tone poems to become prodigious tools of impermanence and contrivances harnessing eternity, examining the dangerous, mysterious energies at the heart of nature and human psychology. The latter are both fragile ecosystems packed with immense (but often elusive) power, equally creative and destructive. He explores how forces which shape and contour the world also impair and destabilize it, for the resourceful mind is also often a detrimental one, networks of ingenuity leading to ruinous mazes of confusion and despair. Above all, Sibelius's music concerns itself with the relationship between a melancholic yet ebullient mind and the wider world outside it; with the function of emotions, the imagination and the intellect in human life; with how art can survey, scrutinize and give meaning to the strangeness of existence.

Frequently, therefore, not only do the abstract and the programmatic coalesce in Sibelius; the elemental – fire, earth, air, water – are also attached to the psychological. Nature painting in his music is never mere sonic landscaping but a penetrating examination of human mental processes, as well as insecurity and instability. The dark forests of *Tapiola* (1926) are the gloomy forests of the mind; the harsh, stark landscapes of the Fourth Symphony (1911) are soundscapes of spiritual, cerebral and ecological anguish; the erotic thrills and dangerous liaisons of *Kullervo* (1892), *Lemminkäinen* (1896), and the First Symphony (1899) serve as prophetic warnings not just about psychosexual licentiousness but environmental debauchery too.

In his extraordinary symphonies and tone poems, Sibelius explores the stimulating forces and shadowy agencies lurking behind the locked doors of nature, the dense layers of myth and the misty windows of the soul. His is a captivating and increasingly pertinent musical mind we would do well to heed. Yet Sibelius never lectures or intimidates, hectors or harasses: he displays; he reveals. His work is an exhibition, not a homily; a demonstration, not a reprimand (even if consequences are often implied). Like all truly great artists, he never tells but merely shows – knowing both psychologically and aesthetically the superior power of the one over the other.

Intermingling illusion and fantasy with truth and reality, Sibelius's distinctive symphonies and tone poems contemplate the timeless and the eternal amid the temporary and the temporal, as they explore legend, life and landscape in musical terms. This mix of approaches gives his music much of its poignancy as well as its compelling power. It is music with a seemingly limitless capacity to grant courage in the face of despondency, to quietly resolve itself into panoramas of assurance despite desolation and isolation. In part, it is the rigour and precision of his work which inspires the confidence to persevere amid misery, doubt or danger, while also sanctioning its dignity and depth. Sibelius is the melancholy man of the dark northern forests, of hard rock and cold water – but he is also a comfort and a consolation, a poet of promise, solace, absolution and transcendence.

Can it be any surprise, then, that despite the sanguinity, reticence ultimately became the only possible answer to such exquisite but delicate visions. Sibelius's journey towards synthesis – of both genre and temperament – was an inexorable excursion towards silence too. But this was not a failure, the symptom of a dark and difficult figure only looking backwards, unable to move ahead; it was a triumph of creative consciousness and fulfilment, of clarity and compression. Yet the development within Sibelius's art, with its progression both inwards and towards tighter models, was a sweeping way of altering not only musical form but also the relationships between nature, personal identity and socio-psychological freedom.

A marriage of instinct and reason, emotion and intellect, Sibelius's music is as synthetic as a skyscraper but as natural and spontaneous as a dividing cell, the complex mechanics hidden by an organic acoustic skin. He assembled his work with painstaking care and attention to detail but wanted the end result to evade its own artificiality, becoming less a creative product and more a part of the environment, a fusion of humanity and the world, art and nature joined.

It is music which asks us to elide the borders of existence, to rethink our connection with the world and consequently with ourselves, inviting us to ponder the constant changes in weather, terrain, climate, season and light – and the impact of such fluctuations on our own actions and states of being. Sibelius did not see swans, lakes, the forest or the infinity of the night sky as an escape into caprice, whim or self-deception but as part of a fundamental, far-reaching project of penetration and renewal. His music, with its meticulous, uncanny sense of texture and space, is a cartography of the soul, a mapping of the mind, an evolving shift into deeper connectivity and communion, sound and mood intimately conversing, imagination working as one with the natural world: flexible, attentive and sympathetic.

Sibelius is a revelation and a warning, a hope and a fear, a caution and a sunrise.

PART ONE

EXPECTATION

Chapter One

Symphony Zero:
Kullervo

Finland did not declare independence from Russia on 6 December 1917. It did so on 28 April 1892, the day Jean Sibelius's massive symphony cum dramatic cantata cum tone poem, *Kullervo*, was given its world premiere, conducted by the twenty-six-year-old composer in the Great Hall of the University of Helsinki. A vast orchestral work with five movements, two vocal soloists and a forty-strong male choir, it was a self-consciously substantial piece, brazen in its scale, unabashed in its vehement bearing and proud of its burly rhetoric. Unparalleled public approval greeted the work, its composer acknowledged as speaking with not only his own unique voice but that of the Finnish people entire, creating not only his own music but the music of a nation that yearned for its freedom.

Kullervo had been given a rapturous reception even before it was performed. Journalists and critics were alive to the budding importance of the work, not only in Finnish music and culture but in its wider sociopolitical ramifications. Hence, on the morning of the concert, indeed in the weeks before *Kullervo*'s parturition, newspapers like *Päivälehti* and *Hufvudstadsbladet* acclaimed its originality and vitality – as well as potential as a catalyst for pro-independence activity. *Kullervo* was a piece which, from the outset, concentrated nationalist feeling and Finnish pride.

A work exploring male lust and violence, female desire and vulnerability, Freudian complexity and nationalist identity, *Kullervo* is a magnificent, even outrageous, synthesis. It takes the spiritual inscrutability and dark sexual narratives of Wagner's musikdrama (especially *Die Walküre*, *Tristan* and *Parsifal*) and fuses them with the orchestral vastness of Bruckner's symphonies. To this are added elements of Strauss's and Liszt's tone poems, as well as echoes of Berlioz's *Symphonie fantastique* and the dramatic symphony *Roméo et Juliette*, along with reverberations of more distant Greek and Shakespearean tragedy: *Oedipus Rex* and *Hamlet*.

Infusing the whole are the ethnic folk idioms of Finland, which Sibelius occasionally claimed never to have used but which are unmistakable in the rhythms and textures of the music.[6] These composite, disparate elements confer Sibelius's first major work not only its distinctiveness, its uniqueness as a work of art, but also its peculiar tensions. *Kullervo*'s audacious hybridity and

---

6 To be fair, Sibelius hardly ever used an authentic Finnish folk motif – though one of Pedri Shemeikka's is cited directly in the first scene of the *Karelia* incidental music – but much of his music is in the *style* of folk melodies. Original in composition and from his own imagination, this music is Sibelius the artist and ardent Finn absorbing his heritage, then singing his own songs.

often rugged, even primitive scoring (all part of the drama) add to the conflict, the friction, the moods, the excitement, of this formidable masterpiece.

Sibelius himself didn't quite agree with this endorsement. Despite the euphoric response *Kullervo* received at its first performances in 1892, after three further complete presentations, in February 1893 the composer withdrew the work and, apart from a few sporadic performances of isolated movements later on, it was never heard again in his long lifetime. The man who would argue for the 'severity of style and profound logic' of the symphony – as opposed to Mahlerian multiplicity – was perhaps concerned by the synthetic, cross-breed nature of his *Kullervo* beast, his five-footed creature with a symphonic head and a cantata tail. It was only in the 1970s, with the activism of conductors such as Paavo Berglund, that the work began to re-emerge onto the concert stage, its fusions and idiosyncrasies – after the chaotic, frenzied developments of twentieth-century music – now something to be embraced and celebrated with new ears.

Yet, as we shall see, despite Sibelius's own reservations, *Kullervo* is full of Sibelian characteristics in both style and technique, and today stands proud not only as a powerful and anticipatory precursor to his superlative achievements in the symphony and tone poem, but on its own eccentric, exclusive terms. A monster, to be sure, but a monster with the brain, the heart and the soul of Finland.

Johan Julius Christian Sibelius was born on 8 December 1865, in Hämeenlinna, an inland city surrounded by hundreds of lakes in the south of the Grand Duchy of Finland, then an autonomous part of the Russian Empire. Known for being a leader in education, governance and the military, Hämeenlinna – like many non-coastal cities – had developed slowly but steadily, its aptness for sensible, logical planning and resourceful forethought (it had opened Finland's first railway line, to Helsinki, in 1862) producing many Finns who would prove to be significant in the country's culture, history and journey towards independence.

Within this diligent, reputable place lies an innocuous yellow wooden house with white windows, barely bigger than a large mobile home: Sibelius's birthplace, now preserved as a museum and occasional concert hall, the pride of this historic provincial city. Crammed full of bourgeois paraphernalia and archaic, absorbing Sibeliana, the *Sibeliuksen syntymäkoti* is a time capsule of a world of middle-class decorum and polite musical enthusiasm. Pianos dominate the space – there seem to be at least two in every room – as do strewn violins and occasional cellos. The wallpaper is respectable, the furniture solid, the fixtures and fittings a model of mid-nineteenth-century aspiration and self-assurance. Yet there is nothing stuffy or oppressive about this house: it breathes intelligence and good taste, and in many ways, like so many birthplace institutions dotted around the globe, it would be a perfectly humdrum relic of the past were it not for the extraordinary life that began there.

Sibelius was the son of Swedish-speaking medical doctor Christian Gustaf Sibelius and Maria Charlotta Sibelius (née Borg). The father died of typhoid fever before the boy's third birthday, plunging the little family into debt, forcing them to sell the house and move across town to live with Charlotta's widowed mother, Katarina Juliana. Sibelius had scant few memories of his father – save the pungent, intoxicating scent of his cigars and the haunting occasion when he showed him a book with a picture inside of an exquisite white swan.

But amid this confusion and upheaval, music began to dominate the young Janne (as he became known; this was a common colloquial form of 'Johan'). While his mother played the piano, the toddler Sibelius would sit underneath trying to match the sounds to colours on the striped rug he sat on, or inventing fairy stories to go with the notes, the first sign of not only his synaesthesia but his need to connect music with narrative, character and imagination. Concerts soon became a permanent part of Janne's life, and his aunt Julia gave him piano lessons on the family upright when he was seven (the boy's knuckles rapped with a knitting needle if he played a wrong note). Janne and his older sister, Linda, had been joined by a younger brother, Christian, in March 1869, and this youngest Sibelius was soon recruited – or was it coerced? – into playing the cello in household family trios, the girl on the piano and their brother Janne surely far outperforming them both on the violin.

His uncle Pehr gave Janne his first violin when the boy was ten, starting a profound passion – even a treacherous obsession – for the instrument that would lead to not only dashed dreams but the creation of one of his most distinctive, astonishing and enduring masterpieces: the violin concerto in D minor. Beyond introducing Janne to the violin, Pehr also encouraged him to pursue composition: he had noticed that at the keyboard, the boy much preferred improvisation to diligently following the notes laid out on the score (Janne doubtless recognizing that this was an expedient means to avoid punishment from his aunt for poor sight-reading). A crucial figure in Sibelius's early life, Uncle Pehr not only replaced the dead father but became a key musical advocate and adviser, leading his nephew down the path that was ultimately to be his destiny and fulfilment.

Before then, however, the irksome business of school. A somewhat distracted, often restless pupil, he had a mind subjugated by musical ideas and fantasies of virtuosic violin playing: musical notes crept into the margins of his exercise books; improvised musical events and plays were put on with his schoolfriends. He also read a great deal, especially poetry and folk tales, again and again connecting the words and images with the music he was surrounded by – playing in either the school orchestra or a local string quartet of which he was a member, their Haydn and Schubert supplemented by thoughts of fires and fairies, lakes, forests and other magical realms.

At school, he did well enough in the more ostensibly serious matters of maths and botany but had to repeat a year before finally, in 1885, passing the exams which enabled him to enrol at the University of Helsinki, then the Imperial Alexander University of Finland. He initially studied law – that respectable pursuit of the conscientious middle classes – but such a monotonous, worthy career was never going to interest this wildly imaginative student for long, and he soon switched to music at the Helsinki Music Institute, now the Sibelius Academy.[7] (It was here that Janne took a name from the business card of a deceased seafaring uncle who had adopted a fashionable French moniker, and 'Jean Sibelius' was born.)

Composition had begun, as we have seen, much earlier – Sibelius was essentially self-taught, though under the kindly observation and sporadic instruction of Uncle Pehr. During his teenage years, extempore improvisations at the piano became

---

7   In fairness, his family had not wanted to hinder his musical enthusiasms, and during his brief stint at the Law Faculty, Sibelius had been allowed to register as a special student at the conservatoire.

mercurial melodies and delightful miniatures, often character pieces, full of invention and delicious tunes. Larger works soon began to take shape: a piano quartet, a suite in D minor for violin and piano. A wonderful pizzicato work for violin and cello (*Vattendroppar*, or *Water Drops*) dates from around 1881;[8] writing what were, by his own admission, a couple of 'rather poor' trios in the summer of 1883 apparently gave the seventeen-year-old Sibelius something to do on rainy days.[9]

At university his first formal music lessons (in harmony, counterpoint, theory and the like) developed his skills as a composer, as did industrious work on his violin playing, in which Sibelius had an advanced technique now considerable enough for him to perform as a virtuoso soloist in various concertos, as well as in corporate fashion with orchestras and quartets. Around this time nicotine and alcohol also made their first entrances into Sibelius's body, the start of a lifelong (and occasionally life-threatening) relationship full of passion and disgust, need and greed.

Working with composer, educationalist and founder of the Helsinki Music Institute Martin Wegelius (1846–1906), Sibelius evolved rapidly – though his teacher claimed he learned more from his pupil than Sibelius ever did from him, and the Helsinki years (1885–89) produced several important milestones in his career. During his childhood, protracted family summers had often been spent at Loviisa, on the southern coast, for Janne

---

[8] It has often been thought this was the work of the ten- or eleven-year-old Janne in the mid-1870s, but it is now more comfortably dated as a later exercise.

[9] Mentioned in a letter from 25 August 1883, this is the first definite reference we have to a Sibelius composition. Thanks to the wonderful work of the BIS music label, all these fascinating, often fragmentary, early pieces – and there are a lot of them – can now be heard, via the Sibelius Edition, which runs to some thirteen volumes.

a place of freedom and discovery, of sun, nature and music (as opposed to the drudgery of school, locked away in Hämeenlinna during the long, dark northern winter). In August 1888 he returned there, writing a fourth and final piano trio, in C major, now known as the *Loviisa* Trio.[10]

This trio represents an important staging post in Sibelius's career, showcasing a move away from the more classically designed chamber works of his adolescence and young maturity and towards formal enlargements characterized by greater passion and intensity. In its compact space, the *Loviisa* Trio coveys an astonishing range of colours, textures and moods, combining humane exuberance with dark, resounding harmonies. It is ambitious, perhaps too ambitious: the form as Sibelius found it could hardly cope with the emotional onslaughts he inflicted upon it. He was going to need a bigger boat in which to navigate his artistic objectives.

A violin sonata in F major (1889), slightly reminiscent of Grieg's (1865), was perhaps his most significant accomplishment to date, a work with promising signs of the mature, distinctive voice to come. Intriguingly, Sibelius wrote to his uncle with an extensive programme – even smaller chamber works were not to be divorced from extramusical identities and agendas. In this work, the F major first movement is energetic and audacious, with some more melancholic passages interspersed, before a 'Finnish' slow movement in A minor of a more extended sombre air. Here, Sibelius told his uncle, a 'true Finnish girl' is crying in the A string, while some country boys dance around her, coaxing her to smile, though she only sings with more feeling and languor than before. The fresh and animated final movement returns to F major, to what Sibelius described as a meadow on Midsummer

---

10 Often spelled with one *i*: *Lovisa*.

Eve, with plenty of singing and dancing. A shooting star pierces the sky, shocking the people into a more meditative frame of mind and an atmosphere of gloomy grandeur before the music closes in tentative joy.

Quite whether this work can sustain the rather involved and complex agenda Sibelius wrote for it is a question. But the violin sonata in F major is no lightweight piece. It makes huge demands on both players and shows Sibelius's to be a swiftly developing musical mind. Moreover, the crucial issue is that Sibelius *did* give it that programme, indicating not only the images and ideas at work in his creative processes but the crucial connection between narrative and feeling which informed his earliest musical experiences.

The work's mixture of classical form with scene setting and more abstract tone painting is a significant marker of the future (and not so far off) Sibelius, as is the nature of the story itself: a definitively Finnish maiden, surrounded by country boys perhaps representing the Russian Empire encircling an ostensibly autonomous Finland which is increasingly undermined, ignored or oppressed in her desire for independence. *Kullervo* will not only unite symphonic form with the tone poem and more literary-theatrical elements, including the tale of a young woman's seduction, but will stand as a defiantly Finnish work of art, unique and self-determining.

Before *Kullervo*, however, came personal and professional disappointments and developments.

During his Helsinki studies, an unfavourable assessment of Sibelius's performance of Mendelssohn's violin concerto in

E minor (1844) proved to be a nail in the coffin of his long-cherished virtuoso career.[11] Sibelius's tone, it was claimed, was thin, harsh and uncompromising. In truth, whatever his considerable talents as a violinist, he knew that he had embarked on a solo career too late: even practicing morning to night from the age of fifteen was not sufficient to prepare for the onerous demands of the calling. Yet his period as a virtuoso was also a diversion. Sibelius disliked what he called 'pen and ink' work, preferring the exquisite elegance of the violin bow to the graft and mess of composition. The elimination of a solo playing career meant that he would be driven to redouble his efforts as a composer, compelling him – despite the incipient distractions of bodies and bottles – to the gruelling grind needed to become a truly original and distinctive musical voice. Sibelius's desire to perform, however, never went away and, as he later said, would manifest itself in several strange ways over the years.

As a student, Sibelius was fortunate to come into the orbit of some of the leading composers and musicians of the age (one of which, of course, he was precipitously becoming himself). In the autumn of 1888, Wegelius scored a significant coup for the Institute when he secured the services of one Ferruccio Busoni (1866–1924) as an instructor of advanced – very advanced – piano studies. A supremely gifted pianist, Busoni would eventually become a crucial futurist composer, incorporating into his music everything from Bach to atonality and North American Indigenous tribal melodies, as well as an important and innovative theorist. He struck up a camaraderie with Sibelius which became a lifelong friendship – the Finn in particular introducing the routinely city-bound Italian to the wonders of communing with nature, showing him how it could inspire

---

11 Sibelius in fact gave only the andante and finale movements.

artistic creativity. Often with them was their mutual acquaintance Armas Järnefelt (1869–1958), a composer and conductor whose advocacy of Sibelius's music would prove so crucial in the years to come (as would Järnefelt's younger sister).

This merry troika – Sibelius, Busoni and Järnefelt – called themselves the Lesko trio, or the Leskovites, after Busoni's huge black Newfoundland, Lesko, a faithful canine companion who had accompanied the Italian during his lonely travels as a pianist and teacher in Germany. Habitually joined by the writer Adolf Paul and Järnefelt's painter brother Erik ('Eero'), these young artists would frequent Helsinki's bars and restaurants for 'meetings' to discuss their latest work, as well as developments in the wider world of politics. It was a time for art and music, booze and bawdy chat, wine and gentle wickedness. Beyond the pub, however, this same autumn, Järnefelt invited Sibelius to his family home for supper and music making. This was to prove a momentous occasion.

Järnefelt's father was General August Alexander Järnefelt (1833–1896), governor of Vaasa, a significant city on the west coast (and future capital of the country for ninety-five days during the Finnish Civil War). A family of considerable high achievers, the Järnefelts were passionate advocates of Finnish language and culture, and in addition to their composer-conductor son Armas and painter son Eero, they had ten other children, all of whom were to prove noteworthy in the politico-cultural life and identity of Finland. One of them was a strikingly beautiful seventeen-year-old daughter, Aino. On first meeting her, Sibelius was instantly smitten (as was Aino).

It took time for their relationship to develop, however – in part due to Sibelius's dalliances with other women, as well as his travels abroad; it also took time to convince old General Järnefelt that this struggling young musician – whose first language was Swedish! – was worthy of his daughter's affections. As it turned out, the success of *Kullervo*, that grand affirmation of Finnish distinctiveness, in the spring of 1892 was the final seal, and they were wed on 10 June that year. Through trial, tribulation and – for Aino at least – exasperation, they would be married for over six decades, a union which bore six daughters and endured love, tragedy, fame and mutual fascination.

In the years between their first meeting and marriage, Sibelius's close contact with this extremely pro-Finnish family changed his attitudes towards his own language and culture (with historic consequences for the country's future). As Pa Järnefelt had balked at, Swedish was Sibelius's mother tongue, as was usual for his class and upbringing at the time. From 1874 Sibelius attended Finnish-speaking schools, but it would take the exposure to the Järnefelt family, as well as the wider influence of the so-called *Päivälehti* circle (after the embryonic pro-Finnish paper), to rouse a new spirit in the composer, transforming him from almost a 'Svecoman' (supporter of Swedish language and culture) to an ardently progressive campaigner for all things Finnish ('Fennoman'). Meeting Aino had changed the direction not just of Sibelius's life but of the whole nation.

Despite, indeed because of, the setback terminating his solo violin career, Sibelius's compositional career was proceeding at a swift pace, and we might single out three works representative of the importance he was now assuming in not only local Helsinki musical life but also the wider culture and aspirations of Finland: a piano suite; a suite for violin, viola and cello; and a string quartet.

In the early spring of 1889, Sibelius fell ill – something of a hypochondriac, he felt himself to be dying – and spent a period of convalescence weighing up his life so far. He now knew that his dream of a solo violin career was not only improbable but a fantasy. It was a bitter pill to swallow, but imbibe it he must if he was to progress elsewhere. And so when his friend Adolf Paul visited the invalid, bringing a huge bouquet of yellow roses, Sibelius returned the favour with a delightful musical posy of his own: a piano suite, *Florestan*. A lyrical, introspective, slightly cyclical work, it is an atmospheric enchantment, full of pleasures and surprises.

Sibelius was keen, as ever, to link ostensibly abstract chamber/solo music to a programme, so he furnished prose sketches of the four parts. In the first movement, Florestan travels to the forest, disconsolate and forlorn. The scene smells of wet bark and wild moss. In the second, our hero comes across a waterfall, whose gushing cascades are transformed into water nymphs. The third movement shows one of these nymphs, with moist black eyes and golden hair. Florestan, naturally, falls in love with her. The last movement depicts Florestan's attempts to seduce her, but she disappears. Resuming his lonely, despondent state, Florestan returns through the forest. As in the F major violin sonata, the role of captivating, enticing but forbidden female figures remained a crucial part of Sibelius's musico-creative psyche, shortly to find its full realization in *Kullervo*.

A suite in A major for violin, viola and cello from this time, slightly bland in character, nonetheless has some of the first indications of identifiably Sibelian metrical designs in his music: its rhythms and configurations are probably recognizable to those familiar only with his symphonies and tone poems. Just as significant as this milestone in developing a well-defined musical personality was the reception of the work at the time. Despite its relative flatness (especially compared to the F major violin sonata or *Loviisa* Trio), critics loved it, feeling it represented 'the boldest hopes' for Finnish art.

Even more lauded was Sibelius's string quartet in A minor – and rightly so, since, along with the F major violin sonata of the same year, it is a key signpost in his career. Technically much more advanced than either, it is a distinct early indicator of the composer's mature style, yet it nonetheless loses none of the brightness, dash and sparkle of *Loviisa* or *Florestan*, while retaining, too, their darker qualities. One especially Sibelian feature is the liberation of the music from the limitations of bar lines, making the metre very hard to detect; familiar triplets colour the background, while what will become a representative Sibelius rhythmical arrangement (short-long-short) is also in evidence. The quartet's finale even anticipates certain themes for the Fourth Symphony, before the work ends with an intrepid incandescence not unlike that of the Fifth.

The A minor quartet was given as Sibelius's graduation piece from the Institute in May 1889 and was an immense success, prompting one critic – Karl Flodin – to claim that 'at a single stroke [Sibelius] has joined the vanguard of those who have been entrusted with the future of the art of music in Finland.' This was high praise indeed for the new graduate. At the same event, Sibelius first met Robert Kajanus (1856–1933) – then a budding composer himself but convinced by the brilliance of his younger colleague's quartet to devote himself to conducting. He would become, despite occasional perhaps understandable resentment, one of Sibelius's key champions and early interpreters, the first to record much of his work – recordings we must treasure.

Sibelius's triumphs with the A minor quartet and A major suite had made him the greatest prospect in Finnish music. Consequently, he was awarded a significant grant to enable him to travel south to two of the great musical cities: Berlin and Vienna. Thus, in the autumn of 1889 he set off on a steamer ship bound first for Tallinn, then Lübeck. In Berlin, at that time in the final months of the Iron Chancellor Bismarck's reign, Sibelius was exposed to not only gargantuan opportunities for alcoholic ingestion but vast amounts of music, both new and established, beyond his wildest desires. His promise to be thrifty swiftly evaporated, and his student grant, along with numerous loans from friends and family, soon disappeared into the coffers of the German capital's bars, restaurants, tailors and opera houses (though the last might have been considered essential homework).

Sibelius was a man who liked to live well, whether he could afford to or not. A system of relinquishing control of his finances to a new friend, Danish violinist Frederik Schnedler-Petersen, quickly came to nothing, and begging telegrams were sent back to Finland. His profligate social and thence sexual life also led him to catch a venereal disease, making him quite poorly for a time. (The relationship with Aino was very much on/off at this stage, and indeed, they didn't write to each other at all during Sibelius's time in Germany.[12])

---

12 Back in Helsinki during the summer vacation between his two years abroad, Sibelius reanimated his relationship with Aino, and they each acknowledged their true feelings for the other. After a concert in Helsinki on 29 September 1890, Jean proposed and Aino accepted (though they kept the engagement secret for a while). When the time came for Aino to leave Helsinki, Sibelius had her entire train compartment filled with her favourite flowers. He could be as extravagant, unrestrained and profligate in romance as he could with whisky and three-piece suits.

Musically, his own work did not proceed a great deal during the first half of his year of study in Berlin. Although some pieces emerged from his pen, parts of which would assume later significance, it was largely a period of exposure and defence, revelation and consolidation, as he subjected himself to the many musical wonders on offer, allowing them to both intentionally and instinctively feed his musical imagination and compositional abilities. On his very first night in the city, he saw *Don Giovanni* at the Kroll Opera; *Tannhäuser* and *Meistersinger* soon followed, inaugurating a relatively short but passionate period of enthusiasm for Wagner's works. He was at the Berlin premiere of Richard Strauss's first great tone poem *Don Juan* and frequently attended the legendary Historische Klavierabend piano recitals given by Hans von Bülow, while a performance of Beethoven's F major string quartet (op.59/1) made a lasting impression.[13]

The spring of 1890, after the sad news of his uncle Pehr's death in January, yielded an important new piece, however: a G minor piano quintet which more than any of his previous works seems to capture the unmissable, unmistakable air of Sibelian melancholy and solemnity. This was a tough, daunting, more rigorous style than he had so far achieved, the themes shared by the constituent parts of the quintet, but with an overall sound immensely orchestral in its range of colours and rich textures. Sibelius had developed the technical skills he needed to progress to larger forms, while still maintaining a gift for covering those procedural proficiencies in magnificent hues, shades and sonic

---

[13] In our age of infinite, instantly accessible (and very often free) music, we perhaps sometimes forget that to actually hear new music, especially large-scale forms like opera and orchestral music, was in Sibelius's early years a relatively rare occurrence. And it cost a significant amount of money to do so, especially when you were as addicted to music as Sibelius was.

surfaces.[14] The quintet also contained more than a glance at Finnish folk music – which Sibelius had recently begun studying – and this, together with its boldness of vision and impudence of expression, unambiguously signalled the route towards *Kullervo*.

For his second year abroad, Sibelius had decided that his education would be better served by spending it in another city: Vienna, where he fantasized about being taught by Bruckner or Brahms.[15] He auditioned for a job as violinist in the Vienna Philharmonic, but nerves got the better of him, as they so often would in his performing life. Here in the imperial city, he was prey to the same kind of lavish living as in Berlin – begging letters frequently found their way back to the family in Finland – and he was exposed to music which seemed to have an even greater effect on him than that he had heard in Germany.

Vienna bestowed a remarkable opportunity to hear the latest developments in European sound, as well as its enduring legacy. Performances of Beethoven symphonies were crucial in teaching Sibelius further lessons in structure and orchestration (he had still taken only tentative steps in larger-scale forms, in his Overture and Scène de ballet), and a performance of the Ninth (1824) – with its dramatic choral finale – was to resonate on his immediate imagination. A presentation of Wagner's *Siegfried* (1871) in the spring of 1891 taught him vital new ways and means of embodying the natural world in music, but two other major works in particular profoundly influenced the

---

14 The work received its premiere in Helsinki on 5 May 1890, while Sibelius was still in Berlin, though lack of rehearsal time meant the work was truncated; its first complete performance took place only in 1965, eight years after its creator's death.

15 Although this didn't come to fruition, he nonetheless received some excellent tuition from composer-teachers such as Karl Goldmark – whose opera *Die Königin von Saba* had made him a fashionable choice of instructor – and Robert Fuchs, who had taught the likes of Mahler, Wolf and Zemlinsky.

temperament, character and musical style of *Kullervo*: Wagner's *Tristan und Isolde* (1865) and Bruckner's Third Symphony (1873; rev. 1877 and 1889).

Tristan's intoxicating evocation of illicit eroticism, metaphysical despair, orchestral intensity and hazardous harmonics Sibelius heard on 21 November 1890. Exactly a month later, on 21 December, he heard a new revised version of Bruckner's Third (the Austrian Anton shared the Finn Jean's predilection for self-doubt and amendment), performed with its composer – who Sibelius fervently claimed the greatest alive – in attendance. Both works made seismic impressions on the young Finn, as they have for so many since. Bruckner's influence, especially, can be detected in the first movement of *Kullervo*, with its sombre, imposing orchestral writing, as well as the majestic hymnal music for brass choirs and a whole range of tremolo and ostinato figurations on the strings – though, as we shall see, all this was devised and expressed in a uniquely Sibelian fashion.

Important as these, and many other, musical stimuli were, something else had an even more powerful impact on Sibelius's path towards *Kullervo*. The day before the Bruckner concert, he wrote to his fiancée, Aino, back in Finland with news that not only was he reading and understanding a lot more Finnish but he was largely doing so by his immersive obsession with a book, one which was deeply infusing all his moods. Although relatively ancient in origin, it struck Sibelius as astonishingly contemporary, and what's more, as pure music, themes and variations. The book became a part of Sibelius, developing into a vital aspect of his flesh and soul. A holy text to him, it was also intimately bound to his relationship with Aino, the love of his life.

This was, of course, the great Finnish epic, the *Kalevala*, one of world literature's supreme achievements and, aside from Aino, set to become the dominant non-musical energy and inspiration in Sibelius's life's work. By mid-April of 1891, he wrote again to his fiancée with the momentous news that he was working on a symphony, 'completely in the Finnish spirit', quoting its first movement's main theme in the letter. Far from Helsinki and Finland's lakes and forests, in the urbane, modern metropolis of Klimt and Freud, *Kullervo* was underway.

The *Kalevala* is an anthology of epic poetry rich in magic and myth, compiled – and occasionally embellished – by philologist Elias Lönnrot (1802–1884) on field trips in the early nineteenth century.[16] He took material from Karelian and Finnish oral folklore and mythology as well as from the songs of prehistoric rural Finns, and Lönnrot's book of tales from 'the land of heroes' is akin to many other poetic traditions from around the world – from the *Iliad*, *Nibelungenlied* and *Gilgamesh* to *Beowulf*, *Os Lusíadas* and *La Chanson de Roland*.[17] Today Finland and Finnish enthusiasts globally observe 28 February as Kalevala Day, a national and international celebration of Finnish culture.

---

16 In this respect, of course, Lönnrot was no different from those peoples who collected the compendium of various religious texts and traditions we now know as the Bible. Assemblage, amelioration and dissemination go together.

17 Karelia is an area in northern Europe of historical and cultural significance for Russia, Finland and Sweden. In the early part of the Middle Ages, settlers from western Finland mixed with the local population to form the Karelian ethnic group, with its own language and sociocultural identity (the Karelian language is closely related to Finnish, especially to dialects in the east of Finland). Today the region is politically divided between land in north-western Russia and in south-eastern Finland, with the latter including popular tourism locations like the Koli National Park. 'Karelianism' was a significant phenomenon in the nineteenth century for Finland in establishing a sense of its own individuality.

Lönnrot's first version of the *Kalevala*, from 1835, had some twelve thousand verses, but a second, much longer version in 1849 extended the collection to approach twenty-three thousand verses, divided into around fifty stories.[18] The chronology of the oral tradition itself is less certain: the oldest themes, such as the creation of the earth, date from around three thousand years ago, and the custom of oral storytelling continued largely until the arrival of written forms, including those from beyond the Karelian/Finnish lands, during the Reformation. Published at a time when Finnish culture and national identity were rapidly beginning to take shape, the *Kalevala*, along with its interpreters, assumed the fundamental sociopolitical position that the Finnish peoples had a glorious shared past and mutual heritage (even if this was a slight elaboration of the more complex truth).

The *Kalevala* tells the story of the creation of the world, along with the various disputes and disagreements between several communities – including numerous, infinitely regressing, retaliatory battles. We encounter the people of Kalevala itself, the Väinölä, and their adversaries, the people of Pohjola, as well as an impressive wealth-making device – the *sampo* – which lies at the heart of many of the stories of love, lust, power and death (and is a little like the horn of plenty in classical antiquity). Kidnapping, theft and seduction form a vital series of plotlines, as do protagonists' attempts to master particular skills (boatbuilding, hunting or ironmongery) or overcome horrendous obstacles, which all too often lead to their humiliation, exile and suicide.

Cosmic mythology and human activity on a stunning scale, the *Kalevala* is poetry which is by turns violent, intimate, affectionate, enigmatic and spectacular. Its interpretation of

---

18 Lönnrot also produced a more lyrical sister collection, the *Kanteletar*, in 1840.

origins and behaviour forms a glorious mixture of religious rites, powerful narratives and profound truths. It blends social hierarchies and cultural anxieties with psychological traumas, heroic deeds with shameful acts, outlandish fantasies and private proceedings with a range of cult and occult images, entities and events. The mysterious object at the centre of the epic – the *sampo* – is precisely that because not only does no one know exactly what it is, but anyone (either in the stories or reading them) can project their own meaning onto it. Is it made of gold or silver? Is it a talisman, a divinity, a spirit, a life-giving force like the sun or air, or is it merely a symbol – a beacon of hope or an article of despair? Like the rings in Tolkien and Wagner, the *Kalevala's sampo* reveals far more about us than it does about itself.

Along with the envy, incest and supernatural artefacts, setting and landscape are crucial elements of the *Kalevala* cycle, as we might expect for such an ancient and rural literary collection, and this aspect was of as vital significance to Sibelius as the compelling narratives and emotional-mystical penetration: indeed, they could not be separated. From season to season and from place to place, we travel in the *Kalevala* through a huge diversity of topographies and meteorological conditions. We witness canorous demigods lost at sea, ethereal swans floating on dark rivers, handsome heroes lost in thick thickets and treacherous woods. Lakes, forests, plains; spring, summer, winter; sun, snow, flames – the *Kalevala* presents an evocative and hazardous world of dread, change and fascination.

The whole work starts with boundless waters and a bird searching for a place to nest: the *Kalevala* is the story of a people often marginalized, afraid and seeking refuge from the hostile world in which they have found themselves. At his grand house, Ainola, in which he would live from 1904 to his death, Sibelius might have enjoyed the comfort of modern accommodation and conveniences – fine linen and a great green fireplace – but he still knew the power of the natural world, as well as its dynamic and metaphorical connections to our mental welfare. Throughout his life, he spent a good deal of time outdoors, needing the isolation and intermittent loneliness within the wild beauty of Finland to enrich his soul, temper his mind and spark his creativity. The Finnish epic both confirmed and extended this outlook.

In terms of structure and form, both of which were crucial in Sibelius's adaptation of the material for his musical purposes, the *Kalevala* was a rich resource, with an intriguing and inimitable employment of various chords, metres, and rhythms and a range of captivating musico-literary devices that could be utilized and developed in new compositions. The poems were often performed as a duo, with alternating, antiphonic verses – almost a singing competition – and sometimes accompanied by the mesmerizing sounds of a kantele (a plucked string instrument, not unlike a zither).

As well as influencing Sibelius, the *Kalevala* has had a significant impact on global music, art and culture. Before Janne, Robert Kajanus's *Kullervo's Funeral March* (1880) and *Aino* (1885)[19] were important early orchestral works inspired by the epic (the latter also significantly brought in a male chorus for its closing sequence), as was a neo-Wagnerian opera *Die Kalewainen in Pochjola* (1890) by the German Karl Müller-Berghaus (which, sadly, has never been performed). During Sibelius's lifetime, and now well beyond it, numerous fellow Finns – such as Leevi Madetoja, Einojuhani Rautavaara, Tauno Marttinen and Aulis

---

19   *Aino* is a remarkable post-Wagnerian symphonic poem, full of rich harmonies and snaking chromaticism, combined with an astounding array of orchestral colours and textures, and its potent inclusion of a male voice chorus had obvious implications for Sibelius's *Kullervo*.

Sallinen – have turned to the *Kalevala* for their own music, and the epic's reach has also extended to folk metal and symphonic metal music, so that bands like Amorphis, Turisas, Korpiklaani and Amberian Dawn have drawn heavily on its poetry for inspiration, as well as some of their lyrics. Albums like *River of Tuoni* (2008) and *Manala* (2012) directly reference the Finnish realm of the dead in their titles.[20]

In art, numerous paintings and sculptures have taken characters and incidents from the *Kalevala* as their subject. Perhaps most famous is the work of Sibelius's soon-to-be friend and drinking buddy Akseli Gallen-Kallela (1865–1931), whose disturbing, intense art depicts Kullervo, Lemminkäinen, and the forging of the *sampo*, among several others. (Gallen-Kallela also created the well-known 1894 work *Symposium*, portraying the boozed-up Sibelius and Kajanus.) Beyond Finland, the epic has inspired numerous artistic products, both popular and more serious. *The Quest for Kalevala* sees Donald Duck on a Finnish adventure, while the young J. R. R. Tolkien claimed the *Kalevala* as one of his sources for *The Silmarillion*; he also drafted *The Story of Kullervo* during the First World War (it was eventually published in the summer of 2015).

Like all epics, the *Kalevala* speaks to a huge range of people on a huge range of subjects. But, as we have seen, one of the first – and perhaps the most important – of its devotees was Jean Sibelius. Its language, images and stories fascinated him, drawing him deeply into himself and expressing things he had often felt and had yearned to say. He found the *Kalevala* to be teeming with stimulating, exhilarating cadences, expedient patterns, muscular

---

20   Sibelius's great-grandson Lauri Porra (1977–) is now an influential metal musician himself: as bass guitarist for Finnish power metal band Stratovarius, as a writer of dark film scores, and as an occasional composer for the Lahti Symphony Orchestra and Finnish Radio Symphony Orchestra.

alliteration and potent parallelism, as well as some enthralling variations on themes, both narrative and musical. These were to be the ingredients for a new kind of music, but one based on a long tradition. It was to be an especially, uniquely, Finnish music, something he had mentioned as 'a new, Finnish type of song' when discussing his setting of Johan Ludvig Runeberg's poem 'Drömmen' ('The Dream'). Sibelius's style would now take in, exploit and explore what he called the 'melodious, strangely melancholic monotony which is in all Finnish melodies.'

The *Kalevala* would inspire numerous works from Sibelius's pen – both directly and indirectly, since all his abstract symphonies as well as his tone poems, whether using *Kalevala* material straightforwardly or not, can trace their origins to the epic. Its reach and effect on Sibelius were profound and total. So while *Lemminkäinen*, *Pohjola's Daughter* and *Luonnotar* have direct connections, associations in works like *Nightride and Sunrise* and the Fifth Symphony are more tangential and implicit. But the link with the epic – its characters, landscapes, legends and themes – is nearly always there, however veiled. It forever haunted his poetico-musical imagination.

It was to be the grave, furious, terrible tale of Kullervo, though, which inspired Sibelius's initial artistic engagement with the *Kalevala*. What was the story, and why did it seem to speak so powerfully to him, as he continued his studies down in Vienna and first cautiously, then urgently began to compose a gigantic symphonic work?

Growing up in the aftermath of his entire tribe's massacre, Kullervo – bequeathed from his youth with prodigious Herculean powers, and a sort of amalgam of Oedipus and Siegmund – comes to realize that the very people who had raised him, the Untamo, are also the tribe who had murdered his family. Sold into slavery as a child, he is mocked and tormented before finally running away from his captors. He discovers some surviving members of his family, only to lose them again. Then, having thought his sister dead, Kullervo goes on to successfully seduce a girl who turns out to be this very sister. After discovering the truth of her lover's origins and connection to herself, she commits suicide. Kullervo becomes mad with rage, returns to Untamo and, using his magical powers, destroys the tribe, before turning his own sword on himself in a fit of guilt and grief. Closing the tale, the old sage Väinämöinen, one of the leading protagonists of the *Kalevala*, warns parents against treating their children too harshly – for there will be repercussions for all.

This was the story as Sibelius encountered it in the epic: a gruesome, electrifying, emotionally and psychologically complex plot, full of fascinating situations, bold characters and a wealth of dramatic detail.[21] It was ripe for extended musico-dramatic treatment, and Sibelius's recent experiences of Wagner and Bruckner in Vienna encouraged him to begin work on a vast new symphonic piece, far bigger in scope and scale than anything he had hitherto managed – or even conceived. That the huge and intense music of major Romantics galvanized the young composer has not surprised those who analyse *Kullervo*; that this fierce and unreservedly Finnish work of art should have been conceived and begun in municipal, bourgeois Vienna has, however, often puzzled commentators.

---

21 Kullervo's role in the first version of the *Kalevala* is relatively small; he becomes far more prominent in Lönnrot's extended 1849 edition.

In fact, of course, Sibelius composed amid the glittering erotic paintings and impending psychoanalysis of the fin-de-siècle city, an invigorating, hallucinogenic world haunted by death, disease and creative self-destruction: the ideal, even obvious, environment to inspire *Kullervo*.[22] A work of Oedipal savagery and despair, crammed with sex, suffering and the lust for revenge, it was in many ways far more likely to spring from late nineteenth-century Vienna than Finland and the *Kalevala*. But, there again, tales of vengeance and desire are common to all peoples, even if the particular insights Sibelius cultivated are especially Freudian in their perceptive reach concerning guilt, excess and corrosion, both moral and physical. Sibelius might not have read Freud, but the issues and attitudes were already about. Freud was a symbol, a symptom, of a damaged, shimmering, agitated world.

The intoxicating mood in Vienna therefore only deepened the composer's fascination with the mythic, archetypal world of the *Kalevala*, both forces combining to discharge a work of great creative vitality and psychological acumen. Sibelius's selection of the Kullervo story was an auspicious coalescence of atmosphere and theme. More than that: given the huge range of material available to him in the *Kalevala*, choosing Kullervo – for what is perhaps his most psychologically powerful work – must have been partly informed, and strengthened, by the new attitudes to sexual practice and a disturbed obsession with death that were swirling through the populace. Vienna was the fuel to the already scorching Kullervo inferno.

---

22   Sigmund Freud first began his work on neurosis, hysteria and the unconscious in the mid- to late 1880s, though his first publications on the subject were not until the mid-1890s, after *Kullervo*'s premiere, with *Studies on Hysteria* (1895) and then the even more groundbreaking *The Interpretation of Dreams* (1899).

Might there also have been more personal reasons? Even if we discount any direct psycho-emotional association between Sibelius and Kullervo, the fatherless boy who submits to forbidden carnal desire followed by stoic resolve, the subject was clearly a compelling one that struck a chord with Sibelius's current world view and much of his reading matter. As such, other key literary influences beyond the *Kalevala* are apparent in *Kullervo*, helping create a work that not only is unequivocally Finnish but cinematically showcases a whole range of other panoramas beyond the (relatively) narrow confines of Finnish folklore. Sibelius was especially preoccupied by naturalist and realist movements, particularly as expressed in the poetry of Johan Ludvig Runeberg (1804–1877) and the novels of Émile Zola (1840–1902), two figures who did not shy away from the harshness of human existence or the power of sexual proclivity.

Runeberg – who, as we saw above, Sibelius had already set to music, which he would do many times again in his extensive song output – was a significant figure in Finnish letters and is today considered the national poet. His epic verse appealed to Sibelius with its concern for a faithful portrayal of human existence, with all its sadnesses and joys, sensual excitements and pangs of pain. Runeberg celebrated the Finnish landscape and its people, taking in first-hand stories of its past and developing them in his art – which included patriotic words that would one day become the national anthem. Serious in his commitment to both Finland and poetry, Runeberg had a freshness – which so appealed to Sibelius – that lies in his fusion of classically orientated themes with Romantic sensitivity, together with the propensity for realism that characterizes his sympathetic identification with rural communities and their wide-ranging lives.

One of the giants of late nineteenth-century French literature, the prolific Zola was intent on creating an art of detachment and determinism, where actions have consequences but where the artist maintains an impassive gaze. Only days before he began *Kullervo* in April 1891, Sibelius was writing ecstatically about his passion for the novelist, and the previous December he had told Aino in a letter that he had just finished reading (and had very much enjoyed) Zola's *Thérèse Raquin* (1867), a brilliant murky tale of murder and sexual depravity (with its magnificent guilt-and-shame-inducing poker-faced cat, François).

Although *Kullervo* is quintessentially Finnish, employing Finnish texts in its third and fifth movements, and irrefutably idealistic (think of the great Romantic opening on the strings or the slow movement's lullaby), Sibelius's fascination with realism (and the wider social concerns the realist movement articulated) pervades the score. Its depiction of sex and seduction was as forthright and convincing as anything from Zola or on the musical stage. Sex, in one form or another, had been in opera for centuries – from Monteverdi's *L'incoronazione di Poppea* (1643) and Mozart's *Don Giovanni* (1787) to Bizet's *Carmen* (1875) – and would become even more prevalent and explicit in the twentieth century, via works like Strauss's *Salome* (1905), Shostakovich's *Lady Macbeth* (1932) and Berg's *Lulu* (1935). Yet somehow including sex in a peculiar hybrid cantata/symphony was even more shocking: such filth, it might be claimed, belonged in the notoriously sordid world of the opera house but not in the supposedly uncontaminated, refined realm of the concert hall.

Certainly, there was no precedent for such blunt, unambiguous sex (and incestuous sex at that) in Finnish music, though recent Finnish literature had contained realistic representations of human sexual activity – indeed, Sibelius had read Juhani Aho's erotic thriller *Yksin* (1890) in the winter before he began *Kullervo*.[23] Perhaps even more than literature, however, music is adept at conjuring sex: its formal arrangements of uncertainty, anticipation, tension, rhythm, climax and release are intrinsically inclined towards sensual representation, communication and analysis. Wagner, for one, knew it: his *Tristan*, which had captured Sibelius so strongly around the time he read *Yksin*, utilized the very mechanics of music – chromaticism, tonal ambiguity, orchestral colour, harmonic suspension – to represent the intricate processes of longing, repression, ecstasy, remorse and liberation as well as other complex workings of the human mind and loins. And Sibelius had been paying attention.

Kullervo might have been based on ancient folkloric poetry, yet it was given urgency by both the modern music contemporary Europe had to offer and by the piquant cultural, intellectual and scientific experiments of contemporary Vienna, as well as by the latest salacious contributions from frantic Finnish and Parisian pens.

---

23 An intoxicating, persuasive combination of realism, Romanticism and erogenous pleasures, its principal female character, Anna, is an unmistakeable literary presentation of Aino Järnefelt, Sibelius's fiancée, with whom Aho was also very much in love. The title *Yksin* means 'alone', and the novel tells the story of a young Finn who plans to travel to Paris to study but becomes ensnared in an obsession with the beautiful Anna. Clearly many of the book's features would have chimed with the presently expatriate student Sibelius, and as with the *Kalevala*, *Yksin* was a key catalyst in driving Sibelius's desire to perfect his understanding of the Finnish language.

Chronologically, musically and thematically, *Kullervo* (1892) seems a link between *Tristan und Isolde* (1865), *Der Ring des Nibelungen* (1876) and *Le Sacre du printemps* (1913), between the shadowy power of Wagner's works and the savage, unrestrained folk energies of Stravinsky's great springtide rite. *Kullervo* connects, too, the symbolist sympathies in Sibelius with his desire to present art in a realist fashion: his dual need to represent absolute truths symbolically through language, sounds and metaphorical images, and to voice the vital needs, sentiments and insights of his age – not least around sexuality and erotic angst – was frankly acknowledged and explored.

With this significant range of literary, musical, cultural and psychological energies at work inside him, as he sat in his student flat in the capital of the Austro-Hungarian Empire, often pining for his beloved Aino as well as his homeland, Sibelius set about creating a new kind of work. It was to be, not least because of its sundry origins and stimuli, a strange restless synthesis which would confuse the boundaries between musical forms, disturb socio-cultural-political complacencies and subject the mythic epic poetry of the north to a brash psychological realism, primitive severity and delicious sensuality.

Listening to his teacher Karl Goldmark, who advised him to craft his themes with the utmost care and attention, Sibelius initially discarded some fifty main subjects for *Kullervo* before he finally arrived at one which suited his desire for an arresting, captivating opening. In a letter to Aino on 18 April 1891, he wrote it out for her (though it was still in F major, not the more sombre E minor we now know), and it is a moving experience to see this extraordinary music appearing in the wider world for the first time, sandwiched between its composer's words to his beloved.

For all this joy, however, he was still a little unsure how to progress, uncertain as to exactly the kind of work he was creating. He knew how different it was, not only from everything he himself had hitherto written (not least in terms of scale) but from other music. Nevertheless, he continued to labour on the first movement for the rest of his stay in Vienna and during the summer back home, and then on the coast in Loviisa in the autumn.

At the end of the year another important ingredient was added to the *Kullervo* pot – with its already rich and piquant stew – when he met Larin Paraske (1833–1904), a singer of Karelian runes, those idiosyncratic poems from the northern lands.[24] Paraske was an Izhorian, one of an Indigenous Finnic people native to Ingria, a small territory now part of north-west Russia, and a passionate advocate and upholder of the distinctive oral poetry of the region. Her memory was astounding: able to intone tens of thousands of lines of verse, she was a living Mnemosyne and haunting, spellbinding personality – as photographs and portraits by Albert Edelfelt and Eero Järnefelt testify.

Sibelius was, of course, fascinated, noting down the melodies and rhythms, hearing in them a means to help forge his own sound world. He was especially intrigued by the way singers prolonged and stressed vowels or a word's last syllables for dramatic effect, and Sibelius twisted his musical language in response. Although he tended to keep a more natural stress at the end of words, we can hear in the third movement of *Kullervo*

---

24 In some of his later recollections, Sibelius thought he had finished *Kullervo* before he met Paraske, though this seems to have been a slip of memory.

– especially at the great moment when the chorus enters – how he has the orchestra maintain a consistent beat, while the voices above stretch their phrases. Added to this is Sibelius's flexible, compound use of melody and harmony, as he incorporates what he learned from Indigenous music into the Western tradition. Harmonies waft and wander away from orthodox major/minor codes, as folk melodies coil and weave around them, producing extraordinary knots and constellations of sound, both frightening and enthralling.

An affectionate love letter to Aino at the turn of the year included the theme for the second movement, and as 1892 progressed, so did the symphony. By March he decided the choral voices should be male ones (taking the somewhat condescending, if well-intentioned, view that a female choir would be embarrassed by the licentiousness of the third movement), and rehearsals were ready to begin at the start of April, firing up a rabble of excited voices in the press about this grand new work for Finland. Sibelius proved himself to be an energetic and competent organizer, not only engaging the Great Hall of the University of Helsinki but coordinating the production of advertisements, programmes, tickets and the endless administrative paraphernalia such events require.

The official language of the Finnish orchestra was, in fact, German, since many – even, at times, most – of the players hailed from more southern lands. As such, communications during the rehearsals were often a little strained and awkward between the Finnish and Swedish speakers and their Teutonic counterparts: various translations and paraphrases were thrown about as everyone tried to master this gigantic, and often very complex, symphonic creation. Those promoters of the Finnish language – the Fennomans – were triumphant: *Kullervo* was clearly granting them victory over their Swedish language rivals, the Svecomans, and the march towards an independent Finnish identity was gathering speed.

Met with near-unanimous praise – most of the cynics came from the Svecoman camp – *Kullervo* marked a turning point in Sibelius's life and career. Not only did its success significantly upgrade his status – as both a composer and as a Finnish national icon – to such an extent that (according to Aino's testimony) the Järnefelts consented to their daughter's marriage, which followed just a few weeks after the premiere, but it encouraged the composer to find his firmest, most original and most compelling voice as a composer of symphonies and orchestral tone poems. So Sibelius's focus now shifted away from chamber works and towards large-scale instrumental and symphonic music, though he would continue to compose songs and piano pieces, as well as important works for the theatre: *Kullervo*'s drama was instinctive within him.

Structurally, Sibelius fashioned a wonder. Written for two soloists, a mezzo-soprano[25] and a baritone, who sing in the third movement only, and male voice choir, who participate in the third and fifth movements, *Kullervo* is scored for a fairly restrained orchestra – certainly a modest vehicle compared to the extravagant forces required by Sibelius's distinguished contemporaries, Mahler and Strauss. *Kullervo* is laid out as follows:

---

25 Although Sibelius's score indicates soprano, the work has almost always been sung with a mezzo voice – including at its 1892 premiere in Helsinki.

I. **Introduction.** The brooding, ominous sonata-form opening movement evokes the heroic sweep of the work's mythical setting in the Finnish landscape, as well as presenting us with the complex, tragic figure of Kullervo.

II. **Kullervo's Youth.** A glowing, luminous lullaby with complementary bucolic episodes and the sounds of nature, which also indicates the hero has been positioned for tragedy since his birth, sold into servitude.

III. **Kullervo and His Sister.** A vast movement, making up a third of the entire work, with the baritone and mezzo presenting Kullervo and his sister, while the male chorus set the scene and offer commentary. Kullervo encounters three women and tries to seduce them; with the third he succeeds, learning too late she is his long-lost sister. When she discovers the truth, she leaps into a stream and drowns. Kullervo laments her death and his crime.

IV. **Kullervo Goes to War.** A gleaming, ghoulish scherzo as Kullervo tries to avenge his tribe, and atone for his own sins, through a glorious massacre on the battlefield.

V. **Kullervo's Death.** A haunting male chorus tell of how Kullervo inadvertently returns to the site of his transgression with his sister, a place marked by dead grass and the barren earth, unable to rejuvenate itself. Here the broken hero meets his dreadful end.

Each of the five movements represents part of Kullervo's life, with the first, second and fourth movements being purely instrumental and the voices joining in for the third and fifth, singing verses from the *Kalevala*.[26] These two tactics in the art of musical storytelling created an alluring combination, though clearly precedents had existed in other forms too (the great orchestral interludes and quasi–tone poems within Wagner's *Ring*, as well as symphonies by Beethoven and Mahler).

Sibelius has an obvious, unavoidable narrative methodology when employing vocalists to sing lines from the *Kalevala* story, combined with a more abstract approach elsewhere. The pair of soloists are highly expressive and dramatically varied, almost performing an opera at the centre of the symphony, while the choir is declamatory in an astounding display of melodramatic-oratorical power (their first entry in the third movement surely one of the most striking and unforgettable moments in all music).

In the three orchestra-only movements, Sibelius the symphonist and tone poet is on full display as he seeks to encapsulate the gist and atmosphere of the story rather than its particulars, using the abstract power of the instruments to brilliantly invoke narrative and mood. Nonetheless, within the vocal sections, too, the orchestra maintains its dazzling ability to depict and represent key narrative elements of the story – such as the crucial climactic moment when the protagonist seduces his sister.

The writing of *Kullervo* has a boldness, a self-assurance, an inspired gait, that nothing in Sibelius's previous music had achieved. Works like the F major violin sonata and G minor piano quintet had exhibited a wonderful range of moods via

---

26 Runos 35 and 36, though the sombre history in Nos. 31–34 is also evoked in the other movements.

remarkable melodies and with an excellent overall structural unity. But Sibelius's conversion of this promise into a large-scale vocal-orchestral symphony was incredible. In *Kullervo*, the thematic material he uses is impressive, haunting, lingering in the memory; his textures and harmonies are effective, stark and audacious; his deployment of instrumental and vocal forces is handled with supreme skill and sonic management.

Indeed, the coherence of the score is staggering. Although *Kullervo* is routinely cited as the black sheep among Sibelius's symphonies, or as the mongrel outsider, in truth it represents his first realization of joining and then merging divergent elements into a compelling, natural whole. In this work, forms and themes weave, entwine and interconnect in ways that unambiguously anticipate the snug organic interdependency of his future music. The 'severity of style and profound logic' that was to become his working methodology, almost a maxim, is readily apparent in *Kullervo* – a troubling, prophetic early masterpiece.

Kullervo, op.7

1. *Introduction. [Allegro moderato.]*

Kullervo opens with a portentous, faraway humming on the strings. Driving above them, in dark and threatening E minor, the clarinets and horns play a motto-like theme that will recur throughout (returning with particular force at the close of the finale). It is a magnificent character portrait of Kullervo, immediately conveying his brooding tragedy and fatalistic determination (the theme's supple harmonization give it a vital elastic power). There are immediate echoes of Bruckner in both the subject itself and its evolution, as well as suggestions of Brahms's dynamic solemnity in the way the lower sounds vigorously determine the overall atmosphere, though the affinity with Finnish folk song is never lacking either. This is ancient Indigenous music refracted through the sonic lenses of modern imperial Vienna.

The movement, in a relatively strict sonata form, has a bravura and resplendent arch which instantly captivates. Eventually, the strings take over the main theme, and the mood not exactly lightens but is allowed to breathe a little easier, expanding further than when the dark subject was sounded on the horns and clarinets. Before long comes a more reflective, quasi-philosophical second subject, with the horn suggesting the inescapability of Kullervo's fate. Sibelius here anticipates a harmonic device which will come into its own in his Fourth Symphony of 1911: the so-called augmented fourth, a kind of tritone – a form of musical interval often known as the devil's music for its especially devious flexibility, distinctiveness and unsettling tonal effect. In *Kullervo*, the tritone's power is not exploited or woven into the fabric of the score in the same way as the Fourth Symphony, but it is troubling nevertheless, alerting us to the hero's precarious personality and dreadful destiny.

This meditative and disturbing episode gradually carries the introduction into a harmonically audacious development section in E major where we hear a variety of especially intrepid writing for the woodwind – in particular some bravely wide-open oboe sextuplets that must have severely challenged the premiere's players (as well as many more since). Mixing memories of Finnish folk sounds with delicious plunges into gorgeous Brucknerian daring, the development is one of *Kullervo*'s most fascinating and boldly inventive passages, quietly lulling us into a false sense of security before the shock and awe of what is to come.

Suddenly, the opening motto theme returns on the brass and woodwind with relentless predictability as Sibelius gives us his hero in all his appalling splendour. It is a section of stunning courage and overconfidence: precisely the tone needed at this still preliminary and exploratory part of the symphonic drama. With similar (and interlinked) inevitability, however, the movement then travels to its conclusion with a coda of crushing defeat, prophesying Kullervo's inexorable annihilation in ignominy and disgrace, a lonely hero to be destroyed by both fate and his own shortcomings.

With exceptional broad but intriguing brushstrokes, the opening movement to *Kullervo* paints a dark and fearsome sonic picture of its hero, contextualized within his ominous background, that is rich with import and anticipation, a symphonic tone poem of immense grandeur, sweep and power.

2. *Kullervo's Youth.* [Grave.]

If Bruckner and Brahms haunt the opening to *Kullervo*, the deflected spirit of Tchaikovsky prowls its slow movement, infiltrating lilting grace with encroaching emotion, discomfort and pain. The overall model of the movement develops that of the andante from Sibelius's G minor piano quintet, written in Berlin the year before *Kullervo*: namely, themes are reiterated but with gradual changes to the rhythm and texture.

The movement is in a plastic rondo form, perhaps a little ironic, and cast as a lullaby in B major with variations that begin haloed in a tender radiance before swelling in psychological concentration as we are told, in instrumental terms, of the hero's hapless, doomed childhood and the growth of his steely willpower. The 'lullaby motif' itself begins with a peaceful, even pacifying, rhythm that turns increasingly agitated and violent, with turbulent, coursing strings, percussive reiterations, and shouty, rough-hewn interruptions on the brass, before passing out in a haze of affliction and fatigue. The progress of the movement is a psychedelic phantasmagoria of changes apprising us of the cumulative woe of Kullervo's existence, and Sibelius's brilliant but often subtle transformation of the motif is one of the key portents of his supreme evolutionary logic in symphonic writing.

Many of the thematic ideas we come across bear a salient resemblance to the local, rural, runic style Sibelius had picked up in his encounters with Finnish folk music. These contrast and engage with pastoral, shepherd-like episodes governed by intentionally artificial and schematic sounds of nature from the woodwind: not only is Sibelius keen to alert us to the harsh world Kullervo inhabits, but the stylized voices accent the tragic inevitability of the protagonist's fate. Moreover, just like runic singers, Sibelius's variations become increasingly complex, altering his themes and rhythms, combining and recombining ideas in a variety of ways. It is a magnificent anticipation of the folk violence and rhythmic intensity to be found in Bartók and Stravinsky (most obviously and alarmingly, of course, in *The Rite of Spring*).

Distinctive, innovative and enduring, *Kullervo*'s slow movement is also effectively a second introduction, coercing the opening to become an even more distant and threatening prelude, a dramatic doubling that only heightens the tension and expectation we feel as we wonder what distressing events lie in store for our hero. They arrive soon enough.

3. *Kullervo and His Sister*. [*Allegro vivace*.]

Vast, alluring and uncompromising, this is the central movement of *Kullervo* in every way. An opera staged in the heart of a symphony, a dramatic cantata erupting in the middle of an orchestral sphere – it is a breathtakingly audacious interjection.

This protracted and multifaceted movement begins with a rushing orchestral prelude in F major portraying Kullervo's windswept journey across the bleak northern lands. It is in a wild dancing 5/4 time, a metre familiar from traditional runic singing while also reminding us that Sibelius had been listening to Beethoven scherzos in Vienna. Everything is wonderfully organized in order to prepare us for the startling, impudent and unforgettable D minor[27] entry of the male choir, who have been patiently seated for half an hour and now function as a kind of dynamic, diabolical Greek chorus: impersonal, non-individualized and utterly indifferent in their ominous dignity.

> Kullervo, Kalervon poika!   Kullervo, Kalervo's child!

Their hymn, which continues, telling of Kullervo's rough ride, has a splendidly antiquated rigour, all monophonic grandeur as Finnish words finally inaugurate what the instruments have hitherto only been hinting at: here is Kullervo, and he is going to fall – and fall hard.

---

27   Though it also has some modal inflections, which only add to the drama.

The role of the orchestra is no less powerful in this movement, however, often providing an unswerving beat and relentless rhythmic momentum over which the voices can stretch and twirl, elongating their lines (in the case of the choir) and vividly varying their expression (in the case of the two soloists). For soon enough, the baritone and mezzo – brother and sister – begin to enact their unwitting transgressions.

Initially, the two singers dramatize brief dialogues between Kullervo and the three maidens he tries to seduce (with added narration from the chorus). The harmonies and rhythms grow in agitation and intensity before he finally succeeds with the third, his inadvertent sibling cum lover. He entices her into his cold, dark sledge on the promise of fruit and nuts in return (an ironic connection with the sister's original disappearance), and the orchestra reassert their dominance by depicting the love scene with an extraordinary erotic vehemence and thrill: a passionate C-sharp major section with an ardent ascending violin theme attended by effervescent throbbing brass below.

From here, as the orchestra, and the lovers, subside, comes a scene freighted with anguish as the siblings discover the truth of their shared origins, the sister's demise captured in a desolate, heartrending monologue for the mezzo. It is a stunning set piece that makes us mourn Sibelius's aborted opera career (but thankful for the hundreds of songs he left us and for *Luonnotar*, still to come). She sings of the strangeness of her life ever since, years before, she became lost when gathering berries, separated until today from her people. (In the *Kalevala* she then drowns herself, though this is not explicitly presented in Sibelius's music.) After this, all that is left is a blunt coda. In grief, isolation and remorse Kullervo furiously curses his fate with his own moving monologue (in a brusque F minor) accompanied by spacious ferocious chords from the orchestra (which foreshadow the end of the Fifth Symphony, a quarter of a century away).

The scene is a tremendous, unimaginable darkening of Wagner's *Die Walküre*. In the *Ring*, the incestuous sexual congress of the twins Siegmund and Sieglinde, though generating much death and suffering, also bears the forbidden fruit of the hero, Siegfried. In *Kullervo* no such promise is forthcoming, and the whole movement is an extraordinary display of Sibelius's raw power – it seems light years away from the lush Romanticism of the late nineteenth century, occupying a more hostile, cruel realm akin to the later symphonies of Shostakovich.

4. *Kullervo Goes to War. [Alla marcia.]*

The work might have ended here, with a sister's horrendous song of lamentation and a brother's guilt-and-grief-stricken monologue. But Sibelius and the *Kalevala* (as well as the composer's other psycho-literary influences) have other plans, and from here, *Kullervo* shifts to something far nimbler and energetic, though with suffering shading the music's conditions. It is almost a modern movie score, reminiscent of the sinister hues amid the dazzle of John Williams's *Superman* (1978), or the flashes of exaltation that pervade the ominous musical language of Hans Zimmer's *The Dark Knight* (2008) and Michael Giacchino's *The Batman* (2022).

Valiant, superhuman and disconcertingly cheerful at times, the fourth movement is *Kullervo*'s unexpected and scintillating scherzo in C major, and a wonderful discharge of tension. The hero's striving for redemption through vengeance is futile (we know that), but it affords him (and us) some measure of release and salvation as he seeks to expunge his guilt via the massacre of his people's enemies.

As with the slow (second) movement, there is an initially Russian air to this music – Borodin and Rimsky-Korsakov on the steppe – as well as a sprightly outdoorsiness anticipating the Stravinsky of *Petrushka* (1911). All is fresh and exciting as Sibelius conveys with a huge variety of tempos, stresses and colours the wild words of the *Kalevala* in orchestral terms, generally reverting to the all-encompassing tone painting of the first two movements, though with some martial fanfares to depict details of Kullervo's derring-do and reprisals on the battlefield.

5. *Kullervo's Death. [Andante.]*

Sibelius was to become known for the extraordinary cumulative power of his symphonic writing along with his sublime organic unity, but these features are already on potent display in the obdurate, unstoppable tramp to the self-scaffold that is *Kullervo*'s last movement. The finale, a poignant, profound movement of fate, time and consequence, brings us the expected ending foretold since that foundational motto in E minor, and the music is infused by echoes from the rest of the work, especially the opening movement (and particularly its recapitulation section).

The male choir returns with abysmal, baleful inevitability, telling the tale of Kullervo's unsuspecting, but obviously inevitable, arrival back at the scene of his crime. They sing in a gloriously old-fashioned and outmoded manner, folk tunes ramped up to phenomenal size, apparently pressing Kullervo towards his dreadful demise. Once an impassive, indifferent outsider, the choir is now the voice of cruel fate, invoking a macabre dialogue between the swordsman and his sword, the blade thirsty for sinful blood and hungry for aberrant flesh.

There is a long pause – often terrifying in performance – before the final scene, where Kullervo skewers himself on his own sword. This silence is the final sentence on Kullervo, and his fate is sealed once and for all. The choir relate his suicide with choral music of furious rising power, followed by a quieter, contemplative orchestral passage which is then brutally overtaken by the momentous coda with its brilliant reprisal of the initial motto theme. *Kullervo* has circled back to its beginning, confirming and satisfying the inevitability of fate that has permeated the work.

Kullervo is a dramatic mural of extraordinary symphonic scope, musical daring and psychological speculation. It has all the grand and fateful events of opera, yet this work's strange configuration – with its weird narrations, deceptive dialogues, abstract mazes, and blurring, alienating points of view – give it perhaps an even greater emotional power than would be possible on the stage. The music takes us deep inside Kullervo's mind, while simultaneously offering a variety of alternative perspectives that are at once confusing and illuminating.

Each of the five movements has its own character, but they are intimately and impressively bound as one. They not only show us the various events of Kullervo's miserable life, but by being trussed together via a symphony offer shifting contexts, both enlightening and bewildering. We are drawn deeper and deeper into the Kullervo enigma but never manage to penetrate its heart. Sibelius was too canny for that. He wanted a remorseless drama and despotic mystery that – like the *sampo* – tells us far more about ourselves than it does about itself.

Kullervo exists at a significant conceptual distance from Sibelius's seven numbered symphonies, as well as from many of his tone poems. And yet it anticipates many of the styles, techniques and concerns the Finn would develop into his own unique blueprint. It was a foundation, and with *Kullervo*'s imposing architecture Sibelius sealed his own fate as one of the outstanding and most original voices in music.

Chapter Two

Invisible Blood:
En Saga, Spring Song & *The Wood Nymph*

For Sibelius, the tone poem was a vehicle for expressing a range of instincts and compulsions, drawing inspiration from psychology, nature, myth and a range of literary, musical and artistic springs. Yet for the Finn, tone painting and tone poetry did not exist to be mere graphic illustration or sonic depiction, textual-pictorial representations in sound. In both his programmatic and his more liberally conceived tone poems, Sibelius sought something more profound and far-reaching. His sensitivity to mythological and psychological nuances elevates his tone poems to become works of immense insight and emotional-intellectual power, the composer exploring the dark undercurrents of existence lurking in memories, stories, seasons – and even in the suggestive rustle of forest trees.

Between *Kullervo* (1892) and his first numbered symphony at the turn of the century, and after his increasing move away from chamber works towards orchestral music, Sibelius focused on a troika of tone poems: *En Saga*, *Spring Song* and *The Wood Nymph*. Along with *Lemminkäinen*, which followed shortly after, these allowed him to write a range of illustrative, narrative music which nonetheless also anticipated the more abstract ideas and musical techniques of his seven symphonies: telescoping themes and fusing motivic and harmonic material on the road towards a shared objective, as well as in the process blurring the divisions of traditional sonata form into his own distinctive formula.

Both symphonic and programmatic elements had been present in *Kullervo* (in the magnificent architecture; in the richly evocative instrumental painting, especially in the orchestra-only movements). And now Sibelius was ready to explore the tone poem form more fully – the genre in which, together with the symphony, he would find his most characteristic and powerful voice. *Kullervo*'s 'volcanic eruption', as the composer Aksel Törnudd had called it after the premiere, paved the way for Sibelius's orchestral lava: a molten material that moved slowly but inexorably through contemporary music, shifting established models and disrupting convenient forms, both a creative and a destructive force.

* * *

Honeymoons can be productive occasions – as well as reproductive ones. The success of *Kullervo* in the spring of 1892 meant that Sibelius could now tie the knot with Aino Järnefelt, and their marriage accordingly took place at her parents' summer residence, Tottesund, on 10 June.[28] The location for their post-wedding holiday could not be more appropriate, given what had accelerated, even enabled, their nuptials: they travelled to Karelia, that northern region of Europe, now split between Finland and Russia, which is home to the *Kalevala* itself.

For a month from mid-June, the couple hired a small wooden house at Monola, situated deep in the rural landscape near Lieksa. This was on the shore of Lake Pielinen, one of Finland's largest bodies of water, well known for its scenic beauty: dappled by islands, surrounded by coniferous forests, it remains a source of immense inspiration and artistic stimulation.[29] On its western bank lies Koli, now a natural park – a territory which was discovered and, to an extent, determined as the Finnish national landscape amid efforts to construct an iconography for an independent Finland. Sibelius, and painters like Akseli Gallen-Kallela, would be crucial in originating and then propagating these emblems of the country, inspired by the landscape to create their art, which would then become such a vital aspect of the national identity.

The Järnefelts, those fierce advocates for Finnish culture and distinctiveness, would, surely, have been proud of their new son-in-law's immediate engagement with and promotion of the Finnish topography to fashion further a new national music, even

---

28   On the Finnish west coast, and now part of a UNESCO World Heritage Site known in Finnish as Merenkurkku ('the throat of the sea'), it is a spectacular location on the Gulf of Bothnia, the northernmost arm of the Baltic Sea, which separates Sweden from Finland.

29   A simple granary building, the Sibelius honeymoon home recently opened to the public in summer. Given its location, amid trees and with a charming veranda overlooking the vast expanse of Pielinen, it is easy to see how it might have distracted the newlywed composer from his marital duties – though it was clearly an idyllic spot to begin what would turn out to be a sixty-five-year marriage, and Aino was already pregnant by the time the honeymoon was over.

as the ink on the marriage certificate was still wet. He composed three Runeberg songs exploring myth and terrain, including one – 'Under strandens granar' ('Under the Fir Trees') – which is a kind of Finnish 'Erlkönig', a ghostly narrative telling of a child's abduction, and squeezes much intensity and possibility from relatively unassuming simplicity (a Sibelian speciality).[30]

He also worked on a more ambitious piece, an orchestral tone poem, which was interrupted but facilitated by a journey even deeper into the countryside. The honeymoon had been paid for in part by a travel grant from the University of Helsinki to study local Karelian poems, as well as kantele playing and rune singing. Accordingly, after their honeymoon, in mid-July Aino went to stay with relatives in Kuopio, while Sibelius trekked through the Karelia lands, across the Ilomantsi, Korpiselkä and Suojärvi regions, on the way meeting singers such as Mikhail Wornanen, Mikko Tolvanen, Stepnaii Kokkonen and Pedri Shemeikka, learning from their unique Finnic styles and profound engagement with the environment around them.[31]

Runic melodies would be taken and replanted in the music Sibelius was cultivating, exceptional rhythms and motifs that would help make his, and Finland's, sound world so distinct, so

---

[30] Something seen to even greater consequence in another song from this period, 'Se'n har jag ej frågat mera' ('Since Then I Have Questioned No Further'), which would be one of Sibelius's greatest. An exquisite, poignant two minutes telling of lost love and lost time, it uses an utterly unpretentious and straightforward tune – with a basic chordal accompaniment – to devastating effect, and it is hard not to be enchanted and heartbroken every time one hears it. Brahms, in Vienna near the end of his life, listened to Ida Ekman sing the song, accompanied by Eduard Hanslick, and was instantly smitten, demanding to hear it a second time, with himself on the piano. Kissing the Finnish soprano on the forehead afterwards, he implored her to sing more Sibelius when next they met – he was a composer who, Brahms said pithily, 'will become something special'.

[31] 'Finnic' – as opposed to 'Finnish' – refers to the broader, and much older, cultural region, its languages and peoples.

idiosyncratic. Rarely did exact quotations from folk music find their way into his music – though one of Pedri Shemeikka's is cited directly in the first scene of the great *Karelia* incidental music of the following year – but the spirit and atmosphere are marvellously preserved, or imitated, throughout Sibelius's work.

By mid-August, his research activities done (in truth, a fairly inexhaustive survey which did little for academic scholarship but much for personal motivation), Sibelius found his way back down to join his wife in Kuopio (the moody, atmospheric nature of the return journey inspiring a tone poem that was to be written some fifteen years later: *Nightride and Sunrise*). In Kuopio, the Sibeliuses mixed with numerous literary types, including the poet-novelist Karl August Tavaststjerna (1860–1898), whose 1891 novel *Hårdar tider* (*Hard Times*) is not unlike its Dickensian namesake in its challenging realism interspersed with inflections of a more lyrical air, as well as the controversial dramatist Minna Canth (1844–1897), whose plays and commitment to social activism were already helping forge Finland as a place for women's rights.

Back in Helsinki by the end of the summer, Jean and Aino moved into a catastrophically expensive four-room apartment in the centre of town, the ruinous rent alleviated only when Janne's brother Christian joined them. Somewhat more financially astute than his older sibling (though so too were Marie Antoinette, Imelda Marcos and the prodigal son himself, compared to Jean Sibelius), Christian contributed to help prevent the early part of the Sibelius marriage from being too unbearably fraught with fiscal worry. Janne himself helped out with some teaching, theory and the violin, as well as playing in his old quartet.

For the most part, however, Sibelius was engaged that autumn and winter with the musical enterprise that he had commenced on his honeymoon at Monola – though some of it he had begun a few months before (or perhaps even in Vienna a year earlier, as a large-scale chamber work for seven or eight players). Robert Kajanus had requested Sibelius write a short 'da capo' piece, but this was not what the now very animated and ambitious post-*Kullervo* composer wanted to limit himself to. Whatever the consequences artistically or financially (though he would know how to pen popular, profitable pieces when he needed to), Sibelius's sights were now set on a grander project. This was to be the tone poem *En Saga*, the first of his great series of orchestral masterpieces exploring landscape, myth and psychology.

However informed *En Saga* was by Sibelius's summer in the Karelian region, it was also coloured and emboldened by a new friendship launched that autumn with a painter who shared not only Sibelius's passion for the Finnish scenery but his fervour for tipples and intoxicants of almost any description: Akseli Gallen-Kallela. Although Aino Sibelius was astute enough to know her husband needed to develop alliances and networks within Finnish artistic communities, she can hardly have been overjoyed that many of these interactions were undertaken at the notorious Hotel Kämp. Here, ostensibly as an opportunity for arty assembly, intellectual discussion and creative promotion, drinking took place on an epic scale, often for days on end.

Sibelius and his cronies formed a group known as the Symposium, and a famous painting by Gallen-Kallela (which exists in different versions) also bore that name and shows the inebriated Sibelius staring blankly into space, surrounded by glasses, bottles and his drinking buddies, and with an intensely emblematic background.[32] A canvas of terror and amusement, it neatly captures what poor Aino had to put up with at that time, lonely at home as her husband disappeared into the black hole of the Kämp – which, like those dark regions of space-time, was both a creative and a destructive force.

The vigorous, vivacious drunken discussions on art and existence, politics and philosophy, were an important part of Sibelius's artistic maturity, acting as a vital impetus to composition, as well as allowing him to make and maintain key connections in Helsinki society. But the after-effects of such constant – and gigantic – alcoholic lubrication were immensely harmful to not only his marriage but his already complex personality, obliging him into bipolar bouts of paranoia, despair and self-hatred that fluctuated uncontrollably with arrogance, egotism and self-importance.

It also had a financial cost. Drinks had to be paid for, and Sibelius sought out various loans at this time, including one from a bank in Loviisa, on what might have been his final visit to the place where he had spent so many childhood summers. The bank manager, it seems, was sympathetic to the local boy done good (and was perhaps flattering himself too), and Sibelius was able to secure credit in order to fund both bouts of boozing and his more enduring creative endeavours.

After having parted ways with Loviisa, a further break with the past in order to fortify the future occurred in early December, after Sibelius's grandmother, Katarina Juliana Borg, died. Following supper and the wake, Sibelius went around the house, touching the books and objects as if in farewell to his childhood home (which would shortly be sold). He sat at the

---

32 The 1894 version is a little rough, with Sibelius looking especially worse for wear. A later, more refined edition has the composer slightly more alert and sober, but still at a table of boozy chaos as the artists contemplate the wings of Osiris.

harmonium, offering for the grieving family a funeral speech in music. When he had finished, he left the house in silence, without saying goodbye, in order to catch his train. The boy Janne was dead. The man Sibelius, architect and father of Finland, was born.[33]

In between Sibelius's bacchanalias and hangovers, as well as a not inconsiderable amount of teaching to help pay the bills, work on *En Saga* had continued in Helsinki through the autumn and winter of 1892/3, the tone poem growing in size and ambition (the drinking no doubt also acting as a pressure-valve release for the artistic intensity). Whatever its possible origins in Kajanus's aborted commission for a short da capo piece, or as a septet/octet from his time in Vienna, the work is on a considerable scale, lasting over twenty minutes in its original version (and much more varied in material than the more unified final edition of 1902).

The first version of *En Saga* is a more primitive work, more clearly connected to the rugged sound world of *Kullervo*. The youthful composer's abrupt key changes, collocation of motifs, and disturbing sonic discords fashion a work of wonderful impact and gratifying emotional contact. It is blunt and forthright, a craggy and compelling soundscape, and it tends to win over listeners and audiences at once – if not always musicians or critics – as was the case at the premiere. The first performance

---

33 What price to have been at this intimate, private event, where Sibelius's melodies on the antique instrument moved his family to tears, or to even now hear the refrains he gave them in consolation. A charming andante cantabile for piano and harmonium in E-flat major, from around 1887, gives us a tantalizing clue.

took place in Helsinki on 16 February 1893, though not until many of the players, believing the work to be overlong and overworked, had been convinced by Robert Kajanus of the imaginative brilliance and inventive foresight of the music. On the premiere programme, Kajanus conducted some recognizable and reputable orchestral fare – Schumann's *Manfred* and Grieg's *Peer Gynt Suite No.2* – given alongside a few well-known opera arias in order to steady the ship before Sibelius conducted his challenging new piece himself.

A decade later, in 1902, the composer was invited by his friend Ferruccio Busoni to conduct the work with the Berlin Philharmonic in the German capital, and the chance to have his relatively youthful work played by one of the continent's best bands caused Sibelius to revise the piece extensively. (He perhaps also used the opportunity to take to heart some of those complaints from the premiere's performers, as well as to implement the more refined musical methods he had been honing during the 1890s.)

In this final version, *En Saga* has a more developed sonic refinement than Sibelius had given *Kullervo*, or any of his early orchestral works. Its general character is more distinguished, more experienced, the tone poem re-cultivated from the composer's advancing techniques of concision, contraction and amalgamation, which were to become the hallmarks of his approach to the orchestra and overall symphonic management. Accordingly, Sibelius condensed *En Saga* by some 150 bars, in some cases disposing of whole motifs, enhancing the instrumentation, removing the long pastoral episode in the middle, and significantly diminishing the frequency of fluctuations in key or tempo. It made the work less heterogeneous and more cohesive, less chaotic and more internally consistent, while also necessarily weakening some of the wildness and idiosyncratic coarseness he had intended for the piece (and which Aino had so loved).

Part of the reason those early musicians/critics were dismissive of *En Saga*, especially in the 1893 version, might lie not only in the relative roughness of the material but also in the elusive nature of its own programme. The many more palpable and descriptive tone poems from Sibelius's pen in the 1890s and 1900s have now allowed us as listeners to unpack more easily that first essay in the genre. That being said, *En Saga* remains one of the composer's most mysterious, indefinable works, deliberately refusing to engage in directness or schematic comprehension because of the abstract nature of its subject.

Sibelius was clear that *En Saga* is a psychological work, the expression of 'a state of mind'. Expressive and spiritually profound, *En Saga*, the composer maintained, contained the whole of his youth, and when writing it he experienced many things that upset him (only one of which was the death of his grandmother and the consequent, successive final departures from the haunts of his childhood). In no other work did Sibelius claim to reveal himself so completely as in *En Saga*, making all interpretations – literary, critical or musical – in some sense alien, since all those we now hear are not given by the composer himself. To some extent, this highly autobiographical work needed, its creator felt, to have its mother-author present at all its births, whether on the page or the podium.

This, however, is the privilege of artists and their artistic vision, and both conductors and critics can hope to interpret the work in ways that are meaningful beyond its own maker's. Naturally, of course, the very denial of a programme has only fuelled speculation as to what one might or could be. Although it is without definite programme or literary source, *En Saga* is demonstrably a *Finnish* tone poem, its first version especially coming from the atmospheric world of the *Kalevala*. However much Sibelius would initially try to deny any such connection, he would, by 1921, concede to an interviewer that the work did evoke the mood of Finland, and that one could not think of anything other than Finnish landscapes and communities when listening to it. As we saw in the chapter on *Kullervo*, the *Kalevala* was, by the time he wrote *En Saga*, deep in Sibelius's soul, and the idea that it could not have influenced him is unthinkable.

That is not to say that other stimuli weren't at work, of course. We have noted Sibelius's reflections on his childhood (both people and places) caused by the passing of so keen a figure as his grandmother; there were the ripe experiences – both emotional and musical – of his honeymoon summer in Karelia. The ancient *Edda*, that rich resource of Icelandic myth and tradition (which influenced Wagner, then later Tolkien, so much), was also an important ambient inspiration, a creative spur which Sibelius felt, especially in the 1930s, was more vital and direct on *En Saga* than the *Kalevala* (though, towards the end of his life, he tended to prefer to revert to the belief that his work's inspiration lay in more purely psychological sources). In some measure, Sibelius in his later years wanted to distance himself from the youthful inspiration of the *Kalevala*, feeling it was either too limiting or too provincial, but its impetus was always there, and whatever else influenced this work, we should never forget the impact the Finnish epic had on him.

The overall effect of *En Saga*, as many of its detractors have pointed out, though it is all part of the appeal to its devotees, is its melancholy atmosphere, its brooding and morbid ambience, as Sibelius ghoulishly reflects on his childhood, his rebirth as a new husband and soon-to-be father – of both his first daughter and, in many ways, a nation. Nonetheless, whatever its competing personal, biographical and psychological foundations, it is a saga, a fairy-tale fiction to be taken not as reality but as a series of sonic-poetic episodes, perhaps as a musical portrait of the artist as a young man, with all the sickly woes and unhealthy obsessions this entails, which are depicted in the music's content and structure, its transgressions and struggles. To censoriously declare *En Saga*, especially in its first incarnation, as unwholesome and preoccupied is surely to miss the point: to expect a phantastic, embroidered depiction of youth and artistic nascency to be clean or consistent is not only futile but woefully misguided.

For these reasons, whatever the refined brilliance of the final version, the energetic unevenness of the original has much to offer and deserves to be performed and recorded much more. In both forms, *En Saga* is an exceptional achievement. It distorts and obscures the generic divisions between symphony and tone poem by telescoping ideas into its single span, uniting harmonic and motivic material towards a common goal, so that the programmatic and psychological elements are inherently bound to the symphonic and musical ones.

Themes themselves tend to shape the music, rather than any strict adherence to sonata form, so that, in structural terms, there is an uninhibited treatment of formal norms. In *En Saga*, you can witness the exposition, development and recapitulation sections, but the boundaries are marvellously fuzzy and imprecise, as Sibelius strives to blend all his musical elements together. Whatever enhancements and advancements Sibelius would undertake in his career – and even if he would also maintain a conscious and identifiable independence between the two forms, for all their mutual techniques – *En Saga* is the innovative template for many of the symphonies and tone poems to come. It was a crucial step forward.

A few weeks after the premiere of *En Saga*, Sibelius became a father for the first time: a girl, Eva, was born on 19 March 1893. Work on several new musical projects continued, and were likely slightly disrupted, by this momentous arrival: an aborted string trio in G minor; a piano sonata in F (his only complete work in the genre and an expansive marvel which seems to beg to become a symphony);[34] a set of six impromptus for piano (which closely exhibit Sibelius's interaction with Finnish folk idioms); a first work for male choir a cappella, 'The Boat Journey' (using a text about the *Kalevala*'s main character, the demigod Väinämöinen).[35] He also made extended progress on the *Karelia* music and began

---

34 Sibelius wrote over two hundred works for the piano, mostly fairly short, covering a range of subjects and variety of styles – dances, romances, souvenirs, miniatures, character pieces – and, to an extent, this sheer volume and diversity has restricted engagement with this fascinating, unduly overlooked portion of the composer's output. These works were often written to bring in much-needed money, especially during the stresses of World War I, which again has nurtured the idea that they are artistically worthless. This is mistaken and unreasonable. Not only do these pieces offer a compelling parallel arc to Sibelius's orchestral career, mirroring many of his stylistic and technical developments in the symphony and tone poem, but they are gems unto themselves. And some of them – like *Florestan* (1889) or the Three Sonatinas (1912), with their marvellous formal contraction, economic articulation and mix of mystery, caprice and exultation – are minor masterpieces.

35 Less than two minutes long, it is a charming engagement with Finnish runic singing and is instantly recognizable as Sibelian in its rhythms and textures. Especially remarkable is the way Sibelius is able to portray, via male voices, the sounds of sailing, waves and maidens. He didn't always need an orchestra to be a marvellous tone poet.

work on a proposed Wagnerian musikdrama (to which we will return in the following chapter).

Sibelius's visits to the Hotel Kämp, with their ensuing days of alcoholic intake, had also increased, doubtless in part because of the twin pressures of composition and fatherhood (though we should not forget his need to maintain socio-musical contacts too). In early 1894 he came second[36] in a choral composition competition with his immensely challenging work *Rakastava* (*The Lover*), a long song/suite which set three texts from the *Kanteletar*, the *Kalevala*'s more lyrical sibling. The first performance of *Rakastava* was for male chorus with some inconspicuous string accompaniment; Sibelius revised it for mixed chorus in 1898 and again in 1912 for strings, triangle and timpani – the version usually known today.

Although not strictly a tone poem, *Rakastava* does bear some connection, especially taking into account its final form, to the developments Sibelius was undertaking at the time, and it is a wonderful depiction of youthful eroticism, a kid sister to *Kullervo*. It moves from an elegiac opening, full of folkloric moods, to passionate joy amid some disturbingly pioneering textures, and finally full circle to the plaintive sadness of departure as it reworks some of the first part's material. A coda evaporates into the forlorn harmonies of an endless northern summer night.

Later in the year, at an ostentatious outdoor concert in Vaasa, on the day of the summer solstice, and with Sibelius's father-in-law, the governor general, in the audience, took place the premiere of a diminutive new orchestral work entitled 'improvisation in D major'. Several other, much grander, pieces from a range of composers were on the programme of this gala event – the Vaasa

---

36   A much more straightforward patriotic piece won, as is usually the case in these events.

National Festival of Song – and Sibelius's innocuous, poetic little work was somewhat forgotten and overlooked. The bashful composer withdrew the piece but revised it the following year: shortening it, changing the key from D to F major, rechristening it *Spring Song* (*Vårsång*) – and declaring it a tone poem.

Compared to many of Sibelius's other works in the genre, with their vast panoramic vistas and dense psychological portraits, *Spring Song* might seem a trivial or insignificant work; certainly, it is much smaller in both scale and ambition, as well as being very approachable, akin to having the salon feel of some of his less important chamber works. But *Spring Song* is not to be dismissed or neglected. Its emphasis on melody and thematic invention is as crisp, fresh and welcome as the very season it depicts, a luxurious portrayal of the tardy northern spring finally arriving, with its attendant Mahlerian mixture of melancholy and joy.[37]

In fact, Mahler himself heard *Spring Song* on his trip to Helsinki in 1907, when the two composers had their famous exchange on the nature of the symphony as a musical form (global totality versus internal rationality).[38] Mahler was not much impressed, however, and his review of *Spring Song* borders on the libellous, not least in its impolite scare quotes:

---

37 Indeed, when the work was revised again and then published in 1902, it was given the French subtitle 'La tristesse du printemps' – 'the sadness of spring'.

38 'I said that I admired [the symphony's] severity of style and the profound logic that created an inner connection between all the motifs. ... Mahler's opinion was just the reverse. "No, a symphony must be like the world. It must embrace everything."' This oft-cited conversation, seemingly in every CD booklet and programme note ever written on either composer, is a little misleading. Not only are Mahler's symphonies, for all their abruptness and disjunction, extremely logical constructions, but Sibelius's are self-contained worlds unto themselves. Moreover, of course, context is important: Mahler had just written his barnstorming, hyper-galactic Eighth, Sibelius his paragon of classical lucidity – the Third.

> Quite ordinary kitsch spiced up with certain 'Nordic' harmonic mannerisms to create a national sauce.

In many ways, this has been the prevailing view ever since: a popular work, 'accessible' in the way concert promoters like and some chin-stroking intellectuals don't. But there is more to *Spring Song* than this, as a composer-conductor of Mahler's insight and intimate connection to landscape and the climate should surely have realized.

Reworked from D major into a more bucolic F major – the key of the *Autumn* Concerto of Vivaldi's *Four Seasons*, and both Beethoven's Sixth Symphony and his rustic op.135 string quartet – *Spring Song* is a study of nature, of changing time and our attitude to such alteration. Just as Beethoven's *Pastoral* evokes the feelings of engagement with nature (rather than being strictly a mere depiction of it), *Spring Song* is about the moods of sadness and joy which accompany the long-awaited advent of spring and its reminder of the changing, ephemeral nature of our existence on the earth.

After the long darkness of winter, the Nordic spring is especially slow to arrive, and is fleeting, too, as the endless days and white nights of summer quickly take over. *Spring Song* captures much of this meteorological variety and emotional multiplicity, as well as its brevity: a short work for a short season. In the wider context of Sibelius's career, *Spring Song* points ahead, in terms of both musical technique and expressive power, to several later works, including perhaps especially the snow country and pure spring water of the Sixth Symphony (1923), where similar patterns of harmonic circumvention help create interconnecting moods of nature and human sentiment.

When, in Helsinki on 17 April 1895, the revised version of *Spring Song* was premiered, it shared the programme with another new tone poem: *The Wood Nymph* (*Skogsrået*). A work that could not be more different from its unassuming neighbour, especially given it came from the same composer at the same time, *The Wood Nymph* offers a neo-Wagnerian narrative based on a specific literary source, reflecting Sibelius's current interest in both the German composer and the wider dramatic modes of opera.

The Wood Nymph itself actually exists, unusually, in three different forms: as an orchestral tone poem, as a solo piano work, and as a powerful melodrama for voice, piano, two horns and strings. This variety both shows the interest Sibelius had in the subject and also reveals the capricious, unstable nature of his still developing musical mind, as he sought out different forms to locate the best one in which to express himself. As we will see more forcefully in the next chapter, with *Lemminkäinen*, the musikdrama would dominate his attention before dissolving into tone poems and symphonies, but its influence remained, in both *Lemminkäinen* and the hypnotic realm of *The Wood Nymph*.

Based on a poem by Viktor Rydberg (1828–1895) – a Swedish poet-novelist often regarded as one of the last great Romantics, whose penetrating fusion of nature mysticism, psychological drama and Nordic myth instinctively appealed to Sibelius[39] – *The Wood Nymph* might be regarded, in Wagnerian terms, as a mixture of *Lohengrin*, *Das Rheingold* and *Parsifal*. It tells the tale of how malicious dwarves lead a handsome, stylish hero awry in the forest. There our gallant protagonist, Björn, makes the fateful mistake of falling in love with a wood nymph,

---

39 The Rydberg-Sibelius melodrama *Snöfrid* (1900), for narrator, mixed choir and orchestra, is also fascinating.

and in so doing surrenders his chances of happiness in the real world: the spell cannot be broken, he can no longer love his wife or perform his intrepid deeds, and he dies a ruined man.

In organizational terms, Sibelius follows the four stanzas of Rydberg's poem, with four informal sections evoking the verses' relevant moods and events:

i) intrepid dynamism: a swaggering portrait of the hero
ii) hectic endeavour: the encounter with the dwarves
iii) sensual love: a tender scene with the wood nymph
iv) heartbroken grief: the inevitable, traumatic conclusion

Although the music closely follows the poem and is episodic in nature, the tone painting at times seems to yearn for a more theatrical quality – reflected in the much shorter melodrama that Sibelius also created by reworking the material, which was staged shortly before the Helsinki premiere of the orchestral version, as well as in the idea that Sibelius may have tangentially planned a *Wood Nymph* opera.

Wagner's long shadow hangs over both the narrative and music of *The Wood Nymph* (Sibelius had visited Bayreuth in the summer of 1894). But, as with folk music, Sibelius refuses to merely imitate what he encounters; rather he assimilates organically certain techniques or styles into his own unique idiom. Similarly, although Rydberg's poem is in Swedish and is unrelated to the *Kalevala*, this is not to say that elements of *The Wood Nymph*'s atmosphere and methods are divorced from Sibelius's now constant and habitual immersion in the Finnish epic.

The then-fashionable symbolist art movement (especially the moody paintings of Arnold Böcklin[40] and Magnus Enckell) also looms over *The Wood Nymph* (as it had in *Kullervo* and would in *Lemminkäinen*). It lurks behind the notes, as Sibelius strove, perhaps a little awkwardly at first, to distance his tone poems from mere pictorialism, creating instead sonic explorations of life's shadowy undertows. Sibelius was far too sensitive and thoughtful an artist to be satisfied with simply depicting a hero or the forest in naturalistic musical colours. A hero is never just a hero; a tree never just a tree; a wood nymph never just a wood nymph. If this can seem a little strained, artificial, even naive, especially when compared to Sibelius's symphonies and later tone poems, it was a powerful creative force as he began to develop his voice as a tone poet and painter.

Despite these optimistic ingredients and an initially positive reception, *The Wood Nymph* languished almost unknown among Sibelius's great tone poems, known to the few who had even heard of it purely as an item in the opus lists. Only in the mid-1990s, when Osmo Vänskä performed and recorded the work with the Lahti Symphony Orchestra, did it become known to audiences, a triumphant rebirth for a fascinating, if less subtle, work now slowly taking its place alongside *En Saga*, *Pohjola* and *Tapiola*.

---

40 Böcklin (1827–1901) had a huge influence on composers. Gustav Mahler, Max Reger, Andreas Hallén, Hans Huber, Karl Weigl, Felix Woyrsch, and many others would all write music inspired by or directly referencing Böcklin's work – but perhaps most famously Sergei Rachmaninov in his great symphonic poem *Isle of the Dead* (1909), from the painting of the same name, which exists in several versions. It was an immensely popular work of art, and as late as 1934 Vladimir Nabokov could have a character in his novel *Despair* wryly remark that a print can be 'found in every Berlin home'. Moody, atmospheric, full of swans, water and death – one can see why Böcklin also appealed to Jean Sibelius.

In truth, *The Wood Nymph* lacks the motivic integration and telescopic concision found in Sibelius's greatest works, that near-miraculous ability to merge units into a symphonic whole, but it still maintains a vital musical argument, its narrative brilliantly and resolutely told. And if, at times, the music maps a little too snugly to its source material, this might also be more encouragingly rephrased: it is a masterly sonic recreation of Rydberg's poem, full of captivating orchestral colours and many charming melodic ideas utilized in order to evoke the story.

Perhaps to desire a more cogent, unified and effortlessly interconnected *Wood Nymph* is to ask the wrong question, to seek to turn a defiantly episodic programme, with less sophisticated links and juxtapositions, into an abstraction. Sibelius tends to 'show his working' much more in this piece, not employing connective features to smooth over the joints and joins. Yet this helps give the work a certain folkloric charm, the feel of a fairy tale, inexperienced and slightly naive.

Although it is unmistakeably a tone poem, *The Wood Nymph* also bears many resemblances and connections to the narrative orchestral style of Wagner, which we should try to perceive in a constructive light, rather than as a derivative failure (especially given our own hindsight of his abandonment of his neo-Wagnerian opera projects). On its own terms, as an orchestral drama and instrumental chronicle, the piece surely succeeds, like its eponymous spirit, as an alluring and captivating addition to the Sibelius canon.

The Wood Nymph was the third of his three mid-1890s tone poems, joining *En Saga* and *Spring Song*, works which show Sibelius developing his art in new directions, laying the foundations for his future music but also existing as important pieces unto themselves, idiosyncratically Sibelian and full of interest.

En Saga, op.9

A bold, richly distinctive symphonic tone poem, bound to both its composer's personal past and wider European heroic traditions of tragedy – from *Medea* to *Mithridate*, *Don Carlos* to *A Doll's House* – *En Saga* inhabits much of the same folkloric style as Sibelius's masterpiece from the year before, *Kullervo*, mixing intimacy with grandeur. We appear to perceive a mythical-aural depiction of the Finnish forests, lakes and hills, as well as some or one of its citizens. More than this, we seem to closely explore this figure's mind, its thoughts and feelings: psychological, as well as topographical, landscapes.

The musical language (especially in the first version) is rugged, powerful, the orchestral textures rough-hewn and weather-beaten. Ostinatos and circular, persistently recurring themes characterize these dense thickets, their melodic scope constrained as if imprisoned in endless rotations of mythic anguish and despair. Change, whether in speed or volume, is usually forceful, unforeseen, as are variances between different instrumental families (it is almost as if the string or woodwind, brass or percussion, are warring tribes). Much of this colourful ferocity and curious freedom was lost with the work's more sleek and efficient 1902 revision, but enough was preserved to capture the angst and mental distress Sibelius desired.

A significant benefit of the revision, to offset the losses, was a clarification of the work's tonal architecture, so that the subtle shifts between C minor and E-flat major are purified, illuminated, increasing much of the understated overall power of the work. Since at least Beethoven, these keys had been closely associated with the tragic – the *Eroica* played on the interchangeability of the two keys, most notably in its contrasting first and second movements – and by its close, *En Saga* has resolved the tonic conflict into a modal mixture, E-flat minor.

Beyond key, throughout the revised work, the licence taken with sonata form, the blending and blurring of its constituent parts, is considerable, with similar processes occurring even and especially in the subsections, making *En Saga* a wonderfully integrated tone poem but one hard to separate into definable segments for analysis. In this respect, it closely matches fluid and indivisible psychological processes (which would be perfectly captured in the literary modernism of James Joyce's 'stream of consciousness' in the century to come), thus confirming Sibelius's own consideration of *En Saga* as the expression of a 'state of mind'.

It opens in a far-flung and isolated A minor, as austere spiccato string arpeggios spin an enigmatically unstable web of sadness, pianissimo, much as Wagner's Norns had in the cold and hostile prologue to *Götterdämmerung*.[41] It is dreamlike but sinister, an ominous nightmare, out of which we are soon brusquely shaken via lumbering archaic woodwinds, hobbling like trolls or goblins from ancient myth and bringing a startling chromatic shift to the sound. The dream and hobgoblin elements compete

---

41 Wagner's musikdrama opens with an icy E-flat minor chord, the ultimate tonal terminus of *En Saga*.

to be the primary and secondary subjects of the work, but both form the initiation and then expression of an expansive, heroic theme which in time will become the main subject, a theme with a substantial sense of drive, purpose and headlong acceleration.

Not long after the introduction, however, the first of many significant differences between versions of the work occur: the first version (1893) is longer, fresher, and more primitive-sounding, as well as more varied in its core material (for both good and ill); the final version (1902) is more streamlined, allowing for greater consistency but a smoothing off of some exhilarating rough edges, slightly dampening the original's vibrant and exotic orchestral colours.

In the final version, the C-sharp minor bassoons offer greater clarity of the subject, before being joined by the horns, with the oscillating strings behind, and then a re-presentation of the anticipated main theme, now suitably developed in stature. After a commanding orchestral culmination, the violas offer a new theme, but one closely related to that submitted by the bassoons, which is then further complicated by the violins bringing in their own version of both the viola and bassoon subjects.

All this material is then progressed, charged and engorged by the orchestra, with the first version offering even more basic material for variation, but essentially undergoing the same processes as in the final version. The latter feels more inherently Sibelian, its inner logic more compellingly connected to his later symphonic style, but most of the techniques in both versions are the same, as Sibelius expands, adjusts and adapts his themes, combining and recombining elements of exposition, development and recapitulation.

Eventually, the main theme returns complete, only to suffer a shattering breakdown on a damaged chord which shows how much Sibelius knew his Wagner. From this devastation, *En Saga* can only wander into a lingering, damaged coda. A chilly extended epilogue follows, with a forlorn clarinet singing a sad song, its gloomy monologue derived from the epic theme heard in the distant past back in the introduction, but now given in a shadowy, sombre E-flat minor, the seemingly inevitable tragic tonal destination of the work.

What does all this signify for the listener, this psychological portrait, this expression of a state of mind? As mental pictures, like cognitive processes themselves (both conscious and unconscious), the tone poem's musical images can be immensely hard to separate, identify or maintain, since they are naturally elusive, abstract, overlapping, interrelating, protracted or arrested. *En Saga*'s 'thoughts' extend to ideas, imagination, memory, problems (and problem-solving), emotions, events, people, objects – the stuff and paraphernalia of the mind, of reminiscence and recollection, of the present, the past and the future, as the mind journeys with its infinite elasticity and freedom through mental states and psychological processes.

Precisely linking a musical motif, phrase or idea with any one of these various thoughts or states of mind is perhaps to be avoided – and risks undermining the very subtle, indefinable sovereignty Sibelius wanted. The tremolando strings; the troll-like woodwind; the misty, murky dissonance; the asymmetrical twirling melodies; the wintry clarinet solo at the close: all these and more cry out for psychological/narratorial interpretation and elucidation. So, too, do *En Saga*'s less specific but highly proficient employment of equilibrium and timbre (which so brilliantly appear to mimic the smooth power of thought), as well as the more violent episodes (which seem to capture the malevolent sway of intrusive thoughts).

Sibelius might have given his piece an abstract title, like his overture in E major of 1891,[42] but he didn't: he deliberately gave it a (semi-) specific (Swedish) title – *En Saga* ('A Story') – and discussed it as a 'state of mind', all of which, as a tone poem, calls out for some form of exposition and explanation. Yet these interpretative processes seem to purposely remain, if not entirely elusive, mostly up to individual players/listeners to re-construct each time they encounter the piece – the moods, thoughts and feelings shifting as liberally as the music does.

En Saga is a story for everyone, a fairy tale of our imaginations, a nightmare narrative which takes us wherever we want it to, subject to the structure and motifs Sibelius has provided us with. It is true that it reflects the composer's state of mind, not ours; but the communicative and connective power of art allows us to take those mental states and transform them into our own. The ominous, melancholy spaciousness of *En Saga* has room for us all.

Coda: In 1894 Akseli Gallen-Kallela painted a diptych inspired by the tone poem. A relatively small work, it has a moody portrait of the composer on the right and a fantastical Finnish landscape on the left, with space left blank below for a quote from *En Saga*. Sibelius eventually received the work but never filled in the third panel. It is likely he did not wish to confirm that the work's 'state of mind' could be substantiated in any tangible sense by either the portrait or the landscape. It was for the listener to undertake for themselves.

---

42 An aborted symphony.

Spring Song, op.16

A short tone poem which evokes in abstract terms the feelings of the slothful arrival of the Nordic spring, as well as marginally more programmatic depictions of the season itself, *Spring Song* initially held the title 'impromptu', which can still help us understand the relatively improvisatory musical architecture Sibelius fashions, extemporizing nature. It is a piece founded on melody and thematic invention, as feelings and flowers bloom and wane, the heart swelling and deflating as the spells of the year shift and change.

The original, al fresco, venue for the work's premiere probably inspired some of the work's more idiosyncratic qualities, such as the affirmatory bells in the concluding sequence with its exaltation of spring, or the bold orchestral lines with their hymnal features to carry more powerfully through the open air.

In terms of harmony and keys, there exists a strongly diatonic quality, as well as shifts to the minor, in much of the writing – especially early on in the work as downhearted thoughts linger or reappear. Harmonies are frequently as elusive and equivocal as the sluggish spring itself, as well as many of the complex emotions attached to it, evading definition and precision in undulations of elation and the blues.

The ever-changing quality and duration of light, fluctuating temperatures and mutable moods are all captured in sound, as *Spring Song* evokes no direct programme or narrative, not even the chronological march of the seasons as such. Instead, it evokes a powerful reflection on human existence via glowing, kaleidoscopic, ever-variable orchestral sonorities. As a tone poem, its abstractions are intensely symphonic; as a musical elucidation of psychology, it is surely as powerful a statement as *En Saga*.

The Wood Nymph, op.15

This episodic tone poem closely follows its source material – indeed, at the premiere, the audience were given copies of Rydberg's text in the programme, indicating the resounding connection Sibelius intended listeners to make between his music and the words which had inspired it. Although officially cast in one movement, there are four clear, if informal, sections corresponding to the stanzas of Rydberg's poem, giving the work the feel of a dramatic tableaux as much as a tone poem.

(The episode titles given below are my own, for ease of navigation, not Sibelius's or Rydberg's.)

1. [The Hero.] *Alla marcia*.

The Wood Nymph opens with a cheerful, sauntering depiction of the hero Björn: a noble brass march theme in C major, proudly played above an upsurge of strings, showing us the 'tall and handsome lad, with broad and mighty shoulders'. It is reminiscent of some of the contemporaneous *Karelia* music, and is majestic, impressive: this magnificent chap is surely as strong as the 'spruce and crag' that surround him. But his striking appearance and swagger attract the attention of 'cunning spirits' as he walks one summer evening and is mesmerized by the 'singing' woods.

2. [The Dwarves.] *Vivace assai – Molto vivace.*

The next section is gloriously strange, conjuring the weird world of the magical Nordic forest and its mischievous dwarves. It is almost minimalist in its approach, with patterns, pulses and repetitions (stubbornly zipped up in A minor) that entice and hypnotize. A short motif, first given on the clarinets, is furiously repeated and reworked into an intense woodwind network: the dwarves weaving a 'web of moonbeams', with off-beat horns and vivacious trombones representing their raucous laughter as they dance around their prey. At the end of this riveting section, the main hero motif returns, as Björn is drawn deeper and deeper into the forest, a prisoner spellbound by the whispers and sighs among the trees.

3. [The Wood Nymph.] *Moderato.*

Next, the inevitable meeting, as Björn encounters and is seduced by the wood nymph herself. We hear the sensual C-sharp major music of a midsummer night, erotic and radiant amid the shadowy forest, with a writhing solo cello representing the nymph's enticements, and support from a horn and pizzicato strings – all glimpses of flesh and suggestion – before a turbulent and outlandish explosion fragments the tranquil tension.

4. [The Conclusion.] *Molto lento.*

In Swedish folklore, a man who falls for a wood nymph is condemned to lose his soul, so Björn is now doomed – able to physically return to the real world, but unable to resume his life within it. The music mutates malevolently from the erotic thrills of C-sharp major to a funereal C-sharp minor, its sombre march limping along via a throbbing, rippling violin theme collapsing into the brass, and Sibelius's preferred 'short-long-short' pulsing patterns of sound. Obsessed with the memory of the wood nymph, the devastated, desolate Björn can no longer love his wife or recommence his heroic exploits. He is full of remorse, but it is in vain. *The Wood Nymph* ends amid a marvellously resonant sound world, full of anguish and regret, as Björn grows old and grumpy, waiting for the release of death, sitting alone and listening to the sighing of the trees.

Whatever the irresistible figure at the centre of *The Wood Nymph* might symbolize – be it an extramarital affair, prostitution, pornography or other non-sexual 'sins' like drink, drugs or gambling – the piece is an immensely powerful piece of moralistic-folkloric musical theatre, told by the orchestra alone (though with significant attachment to its source text). It is a magnificent third panel to close Sibelius's triptych of tone poems from the early 1890s, wonderfully complementing the more abstract and psychological *Spring Song* and *En Saga*.

As a trio, they showcase many of the techniques and styles that Sibelius was to develop in not only his tone poems but symphonies too, the genres constantly intersecting and interacting in his career. But before then, he had to exorcise the Wagnerian ghost. He did so by planning a vast mythic musikdrama – which, ironically, not only ended up becoming some of his greatest tone poems but can also be conceived as a four-movement symphony: *Lemminkäinen*.

Chapter Three

Building Boats:
Lemminkäinen

Even – and especially – if a composer is not well-suited to opera, we like to fantasize about stage works they might have written, or which lie miraculously undiscovered in some distant dusty archive. We boldly marry a combination of musical style and psychological makeup to an existing novel, poem or play, even if such daydreaming inevitably relies on an essentially superficial and disingenuous reading of both the composer and the literature. Thus, we yearn for a Mahler *Hamlet*, the prince of anxiety confronting the prince of Denmark, or Brahms's cycle of Henry James operas, the monarchs of ambiguity, erudition and form convening: *Porträt einer jungen Dame, Die Flügel der Taube, Die Bostoner*. We want to hear Webern's cool concision fastened to Kafka's uneasy brevity; Boulez staging *Waiting for Godot* or *The Bald Soprano*; Grieg tackling Ibsen again (*Ghosts*,

Brand, The Wild Duck?); Edward Elgar turning his attention to Hardy's *Tess* or Kipling's *Kim*.

We do it with prevailing opera composers, too, hankering for more from their theatrical pens. What price for Mozart's *Twelfth Night*, Monteverdi's *Divina commedia*, Berlioz's *Macbeth* or Debussy's *À l'ombre des jeunes filles en fleurs?* We can dream of Strauss's *Oresteia* trilogy, Britten's *Peter Pan*, Kaija Saariaho's *Finn Family Moomintroll*, or Beethoven's *Coriolanus*, his great overture for Collin's tragedy expanded to a full Shakespearean opera. We still yet might see Mark-Anthony Turnage presenting Harold Pinter or Sarah Kane – or even a John Adams follow-up to *Nixon in China*: *Trump in Korea*.

But if such idle fantasies tend to undermine both the self-sufficiency of literature and the autonomous achievements of non-opera composers, it remains true that many musicians attempted and abandoned writing works for the stage, realizing either that the enterprise was beyond them or, more often, that their art was simply not suited to staged musical drama, however dramatic their music might still be.

Jean Sibelius was one of them. *The Building of the Boat* (*Veneen luominen*) was his projected opera, a neo-Wagnerian mythic musikdrama on a grand scale planned from early July 1893 to late August 1894, when it was jettisoned amid an artistic crisis. But the shipwreck of *The Building of the Boat* was not a total disaster. Sibelius salvaged from the musical debris a vast narrative symphony, consisting of four extraordinary tone poems exploring a hero's life, death and rebirth, now known as the *Lemminkäinen* Suite, or *Four Legends from the Kalevala*.

In the second half of the nineteenth century, the political struggles of Finland featured, as we have seen, a tension between the so-called Svecomans, upholders of Swedish-language traditions (and privileges), and the Fennomans, who sought to promote the Finnish language as a means of creating a distinctive national identity. For the Fennomans, having a vernacular opera was regarded as a significant symbol of nationhood, a marker of Finnish distinctiveness, pride and self-worth. Swedish opera had long been played at Helsinki's Swedish Theatre, which was understandably regarded by many as an affront to the dreams of an independent Finland, with its own language, music and culture. Various Finnish opera companies and ensembles were formed but lacked a permanent base or repertoire and tended to swiftly evaporate. The Finnish cause needed a Finnish work.

The Finnish Literature Society decided to act. In 1891, they organized a competition with a significant cash prize going to the composer (and librettist) who could, within five years, present a Finnish-language opera based on Finnish myth or history. By the spring of 1892, with the triumph of *Kullervo*, Sibelius seemed the obvious candidate to bring off such a work. That he was about to marry into an aristocratic family central to the promotion of Finnish language and culture – the Järnefelts – only furthered the cause. Within a year, the mixed reception to Sibelius's first tone poem, *En Saga*, led him to doubt the potential of music without words, and to temporarily believe in the supremacy of opera as a musical form. This great hope of Finnish music was also still under the spell of Richard Wagner, a passion first ignited during stays in Berlin and Vienna. Now, in the aftermath of the *En Saga* disappointment, Sibelius was devouring the German composer's groundbreaking treatise *Oper und Drama* (1851). The stars had aligned.

For his subject, Sibelius turned back to the *Kalevala*, specifically to its eighth and sixteenth runes, where, with the poet and playwright J. H. Erkko (1849–1906), he fashioned a libretto based on the story of Väinämöinen, the leading character of the epic. Bard, wizard and demigod, Väinämöinen tries to seduce the moon goddess Kuutar by building a boat with magic, but his spell is missing three words. He must travel down to Tuonela, the Finnish realm of the dead, in order to find them and complete his mission.

Sibelius began to compose the music – including a deeply evocative prelude (which has become *The Swan of Tuonela* tone poem in *Lemminkäinen*) – but cracks in the project's hull were beginning to show. Initial reaction to the libretto was not positive: opera and theatre promoters wanted a more compelling plot, with what they regarded as significantly eventful and dramatic scenes good for the stage. Sibelius, however, felt that his music would be powerful enough to create the moods and drama. Wagner, it is true, had been able to unite his gift for drama with his supreme abilities as a symphonic composer and tone painter, but only by dramatically developing the art of opera into something new – the musikdrama, with its focus on orchestral music as well as relatively static, highly philosophical, plots. And this, in part, was the problem: the Wagner paradox.

Irresistible force and immovable object, Wagner's work still dominated European music and culture, acting as an endless source of inspiration (for composers, poets, painters, even architects), but it also represented a severe impediment, restricting or stifling imaginations under the weight of the composer's impact. What is more, it still does, forcing many artists, musicians, music lovers (and, it seems, everyone else) into pro- and anti-Wagner camps – and often, of course, a complex, confused mixture of the two. Sibelius, like so many, fell into this last group: deeply attracted to and fascinated by Wagner's art but also repelled and repressed by its power and influence. It was the old story: intoxication followed by revulsion.

Already a committed, if occasionally cautious, Wagner devotee, in the summer of 1894, Sibelius travelled from Helsinki to Bayreuth, that small but prosperous German town where Wagner had inaugurated a festival in order to stage – exclusively – his series of ten operas and musikdramas. For Sibelius, the experience, at the sacred temple of Wagner's art, and midway through composing his own stage work, was to prove decisive – not only for his musical career, but for Finnish opera, culture and history more generally.

Sibelius attended several productions and was intrigued, even spellbound, once again not just by Wagner's powerful music and his fusion of word, image and sound but by his superlative re-creation of the world of Nordic myth. He was fascinated by the insights Wagner was able to mine from ancient legend and saga, as well as the ways in which the German juxtaposed myth with elements of Greek tragedy and contemporary philosophy. Writing to a friend about *Parsifal*, which he saw the day he arrived, Sibelius claimed, 'Nothing in the world has ever made so overpowering an impression on me. ... I can't begin to tell you how *Parsifal* has transported me.'

But enthralment and intoxication had a price, and this pilgrimage down the Rhine[43] did not convert Sibelius to outright Wagnerian fanaticism (though it never made him quite the anti-Wagnerite many, and indeed Sibelius himself, have often liked to maintain). He took a break after seeing *Parsifal*, *Tannhäuser* and

---

43 Literally so: after crossing the Baltic, he travelled in a boat down the famous river from Hamburg to Mainz, with the scores to *Tannhäuser* and *Lohengrin* in his bags.

Lohengrin, and went to Munich to work on his own opera. In a sense, leaving the Wagnerian hothouse did him good, allowing him to breathe and take stock, consolidating and reassessing his feelings towards not only Wagner but his own art. But it was also a brooding time, fuelling a mixture of annoyance, resentment, repugnance – and quiet resolution.

He returned to Bayreuth that summer, seeing another *Parsifal*, plus *Tristan*, *Die Walküre*, *Siegfried* and *Götterdämmerung*, and although often deeply moved by Wagner's use of Nordic myth, the wholesale, even totalitarian, *Gesamtkunstwerk* approach to musikdrama was beginning to overwhelm, then slightly disgust, him.[44] Perhaps the sheer size and scope of the *Ring* was too much, and he wrote about being caught in the Wagnerian labyrinth, dazed and confused, unable to sign up to the Wagner cult quite so enthusiastically as many around him.

We can well imagine the turmoil inside Sibelius, either as he sat in the Festspielhaus or on the train home, thinking of the drafts of *The Building of the Boat* in his suitcase. The turmoil as he listened to Wagner's gorgeously crafted librettos, which so effortlessly absorbed Nordic myth and German legend and then perfectly blended them with vast and compelling symphonic music. The turmoil as his own insecurities and inadequacies were laid bare, night after night after night.

Already from Bayreuth he was writing to Aino about a change in his attitude, seeing his future down a road different from the Wagnerian one and towards Lisztian tone poems. Nonetheless, he returned to Helsinki in September (after a brief vacation in Venice and a visit to friends in Berlin) quite shellshocked and more than a little unsteady. After being ravished by

---

44   He also saw *Die Meistersinger*, and very much enjoyed it – but this, as so often with this work, was the exception, not the rule.

Wagner, Sibelius could sometimes see no future for himself as a musician: a more suitable job, he claimed, would be to work in a factory. Certainly, this experience largely destroyed his aspirations of becoming an opera composer. Not only could he not hope to compete with Wagner's matchless abilities but, paradoxically, he had also been disabused of the supreme significance of opera as a musical genre.

But, as the cliché goes, a crisis is also an opportunity, and from this self-doubt Sibelius was able to find his true evolutionary path as a composer, as a symphonist and tone poet. He literally fashioned his own musical future from the shattered shards of his operatic dreams, reworking the material from *The Building of the Boat* first into *The Wood Nymph* and then *Lemminkäinen*. It was a reforging and repurposing of which Siegfried – and Wagner – would have been proud.[45]

With his Wagnerian ambivalence as a creative spur, Sibelius could now refocus his attention on tone poems. As we have said, some of the music from *The Building of the Boat* went into *The Wood Nymph*, but the bulk of the opera's material became *Lemminkäinen* – though this metamorphosis was not always an easy one, and indeed many parts of its score were still being reworked and jiggled about in the late 1930s.

---

45 Sibelius did not entirely abandon his hopes: a one-act Swedish opera, *The Maiden in the Tower*, a fairly straightforward chivalric tale, was completed in 1896. Although far from a masterpiece – it is severely hampered by a dreadful libretto – it is a modest gem, with small orchestral forces and only four vocal principals. The spectre of Wagner naturally lurks in the wings, but it is full of Sibelian magic and deserves more outings.

Taking time off from his teaching, if not always his drinking, Sibelius sifted through his unfinished opera, seeking to revise and repurpose the sketches – and more substantial matter like *The Swan of Tuonela* – into something usable, meaningful. *Lemminkäinen* was now to take as its subject matter the exploits of a hot-headed and irrepressible young adventurer hero from the *Kalevala*, who is a sort of Finnish combination of Achilles, Don Juan and Siegfried – as well as a bit of Frankenstein's monster.[46]

Such a radical departure from the libretto of *The Building of the Boat*, which focused on Väinämöinen and the moon goddess Kuutar, should immediately indicate that, especially when compared to the more episodic *Wood Nymph*, *Lemminkäinen* is less concerned with observing the narrative sequence of events than in evoking the atmosphere and mood of the story. *The Wood Nymph* was a symbolist tone poem, too, a very powerful one; but *Lemminkäinen* takes things even further, conjuring a complex web of abstract ambient feeling that can allow us to perceive the work as a symphony. This is something its four-part structure also clearly invites, but so too does its imaginative reinterpretation of the constituent parts of a symphony, toying with everything from sonata form to the structure of a scherzo.

Nevertheless, *Lemminkäinen* remains to a considerable degree programmatic music, since it is based on a literary source and retains some semblance of a demarcated story[47] – in such a way that it is also even possible to regard the suite as proto–

---

46 The figure of Lemminkäinen – with his swagger and sexual dexterity – is often cited as the 'Finnish Don Juan', and Strauss's tone poem, *Don Juan* (1889), which Sibelius had heard in Berlin, is a probable overall model for *Lemminkäinen and the Maidens of the Island* – in musical and narratorial terms. Within their single spans, both works contain a network of formal models and numerous contrasts, and both tell the tale of a hero's erotic quests ultimately leading to his downfall.

47 As with *The Wood Nymph*, at *Lemminkäinen*'s premiere the programme note included detailed information regarding the work's source material.

film music, simultaneously accompanying, commenting on and evoking its plot and characters. It is this which further betrays *Lemminkäinen*'s Wagnerian heritage: Wagner was effectively one of the pioneers of film music before the medium even existed. This is partly through the composer's leitmotif configuration, with its brilliant ability to observe and remark on events as well as suggest complex notions of time and psychological change, but also in the grandeur and compass of his vision, as well as his cunning knack for summoning and sustaining pictures through sound.

Because of the tension between programme and abstraction inherent to *Lemminkäinen* – and so much of Sibelius's music – we are drawn, compelled, to create images in our imagination as we listen: the festive orgy on the island; the dark waters with the otherworldly swan; Lemminkäinen's death, dismemberment and rebirth; the furious ride home. It is all fabulously filmic. But, more than this, Sibelius employs the language and techniques of cinema to mesmerizing effect. Jump cuts, deep cuts, cross-cuts, dissolves, dolly shots, establishing shots, truck shots, flashbacks, flashforwards, whips, wipes and zooms – Sibelius finds orchestral equivalents for them all.

Part symphony, part tone poem, part film score, an orphan of an opera with an unstable upbringing, *Lemminkäinen* is a complex work with a complex past.

Over time, after its premiere in Helsinki in April 1896, *Lemminkäinen* underwent a succession of bewildering adjustments, some very significant, in terms of material, structure and scoring. However, as we now have it, in its 'final' version, which – since the *Swan* movement is so often placed either second or third – is still relatively unstable, *Lemminkäinen* unfolds as follows.

1. *Lemminkäinen and the Maidens of the Island.* Based on runo 29 of the *Kalevala*, the hero Lemminkäinen sails his boat to an enchanted and picturesque island where, since the menfolk are away, he is able to seduce many women with his beautiful songs (which also magically turn pebbles to jewels and trees golden red).

2. *The Swan of Tuonela.* Often placed third, the second movement depicts the moody grace of the mystical swan on the dark and holy waters that surround Tuonela, the Finnish underworld and realm of the dead. (This deeply evocative piece was to have been the opening prelude to *The Building of the Boat*.)

3. *Lemminkäinen in Tuonela.* Based on runos 14–15, this movement depicts the hero's quest to kill the Swan of Tuonela and thus win the Daughter of the Northland. However, Lemminkäinen is ambushed and killed by a blind cattle herder next to the sacred river. His body is dismembered and thrown in the waters. After learning of his death, his mother rescues his remains, sews them back together and uses magic – the enchanted honey from a bidden bee – to revitalize his corpse.[48]

---

48 Normal honey doesn't work, and the diligent, if occasionally diffident, insect is sent on a series of journeys ('over the moon and under the sun and between the stars of heaven') before, finally, honey sourced from the seventh and highest paradise of God (Jumala) proves to be an effective medication for Lemminkäinen.

4. *Lemminkäinen's Return.* Based on runo 30, this movement depicts the hero's return home, exhausted after a series of battles and wars (and, indeed, his own death). After a long voyage rich in adventure, he finally arrives in his native land, where he rediscovers places full of childhood memories.

The quite involved events and emotions of *Lemminkäinen's Return*, which was severely shortened in its final version, are more easily observed and understood when listening to their (multiple) original versions. The ordering of the two central movements also presents problems with the narrative/programmatic elements of *Lemminkäinen*. Placed second, the haunting *Swan of Tuonela* offers a vital interlude between the *Maidens of the Island* and *Lemminkäinen in Tuonela*, as well as providing an evocative prelude to and scene setting for those latter events. Placed third, the *Swan* tends to disrupt the narrative arc between Lemminkäinen's death/reanimation and his journey home. There again, *Lemminkäinen in Tuonela* also flows naturally on from his time on the island, and the *Swan* can then serve as a funereal pause and reflection prior to his heroic return.

To an extent, these issues illustrate many of the problems encountered because of *Lemminkäinen's* strange form. Its mixture of narrative, tone painting and symphonic abstraction are often hard to distinguish or decipher – though here we should ask both whether we need to do this and whether it is desirable to do so anyway, since it is clear Sibelius wishes to focus more on underlying moods than on plot.

As we indicated above, in this work Sibelius created an intricate fusion of symphony and tone poem, with filmic premonitions, so that attempting to separate its particular parts is not only futile but misses the point of the multifaceted forms the composer was now creating. Neither wholly programmatic nor abstract, like many of his tone poems (and indeed his seven numbered symphonies), *Lemminkäinen* plays a complex game with structure, genre and interpretation. If we grab at narrative, we likely find it runs through our fingers like sand. And yet it is never entirely abstract music, or even mere mood painting. It is a marvellous, often perplexing and elusive, hybrid innovation.

For all its often caliginous and opaque hues, *Lemminkäinen* is actually an inversion of the tragic trajectories of *Kullervo*, *En Saga* and *The Wood Nymph*. In it, the hero – with the help of his mother and that hymenopteran's sweet magic – turns his misfortunes into optimism and triumph, something wonderfully captured as the music of *Lemminkäinen's Return* gradually moves from C minor fragmentation through to a radiant E-flat major chorale. Despite the furious disorder of its genesis and evolution, *Lemminkäinen* has a remarkable linear development, as melodic, harmonic and textural stability are formed and re-formed, much as Lemminkäinen's mother reconstructs and resuscitates her son's body.

So Lemminkäinen's victory is also Sibelius's, since the score of the *Four Legends from the Kalevala* is one of his finest before the First Symphony, offering a remarkable array of colours, shadows, moods and distilled, sophisticated textures, all housed within a supremely well-designed piece of symphonic architecture. The opera house's loss was very much the concert hall's gain.

Lemminkäinen Suite, or *Four Legends from the Kalevala*, op.22

1. *Lemminkäinen and the Maidens of the Island.*

Lemminkäinen opens with dreamlike E-flat horns – almost foghorns calling out in the mist, with attendant echoes, lost in the gloom. Strings seem to imitate the movement of waves. It is a wistful space, plaintive and evocative, that will soon shift to the exotic sounds of the island Lemminkäinen is to visit: the far-flung sounds of nature arise, as do gentle dance rhythms which increase in strength, prefiguring the erotic revels in store. It is full of midsummer magic, of irrationality, mystery and the murky thrills of being away, abroad, alone. Twisting, tempestuous *Tristan*-esque chromatism further signals the simultaneous magnetism and menace of sensual imbroglio.

The dance music now has an agitated sexual energy. But before long, there arises from this vigour a romantic tune which grows and grows, gathering textural density and a range of harmonic stresses, tumescent and bewitching. Motifs loosely associated with Lemminkäinen and the maidens become interconnected, inseparable, full of genuine passion and unity, mixing longing and playfulness. From this climax, the opening horn call re-emerges, and the music can now achieve some closure and resolution, relaxing into satisfaction and release – Sibelius's own radiant and euphoric Liebestod – while also, in narrative terms, allowing Lemminkäinen to sail away from the island.

There are some elements of sonata form just discernible in this opening movement, as one might expect in a symphony: a development section as the lovemaking proceeds; a post-coital coda. Yet Sibelius treats the form with such liberty, wit and lawlessness that it can be little more than a droll gesture or vague structural device. As he reworked the score over the years, as with *En Saga*, the thematic material became smoother and more cohesive, though again it lost some of its orchestral colour too (the original asks for both a tambourine and glockenspiel). That being said, there was nothing rough about the first version. Clarity and concision rule, and even in its initial incarnation this was Sibelius's most integrated score to date, with not only a remarkable succinctness to the motivic variation and development but a finely ordered orchestration.

2. The Swan of Tuonela.

This famous movement, a marvel of dark orchestration so often detached from its parent work, has a mirror-like calm which is simultaneously uneasy, intimidating in its motionlessness, impassive but threatening (like many a swan). It is a movement of aching melancholic beauty, especially in its extended solo for cor anglais – which clearly references that instrument's poignant employment in the third act of *Tristan und Isolde* as a twin symbol of hope and despair.[49]

The opening is superb, expanding into a seemingly limitless space as an A-minor chord unfurls, taken up and up, one octave at a time. Flutes, clarinets and trumpets are banished, leaving space not only for the muted and divided strings to shimmer and grow towards their highest registers, but also – of course – for the lonely isolation of the cor anglais, floating in exquisite serenity through the score, with occasional support from the cello. A harp offers a glimpse of sunlight, and the movement briefly flickers

---

[49] As well as to *Tristan*, this whole movement is clearly related – in another swan story – to *Lohengrin*'s act one prelude, where Wagner's overlapping violins and woodwind in A major create a beaming luminosity, a bright counterpart to the *Swan*'s shimmering shadows.

in C major before the transcendental swan glides away into the blackness over a quiet drumbeat, strings trembling in the icy air.

Throughout, imaginative timbres, textures and techniques create an exquisite, haunting atmosphere, darkness and light meeting above the waters of Hades. Remote, gleaming, it is also static and hypnotic, transporting us into a realm of fantasy and ecstasy, yearning and fulfilment, beauty and death.

Sibelius had a lifelong fascination with large migratory birds – swans, cranes, geese – and they appear again and again in his work. But perhaps nowhere else is he as able to so powerfully convey their majesty and grace as in *The Swan of Tuonela*, surely one of the most spellbinding and original things in all music.[50]

3. Lemminkäinen in Tuonela.

The third movement, in great contrast to the static stillness of the *Swan*, is highly operatic, full of activity and movement, with blustery, unsettled ostinato figurations and frequent changes in tempo and dynamics at either end of the movement. There are never-ending waves of tremolo strings, as well as intense, stormy music for the brass and woodwind that keenly anticipates Sibelius's music for *The Tempest* three decades away. These, of course, are the swirling whirlpools, rocks and rapids of Tuonela's encircling river – and one of the places in the score where we can be certain of the pictographic element at work.

Amid the eddying strings and brass vortexes, in the middle of the movement is a remote and severe interlude in A minor, full

---

50 It also feels prophetic, for it is hard to think of the employment of stasis in composers like Arvo Pärt, György Ligeti or Kaija Saariaho without *The Swan of Tuonela*. That said, musical stasis is, of course, a technique with a long and diverse history, with notable prominence in West African drumming and the drone backdrops within Indian classical music.

of ice and enigma, and a frightening moment of disquieting calm amid the chaos. In Sibelius's sketches he labelled this passage 'Maiden of Tuoni' (i.e., Death), alluding to the passage in the *Kalevala* where she rows Väinämöinen across the sacred river to the kingdom of the dead. Sibelius had planned such a scene in *The Building of the Boat*, and it is fascinating to have a glimpse, but naturally only a glimpse, of what, to use a Wagnerian vocabulary, 'Väinämöinen's Descent to Tuonela' might have sounded like. In the tone poem, however, this unexpected alteration in register and dynamic evokes the chilly daughter of death as Lemminkäinen encounters her during his migration through the underworld. (Its key – A minor – as well as its general atmosphere serve as either a recollection or portent of the *Swan*, depending on how that movement is ordered.)

From here, the music drifts with a mixture of warmth and sadness towards a lullaby which depicts not so much Lemminkäinen's mother herself, as she gathers the various bits of her dead son ready for his reanimation, but an abstraction: the concept of maternal love. After this, the furious energy of the tremolo strings returns, with determined encouragement from the brass, now representing a mixture of Lemminkäinen's reconstitution and awakening from death.

Although full of masterly writing, this last passage, like its mirror at the start of the movement, is perhaps one of the weakest in the whole *Lemminkäinen* score, in part because it is compelled to offer musical illustrations of the narrative rather than evoke its mood, though Sibelius's writing can never really be said to be formulaic here, and as pure tone painting it is extremely striking.

4. Lemminkäinen's Return.

There is certainly nothing prescribed or mechanical about the rondo final movement. The piece was twice as long in the original and then intermediate versions, and Sibelius's ability to condense themes and merge motifs is on sweeping, glorious display in the short final version of the last movement. He continually adjusts and advances his material but at a steady pace, creating some enthralling illusions and paradoxes – blurs and mirages – as our hero returns. It is all wonderfully cinematic, in full action mode, Tom Cruise or Bruce Willis directed by James Cameron or Paul Verhoeven.

Lemminkäinen's Return begins with a three-note bassoon motif – a sonic embryo that propagates with increasing power and strength through the course of the blazing finale. Initially in fragments of C major/minor, the movement will take on an organic animation as it grows into a heroic, glowing E-flat major chorale: the tonal destiny and homecoming this symphony has been yearning for since those magical horns at the beginning.

The constant speed is extraordinary, with a breakneck and electrifying energy as Lemminkäinen rides wild orchestral waves to return to his native lands. Nearing home, he seems to switch from boat to horse as some faintly galloping figurations come in (though this is never graphically portrayed) to take us to the close. Lemminkäinen has returned, proud and unashamed of his marvellous adventures, a noble son of his mother – and of Finland.

As a series of tone poems, *Lemminkäinen* is an immensely evocative exhibition of atmospheres and sonic moods. As a symphony, even if it lacks the overall architectural unity to be a true example of the form, it generally works in both structural and thematic terms, taking in a quasi-sonata-form first movement, a slow movement, and an extended and devilish scherzo – including a contrasting trio section – before a joyous rondo finale. As proto–film music, it conjures a wealth of images and visual delights, taking us vividly into the world of the *Kalevala*. Yet such threefold interpretations of *Lemminkäinen*, along with lingering misgivings about its origins as an opera, can do the work a disservice, splitting it into various generic pieces much as Lemminkäinen himself is torn to bits and flung in the river. Instead, we should conceive of *Lemminkäinen* much as the hero's mother does – as a reconstituted whole, distinctive, indivisible and unique.

Chapter Four

Russian Borders: The First Symphony & *Finlandia*

Frozen in place by the inconclusive ending to World War II, the geopolitical anxieties of the Cold War placed in the red corner the USSR and its partners, and in the blue corner the USA and its allies. The two superpowers struggled for supremacy across the second half of the twentieth century – and threatened, with their nuclear weapons, to destroy the planet entire. In what was an ideological as well as martial struggle, the capitalist West became a symbol of freedom and choice, while the communist East represented scarcity and oppression (though, of course, it was hardly so straightforward as that).

Amid all this tension and testosterone, spies and the space race, on 21 August 1968 – the day Soviet tanks invaded Czechoslovakia – Russian cellist Mstislav Rostropovich performed the great Czech composer Antonín Dvořák's cello concerto in B minor (1895) with the USSR State Symphony Orchestra at the Proms in London. Preceded by jeers, boos and demonstrations, Rostropovich played with tears in his eyes and – even by his famously fervent standards of intensity – with astonishing passion, making it very clear where he stood politically. The concert ended in triumphant cheers, the soloist holding aloft the score in solidarity with Dvořák's homeland and the people of Prague. It was an extraordinary event that showed the power and potential of art at large, and music in particular, to defy national boundaries and the ephemeral whims of bellicose generals and grim politicians.[51]

Up in Finland, a country technically neutral during the Cold War but subject to severe Soviet influence at the time, the 1968 invasion of Czechoslovakia caused uproar, the streets of Helsinki immediately filling with protestors bearing angry placards. It was not only an instant reaction to contemporary Soviet aggression but an understandable outpouring of rage fuelled by the long and troubled relationship between diminutive, fragile Finland and the belligerent Russian bear.

Situated on the north-western edge of the planet-spanning transcontinental Russian vastness, Finland had long been bound by the culture, impulses and antagonisms of its gigantic noisy neighbour. The eighteenth century saw various occupations by Russian forces – known to Finns as the Great Wrath (1714–21) and the Lesser Wrath (1741–43) – and finally in 1809 came Finland's annexation from Sweden and assimilation into the Russian Empire. An ostensibly autonomous 'grand duchy' under Russian domination, by the 1890s Finland had been – in the

---

51 The performance was captured for posterity, and a recording is available on a BBC Legends CD – raucous protests and all. A few years later, Rostropovich would be denied his Soviet citizenship and forced to live in exile because of his opposition to cultural restrictions.

face of heightened imperial subjugation – increasingly asserting its national voice, not least in the music that Sibelius created during that decade. Most notably, of course, in *Kullervo* (1892), that defiant statement of Finnish pride, but also in a stirring new tone poem that would, even in its very name, assert the 'country of a thousand lakes'[52] as a vigorous sovereign state, becoming a rallying cry for independence in the new century and the de facto national anthem: *Finlandia* (1899, rev. 1900).

But Russian influences on Finnish music drifted over the snow and ice, and for all his vehement patriotic feelings, Sibelius nonetheless strongly identified – psychologically and musically – with the most important Russian symphonist of the nineteenth century: Pyotr Ilyich Tchaikovsky (1840–1893). When, therefore, he finally came to compose a 'pure' symphony, beyond his programmatic ones, *Kullervo* and *Lemminkäinen*, Sibelius allowed certain Tchaikovskian traces to enter his own sound world: an opening motto theme; emotional melodic expressions; lingering, grieving major-minor motifs; an air of tragedy and misfortune (none of which, needless to say, need be exclusively Tchaikovskian in themselves; nor are they absent from earlier Sibelius).

Yet, as with all Sibelian influences – be they Berlioz, Bruckner, Wagner, Tchaikovsky, or indeed his country's own native music – such inspirations were always seamlessly integrated into his own unique and distinctive sonic flavour. They might have been part of the recipe, on the list of ingredients, but the final dish was characteristically *Sibelius*. And what a plat du jour his first official symphony was to be: a rich, convincing work, full of forbidding beauty, suggestive fantasies and quiet

---

52   Even this jubilant sobriquet is woefully inadequate: there are some 187,888 lakes in Finland larger than five hundred square meters.

indulgences in the fertile fields of late Romanticism, albeit with a novel Sibelian concentration and unity.

It is this combination of Romantic mood and motion with Classical focus and frugality that makes Sibelius's symphony No.1 in E minor so persuasive both as an abstract, non-programmatic symphony *and* as a more obviously evocative narrative work, akin to his earlier tone poems and representational pieces, albeit with the story now entirely submerged into the symphonic architecture.[53] Or is it? For, with some cautious elucidation – along with a little help from the composer's own statements that the work had particular and subjective extramusical importance – we can detect and tease out additional concerns within this symphony: personal, as well as folkloric tales of heroes, tempers and atmospheric impressions.

Reasonably hesitant to permit a programme for his first true symphony, in this great orchestral work Sibelius nonetheless articulates several narratives – both elusive and more palpable. Lest we forget, the *Kalevala* remained a vital influence on Sibelius's art, whether tangible or not, and it is certainly not only possible but desirable to see his first symphony as a continuation of the worlds he created in *Kullervo, En Saga, The Wood Nymph* and *Lemminkäinen*. Sibelius's First contains multiple references to – and distortions of – age-old 'heroic journey' symphonies – not all of which, of course, end in triumph. Sibelius's work might even be regarded as a post-Wagnerian 'Siegfried Symphony': it opens in mystery and gloom, and a courageous figure undergoes several psychosexual trials before ultimately meeting their fated

---

53 The symphony shares its key with several other moody masterpieces across the centuries: Haydn's Forty-Fourth, the so-called *Mourning* Symphony (1772), Brahms's Fourth (1885), Tchaikovsky's Fifth (1888), Dvořák's Ninth (1893), Rachmaninov's Second (1907), Vaughan Williams's Sixth (1948) and Ninth (1958), and Shostakovich's Tenth (1953).

doom (itself another key Tchaikovskian motif). Beethoven and Bruckner preferred to resolve the traumas their symphonies explored; Sibelius, following Tchaikovsky and akin to Mahler, would often present more ambiguous conclusions.

The beginning of a famous cycle of seven, this is a symphony that has often been routinely dismissed as 'derivative' (though which work is not?), an imitative offshoot of Russian imperialism. But this is clearly untrue: it is as recognizably a piece from Sibelius's pen as *Pohjola*, *Tapiola* or the violin concerto. If, to some, the authentic Sibelian colours, design and style are not immediately identifiable, this is the more because of their subtlety, their intelligent and cohesive game with the nature of influence and the liminal strangeness of borders: national, musical, chronological and biographical.

Russia, progenitor of so much great art, music and literature – from Gogol to Glazunov, Pushkin to Pasternak, Tolstoy to Tarkovsky – has also been a continually pugnacious actor on the world stage (which could, of course, also be said of Britain, France, Germany, America and empires Roman, Mughal or Mongol). The Russian invasion of Ukraine in 2022 echoed not only 1968 Czechoslovakia but countless other incursions as Russia has attempted over the centuries to either expand or 'consolidate' its immense lands, and Finland has been on the receiving end of several infiltrations from its all too frequently aggressive and insecure eastern neighbour.

Despite (and occasionally because of) politico-military conflict, the musical cultures of Finland and Russia[54] share clear affinities, networks and infiltrations, often embracing – and sometimes shunning – each other according to the fluctuations of time and taste or prevailing diplomatic circumstances. The bleak, picturesque northern landscapes of both countries, with long winters and short summers, cultivated a common air of melancholy in their folk art, though more nostalgic refrains, full of longing and grief, permeated Finland's songs after she was assimilated into the Russian Empire in the early nineteenth century (with the brighter, major-key Swedish influences falling away).

Sibelius is so obviously and evidently an icon of both Finland and Finnish music that, under this protective sway, we can sometimes forget the influence of Russian music on that of Finland. Our distaste for the extreme politics of Russification at work from the 1890s on – when Sibelius was producing his first major works – should not lead us to ignore or downplay how Russian culture shaped that of its diminutive neighbour. In many ways, both politically and culturally, Finland's is a story of triumph, the victory of the underdog against the goliath, as the small nation was able to not only win its constitutional independence but also firmly establish its own distinctive musical voice. But part of that identity needs to recognize the forging forces at work: some of them were from western Europe, the traditions of Beethoven and Brahms; but Sibelius could not avoid hearing the sounds floating over from the east either.

There has been an alarming tendency – now thankfully near extinct – to dismiss Tchaikovsky as a mere tunesmith, to

---

54 We should, of course, be slightly wary of homogenizing Russia. Then, as now, it is an extremely varied place: in landscape, culture, language and traditions. It is only for relative straightforwardness that the term *Russia* is here used.

(deliberately or unintentionally) ignore his complex symphonic structures, his powerful counterpoint, his intricate tonal webs. For many, his music was all emotional flimflam, excessive barbarian blather divorced from the disciplined sentiments of properly ordered and restrained Germanic traditions. Disregarding the prejudiced overtones to so much criticism of Tchaikovsky, and Russian culture in general, such denigration is, more often than not, the product of an imaginative failure to understand the multifaceted role of emotions like nostalgia in Tchaikovsky's art – something composers like Sergei Rachmaninov (1873–1943) and writers like Vladimir Nabokov (1899–1977) would take to an even higher degree of aesthetic concern and complexity. For them, as for Tchaikovsky, nostalgia is a living thing, an element of the future and present as well as the past. Nostalgia is not a negative, foolish sentiment but an active, creative, living force, a means of seeing personal (or familial, local and national) history as existing in as dynamic a fashion as the undecided future.

This Sibelius would explore in his First Symphony, the Finn recognizing both the musical and psychological power of his Russian colleague: Tchaikovsky's extraordinary ability to explore the complexity of our relationship with time and memory, with love and loss. Sibelius saw, too, the need for sophisticated symphonic designs to be properly able to do this. Good tunes weren't enough. Indeed, that was exactly the point: effective, almost overwhelming, melodies did not occur merely to please the ear or soothe the soul. They had a function in terms of symphonic architecture and the journeys and/or emotions the work investigated. It might be something relatively straightforward, even clichéd: a 'beautiful' phrase could represent 'love' or 'passion'; but even that simple idea existed to form either a contrast or the basis for development, distortion, even destruction. Without both a solid plan and an erudite understanding of how musical keys worked, the whole thing would collapse into mush. And Tchaikovsky, for one, would go further, employing that great German tool – counterpoint – in tremendously efficacious ways, to explore divergence, misunderstanding and doubt. Indeed, Tchaikovsky's symphonic style is almost explicitly contrapuntal.

These were all things Sibelius devoured and absorbed. And it was one work in particular that helped indicate to the Finn the path towards his First Symphony: Tchaikovsky's last, the so-called *Pathétique* (1893). A work of immense symphonic power, it has often been read in the context of its creator's untimely demise only nine days after its premiere (in Saint Petersburg, on 28 October 1893). Yet the work hardly needs any such biographical connection: it stands on its own as a commanding universal meditation on life, death and fate, as well as on the meaning of the symphony as a work of art. For Tchaikovsky it was 'the keystone of my entire oeuvre', and it remains one of the most popular of all symphonies, its requiem mood an enthralling experience for music lovers everywhere.

The *Pathétique*'s formal structure – which would influence Mahler so much in his Ninth Symphony (1909) – is unusual, as is its strange choice of movement types; these work together with the fluent melodic figures that are meticulously connected across the piece, quoted, twisted and requoted in a hazy maze of memory and methodical complexity. Much of the work plays with the idea of convention, metaphor and familiarity, inviting us to perceive and then reinterpret common symbols for love, death and mourning (ciphers Tchaikovsky himself, of course, had exploited in his earlier works).

Sibelius heard the symphony twice in Helsinki, in 1894 and 1897. Whatever the political atmosphere in Finland at the time (1899's notorious February Manifesto from Tsar Nicholas II, which severely limited Finnish autonomy, was just round the corner), the *Pathétique* represented the most state-of-the-art symphony about, a model of innovative musical design and progressive urgency. Its Russian origins were one thing, its musical clout and refinement another, and the work was a key influence on Sibelius's First Symphony, part of the Finn's impressive fusion of symphonic concepts and instincts. Tchaikovsky's motto themes, his cyclic constructions, the overall mood of gloom and despair – all were to be keenly present in Sibelius's first true symphonic essay.

But we cannot ignore the politics. By the time of Sibelius's First's premiere (on 26 April 1899), Finnish-Russian tensions were at an all-time high. Not only did the only weeks-old February Manifesto make it possible for the Tsarist government to administer its grand duchy without the consent of the Finnish parliament, but Finnish soldiers could now be conscripted into the Russian army. Whatever autonomy Finland had hitherto enjoyed was now effectively extinguished. Under these circumstances it was always going to be impossible for Sibelius's First Symphony – in that most superhuman of musical forms – to avoid alliance with contemporary discussions about Finnish self-governance and independence. So, whatever wide-ranging heroic and/or musical models we will come to investigate, or whatever purely abstract conversations can be had regarding the symphony – particularly its brilliant organic cohesion of material – it is also crucial to understand the conditions of its arrival and its inescapable status as an allegory of Finnish suppression, courageous struggle and quiet fortitude.

In the winter of 1898/9, Sibelius was beginning to find the political atmosphere of Helsinki intolerable. He longed for the countryside, for time away from urban strife and (alcoholic) temptation, as well as the pressures of his ever-expanding family (Aino and Jean had three young daughters by this time). So in January he took a room in a villa near the railway station in Kerava, now part of the Helsinki metropolitan area but then a small town a few miles north of the city. It gave him the space and peace he needed to complete his first symphony – along with another work that would have its own premiere at the same concert: *Athenarnes sång* (*Song of the Athenians*).

Like the First Symphony, this work – originally in E major and for boys' and men's choirs, plus woodwind, brass, percussion and double bass – has a splendid spirit of rally and remonstration.[55] Setting a text from Viktor Rydberg's poem 'Dexippos', it places us in third-century Greece and tells of the noble deaths of Athenians, fighting their patriotic cause. Quite obviously the ancient Greeks were emblems of contemporary Finns, a geographical and temporal dislocation made merely for aesthetic (and legal) reasons. Just as Verdi in *Nabucco* (1841) had used enslaved Israelites in far-flung Egypt to argue for and accelerate the campaign for Italian emancipation from Austrian rule, Sibelius saw an expedient Hellenic parallel from the past for the cause of his own people.

---

55 As with so many of Sibelius's works, several versions exist: the seditious subtext to *Song of the Athenians* meant it could be more easily performed underground, so to speak, in editions Sibelius wrote for piano solo, for voices and piano, and for voices and limited instruments, as well as a cappella.

A fairly uncomplicated patriotic song with a good rousing tune, *Athenarnes sång* was a big hit with the Helsinki audience, while the symphony was also very well received, especially with the critics. *Kullervo* in 1892 had catapulted Sibelius into Finnish consciousness, but the combination of a fevered political context, a blatantly nationalistic song and a highly sophisticated symphony made the concert of 26 April 1899 a watershed moment for Sibelius and his relationship to his country: there could be no doubting now who the key national figure – musical or otherwise – was. As we will see, the composer was not altogether happy with the symphony, and revisions would promptly take place (indeed the original version has not survived), but the protest song *Athenarnes sång* was to be followed later in the year by an even more famous (and explicit) pro-Finnish work: *Finlandia*.

Finlandia started life as part of a series of tableaux portraying episodes from Finnish history, and was known, a little awkwardly, as the *Press Celebration Music* – it was written in support for the staff of the *Päivälehti* newspaper, which had often been heavily censored, and even temporarily suspended, for its anti-Russian editorials. The whole *Press Celebration* sequence was presented at a gala event on 4 November, ostensibly a press pensions fundraiser but actually a benefit for the suspended *Päivälehti* workforce, as well as a de facto independence rally.

The whole series is worth hearing: a sombre processional prelude takes us to the *Kalevala*'s central hero, Väinämöinen, before we see the god of the forests, Tapio, and the god of the oceans, Ahti, along with Lemminkäinen's poor mother. From this ancient, mythic past, we then see Finland's conversion to Christianity, with some wonderfully archaic bells, before travelling to the sixteenth century and the strange court of Duke John (and his fascination for all things Spanish, for which Sibelius gives us some marvellous quasi-Iberian motifs). The Thirty Years' War (1618–48), an especially hard time for the Finnish peoples, comes next, where a serene domestic opening is invaded by militaristic verve. Further grief and struggle are witnessed in the eighteenth-century fifth tableau, as Finland becomes the ball in a ping-pong of power between Sweden and Russia.

All this wonderful stage management and sequential threading leads to the final tableau: 'Suomi herää', 'Finland Awakes'. It is more sumptuously scored than the earlier movements, and here we witness nineteenth-century Finland slowly emerging as a modern nation state, one capable of and yearning for an independent existence. Sibelius mined the music, subjecting it to a series of revisions, before it eventually became one of his most famous works, *Finlandia* – to all intents and purposes the national anthem of his homeland.

It is a work of astounding emotive power – and not only to Finns. From its craggy, snarling opening chords to poignant woodwinds, reverential strings and impassioned brass, it is a masterpiece of construction and emotion, filling the listener with deep feelings, even if they are entirely unaware of the work's contexts and immediate meanings. Consider, then, the hope and pride that must have consumed that first-night Helsinki audience, and countless Finns since.

Sibelius, and anyone of sense, knew that inspiring music was only one step, and liberation, if it came, would be a long time coming, with death and despair overwhelming the hope and pride for many years to come. Yet, on 4 November 1899, a new century was only weeks away, a century that might need a new tableau to tell a fresh story of Finnish freedom and independence. For now, they had the music.

The New Year 1900, however, began with personal tragedy. On 13 February Jean and Aino's third daughter, Kirsti, just fifteen months old, died of typhoid fever. Aino sank into a deep depression – in part because of the guilt she felt that it had been her who had carried the disease home to the family after a recent trip – while Sibelius, who had particularly adored his youngest daughter, turned to the bottle with an even more alarming need, his drinking turning from something relatively festive to a dark and distressing necessity.[56]

Work, however, did continue. A grand tour of Europe followed in the summer, with Robert Kajanus conducting and Sibelius in a supervisory role, taking his mind off his grief and allowing his works to spread beyond Helsinki's comparatively narrow confines. There were nineteen concerts of Sibelius's music in thirteen cities – Stockholm, Oslo, Gothenburg, Malmö, Copenhagen, Lübeck, Hamburg, Berlin, Amsterdam, The Hague, Rotterdam, Brussels and Paris – along with music by Kajanus and Armas Järnefelt (Aino's brother). The tour was largely a success, a major international breakthrough for Sibelius: German critics in particular praised this bold, unusual and independent new voice, though they were sometimes taken aback by the immediacy and intensity of his music. The French were less enthusiastic;

---

56 The devastation of Kirsti's death led to the extremely swift composition (purportedly in just three hours) of a work for cello and piano: *Malinconia*, op.20, whose melodies and chromatism look far ahead to works like the Fourth Symphony (1911). Commencing with an extraordinary extended solo for the cello, it contains all the forceful, heartfelt music one might expect given its provenance, and it is a supremely virtuosic work for its two soloists, for all its elegiac introspection. It is tempting to see the instruments as representing Aino and Jean, offering each other solace while also coming into conflict as they navigate their grief.

the tour reached France only late in the season, and during a heatwave at that. But the composer returned home in early August pleased with this exciting and significant development for his art, crossing the elusive border from somewhat provincial outsider – albeit rising national hero – to cautiously accepted European figure.

Extracts from *Lemminkäinen* and suites from Sibelius's recent theatre music, *King Christian II*, were a major part of the concert programmes, as was the modified 'Finland Awakes', but it was the new, recently revised, version of the First Symphony that was the star of the show. Amid his heartache at losing his youngest daughter, during the late winter and early spring of 1900, Sibelius had toiled to adjust the work. However, no extant copy of the original survives, so we can only conjecture exactly what Sibelius did to, as he saw it, improve the symphony, though it is likely to have involved a tightening of the motivic and harmonic material, something (as we have seen in earlier chapters) he usually did when revising his orchestral works.

Whatever the important Russian musical inspirations, and complex political contexts, of this symphony, these are far from its only influences or interpretative possibilities. When he began work on the symphony, Sibelius had conceived of a programmatic piece, with a 'musical dialogue' – perhaps between Finland and Russia, as well as a range of other European literary and musical traditions.

The motto for the first movement was initially to be a 'cold, cold wind blowing in from the sea'. The second movement was to be based on Heinrich Heine (1797–1856), the lyrical – and later politically radical – German poet so important to Schubert and Schumann: 'the pine of the north is dreaming of the palm of the south'. The third movement was to be 'A Winter's Tale' (though whether connected to Shakespeare's tragicomedy is unclear). The fourth and final movement was to be called 'Jorma's Heaven' and draw inspiration from Juhani Aho's 1897 neoromantic novel *Panu*. (We met Aho earlier, in the *Kullervo* chapter, infatuated with Aino Järnefelt, Sibelius's then fiancée.)

This programme, however, was never carried out, and it is a matter of some speculation as to how far such titles and descriptions characterize the music as we now have it. Nonetheless, it's worth keeping in mind these early thoughts Sibelius had for his symphony, not least as he made the uneasy transition from programmatic / tone poem works into a more definitely – and defiantly – abstract symphony. Sibelius's music always has an extramusical element lurking somewhere. And once you've heard the idea that the symphony's opening might be 'a cold, cold wind blowing in from the sea', it's hard to break the link, so perfectly does it seem to match the symphony's famously frigid first sounds, as a solo clarinet sings its desolate magic (and presenting to us all the work's basic motifs).

In the same sketchbook where Sibelius talks of Heine and Aho are excited mentions of Hector Berlioz (1803–1869) – and, indeed, one of the drafts marked 'Berlioz?' found its way into the finale of the symphony. Sibelius had heard the French *maître*'s *Symphonie fantastique* (1830) in Berlin in 1898, just as he was beginning work on his First, and had been dumbfounded by the experience. There was Berlioz's extraordinary development of symphonic form, with its dazzling sonic storytelling and pictographic music (the narrative of the symphony moving from daydreams and a ball to the countryside, scaffold and dreams of a witches' sabbath), but so, too, was there the daring orchestration the Frenchman devised (and required) to tell such a strange symphonic tale.

As we have indicated, it is in the finale to Sibelius's First Symphony that the Berliozian influence comes to the fore: not only did certain sketches end up there, but the very subtitle of the movement ('Quasi una fantasia') links it with the peculiar and exorbitant goings-on in the *Symphonie fantastique* (as well as, as we will see, many other works in European music). The disjointedness, incoherence, secrets and hidden meanings of dreams were ripe for musical, especially symphonic, treatment (Wagner would keep returning to such concepts), as love, sex, art, imagination, power and the sublime commingle in the sleeping mind, and Sibelius's First Symphony is an important, if less apparent, part of this tradition. Struggle, desperation, hyperbole, irony, nostalgia – all are present in both the Berlioz and the Sibelius as their symphonies travel through obsession, oppression and delusion to misery and madness, interrogating the nature of musico-literary traditions and conventions while they're at it.

Other European voices are also part of the complex synthesis of Sibelius's First Symphony. As in *Kullervo*, Bruckner's potent influence on the orchestration is readily discernible: the rugged, sometimes deliberately uneven, brass writing in the first movement; the throbbing, vigorous repetitive patterns of the scherzo, perhaps Sibelius's most Brucknerian movement. More broadly, the organic teleology so profoundly important to Bruckner, as well as to Brahms, is a vital part of this symphony – as crucial (and connected) as its flashes of erotic delight. The narrative of the work is a decisive mixture of the two, the strictures and structures of fate directing and overwhelming the dangerous ambitions of the anonymous protagonist.

Bruckner's great hero, Wagner, also inadvertently shaped many narrative/thematic elements of Sibelius's symphony. As we saw in this chapter's introduction, it is possible to view this work as a 'Siegfried Symphony', as nature, destiny and desire generate a profusion of evocative material reminiscent of music and events in Wagner's great musikdramas *Siegfried* (1871) and *Götterdämmerung* (1874). Following the fraught trials of Sibelius's opening movement, the andante mixes tempestuous, hot-blooded sections with more lyrical music (all of which might mirror several of Siegfried's adventures: taming bears, forging swords, slaying dragons, riding rivers, and so on).

The 'Brucknerian' third-movement scherzo in C major is certainly progeny of the grand Viennese tradition, but it is also naive, animated, careering like Siegfried towards its mysterious fate. The faraway trio in E major features a quietly longing horn motif, in addition to flickering, dancing woodwind and baleful drum rolls, so that, in this suggestive Sibelian passage, we are gently reminded of both Siegfried's daydreaming in act two of *Siegfried* (the so-called Forest Murmurs, or Waldweben, section) and the Idyll section at the end of that work, as Siegfried and Brünnhilde meet – an erotic encounter laden with tension, release and far-reaching implications not unlike those of the symphony's nameless hero.[57]

Sibelius's First Symphony's finale, as we saw in its connections with Berlioz, will develop from dream to nightmare as its fantastical journey remorselessly thunders its hero towards his *Götterdämmerung*-like fate, employing a sonata-form design to emphasize the inexorable situation. With an ominous mythical allure consistent with both Finnish folklore and Wagnerian musikdrama, Sibelius's finale immediately brings back the clarinet solo from the very opening of the symphony, now powerfully

---

57 Forests, of course, will make a majestic final appearance in Sibelius's oeuvre, with his last great work: the extraordinary tone poem *Tapiola* (1926).

orchestrated, just as Wagner's *Ring*[58] had employed a handful of linked – but exceptionally malleable and metamorphosed – motifs which not only helped unify the work musically but allowed for dramatic presentations of inevitable calamity (and closure).

Wagner's *Ring*, like many a Tchaikovsky symphony, is a cyclical work, and Sibelius's First Symphony concludes in this tradition: by closing, but not escaping, the grim loop of life/fate. By redeploying the opening idea of the entire symphony, it seeks to rewrite its own history, as well as to redeem itself. But after the two initial returns, the theme is never heard again. The finale will need another one, and the dynamic forces of the symphony produce a goal-orientated motif that offers hope for some measure of deliverance. This will not be enough, however, and the symphony closes darkly in E minor, unable to locate a truly redemptive major-key conclusion that might break the cycle of doom: the work ends in grim inevitability with a portentous drum roll and then two gentle pizzicato chords that quietly seal the circle.

Sibelius's First Symphony is a masterpiece of integration and cohesion – on its own terms, but also as a hybrid, synthetic work exploring and engaging with several musical traditions: Finnish, Russian, French and Austro-German. It also exploits and interrogates notions of circularity and linear musical forms, showing just how skilful Sibelius had become at symphonic

---

58 Written between 1848 and 1874, premiered complete in 1876, and of which *Siegfried* and *Götterdämmerung* are the third and fourth parts.

transitions, mutations, echoes and reappearances, dexterously organizing and then recontextualizing his material for new and powerful purposes.

For the 'hero' of this restless, wonderfully troubled work, victory comes tantalizingly within reach, before being snatched away by a daring symphonic refusal to structurally resolve itself. That 'hero' might well be Finland itself, since the work stood as a formidable allegory for Finnish resistance against continued Russian subjugation: in both the music and politics, total resolution/liberation did not come. Finland, like the symphony, would have to wait. For Sibelius himself, however, the work was truly triumphant, an extraordinary and novel essay in the form which immediately received the plaudits it deserved.

Together with 'Finland Awakes' / *Finlandia*, the First Symphony paved a new path for Sibelius, musically and in wider cultural terms, representing both important compositional steps and landmarks in the development and recognition of Finland as a unique and compelling voice on the international stage. The Sibelian – and Finnish – century had begun.

Symphony No.1 in E minor, op.39

1. Andante, ma non troppo.

Given the theatrical and narrative elements this symphony contains, it is appropriate that it begins with both a quiet drum roll and music that sounds like the sonic equivalent of the traditional 'Once upon a time …' opening to countless folk and fairy tales the world over: a meandering solo clarinet.[59] Unadorned, wide-ranging, sorrowful, this long improvisatory solo is immediately comparable to the runic style of Finnish folk singing from the Karelia region Sibelius knew so well. It instantly establishes an atmosphere of mystery and pain, as well as structural ambiguity and anticipation as we await the symphonic drama to come.[60]

Beyond its enigmatic mood and placement, the landscape of the long haunting solo is also crucial in presenting all the symphony's main thematic material. To maintain the folkloric theme, it is like a puzzling map, full of vital information – fair maidens, diabolical dragons, buried treasure – for the adventure ahead. The start of the finale will briefly reuse/rewrite this music, connecting the work at a fundamental thematic level, so that the work from its very beginning presents shadowy tensions between linear and circular symphonic paths.[61]

A quiet timpani roll introduces the solo clarinet, which lingers in tonally vague areas as it tells its sad, inscrutable stories, which will shortly begin to take on meaning. It finishes its forlorn meditation, and a sonata-form movement commences: the second violins hurry in with a towering tremolando, while the first violins cultivate an arresting new motif. This assertive main theme is rhythmically tense – and not unlike the energetic first movements

---

59 I am indebted to Stephen Johnson for this idea.

60 We recall that Sibelius's original motto for the first movement was to be 'a cold, cold wind blowing in from the sea'.

61 Given its forward-looking purpose, it is fascinating, if not surprising, that this clarinet preamble was in fact a late addendum to the score: a reconsideration and inspired addition rather than the catalytic or original spur of the work. Clearly Sibelius later saw the musico-dramatic benefits of a pre-emptive prelude.

of Beethoven's Seventh (1812), Borodin's First (1867)[62] and Tchaikovsky's Fifth (1888), all of which, like Sibelius's First, contain slow introductory sections. The enormous vitality of the music makes it clear that, as with many other symphonies earlier in the century (if not necessarily the trio just mentioned), we are to consider this as a presentation of a courageous hero: young, hearty and full of strength.

Everything is urgent, compelling, vital. We barely touch E minor – finding it only in the movement's closing bars as fate begins to take a grip – and instead tend to stay around G major, though with ambiguous flirtations towards the symphony's true tonic key. A clap of thunder from timpani and tuba leads to a restoration of the movement's energy: a restatement of the hero's opening gesture, now on brass and timpani, which builds towards a furious climax that then subsides into F sharp.

Iridescent strings and an archaic harp initiate the second main theme on chirrupy flutes and other avian-pastoral woodwind: we have entered a mythical bucolic world, though before long it is swept away by an orgiastic dance reminiscent of passages from *Lemminkäinen*. But this section, too, is terminated – by a brusque staccato resolution that ends the exposition.

The development section – Sibelius pays lip service to sonata form in this movement, but it is crucially there – is a stormy affair, repeating certain patterns until the bucolic sequence returns with a pair of solo violins rapturously entwinned and clearly showing us the hero's romantic adventures. (Did he spot a fair maiden in the first presentation of the bucolic section and then go back to meet her in the development?)

---

62 Borodin's First had been played in Helsinki in 1896, though Sibelius was not present at the concert.

From here, the development builds swirls of motion that lead to an abbreviated recapitulation that Sibelius will go on to make a speciality in his symphonies: compressing form was one of his key novelties as a symphonist, and it is readily apparent here, even in his first essay. We are given no firm E minor warning: instead, the heroic first theme is steadily reaffirmed, building in rugged, precipitous power – pure granite strength – to a brass fortissimo of great Romantic power (it is truly sublime), before a vast timpani crescendo is curtly cut off in the final bars. It is a ghastly, furious gesture: two very low E minor chords from sombre plucked strings and harp.[63] All our hero's vehement energy has seemingly come to nought, only to doubt and despair.

The whole movement has been a battle between adventurous exploits (including amorous deeds) and destructive elements – and, just as the protagonist's actions serve to also undermine him, so too the conventional sonata-form sections of exposition, development and recapitulation are destabilized, squeezed, deformed. The symphony's heroic narrative is wedded to its musical technique.

2. Andante (ma non troppo lento).

The slow movement in E flat is a sudden shift in not only mood but time and place too. We seem to sink into a world of charm and changeless wonder (at least at first). It is a fantasy, an escape, perhaps a more extended return, though in dream form, to the bucolic section of the opening movement. Perhaps we are in a Finnish folk heaven, a Nordic Valhalla for heroes.

---

[63] The effect sounds a little like the kantele, or Finnish harp/zither, which Sibelius had been so fascinated by on his post-honeymoon trip around the Karelia region in 1892.

The movement is a form of rondo – though this reveals little of its emotional variety, which is all superbly bound together. It begins with a Tchaikovskian lullaby of exquisite grace on muted violins and cellos (which also recalls elements of the 'Kullervo's Youth' movement in that work), which is joined by a more determined melody for the horns and woodwind. The lullaby is simple, sentimental, powerful – calming the symphony and allowing the mind and memory to wander.

There are a wealth of fascinating passages throughout this movement – especially a creepy sequence for woodwind, timpani and solo cello – but essentially the movement is a series of reiterations and augmentations of the opening material, repeating and intensifying the mood and memories. Over time, these cyclic amplifications gain a culminative power, eventually flaring up into C minor.

The Tchaikovskian lullaby does return, but it is tautly compressed, and its earlier sense of serenity has been disturbed by its own dark intensifications. Sentimentality and nostalgia are at their dynamic best, changing memories and our relationship with them, making the past as unstable as the future. (The movement is also clearly a dreamworld, memories taking on the strange, supple and manipulative magic of *Alice's Adventures in Wonderland* or *Finnegans Wake*.)

3. Scherzo: Allegro.

The Brucknerian/Siegfried scherzo (discussed in the essay above) is in some ways a generic mood piece, an artificial return to folk idioms or country dances, the latter especially familiar to Mahler, particularly in his ländler movements. This is significant, for Sibelius is clearly setting up a range of musico-cultural networks by this startling summons to custom and convention. Viennese traditions, Wagnerian mythology, Finnish folklore – all are to be referenced, synthesized (and distorted) in this extraordinary movement.

It begins with the pulse of pizzicato string chords, along with the timpani, which provide a tersely animated motif of their own, soon adopted by other orchestral zones. The music takes on an increasingly impulsive, unpredictable nature as it develops: we can probably add some Shakespearean midsummer madness to the eclectic mix.

Scherzos usually have a 'scherzo-trio-scherzo' structure, and Sibelius's here is no different, with the outer sections presenting a vigorous circular dance, with sharp metrical intrusions from the timpani and some weird fugato for the woodwind and strings. The central trio slows the pace to return to the bucolic world of the first movement as well as the second-movement lullaby (and its intensifications). Whatever the Wagnerian Waldweben associations, the trio is also a delightful invocation of the Nordic forest, full of rustling trees, peculiar sounds and eerie light.

4. Finale (Quasi una fantasia): Andante.

Sibelius labels his first symphony's last movement 'Quasi una fantasia' ('Almost like a fantasy') not only to justify the remarkable liberty with which he indulges established forms but also to display how the pan-European nexus of his work continues in the finale.

Several celebrated classical works had used the term *fantasy* (and its cognates) to signal freer forms, departures from orthodoxy and potentially asphyxiating parameters, especially when conjuring up worlds of love, night and dream. Mozart's fantasia No.3 in D minor (1782) is a wonderful elicitation of murky nocturnal shadows; Beethoven's *Moonlight* Piano Sonata in C-sharp minor (1801) carries an identical marking to Sibelius's finale; one of Schubert's final, and bleakest, piano works, the fantasia in F minor for four hands (1828), is a dynamic, funereal masterpiece. Tchaikovskian links are also apparent: the turbulent, ardent atmospheres of the 'symphonic fantasy' *Francesca da Rimini* (1877) and the 'fantasy overture' *Romeo and Juliet* (1880) were surely in Sibelius's mind when he came to compose his own fantasia.

Appropriately, for all this historical referencing, the finale of Sibelius's First opens back at the beginning of the symphony – almost. It rewrites the solo clarinet's long, lonely melody with some substantial strings, plus some softer reverberations from the woodwind. The theme's re-emergence is histrionic, hyperbolic, almost comic – but distressingly so, like a confused old general wheeled out by politicians for their own sordid purposes. The theme is war-weary, tired, the memories of previous campaigns seen now from a contemporary, and darker, perspective.

This is as far as the reappearance of the subject will go, however. If the hero is to escape the torments of fate, he will need another theme. One comes, amid a torrent of tragic musical ideas, each clambering for attention: laconic, aphoristic motifs emerging with a startling impetus and intensity. Eventually a lyrical cantilena for strings begins to drive the movement forward with more purpose and optimism, and its recurrence – with lush, eager strings and confident brass fanfares – is especially positive: another of the symphony's great Romantic moments. Can our protagonist finally find peace – or even victory?

But there is another twist to come, and the ending of Sibelius's First Symphony is one of huge imagination and audacious drama, one to match the daring opening to the work. The movement builds to a vigorous, compelling fortissimo, not unlike that at the climax of the first movement. But, just as at that point in the symphony the hero dwindled into doubt and despair, in a devastating coda to the finale, the hero is snuffed out with a repeat of those two grim E minor pizzicato chords. The optimistic new themes were not enough, nor could there be any major-key version of the motto theme. The symphony's destiny has been to slaughter its star, to maintain the macabre cycle of fate, to obstinately refuse to achieve any kind of musical/structural resolution and merely to abscond with a pair of cackling plucked strings.

This final movement seems very close to being a tone poem; indeed, the whole symphony may be heard as a cycle of tone poems, showing us the life and death of an unknown, unnamed hero – and many programmatic or allegorical readings of the work are possible, even desirable. Yet we are not left only with a glorious enigma. The motivic and harmonic cohesion of Sibelius's work, its brilliant structural organization, organic unity and subjective momentum, is proof of its enduring status as one of the great symphonies: no more, no less. And this was only the beginning.

Finlandia, op.26

Finlandia, that distinguished refrain of a nation, opens in immensely evocative fashion with a menacing, snarling motif in the brass that moves swiftly from forte to fortissimo. Woodwinds answer with a sanctified sense of elevation and awe before the strings offer a more compassionate element, almost the sound of the human voice.

This slow introductory material yields to a tempo change into allegro moderato and brass fanfares that herald a courageous national spirit of fight and fervour, the confidence of the music growing and growing.

From within this sonic self-assurance, on the woodwind comes the famous – the world-famous – tune: the great hymn motif of *Finlandia*, a tremendously stirring theme and the superficial second subject of the work, though such technicalities are lost in the emotion. The strings continue to play the hymn theme with astonishing reverence, respect and nobility.

This gives way to an increasing tempo, the momentum surging and swelling in the wind and then the whole orchestra, crowned by a return of the brass fanfares. The music gushes towards its triumphant conclusion with great crashes of percussion and timpani rolls as the mighty motif continues to ring out in a telescoped version of itself, amplified like a turbo engine, a potent symbol of coiled power and belief, self-formation and self-proclamation.

Finland is now certainly awake, a mighty machine ready for the future.

Chapter Five

A Confession of the Soul: The Second Symphony

We saw in the previous chapter how a range of ideas and images – cold sea winds, German Romantic poetry, a contemporary Finnish novel – initially nourished Sibelius's First Symphony (1899). These concepts were then overhauled by a network of complex musical strands (Russian, French, Austro-German) to create an ostensibly abstract work, but nonetheless one with a heroic narrative never far from the surface.

For his Second Symphony (1902), completed only three years later, a similar programmatic derivation fed Sibelius's creative mind. The work originated in sketches for a cycle of four tone poems, not unlike *Lemminkäinen*, entitled *En Fest* ('A Festival,' or 'A Celebration'). And Sibelius chose well for himself: among his sources of inspiration were the legend of Don Juan, the Spanish libertine who had inspired Mozart and Richard

Strauss; the *Divina commedia*, Dante's great poetic study of heaven, hell, and everything in between; and Liszt's oratorio *Christus* (1866), based on the traditional life of Jesus.

More personal stimuli were also at work: the magnificent transformation of the main theme in the finale's coda was said to have been inspired by the sight of his friend the painter Akseli Gallen-Kallela's villa deep in the Karelian forests. One theme was apparently improvised during the christening of Gallen-Kallela's son, while another is purported to have emerged when Sibelius was asked to judge the composition of a seven-year-old girl (though whether Sibelius simply purloined his youthful colleague's material is lost to time). The mournful second theme of the finale was supposedly composed as a memorial to Sibelius's sister-in-law, Elli Järnefelt, who took her own life in July 1901. The still raw memory of his daughter Kirsti's death in February 1900 is also likely to have influenced aspects of the work's creation.

As with the First Symphony, however, the Second discarded traces of its literary and personal origins as Sibelius sought to achieve greater progress with his orchestral music as a non-representational and conceptual expressive conduit: a vehicle of musical logic and momentum. But these preliminary ideas were more than naive drafts or discarded scaffolding. They help us understand not only the evolution of Sibelius as a composer but also how his symphonies remain close (in both design and meaning) to the tone poems he would also write all his creative life. We need not interpret the Second as the *Don Juan* or *Dante* or *Kirsti* Symphony – this is too reductive and restrictive; but we can use these elements to unpack and develop our understanding of Sibelius's imagination, ambitions and concerns.

Certainly, however far we might try (or wish) to interpret Sibelius's Second as a tone poem or programmatic symphony, it is as a cogent, compelling symphonic construction that it most obviously succeeds. Full of mystical, personal and literary material, it is true, but all woven impeccably into the fabric of the work, the mastery of form ingesting – but not destroying – its 'confession of the soul', to use Sibelius's own phrase.

We can appreciate Sibelius's Second Symphony, like all his essays in the medium, on a purely abstract level, as connoisseurs of symphonic logic and structure, meticulous dynamics and exquisitely compressed ideas (the first movement in particular is his finest accomplishment yet in terms of realizing his personal musical dogma, 'inner connection between motifs'). But we can also be musical pathologists, studying cause and effect, origin and upshot, using our sonic scalpels to probe beneath the supreme symphonic skins Sibelius produces. Relegate Sibelius to mere logician and we miss much of what that lucidity is intended to communicate. After all, Johann Sebastian Bach, one of the great musical theorists, and Kurt Gödel, the matchless mathematical logician of the twentieth century, both saw their very different endeavours as a means to comprehend a theistic, personal, loving God: logic and emotion are connected.[64]

If Sibelius's enterprise is not expressly evangelical (at least in any doctrinal sense, though his work is deeply spiritual), it is certainly far more than a dour exercise in symphonic logic. The 'Big Tune' of the finale reveals as much to us, disclosing this work as – like Beethoven's Ninth, whose finale had a decent melody of its own – a channel of aspiration and liberation: for Sibelius the symphonist and Finland the nation.

---

64 We should always be wary of regarding Bach as only a musical mathematician: whatever his theoretical and analytical gifts, he was a full-blooded, practical, earthy composer, too, something apparent especially in his two hundred–plus church cantatas, some of the most humane documents in musical history. They could never have been written by an exclusively cold, rational mind; their composer had to recognize the complex, vulnerable nature of the human condition.

All Sibelius's seven symphonies are cousins, clearly from the same immediate musical family; but the First and Second are brothers (if not twins), and the Second Symphony would become what the First strove to be: a heroic, nationalist statement of freedom and independence.

The First showed the struggle; the Second, the triumph.

We last saw Sibelius returning home quietly elated by the, on the whole, successful European tour of his First Symphony in the summer of 1900, a milestone for his music on a bigger stage than Finland could offer. Sibelius had intended to surprise his wife and the girls, but Aino's letter telling him that they were away in Kuopio never reached him, so his return was a slight anticlimax. When they were reunited, however, Aino was delighted to see her often morose husband in good spirits. Success could never bring their darling Kirsti back, but it surely helped them be more positive about the future, not least because whatever the achievements of the continental peregrination, Sibelius's musical future – and finances – were still very uncertain.[65]

Before the tour itself, bizarre anonymous letters of support and advice had kept turning up, including a suggestion for a

---

[65] In the late summer and early autumn, Sibelius composed the patriotic allegory *Snöfrid*, a melodrama for choir and orchestra, and a haunting series of songs. Among them, 'Den första kyssen' ('The First Kiss') is an agonizing reflection on lost innocence, with a neo-Wagnerian, *Tristan*-like chord that punctures the narrator's naivety; 'Marssnön' ('March Snow') is an upbeat expectation of spring, while 'Demanten på Marssnön' ('The Diamond on the March Snow') is a captivating gem (as its title suggests). A final song, 'Säv, säv, susa' ('Reeds, Reeds, Sigh') concerns a drowned girl, and the song seems a poignant mini requiem for the recently departed Kirsti.

new name for the sixth tableau of the *Press Celebration Music – Finlandia* – as well as the opinion that Sibelius should undertake a trip to Italy, 'where one learns *cantabile*, moderation and harmony, plasticity and symmetry of line.' After the tour, their source was revealed to be the eccentric musician and writer Baron Axel Carpelan (1858–1919), a minor Swedish Finnish aristocrat who existed in poverty but had numerous contacts with wealthy patrons and used these connections to raise funds for Sibelius, whose music he could see was not only innovative and new but potentially prophetic.

The two men became firm friends, and in the autumn of 1900, Sibelius took Carpelan's advice to travel to Italy. Carpelan had secured a bursary for travel,[66] and being back home had only served to remind Sibelius of the daughter he had lost. The family left Finland on 27 October, stopping first in Berlin – Sibelius felt it important to consolidate the success of his German tour. They ended up staying for several months, living in a luxurious hotel and quickly devouring the funds designated for the trip to Italy: by January 1901 the money was all gone. This was an early test of the friendship with Carpelan, who – with Aino – was, quite reasonably, dismayed that the money he had raised had not been used for the purposes it had been intended.

Ever the resourceful chancer, Sibelius managed to secure funds from another Finnish source, and in late January the family finally left Germany, crossed the Alps, and travelled down to Rapallo, a small town on the Ligurian coast between Portofino and Chiavari, near Genoa.[67] Aino and the two girls stayed in a

---

66 Around €18,000 in today's money, part of which Sibelius used to clear a few outstanding debts.

67 Just before they left, Sibelius composed one of his most celebrated, lush and romantic songs: 'Flickan kom ifrån sin älsklings möte' ('The Tryst'). Setting Runeberg, the song traces how a young sweetheart hides her romantic liaisons from her mother before admitting everything when he breaks her heart with his faithless behaviour.

guesthouse, while Sibelius drifted into the aromatic hills above the sea, renting a study in a villa surrounded by a garden full of roses, camellias and magnolias, as well as citrus, palm and almond trees. Liguria in mid-February is not hot, but it is usually mild – and it is certainly more agreeable than metropolitan Berlin in winter. These serene surroundings began to stimulate Sibelius's musical imagination (as we will see).

Health and money worries persisted, however: not only did the new funds rapidly begin to disappear (plus ça change), but their second daughter, Ruth, then aged six, fell acutely ill with a fever. Typhus was feared, but the illness turned out not to be as serious as initially thought (peritonitis), and she made a full recovery (and lived into her eighties). While the stress of this so soon after Kirsti's death must have been indescribably painful, Sibelius's response was both astonishing and deeply selfish. As soon as Ruth was out of danger, in late March he disappeared without warning to Rome, staying in a hotel, composing, and visiting the opera and assorted antiquities such as the Colosseum. It is not only hard to offer Sibelius any sympathy for his shameful conduct but difficult to imagine the trauma and pressure placed on Aino – not least because of her husband's not infrequent alcoholic vanishings into the bars and restaurants of Helsinki and Berlin, where he wouldn't be seen again for days on end.[68]

Nonetheless, judgement is easy; composition is not. The demands of his domestic, marital and paternal responsibilities were often in conflict with the millstone of creative expectancy: he was now not only a vital national figure but a coming voice on

---

68 In Helsinki, Sibelius would sometimes send strange little notes home, promising to be back 'soon' or 'tomorrow', which was rarely an accurate proclamation. When her husband died, Aino came across a batch of these curious, perhaps well-intentioned but ultimately unkind dispatches and was filled with horror at the pain of those years. 'Unpleasant letters. Not to be saved', she wrote on the back.

the European musical stage. And, it has to be said, the Roman trip did bear musical fruit: among other bounty, he penned the first sketches for what would become two of his greatest tone poems, *Pohjola's Daughter* and *Nightride and Sunrise* (which we will explore in the next chapter).

Sibelius did write to Aino from Rome, full of his usual remorse. He was, at least, very aware of the pain he could cause given his unpredictable nature and complex obligations. But the amounts of love, kindness and patience Aino Sibelius held within her must surely be measured in oceans and galaxies. She forgave him, and the family returned home to Finland in May 1901, detouring briefly to Florence in order to visit the Uffizi Gallery, as well as making fleeting stops in Vienna and Prague (where Sibelius briefly met Dvořák, whom he considered 'humility incarnate').

It was this Florentine excursion that helped generate significant material for the Second Symphony, some of which had also come during the stay in Rapallo. Ideas for a setting of part of Dante's *Divina commedia* came to Sibelius in the great medieval city that the poet had been born in and was exiled from. The poem's extraordinary exploration of a soul's punitive, purifying journey after death profoundly appealed to Sibelius's complex personality – as well as, perhaps, his sense of guilt over his recent behaviour.

Sibelius also made sketches for strings in what would eventually become the symphony's slow movement. He labelled this warm, major-key melody 'Christus', after Liszt's oratorio on the life of Jesus, which Sibelius had seen with Aino in Berlin, but also because of his own desire to engage with Christological and religious ideas – an obvious choice of both narrative and thematic material. Taken with the Dantean theology fizzing in his head, Sibelius seems to have been conceiving a programmatic work (he was not yet considering it a symphony) with some kind of battle between life and death, or a fight for a man's soul, the struggle perhaps personified by a range of familiar figures. Given the eventual ending of the movement – with its bleak coda for brass and woodwind – it seems that this campaign is, inevitably, won by Death.

One further element fed the creation of the slow movement and occurred a little earlier than in Florence or Rome. This originated back in the rose-scented garden of Rapallo and was, of course, the legend of Don Juan, Iberian debauchee and folk hero who had inspired Mozart's and Da Ponte's landmark opera *Don Giovanni* (1787), Byron's satirical epic *Don Juan* (1824), and Richard Strauss's eponymous first major tone poem (1888), along with a wealth of works from other creative minds, from Buddy Holly to Ingmar Bergman, Søren Kierkegaard to Albert Camus.

Utilizing the image of the Stone Guest who beckons the Don to his destiny, Sibelius drafted an intricate scenario to go with his musical sketches (which, we remember, were still being conceived as a part of a tone poem rather than the slow movement of a symphony):

> Sit in the twilight in my castle; a stranger enters. I ask him several times who he is – but never with any answer. I try to entertain him. Still no answer. Eventually this unknown guest begins to sing a song and Don Juan realizes who he is: Death.

As you listen to the first part of the Second Symphony's slow movement you can, should you be so inclined, map this little Don Juan set-up onto the music – which includes a menacing bassoon (supernatural footsteps?), fretful repeated figurations (the Don's increasingly anxious questions?), and a violent brass fortissimo (perhaps related to the actual announcement of Death?). All this is then followed, in the score, by the more tender 'Christus' sketches.

Clearly there are thematic links between all three of the situations Sibelius drafted: Don Juan, Dante and Christ are all figures in narratives fixated on vice, punishment and human transience. They are also the stuff of religion and drama the world over since time immemorial, and the basis of many an exciting opera or even symphony. Listeners can take as much or as little from the primary stimulus as they wish – though it has to be said that the movement based on this material is probably the least pleasing, at least from a purely symphonic standpoint, in the work, betraying a little its programmatic heritage.

Italy more generally, however, might be said to still govern certain areas of the symphony, as well as its overall philosophy. Although the work can't be considered Sibelius's 'Italian symphony' in the same way that Mendelssohn's Fourth (1833)[69] or Berlioz's *Harold en Italie* Symphony (1834)[70] are clearly works to be considered in relation to the Italian landscape, people and so forth, we can consider a biographical aspect that seems pertinent to the final work.

---

69 Directly intended to convey the colour and atmosphere of Italy in symphonic form, Mendelssohn's work includes Roman saltarello and Neapolitan tarantella dances in the finale.

70 Inspired by Byron's long narrative poem *Childe Harold's Pilgrimage* (1818), Berlioz's 'symphony with viola obbligato' is divided into four parts: Harold in the Mountains; March of the Pilgrims; Serenade of an Abruzzo Mountaineer; Orgy of Bandits.

The opening movement, for example, seems to breathe the relief of arriving in the warm south after a harsh northern winter – not unlike the parallel opening movements to Beethoven's 1808 *Pastoral* ('pleasant feelings on arriving in the countryside') or Brahms's Second (1877), another countrified symphony. In the Sibelius everything seems to collect momentum and spread out as if this is the dawn of a new day and season, its strength growing like the spring sunshine. And it is the first rising rays of that sunlight, the work's initial climbing three-note phrase (F sharp–G–A), which will go on to generate almost everything in the symphony, an extraordinarily unified internal network coming from a tiny unfurling source heard in the symphony's first moments.

For Sibelius, his symphonies were 'confessions of faith' (each from a different period of his life), and the Second might be perceived as an admission of hesitation, impulse, compulsion, self-reproach, trauma and renaissance, spiritual or otherwise. Transcendent affirmation is forged out of terrestrial suffering.

Beyond personal, biographical or mystical readings, however, come more potentially momentous political-historical ones. The tensions at the heart of the symphony, as well as its push towards celestial luminosity, can, as we've seen, be regarded as a figurative eschatological battle against mortality and eternal damnation, but a more earthly conception is also important. There is a Nietzschean drama at work as well as a Dantean one, with a defiant Übermensch trajectory towards a this-world liberty, grasping the earth with gratitude and joy, which can be closely identified with the Finns' struggle against Russian imperial oppression that we pondered in the last chapter.

There, the First Symphony was unable to break into a major key to evade the grim cycle of fate; here in the Second, a more resilient overall shape allows a form of emancipation to be achieved. The finale has an immense battle and concluding shout of triumph – arguably on an epic scale worthy of geopolitical and nationalist explanations. Sibelius, understandably, was keen to play down any such links: he had, after all, worked hard to create a severe, abstract symphony based on acute internal reasoning, not some Russia-bashing, tub-thumping cry for freedom. (Sibelius was probably also keen not to become even further embroiled in political affairs that not only were potentially dangerous but also distracted him from his family and, ironically, composition.)

Nevertheless, Sibelius's Second is a work of vast communicative capacity, of enormous dramatic and interpretative potential, something it retained from its most primitive early drafts. The debts to the apotheoses of Beethoven's Fifth (1808), in the tense transition from third-movement scherzo to conquering finale, and Ninth (1824), in that finale's Big Tune and complex drive towards freedom and joy, are clear. And Beethoven's symphonies, then as now, stand for (among many other things) political liberty, for journeys from chaos to creation, darkness to light, struggle to victory.

Sibelius's friend, colleague and most important early interpreter, Robert Kajanus, emphatically saw the work in this way, as a political manifesto, writing that the andante was an image of heartbroken protest against contemporary injustices which threatened to 'deprive the sun of its light and our flowers of their fragrance'. For Kajanus, the scherzo represented furious, intense groundwork, preparing for the finale, which progressed on the way to a glorious, victorious close meant to stimulate in the listener a 'picture of lighter and more positive prospects for the future.'[71]

Others, of course, will – reasonably – want only safer, exclusively musicological, interpretations. For them, Sibelius's Second is an intellectual essay on the very character of the symphonic endeavour, an exercise examining symphonic expression, growth and manifestation. It is, for them, above all about musical objective finding, about sonic and symphonic orienteering. It involves the enunciation of structural concerns and the interplay between musical keys, an epic abstract expedition to locate the great final hymn in D major.

The point, surely, is that no single interpretation – Finnish nationalist, Nietzschean, Dantean, biographical, eschatological or purely musicological – is 'right'. All have their role in our understanding of the symphony, which, like all truly great works of art, exists far beyond its creator's own limitations or intentions, only some of which may be realized at a conscious level.

What can be stated with some confidence is that the Second Symphony marked a turning point in Sibelius's career, especially as a symphonist. In some ways, the Second denoted a crisis as much as a crossroads, and as such it is a touching musical document. It shows an outstanding, if still developing, gift for symphonic logic and motivic compression. But whatever the Second's undoubted originality – of technique, form and personal expression – there is a good case to be made for arguing that this work, as well as the other of his first two 'pure' essays in the symphonic medium, existed somewhat in the seductive shadow

---

[71] An attitude echoed by the Finnish musicologist Ilmari Krohn, who, in the aftermath of the Winter War (1939–40) between Finland and the Soviet Union, and the Second World War more generally, hailed the Second as the *Liberation* Symphony.

of their broader symphonic predecessors. It is reductive (and misleading) to call Sibelius's First and Second his *Tchaikovsky* and *Beethoven* Symphonies, but there is a hint of truth to the statement. It is also true that they both contained, and to some extent held on to, a programmatic derivation far more than any of their successors would.

But none of this prevented the Second Symphony from becoming, justifiably, an instant sensation.

When Sibelius returned home from his Italian sojourn in the spring of 1901, he spent most of the rest of the year working on the symphony before, on 8 March 1902, it received its world premiere in Helsinki University's Great Hall. It was a roaring critical and commercial success, with several repeat concerts selling out – an unparalleled accomplishment for a new orchestral work in Finland.[72] It soon travelled abroad, attaining a significant international following (especially in Britain and America, countries which would have huge consequence for Sibelius's long-term standing). To this day the Second remains probably the most popular, most performed and most recorded of all Sibelius's symphonies.

For Sibelius himself, however, matters were more complex. He turned thirty-seven at the end of 1902, and his career as

---

72 Spending some time alone on the coast at Tvärminne during the summer of 1902, after the premiere of the Second, Sibelius composed one of his most popular songs, 'Var det en dröm?' ('Was It a Dream?'), setting a poem by Josef Julius Wecksell. The words seem to echo the dreamy premiere of the symphony, telling of a lost love of such mysterious enchantment that it appears surreal, almost a hallucination, and Sibelius gives the song a wonderful far-reaching theme.

a composer (he was still conducting here and there) needed onerous attention on two, often rival, fronts. First, there was maintaining his domestic reputation as a nationalist hero, a Finnish Verdi/Wagner, with all its substantial burdens and benefits. Second, the problem of preserving and then developing his wider international status as a noteworthy, auspicious and original voice in the congested marketplace of the new century's music. It was a double challenge of immense, and escalating, psychological and organizational proportions. And it would frequently require gargantuan quantities of nefarious substances – swimming pools of alcohol plus vast jungles of tobacco – not only to manage the anxieties it caused but to oil the wheels of the creative muse herself.

Despite all this, 1903 dawned brightly. Sibelius was making progress on a new work, and a particular pet project at that: a violin concerto. Another daughter (their fourth), Katarina, arrived on 12 January. To top it all, a small legacy from an uncle meant that Sibelius and his family could finally escape the tedium and stress of cramped rented accommodation in/around Helsinki and move outside the capital – which, as far as Aino was concerned, also had the not inconsiderable advantage of being a long way from the all-night-and-next-day drinking sessions at the Kämp or König restaurants. Here, Sibelius would build his own house amid his beloved countryside, in the forest and lake surroundings of Järvenpää, a sanctuary that was also a workshop, giving him the relative peace and routine to more firmly commit himself to his art (and his family).

This would be Ainola, the home in which he would spend the rest of his long life.

Symphony No.2 in D major, op.43

1. Allegretto.

Sibelius's First Symphony opened with a desolate clarinet solo which presented all the main themes of that work in a condensed embryonic prelude. The Second Symphony goes even further, disclosing its primary material in its first trio of notes: the rising three-note progression not only forms a motto for the work but is the basis from which all its subsequent matter will flow. It is not unlike the nascent, bourgeoning 'Nature' motif at the opening of Wagner's enormous fifteen-hour *Ring* cycle, and from this rudimentary initial seed Sibelius, like his musikdramatist colleague, produces a continuously evolving symphonic development, where all its psychology and theatre is intimately bound to its germinal sound. It is an immense achievement of musical organization and organic unity.

The D major opening on strings is a pastoral hymn to spring and the sun, those three ascending notes a song to light, hope and growth. The impression is cheery, rustic, full of freshness and subjective feeling. But, as in Sibelius's tone poem *Spring Song*, there is more than a hint of Nordic melancholy too. From here ideas will be exhibited one at a time, before being conjoined in a variety of ways and from different perspectives, offering new contexts and novel commentaries on the material. This allows Sibelius to present a huge range of emotional-intellectual angles, which nonetheless still gives the (very accurate) impression of evolving from both the same source and each other.

In the *Ring*, Wagner inverts the ascending 'Nature' motif to powerfully create its own opposite (the descending one of the 'Twilight of the Gods') and in so doing turns it from a magnificent source of life and growth into an instrument fit only for corruption, corrosion and death. Likewise, in his Second Symphony, Sibelius almost immediately flips the simple F sharp–G–A opening theme to provide the woodwind's response – but, unlike the dark metamorphoses of the *Ring*, its alteration merely develops the vernal song into a subsiding, somewhat equivocal, rustic dance on clarinets and oboes (both the song and its woodwind retort will be mightily transformed at the start of the finale). Horns echo but with shifts to E minor, lending a characteristically mournful strain to this arrival of the northern spring. The horns are interrupted by the return of the string song but insist upon their elegiac point of view.

After a strange pause, flutes and bassoons try to suggest an alternative way forward, away from D major: the B-flat route? The pleasant spring journey, the march south, is being quizzed, mistrusted. Timpani rolls offer their menacing opinion, perhaps some threatening thunder to remind us spring is not all lambs and lilacs. An extended, transitional tune for the violins alone reaffirms the desire to proceed, but it is a solitary, almost helpless voice which closes in a lugubrious E minor that seems to end up agreeing with the earlier horns.

A backwards version of the opening notes helps create the (indefinite) second subject on woodwind, and strings yearn for the lost hope of the opening moments, when everything seemed so straightforward. Mounting pizzicato strings accelerate the music, the movement gathering its rhythmic momentum, growing and widening all the time as the material expands and transforms itself. Everything is moving forward, with a now inspiring energy, captivating syncopations pushing the music along towards the end of the sonata-form exposition with frequent reminders of those expectant first sounds.

This symphony's exposition has been a masterclass in goal-directed regulation: despite the immense atmospheric ambiguity and variety, Sibelius's control of the material within his structure is faultless. The development is no less proficient, organized as a sequence of upsurges, and slightly smaller tendencies, towards a range of keys: D flat and especially B flat, which begin to dominate the mood. Keen to preserve its energy, the movement courses on, tunes and transformations continuing, especially music based on the earlier sequestered violins. Whereas the overlaying of material is more conventionally typical of the recapitulation section of sonata form, Sibelius's brilliant evolutionary unity brings it in a little early. Faint woodland whispers on the woodwind, previously a little ominous in character, become frisky, then rapturous songs of delight alongside a persuasively formidable brass chorale, and the recapitulation is a magnificent synthesis of the opening movement's very diverse music – which, given its common heritage, never sounds overwrought or insincere.

The movement, and the journey, end in unobtrusive fashion, with a Classical tidiness and almost calculated certainty, like a train pulling into a railway terminus. The inaugural string figures return, slowly climbing and then inclining (the final puffs of the locomotive's engine), so that the allegretto closes in a firm D major.

As with the opening movement of Brahms's own rustic Second Symphony (also in D major), Sibelius's offers a cryptic, elliptic, often very equivocal sonic mood, something arguably heighted in the Finn's work, given the more subtle technique by which he is able to both bind and evolve his material. Sibelius claimed the main theme one of his sunniest (and often lamented the movement being played too slowly), but it is also restrained by the obstruse sorrow that is a key feature of his music, and from which derives much of its attraction and power. It is never blithely contented, nor is it as deeply despondent as many other Nordic composers.

Travel, nature, time and the seasons are complex features of human existence; none are as straightforwardly 'happy' or 'sad' as we might suppose.

2. *Tempo andante, ma rubato.*

Compared to the outstanding fluidity and cohesion of the opening movement, the second is more partial, even factional, betraying both the complex, miscellaneous origins of much of the material (discussed above), as well as, perhaps, its reflection of 'heartbroken protest' against Russian oppression, which Robert Kajanus observed. Is it also a manifestation of Sibelius's own inward glances, towards the nature of his soul and the conduct of his character?

The three key ideas which inspired the movement – Dante's *Divina commedia*, Death visiting Don Juan, and the 'Christus' motif – are in effect condensed into one distinct lyrical concept, but given the underlying conflict and struggle inherent to each, between love and temptation, desire and death, this single subject is splintered, ruptured into the shifting moods of the movement, from solemnity to an expressionistic anguish and dissonance, reminiscent of Wagner's *Tristan* (1865), Strauss's *Elektra* (1909) and Bartók's *Bluebeard* (1918).

It begins with a protracted introductory section for pizzicato lower strings. Sombre cellos and double basses in D minor tread slowly, even chanting like penitent pilgrims, occasionally writhing in agony to try to extract themselves from the incarceration of sin / D minor. The bassoons, suggestive of the visitation of Death in the 'Nordic Don Juan' scenario Sibelius sketched, creep along with the first main theme of the movement, joined by restless repetitive figurations and an uneven violin motif, before travelling to a ferocious brass fortissimo that seems to announce death itself.

Following a prolonged pause, the uneven violin motif is wondrously transformed into the affectionate, exquisite and otherworldly F-sharp major 'Christus' theme, the hopeful message of Jesus and his offer of redemption, which is then swept aside by indifferent gestures from the bass. A war ensues, between death and salvation, for the subject's soul, the movement's themes undergoing a series of violent metamorphoses. The momentum gradually subsides only to suddenly erupt in a shout of discomfort/disobedience from the orchestra before the andante closes with a pair of grave pizzicato chords (not unlike those which ended the First Symphony's first movement), perhaps a coffin entering the ground, followed by two thuds of earth.

It is immensely theatrical – and profoundly ambiguous, as the hero seems to enter the nebulous realm of judgement amid the fellow dead.

3. *Vivacissimo.*

The dust and dirt of the grave which closed the slow movement are swept away with a relatively traditional scherzo of Beethovenian wildness and energy, along with some Mendelssohnian lilt and charm, aspects which will continue into the last movement. The movement maintains the usual divisions of the form, alternating B-flat *vivacissimo* scherzo sections with G-flat *lento e soave* trios before an enthralling transition without break into the finale, aided by a slowing of the second trio – and akin to the corresponding movement in Beethoven's Fifth (1808).

Full of turbulent flashes and dashing energy, as well as several keen reminders of the symphony's opening three-note motifs, the scherzo sections are interposed by the lyrical trios, with their detached, hypnotic (proto-minimalist) oboes and air of expanding rural peace. Eventually, an ascending three-note theme (G flat, A flat and B flat) constructs a brilliant bridge to the last movement, taking us across from our pastoral idyll into the serious business of the finale.

4. Finale: Allegro moderato.

Sibelius's themes are always elemental, and nowhere are they more valuably so than in the last movement to the Second. He assembles his symphonic viaduct from the scherzo with a breathtaking elegance and subtle strength, utilizing the work's primary, embryonic idea into something that will become monumental, world-changing, expediently sublime. (There is also a sense that the rhythms of the finale closely follow those of the Finnish language – especially the frequent strong downbeats – so that it is not impossible to say that the last movement 'speaks' Finnish: handy for a work destined to take on such nationalistic scope.)

After a tense but beautifully judged crescendo, the radiant, memorable Big Tune theme of the finale materializes like the light of a dozen suns, on glorious strings supported by intrepid brass fanfares: luminous, heavenly trumpets, wonderfully resonant horns (and some slightly intimidating trombones). It is simply a version of the symphony's opening spring song for strings, with its equivocal woodwind replies now given infinite courageous power by the brass labrophones. This might be familiar material, but such is its new context, as well as the journey it has undertaken, that it all sounds as fresh as the first day of the world: emotion and evolution in perfect harmony.

But no war is won without pain. A second, muted, folk-like theme from the oboe reintroduces the threats and uncertainties of the doubt-and-death-ridden slow movement (according to Aino, the theme was written in memory of her sister, Elli, who had recently died by her own hand). A more spiritual-pastoral mood, as if in remembrance of all the dead, takes over before the energy of the movement begins to build again with the kind of elusive momentum that is a unique speciality of Jean Sibelius. Everything is rigidly regulated (the development is stringently contrapuntal) but made to seem as natural and sinuous as any of the metaphorical rivers his art so ceaselessly invites.

Sibelius's Second's finale is long, almost as long as the slow movement and much longer than the first movement. As such it needs on the podium a musician of exceptional ability to keep the organic impetus flowing as the composer expected, to avoid the repeated material sounding stale or even dangerously hackneyed (in both its slower and faster sections). The conductor must trust that Sibelius knows – musically and psychologically – exactly what he is doing. For the great Finn has a majestic, thrilling surprise in store for us.

The recapitulation develops with an unstoppable, inevitable motion towards the passionate final orchestral culmination and its victorious coda. Our three-note motif, subject to countless repetitions and logical explorations across the stormy span of this extraordinary symphony, reaches up to emphatically grasp a fourth note, with the ascent on a strong downbeat. It is almost as if the symphony is shouting in Finnish, and the subsequent euphoria is one of the most transcendent – and physically potent – in all Sibelius. At last, the epic struggle is over, and the symphony can end exultantly in its well-earned major-key resolution.[73]

---

73 After the Second's premiere, Sibelius made several changes to the score prior to publication. The opening was reworked to begin after the second beat of the bar, making the transition to the horn motif more persuasive; two bars for clarinet were eliminated, and a climbing theme for bassoon was bestowed instead to the violas and cellos. In the second movement, the 'Christus' theme was lengthened, with the evolution back to the opening music also prolonged. We are lucky to know of these changes. The original manuscript was presented to Sibelius's friend Ludwig Hjelt: many years later, his house caught fire, and only the quick thinking of the family saved the score; it was the only item salvaged from the inferno. The manuscript – scorched edges and all – can be seen in Turku's Sibelius Museum.

PART TWO

AMPLIFICATION

Chapter Six

Progeny of the North:
Pohjola's Daughter, Nightride and Sunrise & *The Dryad*

Music, with its sequence of sounds progressing from one place to another, naturally lends itself to depicting or discussing journeys. Inspired by the same pair of Goethe poems, Beethoven (1815) and Mendelssohn (1828) wrote a cantata and concert overture respectively, *Calm Sea and Prosperous Voyage*, each illustrating the anxiety of serene waters before the wind picks up to allow good passage. Setting Baudelaire's verse, Duparc's great *mélodie* 'L'invitation au voyage' (1870) navigates the exotic, illusory landscapes of the Dutch East Indies, while Mahler's early song cycle *Lieder eines fahrenden Gesellen* (1885) portrays a young man's hopeless attempt to forget his lost love by meandering around the countryside. More recent composers have showcased the conveyances of contemporary travel: train enthusiast Arthur Honegger's *Pacific 231* (1923) depicts a demonic steam locomotive, the music's momentum building in menace, the scenery shifting from pastoral idyll to industrial abyss, and John Adams's brief orchestral fanfare *Short Ride in a Fast Machine* (1986) has a pulse of clarinets and synthesizers to impart a remorseless (and possibly remorseful) jaunt in a sports car.

After *Lemminkäinen*, Sibelius's next three tone poems – *Pohjola's Daughter* (1906), *Nightride and Sunrise* (1909) and *The Dryad* (1910) – all play with our sense of movement, stasis and energy. They also reflect Sibelius's further, and deeper, engagement with the natural world, his withdrawal into the forests of the mind and literal woods that would surround his new home at Ainola. Somewhat marginalized from the (apparent) mainstream European music scene ('not everyone can be an innovating genius!' he would write in his diary), his music reflects both his professional and personal awareness of, and appreciation for, isolation. Sibelius would not be an ostentatious genius, a violent revolutionary; instead, he would cultivate a quiet rebellion, changing form and feeling in extraordinary ways that are still only just becoming apparent.

A lonely spirit in the woods, Sibelius now composed tone poems that are journeys into the soul as much as the landscape, channels to demonstrate (and cope with) his differences. But this was not negativity or pessimism. Composition was also an agency of definition and assertion, a pronouncement of his individual character and unique voice – for these works, along with the Third Symphony, were crucial markers in his musical development, as Sibelius developed a more focused, concentrated sonic language in which he would realize some of his most astonishing creations of all.

At the end of 1903, after a busy year of composition and conducting, Sibelius wrote some incidental music for his dramatist brother-in-law Arvid Järnefelt's new work *Kuolema* ('Death'). One of the pieces, *Valse triste*, was to become orphaned from its parent play and take on a life (and earning capacity) of its own: a sad waltz, it meanders in luxurious pain and melancholic recollection around memory and mortality. It eventually became Sibelius's most popular work to date – though, unfortunately, he had sold the rights for a pittance to the publishers Helsingfors Nya Musikhandel due to a lack of funds; shortly afterwards the piece went supernova, becoming a celebrated global hit and netting its buyer a vast sum. Sibelius must have worn a sardonic smile each time he heard the infernal piece played by the little salon orchestra in every restaurant, bar and tearoom he frequented.

And frequent he did, frequently. For his wining and dining, to use a polite expression, were still considerable at this time, despite both his many musical commitments and attempts to rein in the spending. In fact, according to Sibelius's friend Sigurd Wettenhovi-Aspa, an unconventional linguist and sculptor, *Valse triste* had been composed on the upper gallery of – where else? – the Hotel Kämp. (On this occasion, as it happens, Sibelius had a heavy cold, so was temporarily off the booze but medicating heavily on vast quantities of quinine, along with some oysters for sustenance.)

More generally, however, Sibelius's family were deeply concerned about his drinking, worried that he was by now performing his own dance with death via the bottle. On 19 November 1903, a few weeks before the *Kuolema* premiere,

Sibelius's brother Christian, a doctor, wrote to his sibling begging him to cut down on his alcohol intake: he was forceful, outspoken, telling of the terrible consequences of abusing drink that he had witnessed in his profession. A day earlier, in fact, Jean had undertaken some measures to get away from the temptations of Helsinki's saloons and eateries: he had purchased some land by Lake Tuusula, in Järvenpää, some thirty miles north of the capital, far from the disreputable dens of the Kämp and König, in order to build his own house, a permanent residence for work and family.

Construction began in the new year, with the carpenters' wages swallowing money almost as quickly as Sibelius could have drunk it. To some extent, however, he eased off the booze, giving concerts in Helsinki, Turku and Vaasa to help foot the bill for the building work, and at the end of April 1904 he proudly wrote to his brother in Berlin that he had been abstentious for two weeks. Further concerts followed that summer, in Estonia and Latvia, including performances of the Second Symphony.

On 16 June 1904, a young Finnish patriot shot the hated Russian governor general Nikolay Bobrikov before turning the gun on himself. Sibelius and his friends, along with a good percentage of the populace, were jubilant. Celebrations went on until late into the white night, and to such an extent that many of the revellers – including Sibelius – were arrested, for the rather innocuous misdemeanour of exhibiting 'unmotivated joy'.

Custodial intervals aside, by the summer the composer, his wife and their daughters had relocated to Tuusula to supervise the final work on the house, and on 24 September 1904, Sibelius and his family moved into their new home. It was to be called Ainola ('Aino's Place'), in honour of Sibelius's long-suffering, infinitely patient wife (who herself would live in the building for sixty-five years, dying there two months before her ninety-eighth birthday, in the summer of 1969).

It was a little overcrowded at first (the upper floor did not arrive until 1911), and Sibelius was usually compelled to compose at night, when the children were in bed. Theirs was a simple existence: there was a telephone, and a sauna was soon added, but it had no electricity or running water, and the modern town of Järvenpää had not yet been built. A handful of shops supplied local needs, and there were some interesting neighbours – the painters Pekka Halonen and Eero Järnefelt (another brother-in-law) and writer Juhani Aho also lived on the shores of Lake Tuusula.

With the new house, however, old habits died hard. The bouts of alcoholic self-restraint Sibelius had experimented with earlier in the year were short-lived, sporadic, and scarce, and when he was away on a conducting tour in the weeks before Christmas, Aino would write to her husband begging him to consider both his own health and their relationship. At one point, he phoned Aino at home while severely intoxicated – which can hardly have helped matters. It would be one of the most traumatic periods of their long union, which nearly reached breaking point on several occasions. Sibelius knew the problems but not the solutions. He revelled in the energy, escape and release of booze but hated the painful price it exacted: on his body, on his marriage – and on his work.

The day before the big move on 24 September 1904, Sibelius had completed a short three-movement piano piece, *Kyllikki* (op.41), a work its composer denied was related to the *Kalevala* story of Lemminkäinen and Kyllikki but which certainly seems to evoke the sex, war and dances of the tale. Although little-known, *Kyllikki* not only is a fascinating, ambitious work (reminiscent of Schubert or Schumann, and perhaps stimulated by Sibelius's friendship with the composer-pianist Ferruccio Busoni) but is also significant in being probably the last piano work that engages with Kalevalan nostalgia and fantasy – just as another, much larger, orchestral work completed at the beginning of the year represented his last major piece in what we might call a nationalist Romantic style. From now on a more exceptionally Sibelian sound world emerges, more concentrated, uniquely expressive, distinctively and outstandingly his own.[74]

The orchestral work was, of course, the violin concerto in D minor, op.47, completed early in 1904 but subject to severe revisions the following year after a disastrous premiere on 8

---

74 In 1903, and then in 1904, just before the Ainola move, Sibelius composed five songs now known as his op.38, an astonishing quintet containing perhaps his most profound and moving works in the genre. 'Höstkväll' ('Autumn Evening') is an almost symphonic lament for the changing patterns of the landscape, full of pantheism and other tributes to nature, with a lone traveller considering the world in all its ominous and astonishing splendour. The next, 'På verandan vid havet' ('On a Veranda by the Sea'), anticipates the dark and brooding sound world of the Fourth Symphony (1911). It contemplates the sea and stars, reflecting that all are destined for oblivion in their 'thirst for eternity', and Sibelius ended the song with a huge and terrifying climax. The third, 'I natten' ('In the Night'), is less chromatically tense, deliberating the range of moods darkness can bring, while the fourth, 'Harpolekaren och hans son' (The Harper and His Son'), has the piano impersonate a harp as the singer tells of a journey to a 'temple hall, built of firs and pines'. The first four songs set Viktor Rydberg; the fifth uses a poem by Gustaf Fröding: 'Jag ville, jag vore i Indialand' ('I wish I were in India'). In this colourful, highly philosophical song, the singer yearns for the mysteries and magic of the exotic unknown, of a release from this world into the comforting promises of Eastern religions: the peace of extinction, of freedom from the 'bleak shore of consciousness.'

February. Not only was building work on Ainola due to begin two days later, on 10 February, but Sibelius had – as with *Valse triste* – sold out because of a desperate need to earn money sooner: a more lavish, prepared premiere with Willy Burmester in Berlin had been scratched (much to the celebrated violinist's ire) in favour of an earlier date in Helsinki with a less gifted soloist, Victor Nováček, and Sibelius conducting. Nováček could not cope with the considerable challenges Sibelius had presented – in what was, after all, his own instrument, the instrument in which he himself had harboured hopes for a stellar concert career.

Disappointed by the poor first performances, as well as its critical mauling in the press, Sibelius nonetheless did not give up on the concerto for his beloved violin and, in the summer of 1905, sat down to revise it. This was a work he had been anxiously toying with for years – in some respects, he had been ever since his adolescence, in his first experimental engagements with musical colour and melodic enunciation (and during those early dreams of a glitzy performing career). As with most of Sibelius's orchestral revisions, he sought to condense the material: shortening, streamlining, *purifying* it – and, as a consequence, removing much excellent, and very idiosyncratic, music. Aino always preferred the more subjective roughness and spirit of the original, though fortunately today we have both versions to listen to, compare and enjoy.[75]

Sibelius's violin concerto is a highly original musical document – an expression of agony and eloquence, sumptuousness and suffering – though it does share some of the grandeur and mercy of Beethoven's, along with the more lyrical tendencies

---

75   The premiere of the new version took place, in Sibelius's absence, in Berlin on 19 October 1905. Richard Strauss conducted the Berlin Philharmonic, and the soloist was the orchestra's leader, Karel Halíř (Burmester, rather sulky at having had the original premiere taken from him, claimed he was too busy to do it).

of Mendelssohn's or Bruch's (though it is not symphonic in the same way as the one from Brahms). The work displays an immense, enthralling tension between the virtuosic, expansive demands of the soloist's part and Sibelius's growing fixation on tauter structures and formal advances.

A vast (even in the revision) opening movement shimmers into life, the hazy atmosphere instantly transporting us to a northern landscape of mystery, beauty and wonder, as puzzling and exquisite as a folk tale but charged with the majesty of the topography. It is in sonata form but ruthlessly compressed, allowing the violin part to sparkle and shine with some of the soaring elegance and intellectual heft of Bach's sonatas and partitas but with Sibelius's gift for exoticism and fluid lethargy. The orchestral writing is hardly forgettable either: enigmatic panoramas engage with brassy flourishes and energetic string sections. The revision removed the huge Bach-like cadenza, but this only served to heighten the remaining cadenza's purpose as a substitution for the development: an outstanding example of Sibelius's innovation in form via tighter, stricter designs. A stormy coda allows the soloist to float and fly before their material is swallowed by the vast orchestral ocean.

Princely and precious, in the second movement the woodwind drifts around the keys before the soloist enters, with a phrase of infinite warmth and nobility, expanding in restrained dignity and quiet grace. More anxious modulations come in, especially from the orchestra, the music darkening and marked by syncopation mechanisms (short-long-short) that propel the music ahead. The soloist asserts flamboyant versions of the opening tune, material that briefly returns with rapturous verve in the whole orchestra before a whispered coda of sublime retrospection.

After the nocturnal reflections of the adagio, the finale is a dazzling firework display, full of luminous ornamentations and mechanical sorcery from the soloist. Especially in its initial conception, it ceaselessly invents, contriving new means to show off, boast and brag. Pity the soloist not on top form the day they have to perform it. Progressively astonishing sequences hurry the concerto towards its conclusion – which comes out of nowhere, a terse and curt finish that seems almost embarrassed at all the exhibitionism.[76]

Sibelius never became the global superstar violinist he always dreamed of being. But he lived that life vicariously through one of the most alluring, moving and desperately difficult works for the violin ever written, a piece worthy of Paganini at his most satanic. More than this, his violin concerto is an orchestral masterpiece that simultaneously developed Sibelius's formal techniques in compression and expression while also calling an end to the more idealistic public style he had hitherto explored. It could never be repeated and stands magnificently alone.

Between the first and second versions of his violin concerto, and as intermittent, frustrating early work on a third symphony continued, Sibelius wrote incidental music to Maurice Maeterlinck's symbolist play *Pelléas et Mélisande* (1893), for a production at the Swedish Theatre in Helsinki in the spring

---

76 Musicologist Donald Tovey once memorably described the movement as a 'polonaise for polar bears' – but the lithest, most dexterous *Ursus maritimus*, a Fred Astaire of the arctic ice and snow, could not cope with the vertiginous angles and savage pirouettes Sibelius's finale asks of its dancing soloist.

of 1905, with the musical parts conducted by their composer. Writing music for the theatre was an addictive habit Sibelius relished throughout his career, and this was his first major example since *King Christian II* in 1898. He had forgotten nothing of his eerie dramaturgical talent.

Closer to Fauré's (1898) than Debussy's (1902) or Schoenberg's (1903), and with ten numbers for a fairly modest orchestra, Sibelius's *Pelléas* (1905) is by turns sombre, grand and mysterious.[77] It is a richly evocative score (later turned into a suite), displaying this composer's uncanny ability to summon character, event and emotion with great economy of means – colour and drama aroused by the slightest gestures. But then, of course, this was the veteran author of several outstanding tone poems, a genre to which Sibelius now returned, picking up pieces he had begun a few years before.

The iridescent elegance of *Pelléas* showed to some extent the refinement Sibelius's music had undergone since the raw violence of *Kullervo*, *The Wood Nymph* and *Lemminkäinen* (though writing music of gleaming sensitivity was hardly new to him: *The Swan of Tuonela* had proved that). *Pelléas* is all about suggestion, insinuation, an elusive and inscrutably kaleidoscopic atmosphere very close to Maeterlinck's text. Yet for all its moody brilliance and seductive scoring, there is something slightly outmoded about the tone and direction of this work, which seems to belong in the 1890s. Naturally, part of this is precisely the effect Sibelius wanted to conjure up: *Pelléas* is a work about obscurity, pensive recollection, the various provinces of loss and the past. It *had* to seem archaic. For his next tone poems,

---

[77] In Britain, BBC Television would bring the piece to countless millions by choosing the number 'At the Castle Gate' – all cosmic splendour and intensity – as the theme music for its long-running monthly astronomy programme, *The Sky at Night* (1957–).

however, the sound was to be as sharp and cutting edge as the sleigh skis on which their heroes ride.

Despite the sanctuary of a permanent house, Sibelius travelled extensively at this time, largely to promote his own music beyond the frontiers of Finland, but also to hear new music. At the beginning of 1905, in Berlin, he became acquainted with a number of important recent works: Strauss's *Ein Heldenleben* (1898), Debussy's *Nocturnes* (1899) and Mahler's Fifth Symphony (1904).

In November, his first visit to Britain followed trips to Copenhagen and Berlin. Despite being fined at Dover for entering the country with undeclared cigars (so typically Sibelian), the composer had an excellent time in London, staying at the opulent Langham Hotel on the fringes of Regent's Park and opposite the capital's foremost concert venue, the Queen's Hall. The pleasure continued as Sibelius travelled north to Birmingham and Liverpool, where he conducted *Finlandia* and his First Symphony to thrilled audiences and made friends with conductor Henry Wood, critic Ernest Newman and composer Granville Bantock. All three, and others, would play a crucial role in promoting Sibelius's music in the English-speaking world over the coming decades. From here it was on to Paris, where he celebrated his fortieth birthday on 8 December, then back to Berlin, before he finally returned to Ainola and his family in February 1906. It was time to get back into serious composition: for several months, he barely left his desk, save for meals, sleep and the all-important daily walks.

Towards the end of 1905, Sibelius had begun work on a new tone poem that he called 'Luonnotar'. Regrettably, it was abandoned – though just as some of its material had derived from a similarly discarded oratorio (*Marjatta*), much of its music was repurposed for the tone poem (or 'symphonic fantasia', as Sibelius also called it) we now know as *Pohjola's Daughter*, as well as the slow movement of the Third Symphony. (The tone poem for soprano and orchestra discussed in chapter nine, *Luonnotar*, is a different work.)

Although the musical material for *Pohjola's Daughter* grew out of that written for 'Luonnotar', it was subject to extensive recomposition: a complete alteration of its fundamental elements, a rearrangement of its tonal and formal structure. There was also a complete change to the tone poem's subject matter: 'Luonnotar' was concerned, like the later *Luonnotar* for soprano and orchestra, with the *Kalevala*'s creative myth; instead, *Pohjola's Daughter* would tell the story of Väinämöinen from runo 8 of the *Kalevala*, of his sledge journey home from Pohjola, the Northland, and his subsequent falling in love with Pohjola's daughter and the impossible challenges she sets him.

Given the comprehensive adjustments – the wholesale change – to both the narrative and music of this tone poem, it is unsurprising that the score does not closely follow its new story with any degree of fastidiousness, instead presenting the characters, events and emotions in much broader lines. Even if the origins of the work had been less complex, however, it is likely to have remained in a similar mould: Sibelius's style by now was much more abstract than in works like *Kullervo* or *The Wood Nymph*, the orchestra proceeding according to its own inner logic rather than relying on the minutiae of its narrative. (It can be no surprise that at various points the composer considered turning the work into a symphony, and its 'symphonic fantasia' moniker, as much as its streamlined design, attests to this.)

The white-bearded antediluvian soothsayer Väinämöinen is the primary creative force of the *Kalevala*: perpetually wise, he is possessed of a magical singing voice (the earliest accounts, those prior to Elias Lönnrot's *Kalevala*, make him the god of chanting, singing and poetry). His story is not divorced from that of the creation of the world, so Sibelius's narrative change to *Pohjola's Daughter* is perhaps not as drastic as it might have been, though Lönnrot was keen to disrobe Väinämöinen of many of the more extreme divine aspects of his character, demythologizing him to a shaman-like person, the son of the primal goddess Ilmatar.

In the *Kalevala*, we witness Väinämöinen as an eternal bard, a figure who exerts order over chaos, establishing the land of Kalevala, where so many of the epic's events take place. Typical of his activities is slaying a giant pike and turning its jawbone into the kantele, the Finnish harp that so intrigued Sibelius, which produced music of such beauty that it drew all the creatures from the forest to marvel at its sound. Väinämöinen's long search for a suitable wife leads the people of Kalevala to interact with their shadowy, intimidating neighbour in the north, Pohjola – at first on friendly terms but gradually turning to more hostile and antagonistic dealings. (This conflict culminates in the creation, and then theft, of the *sampo*, a magical artefact which is later split into many pieces and widely dispersed around the world.)

The *Kalevala* thus sets up a polarized world, with the people of Kalevala (or Väinölä, as it is sometimes called) in opposition to those of Pohjola. Many have been keen to establish the real, non-mythic, origins of Pohjola, though it is clear that it represents a classic literary trope, especially in north European traditions: an unknowable place, a source of evil, a cold and foreboding distant land not unlike Grendel's swamps in *Beowulf* or Mordor in Tolkien's *Lord of the Rings*.

It is Väinämöinen's hunt for a companion in these far-flung unfriendly northern domains that forms the narrative of Sibelius's *Pohjola's Daughter*. During his journeying, Väinämöinen speeds through the Finnish landscape on his sleigh when suddenly he hears the beautiful Maiden of Pohjola – i.e., Pohjola's daughter – spinning a golden thread on her spinning wheel in the sky. Entranced, Väinämöinen implores her to descend from the heavens and join him on his sleigh as his wife. The maiden agrees but first requires him to perform heroic deeds and sets a series of unfeasible tasks, including tying an egg into invisible knots and carving a boat from the fragments of her spindle. With the assistance of his magic, Väinämöinen succeeds in most of the assignments, but evil spirits intervene, and he injures himself with his own axe. Wounded and overwhelmed, he abandons his attempts to woo the daughter of Pohjola and continues his journey alone.

There is a clear association between this scenario and the second libretto draft of Sibelius's projected opera *The Building of the Boat*, which we discussed in chapter 3. There, Väinämöinen falls in love with the daughter of Nature and accomplishes a series of miracles, visiting Tuonela and building the magic boat of the title, before finally becoming disillusioned with the icy remoteness of the daughter and departing alone.

Given the messy and varied genesis of *Pohjola's Daughter*, it is unsurprising that choosing its title caused several headaches. Initially, Sibelius told his publisher that the work should be called *Väinämöinen*, but they considered that to be too difficult a name, suggesting instead the *Pohjola's Daughter* that has stuck. Sibelius countered by proposing *L'aventure d'un héros* (*The Adventure of a Hero*), but this was deemed to be too similar to Strauss's *Heldenleben*. They finally agreed on *Pohjola's Daughter*, printing some clarifying passages from the *Kalevala* at the head of the score, and the work received its premiere in Saint Petersburg on 29 December 1906. Sibelius himself conducted the Mariinsky Theatre Orchestra, and the piece was enthusiastically received: 'a tremendously talented and imaginative composer', wrote the magazine *Rusj*.

A tragic-heroic tone poem that returned to the world of *Kullervo* and *Lemminkäinen*, *Pohjola's Daughter* is full of rich orchestral details and an enormous range of colours, tones and textures. Like his First Symphony, plus *En Saga* and *The Wood Nymph*, this magnificently brooding work depicts a valiant pursuit, an epic quest, that ends in defeat and/or exile for its hero. In this sense, *Pohjola* is almost the opposite of a Straussian tone poem of daring and triumph, though the scoring is in many ways very similar to his German colleague's (Sibelius had written passionately home to Aino after hearing *Heldenleben* in Berlin a few months before he began work on *Pohjola*, claiming not only that was he fascinated by the score but that he had learned a lot from Strauss's virtuoso style and technique).

Where Sibelius strongly diverges from Strauss, however, is the use to which the orchestral detail is put. For Strauss, it is a vital part of the programme, illustrative and descriptive, telling the story in sound; for Sibelius, a more abstract world is evoked, though of course many programmatic elements remain (especially the notion of Väinämöinen's riding his sleigh). In a letter to Aino long before the final form of *Pohjola* had been reached, Sibelius was clear that this work would be a 'symphonic fantasy', adding for good measure that 'this is my genre! Here I can move freely without feeling the weight of tradition.'

Sibelius's comments offer a stimulating perspective on the formal method of *Pohjola*, its tonal structure and motivic erudition, as well as on this work's outstanding symphonic intensity, its wonderful contrapuntal concentration. It tends to hover in the tragic space between G minor and B-flat major, the latter the key in which Väinämöinen's stability lies, though his heroic fanfares are continually repelled and redirected by the F-sharp minor of the theme associated with the daughter of the north herself. By the end of the work, Väinämöinen's defeat and lonely departure, the music cannot locate a definite closure; instead the coda floats away into unfulfilled oblivion and a harmonic void. It is impressively bleak, without redemption, liberation or transfiguration, an isolated hero aggrieved and alone.

Its austerity and imposing sense of accession to the chilly nature of existence appealed to Arnold Bax, who had a strong affinity with Nordic culture, but *Pohjola's Daughter* is also one of Sibelius's most humane statements, showing the contradictions of power and fame (which he himself must have felt keenly at the time). His symphonic fantasy is a journey into pain and humiliation, but it is also a voyage of self-discovery, a mythical vision of acquiescence, acceptance and contingency, with isolation and seclusion the great teachers.

Many sunrises illuminate music, inevitably with big crescendos as composers try to reproduce the daily reappearance of our life-giving star. Haydn's magical op.76/4 string quartet (1797) is nicknamed the *Sunrise* for the ascending chords at its opening, while Richard Strauss's depiction of a day in the mountains – *Eine*

Alpensinfonie (1915) – begins with 'Night' followed by the sound of the sun surging across the alps. Puccini's *Turandot* (1924) ends with a sunrise, the crowd celebrating to the famous tune of 'Nessun dorma', and Delius's *Florida* Suite (1887) portrays a tender sunrise – composed in Leipzig but recalling his stint as manager of an orange grove in the Sunshine State. Carl Nielsen spent a Greek holiday in 1903 writing his *Helios* Overture, its jubilant music illustrating the sun soaring over the Aegean in a golden arc across the sky. Also staying in Greece, Maurice Ravel likewise depicts the sun rising over the glittering sea in his ballet *Daphnis et Chloé* (1912) – serene woodwinds ripple over the waters as birds drift overhead, the music swelling towards a rapturous solar climax.

Sibelius, too, would join this luminous band of sonic sunrises, and with one of the most euphoric depictions of all. After *Pohjola's Daughter*, the Finn's next major projects were incidental music for *Belshazzar's Feast* (a play by Hjalmar Procopé) and the Third Symphony, to which we will return in the next chapter. However, through depicting an expedition of hard-won release and renewal after a protracted phase of contemplation and even difficulty – something not exactly absent from the composer's own life at the time – Sibelius's next tone poem continued the journey undertaken by the Third Symphony, and both works inaugurated a new phase of artistic creation, one of exquisite poise, concentration and critical self-examination.

But this new tone poem, *Nightride and Sunrise*, looked backwards as well as forward, its delineation of a flight across the gloomy Nordic landscape mirroring that of Väinämöinen's in *Pohjola's Daughter* and sharing its predecessor's preoccupation with images of landscape and nature, in addition to human interactions with both. The last was a theme which would now consume Sibelius in all his remaining tone poems (though features are of course also present in the earlier ones). Väinämöinen's introspective glances in *Pohjola's Daughter* are also taken further, as the *Nightride* becomes a vehicle for self-analysis and doubt, which are then thrillingly overtaken by the grandeur of nature and the birth of a new day.

For many, Sibelius's is the supreme sonic expression of Finnish scenery, of Nordic topographies in all their beauty, magnificence and mystery – and it is this final sense of ambiguity and inscrutability which is so crucial to the Sibelian method. His tone poems (and symphonies) are not mere aural depictions of northern panoramas; they are complex docudramas examining internal as well as external worlds, exploring our intricate relationship with the air and land, water and flora. Sibelius does not merely paint, he probes, combining landscape and psychology with exceptional penetrative insight, taking us to remarkable locations in the mind as well as the environment (which will receive perhaps its most extraordinary examination in the Fourth Symphony of 1911).

Many of Sibelius's works have an uncanny ability to play with our sense of time as well as place: landscapes unfurl in front of us, with incredible distancing or foreshortening effects from the orchestra, but so too do forays into temporal or mythological history. In Sibelius, storytellers seem to begin their tales with both an inward and outward gesture, wrapping us in their embrace as they take us on their narratorial-musical journeys. They enclose us in the mystery and magic of myth, with strange impressions of both supernatural and geographical space, as well as a sense of immeasurable time, inestimable history and the sagas of the past that can inform us in the present.

As a journey through the landscape, *Nightride and Sunrise* is surely an ideal display of the interaction between humanity and nature. It was sketched in the autumn of 1908 and premiered in Saint Petersburg in January 1909, and Sibelius gave several differing accounts of the work's origin: some of the music was drafted in Rome in 1901, apparently after seeing the Colosseum in the spring moonlight; elsewhere, towards the end of his life, he claimed it was inspired by a night-time horse ride from Helsinki to Kerava 'around the turn of the century', when he witnessed an outstanding sunrise, the heavens blazing in a range of sumptuous colours. It is also likely to have been stimulated by the huge nocturnal journey in the wilderness between Suojärvi and Värtsilä which Sibelius took after his honeymoon in the summer of 1892, when collecting poetry and folk music in the Karelia region.[78]

For all these likely, even collaborative, sources, the essence of the work is perhaps best encapsulated in remarks the composer made to his English friend Rosa Newmarch:

> [The] inner experiences of an average man riding solitary through the forest gloom; sometimes glad to be alone with Nature; occasionally awe-stricken by the stillness or the strange sounds which break it; not filled with undue foreboding, but thankful and rejoicing in the daybreak.

The work is a splendid spiritual experience of the natural world, of galloping figures and the strain of movement – both through the forest and over the icy expanse of the frozen landscape. There is an unrelenting forward motion (with great impetus, drive and cumulative vitality), but there is also a sense of stasis

---

78 A distance of some 130 kilometres or 80 miles.

and of reflection: perhaps the brooding thoughts of the traveller, but also the immobility of the endless, unbroken topography. It is a magnificently constructed world of tension and confusion. Disconsolate voices materialize and then evaporate from within the trees or hostile mists; but then, a miracle: the sun arrives on the horns, one of Sibelius's most dazzling representations of nature, music filled with serene opulence and anticipating the tranquil majesty and celestial reassurance of the Fifth and Seventh Symphonies.

Nightride and Sunrise is palpably pictorial and episodic, depicting a journey and a dawn with vivid energy and colours, but it is also a reflection on the symbolic quality of landscapes, on the meanings and values of the natural world as we live through it. Moreover, the chronological, sequential experience of listening to the work is comparable to our optical perception of the changing landscape: the audio and the visual, time and space, work together to create a thrilling multisensory jaunt.

For his next tone poem, *The Dryad*, op.45/1, of 1910, Sibelius wrote a brief, impressionistic piece that is often forgotten amid the might and majesty of his other works. Not unlike his earlier character piece *Pan and Echo* (1906), *The Dryad* is a miniature maze of tempo changes and quizzical gestures, in this sense anticipating the incidental music to *The Tempest*, especially the 'Oak Tree' movement (and, indeed, a dryad is a nymph that lives in a forest, especially in oak trees).

Unlike his other, post-*Nightride*, tone poems, *The Dryad* keeps landscape firmly in the background, allowing the dryad of the title to flit about centre stage. The work is designed in three parts, with a pensive introduction and contemplative coda framing a waltz which is presented to us in a teasing fashion, seeming never to be fully heard and given a mildly exotic coloration through the scoring of some castanets and short, bouncing string writing. The mildest whispers and mutterings interchange with ardent, yearning motifs along with some hyperactive dance music, everything fluctuating and oscillating in a bewildering labyrinth.

The Dryad has an appropriately weightless feel, something Sibelius would explore further in his Fourth Symphony (1911), and which also reflects the Finn's increasing appreciation for his French colleague Debussy's work. Sibelius had heard the *Nocturnes* again in London the year before he wrote *The Dryad*, and that masterpiece's sense of light, space and movement are strongly carried over in this diminutive tone poem's enigmatic colours and curious rhythms.[79]

Written as he was engaged on both his Third and then Fourth Symphonies, *Pohjola's Daughter*, *Nightride and Sunrise* and *The Dryad* – along with the violin concerto – were all important steps in Sibelius's musical progress, ushering in a style that was more determined, resolute and subtly expressive, and with important implications for all the major orchestral works to come.

---

79 *The Dryad* – op.45/1 – has a flamboyant twin: the Dance Intermezzo, op.45/2. Shamelessly good-natured and with a rollicking tune, it won't win any awards for penetrating psychological insight, but the Dance Intermezzo is a charming little piece, worth three minutes of anyone's time.

Pohjola's Daughter, op.49

Pohjola's Daughter begins in gloomy majesty, with the forbidding obscurity of the Nordic terrain. An introduction in G minor (with divided cellos, horns and bassoons) evokes a murky, brooding atmosphere of fable, legend and landscape. Everything seems desolate and timeless, even formless, as we enter mythological realms and the primordial dynamisms which create and sustain the world. A subdued, lugubrious solo cello sings like a poignant storyteller, an incantation that imparts an impending sorry tale. The bassoon, plus detached growls on the timpani, joins the misty scene, which then begins to imperceptibly brighten as woodwind voices start to speak, something noticed and followed by the strings.

Before long we are swept up by the spine-tingling and invigorating forward momentum of Väinämöinen's sleigh, with a rugged brass statement representing the dignity and grandeur of our hero, which tries to proclaim B flat as an intrepid new key. Suddenly, however, Väinämöinen's journey is interrupted: a harmonic deflection to F-sharp minor exhibits the glistening mystical image of the daughter of Pohjola herself, seated on a rainbow, and there follows a pensive pastoral section, with some exquisite writing for oboe, cor anglais and flute as the beautiful maiden weaves across the sky.

From here the middle of the tone poem portrays Väinämöinen's progressively angry and exasperated attempts to complete the impossible tasks the Maiden of the Northland has set him. Agitated pizzicato strings begin a development and an exhilarating series of displays where we witness birdsong on woodwind cadenzas, plus Väinämöinen's valiant exertions along with the maiden's ridicule and scorn. At several points the daughter shrieks with mocking laughter, in bursts that sound almost exactly like the legendary violin screeches from composer Bernard Herrmann in the shower scene of Alfred Hitchcock's 1960 thriller *Psycho*.

In the Sibelius, the daughter's dark mirth is a tense moment, leading to some rigorous motivic expansion and an alarmingly compressed repeat, the score gradually beginning to replenish with Väinämöinen's B-flat majesty as optimism and anticipation are restored – only for the hero to be frustrated one last time, just at the moment he thought he was victorious. Väinämöinen's bold music vanishes into the harsh landscape, the nebulous, funereal coda a sequence of gradually rising string lines, bleak strands of sound haunted by tonal mists and memories. A progression from G to A to B flat in the cellos and double basses fades out, and our hero returns to his brooding sleigh journey alone.

Pohjola's Daughter has all the qualities of a dream or a mirage: an eerie, ephemeral and perplexing vision. It is a masterpiece, one of the finest of all Sibelius's tone poems.

Nightride and Sunrise, op.55

In tonal terms, *Nightride and Sunrise* tracks a journey from C minor to E-flat major, a familiar coupling of keys (Beethoven exploits them to electrifying effect in the *Eroica*; Sibelius himself had done so in *Lemminkäinen*), but it is the tempo and timbre of the work that most obviously dictates its articulation (themes, too, are relatively minimal).

It opens with an abortive brass cadence in E flat that is promptly directed downwards: a galvanizing gesture that acts as a tense lift-off for the journey (perhaps the crack of the driver's whip, or a burst of snow under the skis).[80] The prolonged ride sequence swiftly follows, full of dogged determination and icy strangeness, ideas crystalizing in a fashion not unlike the finale of the Third Symphony. Shards of ostinato – remnants of the volatile opening – begin to coalesce and re-form (a bit like the shapeshifting assassin in *Terminator 2*, the T-1000), establishing a more secure sonic background. Projected in front of this is a new melodic phrase on the violas and cellos known as the 'ride monologue', along with an elegiac woodwind theme, which are accompanied by a subtle shift in the rhythm into a more regular beat: the journey is underway, and the rider is gathering speed.

Nightride and Sunrise is a thrilling aural representation of moving through space, of passing time, and contains a number of compressed statements and developmental gestures. In this sense, the tone poem is highly symphonic, a pattern of perpetual exposition, repetition and elaboration with continuous thematic progression. This procedure is reiterated by the ride's second phase, where a turbulent culmination has several ostinato layers overlaid and superimposed on one another before a short-lived pause and transition on strings towards the 'Sunrise' section of the work.

---

80   Sibelius's drafts bear painful witness that it took a while to get this inaugural gesture just right. Several reworkings show the composer cleaning up the scoring, honing the harmony for the greatest shock value.

Leading in with the strings (a miracle of musical imagination and sonic ingenuity), a gleaming horn chorale softly announces the first golden rays of the dawn. The tone poem's focus gradually sharpens towards a second declaration, in which the chorale is given by the trumpets and trombones before being reaffirmed by the trumpets together, the theme becoming more intense all the time as the sunrise advances. A fleeting display from the clarinet yields a spark of light from the strings, then silence, before the brass solve the riddle of the abortive opening cadence by taking the work to a luminous, dazzling affirmation of E flat.

Reminiscent of the two dawns in *Götterdämmerung*, or the opening prelude to *Das Rheingold*, it is nonetheless pure Sibelius. A stunning portrayal of the natural world – but, more crucially, also a statement about our relationship with the environment, of our unity with the landscape, sun and sky. *Nightride and Sunrise* is a breathtaking, awe-inspiring hymn to nature and our amazement in its presence, a life-enhancing celebration of hope and regeneration, confidence and rejuvenation (something possible with the dawning of each new day). To listen to it is to hear Sibelius at his most majestic, filled with peaceful dignity and tranquil splendour.

The Dryad, op.45/1

(See main essay.)

Chapter Seven

Pale Fire:
The Third Symphony

The opening years of the twentieth century saw an abundance of gaudy, opulent musical showstoppers. Alexander Scriabin's symphonic *Poem of Ecstasy* (1908), as its title suggests, was a giddy, psychedelic world of unstable harmonic intensity exploring the mystical and the sensual.[81] Gustav Mahler's Eighth (1906) was his most unusual and extravagant symphony, employing gigantic vocal and orchestral forces in a dramatic fusion of religious hymn with secular drama that continues to thrill, overwhelm and bamboozle in equal measure.[82] Richard Strauss had shifted his attention away from lavish tone

---

81 At one point, the work was to be called 'Poème orgiaque' ('Orgiastic Poem'), and even the finished score includes unusual expressive markings like 'growing intoxication' and 'very perfumed'.

82 And now known, of course, as the 'Symphony of a Thousand'.

poems, but his new operas – especially *Salome* (1905) and *Elektra* (1909) – maintained his elaborate instrumental technique and, like Scriabin and Mahler, employed vast augmented orchestras in a collective orgy of late Romantic colour, power and excess. It was an age of technical and cultural innovations, of conspicuous wealth, noisy superfluity and immoderate dissipation, as the new century hurtled towards the chaos and catastrophe of 1914.

Against this lurid backdrop, and with the imposing heroic/romantic journeys of his own First and Second Symphonies under his belt, Sibelius produced his lucid Third (1907), a modernized, Nordic 'classical' work of astonishing economy, discretion and cumulative power. Its incisive musico-symphonic language is one of self-control, delicacy and integrated voices, the composer assimilating what he had learned from Wagner, from Bruckner, from Tchaikovsky – from himself – and transforming it into something clean and fresh. The architecture is reduced, concentrated, and not only in its motivic material. Four movements have become three, scherzo and finale blended together even more organically than in the Second.[83] The orchestra's size, too, is more restrained, functional, reflecting the dimensions of a century before, not the immense armies of musicians the new era habitually engaged.

For all this temperance and refinement, Sibelius's Third is no wallflower, no unadventurous homebody. Quite the reverse: its self-discipline and matchless mastery of construction are aligned to themes and orchestration of unnerving expressive capacity, the strict logic of its technique used to evoke enigmas and enchanting ambiguities. At times the Third has the aura of a country house whodunit, with an amateur sleuth's shrewd

---

[83] Where a bridge, not unlike that between the third and fourth movements of Beethoven's Fifth, occurs.

intelligence and probing power beneath the gentle old-fashioned exterior – a *Miss Marple* Symphony?

Yet, as with any good murder mystery, darkness and diversity lie behind the symphony's cool, classical facade: Sibelius's drinking and carousing with artists in Paris; a painting about the death of a child; new theatrical projects; an oratorio about the Virgin Mary; several abandoned works concerning the birth of the world, supernatural fruit, and the life of Christ. Sibelius would pool and purge all these resources, merging a range of inspirational material into a cogent, sparing modern work that would both establish and define his highly original symphonic style.

The Third has a structural design of immense and supple might, though its milder manner and more pallid, pastel colours can conceal this silent strength. Its fires are paler than those of Sibelius's other symphonies – but perhaps burn longer because of it. For this work was not a transition towards revolution: it was the revolution itself.

In the previous chapter we saw Sibelius undertaking a European tour during the winter of 1905/6, taking in Copenhagen, Berlin, London, Liverpool and Paris. It was in the French capital that he spent the most time – and money.

Unlike in Britain, where Henry Wood, Ernest Newman, Granville Bantock[84] and Rosa Newmarch (among others) had

---

84 A composer Sibelius championed (and vice versa), even becoming the first president of the Bantock Society, Sir Granville Bantock (1868–1946) was an astonishing voice in twentieth-century British music. Strongly influenced by both Scottish folk music and the musikdramas of Richard Wagner, among his finest works are the *Celtic* Symphony (1940), the *Hebridean* Symphony (1916), the choral epic *Omar Khayyám* (1909) and the Tchaikovskian tone poem *Thalaba the Destroyer* (1900). Sibelius dedicated the Third Symphony to Bantock.

welcomed Sibelius and his music (and would go on to promote its cause for decades), in France the Finn received a cool reception – something which arguably persists, despite some occasional interest, to this day. The few performances of his works had been largely met with indifference or bemusement, and the little positivity which occurred was insufficient to establish him on the French concert calendar. Sibelius himself, however, remained upbeat about Paris, acknowledging its greatness as a city and the sponge-like nature of his interaction with it, as he soaked up ideas and absorbed what it had to offer. Graft on his music continued, especially on the 'Luonnotar' project (concerning the Finnish creation myth) discussed in chapter 6 (and part of which became *Pohjola's Daughter*), and he once again considered modifying the piece into a symphonic work.

A significant Finnish community existed in Paris, either expats or short-term visitors like Sibelius, and they welcomed this leviathan of their number warmly. Sibelius struck up a particular friendship with the young painter Oscar Parviainen (1880–1938), a relationship cultivated and maintained by copious amounts of drinking. At one point, a commemorative evening was held among the Finns for their beloved national poet Johan Ludvig Runeberg (1804–1877), an event which seems to have been especially raucous, Sibelius enjoying the festivities so much that he embarked on one of his near customary multi-day binges, sopping up a good deal of the city's supply of wine and spirits in the process. Parviainen found him several days later sitting bemused in the Café de la Régence on rue Saint-Honoré, still in his tattered tailcoat and wearing a white shirt that had certainly seen crisper, cleaner days.

Repairing to Sibelius's hotel room and its resident piano, the composer improvised for the painter while the painter sketched the composer. Sibelius evidently extemporized on some themes taken from his (by now) defunct oratorio *Marjatta* – a project based on the final story[85] from the *Kalevala*, with a libretto offered to the composer by the writer Jalmari Finne (1874–1938). The innocent virgin Marjatta eats a red berry (*marja*) in the forest and becomes miraculously pregnant. When she asks for a sauna to carry out her parturition (a common means of easing labour pains), she is shunned by her parents, and eventually gives birth, with a horse's breath functioning as her steam room, to a baby boy. He is baptized and confronts Väinämöinen – the *Kalevala*'s primary protagonist – and a series of legends occur, forming a mythological symbol of Christ's life that plays on the linguistic connections between Marjatta, *marja* and Mary. Eventually Väinämöinen is exiled to sea, inaugurating the close of the heathen era and with it the birth of Finnish Christianity. (Here endeth the *Kalevala*.)

Parviainen was captivated by the musical material, unable especially to get either the 'Great Feast' ('Stor fest') or 'Funeral March' ('Sorg marsch') out of his head for days after his hangover hang-out with Sibelius, the tune spawning numerous sketches. He also loved a part known as the 'Prayer to God' ('Bönen till Gud'), its sound generating a range of synaesthetic painterly responses: 'the most vivid red and darkest black'. This 'Prayer to God' theme was not, however, to remain only in the ears of a couple of katzenjammered Finns: Sibelius later remarked to Parviainen that it had been employed as the chorale-like section in the second half of the Third Symphony's finale.

Indeed, there are psalm or chorale-like parts in all three movements of the Third, indicating perhaps that some sort of connection to the Virgin Mary is part of the symphony's elusive

---

85 Runo 50, 'The New-Born King'.

underbelly. This need not suggest, of course, that the work carries a 'hidden meaning', that it is a cipher for Christianity – Sibelius was not much interested in such furtive proclamations of faith – but it can help us comprehend some of the origins of the symphony as well as broad ways of interpreting its intangible surfaces.

For his part, Parviainen could not let either the 'Funeral March' or 'Prayer to God' rest, and their music became reworked and recontextualized, transformed into important paintings (which he would give to Sibelius as presents: both works still hang in Ainola). *The Spanish Commander's Funeral Procession* (also known as *The Cortège*) is a swirling riot of yellow, red and black, a grand and luxurious image said to be the composer's favourite painting. The other work, *Prayer to God*, could not be more different: lit by a single candle, a sick child – serene and angelic – lies in bed, either dying or recently deceased. A woman, evidently her mother, rests distraught and helpless upon her daughter as a figure of Death watches over the scene. White and black dominate the canvas, with the candle's flame offering respite and hope.

Parviainen was aware of the Sibelius family history and was perhaps consciously painting the death of their little girl Kirsti (1898–1900) from a few years before. He gave *Prayer to God* to the composer in around 1910, and at Ainola the work was known as *The Death of a Child* (though in a 1924 interview the composer also referred to it as *Valse triste*). Hanging the painting in a prominent position above his grand piano, Sibelius claimed he wanted to be reminded of his daughter every day, and especially when he wrote music. It is fitting that this work, inspired by Sibelius's music, could then generate more art in return, a virtuous aesthetic circle, and all lasting tributes to Kirsti.

When he returned to Ainola after his European tour, work continued on the various projects that would become the 'symphonic fantasia' tone poem *Pohjola's Daughter*; he also worked intermittently on the Third Symphony. The two enterprises were certainly linked in Sibelius's musical imagination (and therefore perhaps, too, in his programmatic one), since discarded sketches for *Pohjola* contain material which found its way into the new symphony. Given that Sibelius was rarely bereft of material and might easily have developed fresh-minted music for the symphony, it seems likely there was some sort of connection at work (though it is also just as probable that the material shook off and evaded all its extramusical meanings once it was redrafted into the symphony).

It worked the other way too: some of the discarded material from the Third found its way into the piano suite *Kyllikki* (1904) and the string quartet *Voces intimae* (1909). We are often fed an image of artistic geniuses creating in pure, white-hot inspiration: think of the Hollywood Mozart in *Amadeus* (1984), with his flawless notes emerging from his flawless brain (plus the odd maniacal laugh or scatological gag), or the popular picture of Shakespeare, his honeyed words flowing smoothly onto the page. The reality, of course, was far different, far scruffier, even for Mozart and Shakespeare.

Sibelius's compositional processes were often messy – and the abundance of sketches for the Third Symphony, as well as their derivation and eventual homes, show just how complex composition could be. It was a multifaceted procedure, fluctuating over time, amalgamating forces and resources in order to shape something cohesive, unified, sublime: a Siegfried forging a symphonic Nothung from manifold literary, musical and personal splinters. The end product is what chiefly concerns us, but the processes can be revelatory as well: the three texts of *Hamlet*, or the changes to the Cinthio source material for *Othello*, divulge as much as we are likely to know about Shakespeare's working methods; likewise, in Sibelius we can witness the ways in which he repurposed material as he suddenly saw new (or different) potential for this embryonic theme or that harmonic argument.

The hymn-like, quasi-religious aspects of the Third Symphony are a feature apparent in its very construction and final form as well as the work's complex genesis. Claiming that its design as a three-movement work references the Trinity, as some have done, might be going too far, but there can be no doubting the spiritual ideas that initially drove much of the music as well as its overall transcendent, incantatory character. Although Sibelius's techniques have essentially purged the symphony of anything obviously programmatic, there is still room for speculative interpretation, as we seek to comprehend this work beyond its solely musicological significances.

In the gently rocking, lullaby motion of the second movement there seems a further nod to the *Marjatta* oratorio; so too the scherzo-finale's gradual movement towards first exhilaration and then mystical expansion appears closely related to the general narrative trajectory of the choral work Sibelius sketched and then discarded. This might also be related to the connections to the Christ narrative in *Marjatta* and the *Kalevala*. Here the symphony's flowing first movement might symbolize the life of Jesus, its F-sharp and B minor tangents lying outside the C major revivification, which plays a progressively more significant role as the symphony proceeds. The more reserved and introvert second movement then becomes Christ's Passion, before the high-spirited sequence and elevation of the 'resurrection' finale.

If all this seems far-fetched, fanciful, an injustice to Sibelius's extraordinary symphonic logic and structural design, it is not intended to be taken too literally. And yet by 'reverse-engineering' his music, we can see the remarkable way in which he took so many latent and varied ideas and crafted them seamlessly into such an extraordinary example of new symphonic form. That being said, such proposals are only suggestions and reflections, and it is the abstract musical and emotional power of the symphony that is its main concern and achievement.

The completed artefact of the Third feels as if it has been created almost ex nihilo, fully formed from nothing into a miracle of unity and organic growth. Although we can detect, with a scrupulous scalpel, some of the symphony's metaphorical birth pangs, it also feels eternal, timeless, an inspired vision which acknowledges music's own hypostatic union between the human and the divine. (Which need not imply anything directly Christian or theistic: all of us can acknowledge the presence of, and need for, the spiritual in our lives.)

Work on the Third Symphony was patchy and irregular for several years, as Sibelius assembled and reassembled his materials to forge a new way forward. We recognized above the often cluttered nature of composition, but Sibelius was not as disordered as a Beethoven, nor – of course – was either composer working in some sort of entirely chaotic world. And when he wanted to work, Sibelius could truly focus, rarely leaving his desk, especially when a work was reaching its final form – like a musical midwife, he vigilantly prepared his new child for entry into the world. (Slumber and nutrition could often be taken *al desko*, though he did leave for his essential perambulations in the countryside.) The Sibelius girls might sometimes be noisy – in 1906 Eva was thirteen, Ruth twelve, and little Katarina three – but, as Aino recalled, they also knew when they had to behave and be quiet, out of respect for their father's work.

In 1906, that work included the short character piece *Pan and Echo*, a cantata called *The Captive Queen* (op.48), the six op.50 songs, and incidental music for *Belshazzar's Feast*, as well as *Pohjola's Daughter* and the Third Symphony. *Belshazzar*, based on the Old Testament tale from the book of Daniel, has sometimes – understandably – been written off as a waste of musical ideas (and it is true that the text of the play Sibelius set is not particularly original). Nevertheless, the music was still an important work, the only real occasion in which 'orientalism' enters into his music, generating a fascinating range of exotic tone colours (which imperceptibly wriggle their way into some of his other works).

The hard graft of 1906 (not only composing but conducting in Oulu, Vyborg, Vaasa and Saint Petersburg) gradually took its toll in the new year when indulgent binges in Helsinki began to resume. On one particularly infamous evening – 27 January 1907 – he spent the equivalent of €500 on champagne, brandy and lobster. Aino, exhausted, panic-stricken and distressed at her husband's relapse into his chronic gorging and splurging, went to a sanatorium to recover. That spring, the composer confided to a friend in a letter: 'This drinking, in itself so pleasant an occupation, has really gone too far now.'

Boozing was also disrupting continued work on his new symphony, the first performance of which had to be postponed. In August, with Sibelius reconciled to his infinitely fortitudinous wife, the couple took a trip together to Berlin, patient Aino steering thirsty Jean away from the bars and restaurants and into the city's museums and galleries. This kept him sober but also hindered work on the Third, which was at long last complete only after they returned to Finland. With the pages to the finale still wet, the premiere took place in Helsinki on 25 September 1907, joined on the programme by other recent works – *Pohjola's Daughter* and a suite from *Belshazzar's Feast* – and conducted by their composer.

Most of the audience, expecting a work in the grand national/Romantic school of the first two symphonies, were confounded by the new piece's classical proportions and contemporary mode. Some of the critics, however, enthused over this urbane updating of symphonic form: 'it meets all the requirements for a symphonic work of art in the modern sense', raved one, though another felt it did not make quite the same impact as the earlier pair from Sibelius's pen – just as the composer himself had predicted. A similar response arose when Sibelius repeated the work in Saint Petersburg a month later (though Muscovites were more approving).

The Third's more subtle approach to the development of the symphony would take time for people to appreciate.[86]

---

86 It was in Helsinki, only a few weeks after the début of Sibelius's Third, that Mahler visited his colleague in his capital, and they had their famous conversation, mentioned earlier, about the nature of the symphony. The Austro-Bohemian, fresh from writing his gargantuan Eighth the summer before, argued that the symphony must be like the world, 'embracing everything'; the Finn, unsurprisingly so soon after completing his Third, argued for the importance of inner logic.

When it comes to a work so often referred to – including by this chapter – as Sibelius's most 'classical' symphony, we might take a moment to reflect on what that means, especially within the context of the new century in which it was composed.

Neoclassism, in music, emerged as a reaction to the disintegrating chromaticism within late Romanticism and modernism – many elements of which sought to eradicate traditional tonality altogether. The movement also coveted a cleaner, more straightforward style: gallant rhythms, self-confident harmonies, diatonic tonalities and well-defined sectional forms (including dance suites, concerti grossi, and so on). The key proponent of this style, Igor Stravinsky (1882–1971), adopted it in the 1920s, '30s and '40s, following on from his earlier Russian period and prior to his late serial one. Works like *Pulcinella* and *Symphonies of Wind Instruments* (both 1920), *Apollo* and *Oedipus Rex* (both 1927), *Symphony of Psalms* (1930), *Perséphone* (1934), *Orpheus* (1947) and, finally, *The Rake's Progress* (1951) would make flamboyant use of antiquated techniques intentionally juxtaposed with a disconcerting hauteur to create some magnificent dramatic and orchestral effects.

All these sardonic, often mischief-making 'cocktails' seem a long way from Sibelius's 'pure spring water', as he was later to characterize his own music in a none-too-subtle dig at Stravinsky's significant achievements. Sibelius's Third is quite the pioneer, preceding the Neoclassical Stravinsky as well as works like Ravel's *Tombeau de Couperin* or Respighi's *Ancient Airs and Dances* (both 1917), though of course such backward glances and retro borrowings had always existed in music.

Where Sibelius differs from Stravinsky and the Neoclassicists is the essentially sincere nature of his work, with its absence of pastiche or irony. His work is closer to the *junge Klassizität* (young classicism) movement, which asserted the primacy of both melody and absolute music, doing away with programmatic inclinations that dominated Wagner, Liszt, Debussy, Strauss, et al. A key figure in this crusade was Sibelius's friend Ferruccio Busoni, who would argue that artistic experiments should come through musical necessity and only within the context of 'firm, rounded forms'.

Sibelius's Third (1907) seems to be an exemplary ideal that is likely to have been central to Busoni's much later formulations.[87] An exceptionally original work, it reinvented the classical symphony in a modern, streamlined fashion. It was like a sophisticated Rolls-Royce motor car redesigned for the twenty-first century: retaining all the elegant, enduring style and power of old but with a contemporary twist. The Third Symphony's linear logic and exacting counterpoint, its strong sense of purpose and direction, especially in the outer movements, are born of its heritage, even as its more subtle reconsiderations – in tonality or motivic expression – push forward and define the medium in new ways.

The composer was very clear about the earlier paradigms his music was echoing if not duplicating: 'a Mozart allegro,' he observed, 'is the perfect model for a symphonic movement.' The concord and consistency in Mozart, the continual and elegant expansion of ideas, with nothing protruding or impinging upon the rest, were, for Sibelius, the epitome of simple but formidable expressive power, which he sought to embrace in his own new symphonic compositions.[88]

---

87   Busoni's *On Young Classicism* was published in 1920.
88   Though, of course, we should not forget that a great deal of Mozart's energy and interest comes when he *disrupts* elegance, using minor keys, dangerous harmonics or perilous rhythms.

Crucially, there was also the question of key. To write in C major was a bold statement in 1907 (and it would be an even bolder one with his Seventh Symphony in 1924). Not only was this the key of Haydn's *Midi* and *Bear*, Mozart's *Linz* and *Jupiter*, Beethoven's First, Schubert's *Great* and Schumann's Second Symphonies, but it was the foundation of centuries of Western classical music. But these pre-eminent symphonies, along with other radical works (like Beethoven's *Waldstein* Piano Sonata and first *Razumovsky* Quartet), had shown that the key was as malleable as it was time-honoured. It was the ideal renaissance key for Sibelius to anticipate Busoni's articulations of experiments *within* 'firm, rounded forms', reimagining the whole concept of a symphony in C major.

This work, which to many has seemed to be a throwback, a regression, is actually a far-reaching and revolutionary as well as marvellously original and convincing achievement. Shunning a Che Guevara beret or Mao jacket, spurning atonality or serialism, Sibelius's Third Symphony instead ingeniously advanced symphonic form wearing a tasteful business suit – but with some surprises hidden beneath its well-cut cloth.

Symphony No.3 in C major, op.52

1. Allegro moderato.

Sibelius often talked about the compelling forward momentum which holds his symphonies together, and this feature is readily apparent in his Third, as it surges onward with glorious movement, a voyage to match those undertaken in *Pohjola's Daughter* and *Nightride and Sunrise*. But all journeys start somewhere, and this symphony begins with a recurrent aphoristic folk gesture on the cellos and basses, reminiscent of *Kullervo* and ideas Sibelius later derived from his tour of the Karelia region in 1892, as he collected traditional poems and songs.

Seeking economy and focus, Sibelius's Third begins with a single melodic thread, in C major but lacking any harmonic support, making it full of nervous energy and coiled symphonic potential. The opening music feels like a blithe rural dance, organizing and reorganizing itself as it resolves the right motivic combination to best move forward. And, as in so much Sibelius, the rhythm and tempo in this movement will be as important as the melodic material. Succinct, steady, the Third's inaugural theme is methodical and orderly: checking it has everything in the rucksack ready for its expedition ahead.

Other material progressively begins to join in; the music sweeps along, vigorous and bracing. This builds to our trip's first magnificent panorama: a climax on brass, trumpets and trombones, which call out before their figure is adopted by the woodwind and horns, featuring Sibelius's hallmark short-long-short rhythms. Hints of an invasive F sharp pivot us to a subsidiary second theme – in B minor – which, like the first, is given initially on the cellos. It becomes an impressive, ambitious, almost epic idea – singing, but with a strong pulse for support in the background. It is our first look at a musical idea that will ultimately spawn the hymn-like exaltations of the finale.

As this music fades, the tempo changes for the first time in the symphony: the exposition of this neat sonata form ends, and we enter a strange tranquil realm (*pianississimo*), a brief pause to reflect and catch our breath after our striving start. Rising, we continue in an obscure landscape, clutching in the mist for recognizable signposts: woodwind offer lugubrious versions of the B minor theme, with an especially despondent extended solo for the bassoon. Fragments of the main theme waft by. Tendrils gather on the strings, together with hints of that 'devil in music', the tritone interval.[89]

Our fear begins to escalate – are we lost? are we going mad? – before suddenly this sonata-form development section ends and, bang on time, the opening theme reappears complete to proclaim the start of the recapitulation. Back on familiar ground, our journey can continue in straightforward fashion. And so it does, the final march to the day's designated end – hostel, hotel, palace – spirited, robust and unswerving. The movement then closes in unqualified spontaneity with a distinguished coda-hymn on the woodwind, horns and strings, which seems to herald our advent like the tolling of welcoming bells. We have arrived.[90]

2. Andantino con moto, quasi allegretto.[91]

After the journey, the night. We enter an inexplicable and motionless world, a nocturne of the Nordic midsummer carrying a peculiar light and mystical sense of foreboding mixed with

---

89   Which will come to dominate Sibelius's Fourth Symphony (1911).

90   On the tentative 'Christ narrative' analogy mentioned in passing during the essay, this might represent Jesus's triumphal entry into Jerusalem on Palm Sunday – and with the movement's ghostly development section, perhaps his temptations in the wilderness?

91   This tempo has long been a source of controversy: many have played the movement too fast (understandably, given the unambiguous marking in the score), disturbing its powerful impact. Despite the marking, Sibelius himself seems to have been very clear on preferring a slower tempo, but the issue is further complicated by the extraordinary demands the movement makes with its rhythmical relations.

charm. The movement has a simple surface, but it is an illusion, for the complex interior is an ambiguous hybrid form – part meandering rondo, part collection of variations, part sonata form – all of which is continually sustained by the rhythmic instincts of pizzicato strings haunting the background with their insomniac pulse.

These recurrent, circular, static motifs seem to reference not only Finnish folk music but their shared heritage in the seasons of the north. The usual rotations of day/night are replaced by endless periods of light or half light, enchanted but with their own sense of dread. And then long dark winters, agonizing and intense. In chilly, hostile G-sharp minor we drift and equivocate among our night-time concerns and supplications, the music full of menacing monotony. No mere intermission between the energetic, goal-orientated outer movements, the Third Symphony's andantino is an invocation, a prayer, a vigil, a gently swaying lullaby against the forces of despair.[92]

Everything is nuanced, spare, brooding. Pizzicato lower strings (viola, cello, bass) play the same rising three-note motif the brass had in the first movement, and from this slowly materializes the meditative but often anxious main theme, first on the flutes and clarinets, then assumed by the first violins. The lingering blue-grey summer night is generated by poignant, gently dancing cellos, who are answered by twinkles and flashes of woodwind light. These passages alternate and return, imperceptibly increasing in speed and character, before a heavier, more dignified, re-emergence of the main theme has the disturbing appearance of a funeral procession. The strange ominous midsummer nights of the north can do puzzling things to your thoughts.

---

92 Perhaps a prayer to God concerning the death of a child?

The movement ends in withdrawal, drained and even a little bitter, but with emotional self-possession and forbearance, too, the darker reflections drifting away with the dawn. It is an extraordinary movement, full of organic, binding unity across the symphony, breathing an atmosphere that is both disquieting and reassuring, able to trouble and to soothe, moving but never maudlin, its hypnotic magic a brilliant construction of great subtlety.

3. Moderato – Allegro (ma non tanto).

Beginning with suggestive fragments and loose memories of the first two movements' themes, the last movement is a compressed scherzo-finale whose energy and occupation effectively expel the penumbral ruminations of the andantino to lead towards a hymn of happiness. Rarely loud, the music is relentless in its speed and mobilizing momentum: 'the crystallization of thought from chaos', Sibelius remarked.[93]

The thematic threads are initially tangled and disordered, as we might expect in a scherzo, as the symphony teases with a range of tempos and motifs. The whole symphony seems to be in a time warp: its past, present and future all coexisting, the work's magnificent unity now fallen sway to an almost Nabokovian sport or even Kafkaesque nightmare. Gradually the themes begin to weave together in a miracle of evolutionary consolidation that rises towards an exuberant climax. This coagulation of themes suddenly becomes stranded, forsaken, and the music draws back into its muddled restlessness and agitation. As in the slow movement, and the spectral development section of the opening

---

93 The tone poem *Nightride and Sunrise*, discussed in the previous chapter, will also shortly adopt the scherzo-finale model and mood of the Third Symphony's finale.

allegro moderato, we fall into fog and seclusion. It is hazy, grey, with woodwind calls threatened by an unnerving string ostinato.

Trying to evade this obscure mist, the preliminary 'scherzo' music is repeated, its game of 'tempos and motifs' now slightly lighter in tone and gaining a more purposeful direction. From here the movement progresses into one of Sibelius's most harmonically adventurous passages, with a dense, highly chromatic development section.[94] We are tonally adrift, a disorientation that slowly dissolves to allow a mysterious new melody to transpire.

Based on a tiny descending motif heard earlier, this theme emerges loosely on the horns before being taken up by the lower strings: first the violas, gradually augmenting the theme, then the cellos, asserting it as a magnificent hymn in a bright, confident C major. This new idea is inspiring, boldly – almost wilfully – diatonic, a C major sunrise that will provide the foundation for the rest of the symphony.[95]

Troublesome F-sharp dissonance is snatched into the sunlight and then literally drummed out of existence as the C major hymn gains impetus and motion, picking up any lingering nervous energy. The modest orchestra's entire ensemble begins – for practically the first time in the symphony – to sing together with one voice, the instrumental tutti joining the intrepid harmonic, motivic and rhythmic swell. The hymn repeats again and again, with jubilant horn trills and dangerously pulsating

---

94 'Experiments,' as Busoni might say, 'that come through musical necessity and only within the wider context of 'firm, rounded forms'.

95 Which we might wish to regard as a 'resurrection' idea linked to the 'Christ narrative' cautiously floated in the essay. Nonetheless, such theological interpretations are obviously of extremely limited value, not least because this non-programmatic, abstract symphony is very clearly promoting a resurgence and revivification of C major far more than any potential reference to Christ's restoration and ascension.

strings, everything flourishing into a resplendent orchestral chorus of praise and triumph.

The ending itself, after these orations of acclaim, is superbly succinct – and entirely Sibelian. Just a vast three-note Nordic figure, backed up by the unflinching granite sounds of the timpani and brass.

The technical processes Sibelius developed carry an enormous musical, intellectual and emotional persuasion, and his Third Symphony is a staggering original achievement of extraordinary cumulative power and logical integration. The apparent spontaneity and inevitability Sibelius produces as a result of his subtle, refined methods – evolving, repeating, coalescing – are a compelling testimony to not only his originality but his commitment to his own path, his refusal to be lured into fashionable or ephemeral means.

Sibelius's private revolution was underway.

Chapter Eight

Landscape/Mind: The Fourth Symphony

Finland is rising from the sea.[96]

Compressed for aeons under the immense weight of glaciers, the retreat of these vast sheets of frozen water has, in the twelve thousand years since the end of the last ice age, allowed a post-glacial rebound to take place, creating the iconic lakes, forests and humble hills of the Finnish countryside. This generally low-lying topography – with few hills and fewer mountains – means that any significant elevation in the terrain not only is rare but can offer remarkable panoramic views of the surrounding landscapes.

---

96 Throughout most of the world, sea levels are currently rising around three millimetres a year, but in Finland, and much of the surrounding region, in relative terms they are falling around nine millimetres.

One such prominence is located in the far east of Finland, in the Karelia region, above the shores of Lake Pielinen. A long, sequestered ridge known as Koli, it is made mostly of white quartzite and forms a strange expanse of smooth, rounded rock that stands apart from its environment. Its three main summits, none higher than 350 metres – Ukko, Akka, Paha – refer to the Sky God, Female Spirit and Evil Spirit, respectively, from Finnish folklore and mythology, while a fourth, Pieni, is known as the Little Hill.

Koli is an obvious viewing point, a place to gasp and wonder, rest and reflect – given both the natural platform it affords and the vistas lying beyond. It has become the location for countless travel brochure spreads, tourism websites and hackneyed social media postings. We've all done it, somewhere: standing tall, arms akimbo, gazing into the distance – we all, it seems, want to ape Caspar David Friedrich's 1818 masterpiece *Wanderer Above the Sea of Fog*, that emblematic image of *deutsche Romantik*, whether ironically or not.[97]

Such sentimentalizing of the landscape, not least in Finland, is hardly new, however. At the end of the nineteenth, and into the early twentieth, century, several prominent Finns made use of this far-flung region's exceptional scenery to generate an iconography for Finland, as part of a wider campaign for its independence from the Russian yoke. Two such figures were the painter Eero Järnefelt and his brother-in-law Jean Sibelius, who, in the early autumn of 1909, took a trip together to Karelia, to listen to the 'sighing of the winds and the roaring of the storms', as the composer put it. Even then – in part because of the art and music they had already completed – it was known as a

---

[97] It is, perhaps, an innate human wish, to assert our simultaneous pride and wonder, both mastering and respecting the landscape – a phenomenon nature writer Robert Macfarlane attributes largely to Friedrich's great painting.

celebrated beauty spot, a place of natural splendour burdened with nationalistic pride and hope, both a symbol of freedom and a graphic assertion of Finnish uniqueness. There is substantial irony in this: for all its isolation and magnificence, it was no pure, unspoiled wilderness but rather already a nexus of heavy creative, intellectual and political negotiation.

'One of the great experiences of my life,' said Sibelius of this 1909 expedition, and Koli and its sublime environs helped inspire one of the most revered of all Finnish compositions, a work laden with meaning of an almost biblical nature for many Finns to this day. It is a symphony containing chamber like transparency of orchestration but a densely expressive intensity, the two operating in extraordinary creative tension. It is impressively, beguilingly, modern – yet it is also, in its composer's own words, 'a protest against present-day music'. It is stark, unyielding, almost maliciously callous and cruel, full of searching introspection, but at the same time a comfort, a solace, an abode of acceptance, as well as a sonic space incorporating many more moods than its reputation for grim cheerlessness suggests. It dismantles and reconfigures symphonic DNA: harmony, melody, rhythm, form – all the fundamental components of music – are destabilized as we follow Sibelius's profound, mysterious vision, his probing reflection on the nature of time and space, on the limits of human fragility and endurance, on the relationship between particular spaces and existential states of being. It is a work of ceaseless fascination where nothing is trivial, a journey into awareness and disclosure, forfeiture and desertion.

The chilly pages of its score transcribe an anxious mind. A psychological symphony in A minor, with spare grey textures and bleak abstaining chords, its composition was influenced by a complex vortex of competing forces: a classically minded string quartet, loneliness, cancer, alcoholic withdrawal, intellectual liberation, a devilish musical device, a threateningly repetitive narrative poem – and, of course, the unforgiving landscapes of northern Europe. It is a work that is mutually claustrophobic and agoraphobic, afraid equally of confinement and open spaces, even as it also seeks to embrace the conditions of both. It needs and fears nature; it dreads and demands a welcoming drink by a roaring fire on a frozen day.

Froward, alien, intense – Sibelius's Fourth Symphony (1911) is a dark, austere masterpiece lying at the literal and symbolic centre of his art. Like the Finnish landscape, it encompasses both beauty and severity; like its Finnish maker, it is intangible, withdrawn, even a little remote. It is a work born from pain, from solitude, from a heightened awareness of mortality. At times it can seem a sly, elusive work, the composer moving like a double agent through the music; at others it is disconcertingly raw and honest, a candid confession of sin and suffering.

The Fourth is a work that can be hard to listen to – its dissonant abyss can feel overwhelming – but it contains a magnetic power, an elemental persuasiveness, a hypnotic internal cohesion that confers its status as one of the most important of all Sibelius's works, and one of the most significant orchestral pieces of the twentieth century.

By the beginning of 1908, Sibelius's boozing caught up with him. Already subjecting the composer to spells of depression and paranoia – the spirits dampening his spirits, so to speak – it now recalled its physical debt. During a trip to Saint Petersburg the previous autumn to conduct his Third Symphony, Sibelius had written to Aino complaining of a certain hoarseness of voice, which persisted through the winter into the new year. He was taken to the Deaconess Hospital, Helsinki, for a fortnight's treatment (though it seems to have been largely fruitless, little more than a drying out). His friend Axel Carpelan wrote to Sibelius's friend and colleague Robert Kajanus about a dream he'd had in which, unless 'Sibbe' stopped smoking and drinking hard liquor – two key emotional crutches for him – the composer would be dead: 'This illness must surely be his final warning.'

For a time, it was. Too ill to maintain his continent-scurrying lifestyle (with food and wine in the best hotels and finest restaurants as he toured his music around Europe), he was compelled to cancel trips to Berlin, Warsaw and Rome. Aino must have breathed a sigh of relief. By the end of February, however, a return visit to London was arranged, including another stay at the lavish Langham Hotel, Regent's Park, and a performance of his Third at the Queen's Hall, which Sibelius conducted himself. He caught up with his English friends, Rosa Newmarch, Henry Wood and Granville Bantock (the latter the dedicatee of the symphony), though Newmarch was concerned not only by Sibelius's self-destructive drinking – which had clearly resumed – but by its attendant sore throat and his countenance, which was much older than she had been used to.

It was, indeed, a foretaste of something very nasty round the corner, and perhaps Sibelius knew it. He spent most of his free time in London in blithely nonchalant cheerfulness, writing postcards back home. One such missive has an image of Westminster Bridge and the Houses of Parliament and includes not only a brief quotation from the Third's finale but a cartoon sketch of an empty wine bottle floating down the Thames. Is it a wry reference to Gallen-Kallela's infamous drunken-symposium painting, a droll acknowledgement of habitual drinking that needed to stop before it was too late?

Early 1908 was taken up with the composition of incidental music for *Swanwhite*, a new play by August Strindberg, while the latter part of the year was focused on the tone poem *Nightride and Sunrise* (discussed in chapter 6).[98] Among several more minor works in between was a song, 'Jubal', op.35/1, involving an irresponsible and naive youth who, like Parsifal and Lemminkäinen, recklessly chases a swan. The bird is killed, its dying swansong reproaching the hunter and compelling him to 'bind string to string' in order to play music for the world, which he will now do every night. Was this swan representative of Sibelius's own guilty conscience? Was his own youthful drinking now nothing less than a death wish? Perhaps it was time for his own evenings to be filled by not whisky and wine but, like Jubal's, music?

By May 1908, Sibelius's tickly throat was considerably worse, now acutely painful, and he sought medical advice in Helsinki. Although the composer was given to bouts of hypochondria, this consultation probably saved his life: a cancerous tumour was identified, and an initial operation took place on 12 May, followed by an additional procedure with the leading specialist, Dr Fränkel, in Berlin (the city of so many of Sibelius's alcoholic hijinks; the irony was unlikely to have been lost on the composer). With Aino pregnant[99] and money (as usual) in short supply, it was hardly a desirable trip, even disregarding its gloomy itinerary – but it was an absolutely necessary one. Frantic efforts were

---

98 Strindberg's *Swanwhite* and Sibelius's music both received their world premieres, to critical acclaim, at the Swedish Theatre in Helsinki on 8 April 1908.

99 Their fifth daughter, Margareta (1908–1988), arrived on 10 September.

made to borrow money, with Sibelius's fame probably the only factor that brought forth credit (who, after all, would want to advance currency to a notoriously bad debtor who might also be seriously ill?).

In late May, Jean and Aino set off for the German capital, and in the summer of 1908 a series of thirteen operations took place under Fränkel's scalpel – yet the doctors could not solve the problem. A young assistant offered to 'have a go'. He lowered his various instruments into the throat of Finland's finest composer and located the pernicious obstruction. A yank, a shout, and Sibelius was freed from his torment. (That autumn, he wrote *Nightride and Sunrise*, and it is tempting, if excessive, to see this work as a musical representation of his journey flitting through the jaws of everlasting night and emerging into new light and life.)

This was not the end of the malady, however. Sibelius was incapable of speech for several weeks during his convalescence, and there was a strong prospect that the operation had not been a total success, or that the growth would reappear. Moreover, and perhaps most personally devastating to this enthusiastic imbiber of luxurious wines and punishing liquor, booze was off the menu. So, too, was smoking of any description.

Alcohol and tobacco disappeared from Sibelius's life for seven years – seven years that Aino claimed were the happiest of her entire existence. In this sense, we might see the throat tumour as a positive thing: a middle-aged dice with death that made Sibelius see sense and mend his ways, as well as his marriage. But it was not so straightforward as this. Drinking was a vital source of consolation, reassurance and pleasure for Sibelius, an invigoration and an escape. As well as losing part of his identity to sobriety, it was like the loss of a friend – two friends, since cigars were a companion comfort – and he had to mourn. Suddenly having this vital emotional support removed was only partially liberating: it improved his marriage and his general health; it sharpened his intellectual faculties and honed his mind. But it also compelled him to encounter himself and the cosmos naked and alone.

We can hear some of that confrontation in the Fourth Symphony, its implacable austerity telling of abstention even as its precision showcases its creator's clearer brain.

The years that followed the throat operation were productive, the sober composer creating a series of introspective masterpieces that further developed the character and quality of his art. This previously often irritable (read *hungover*) artist even did something he hadn't undertaken for years: teaching. He even took on specific pupils for the first time – two of the most talented young composers of the next generation, Toivo Kuula and Leevi Madetoja. Sibelius was a little unsure of his position as an educator, as a developer of musical identities. He knew that his own style was too idiosyncratic a foundation upon which to establish a school of musical thought, but he was also a little wary of a young pretender toppling his status as musical father of the nation – though he did enjoy operating as a paternal figure to these new voices (which, to an extent, probably helped him stay teetotal).[100]

---

100 Toivo Kuula (1883–1918) wrote mainly for voice and orchestra – his *Sea-Bathing Maidens* (1910) and *The Maiden and the Boyar's Son* (1912) are certainly worth

Sibelius did not travel to Saint Petersburg for the premiere of *Nightride and Sunrise* on 23 January 1909,[101] but he was able to travel again to England in February, staying another time at the Langham and gradually mixing more and more within the country's elite social and musical circles (often being bored by the pretensions of affluent music lovers and blue-blooded benefactors keen to display their artistic and intellectual acumen). The social events must have been hard for this newly abstemious bon viveur. His letters home to Aino, from a city he loved, are a little grumpy: his colleagues and rivals have positions in society he sometimes seems to envy – though only to an extent. In reality, he knew he neither needed nor wanted such obligations, preferring his own moody isolation and freedom, something he would begin to wear as a badge of honour. The composer was turning increasingly to the sphere of his own inner creativity. ('I no longer feel at home in the town. The solitude of my life is beginning,' he confided to his diary the following year, on 10 January 1910.)

Sibelius had the opportunity to hear a good deal of music while in the English capital, most notably at the Queen's Hall on 27 February, when he saw Debussy conduct two of his own masterpieces: the *Nocturnes* and *Prélude à l'après-midi d'un*

---

exploring – along with some two dozen songs and several intriguing piano and chamber works. He died in a drunken brawl, a few weeks before his thirty-fifth birthday. Leevi Madetoja (1887–1947) would live longer and achieve more, becoming a stimulating composer of many works, including two operas and three late Romantic symphonies (1916, 1918 and 1926) that should be of interest to anyone who values Sibelius. (A fourth symphony is presumed lost: the near-complete manuscript disappeared at a Paris railway station in 1938 when Madetoja's suitcase was stolen. We live in hope that it will one day materialize from the bowels of a French *bureau des objets trouvés* ...)

101 It was given by Alexander Siloti and received a hostile reception (the conductor later admitted he had made cuts to the score which likely disturbed the work's delicate balance). Glazunov, however, loved the piece, writing enthusiastically to its composer to congratulate him.

faune.[102] (Not to be outdone, Sibelius also performed *En Saga* and *Finlandia* there during his stay.) Finding himself with some time off, he visited the British Museum, a place which fascinated him,[103] while an excursion out west to Cheltenham saw him conduct *Valse triste* and *Spring Song*. Returning to London, Sibelius decided to stay a little longer in the city in order to compose. Checking out of the ruinously expensive Langham, he rented a room at a private house in Kensington, an establishment run by a certain 'Mrs Dodd'. The location is commemorated today by a blue plaque,[104] though unfortunately one of his landlady's neighbours was a budding amateur pianist, and before long Sibelius had to move out, to 15 Gordon Place, just round the block.

It was here that Sibelius toiled on his latest work, a string quartet – the first since his youth – now known as *Voces intimae*, op.56.[105] For the most part it was completed in London, though Sibelius was still grappling with its final form later in Paris and Berlin (where his doctor, Fränkel, examined his throat again and gave a tentative all-clear). In some ways, the health-and-

---

102 Afterwards the two composers exchanged compliments, and Sibelius, always so insecure but especially *sans vin*, particularly appreciated the great Frenchman's praises. This was surely reciprocated: the transparent textures and aural charisma of Debussy's orchestral masterpieces are readily apparent in *The Oceanides* (1914) and *Tapiola* (1926), whatever their differences in approach or structuring.

103 The institution has repaid the favour by finding the composer fascinating too: it now contains, as part of its numismatic collection, a hundred-mark banknote issued by the Bank of Finland (in circulation prior to the country adopting the euro) with a portrait of Sibelius on one side and four flying swans with pine trees on the reverse.

104 For the curious, it is located above the front door at 15 Gloucester Walk, London, W8 4HZ, between the city's Holland and Hyde Parks.

105 The name 'intimate voices' comes from a note from Sibelius to Axel Carpelan on a copy of the score near the beginning of the slow movement, where some ethereal E minor chords speak of familiarity, affection and confession.

recovery background to this work was providential since, as a five-movement string quartet, *Voces intimae* also owed something to the formidable reputation of Beethoven's great quartet in A minor, op.132, with its famous central 'Heiliger Dankgesang eines Genesenen an die Gottheit, in der lydischen Tonart' ('Holy song of thanksgiving of a convalescent to the deity, in the Lydian mode'), written in the aftermath of Beethoven's own recovery from serious illness in the spring of 1825. Moreover, just as Beethoven composed the quirky *alla marcia* as a supplementary accessory to the Heiliger Dankgesang, Sibelius appends his first movement with a whimsical scherzo.

Although the shifting musical sands of the twentieth century produced many great cycles of string quartets – from Bartók, Nielsen, Shostakovich, Maconchy, Bacewicz, Villa-Lobos, Simpson and Holmboe – it is also notable for several stand-alone works from major composers: Sibelius, Debussy, Ravel, Grieg, Delius, Elgar and Fauré each wrote only one mature piece for the medium. For Sibelius, his *Voces intimae* was an important achievement, a singular return to a form he had engaged with several times in his youth. (These forays, although not of the same standard as op.56, are worth discovering.) In some ways the string quartet – with its severity of form and remorseless logic – seems tailor-made for Sibelius; yet there is also an important sense in which he needed the full colours, textures and relationships of the whole orchestra in order to realize his full effects, as well as to engage with more pantheistic tone painting than might be possible with just four string instruments.

Either way, *Voces intimae* was a significant re-directioning for Sibelius and an important step on the journey towards the Fourth Symphony – not least since some sketches for the slow movements of both works, which share many of the same rhythms as well as melodic outlines, occupy the very same piece of paper (and where the symphony is scored for string quartet). *Voces intimae* is inward, dialectical, mixing cordiality and impenetrability, a work of abstract discussion and private sentiment. It lacks any programme but obliges responses that are both emotional and intellectual, as it freely juxtaposes psychological insight and philosophical consideration with more subjective feeling.

A figure no longer able (or willing) to enjoy the various pleasures of metropolitan existence, Sibelius was increasingly turning to self-examination and analysis, and so was his music. The brilliant work of a relatively lonely man far from his home and his family, holed up (not unhappily) in a rented room in West London, this quartet of 'intimate voices' seems to speak in a personal, even secretive language. A complex hybrid, its musical syntax is both classical and related to the runic rhythms of Sibelius's beloved Karelia – a place to which he would soon return.

It was during this stay in London in the late winter and early spring of 1909 that Sibelius began writing his (now legendary) diary, which he largely maintained until the 1940s, though some of the later entries are very sparse indeed. More methodical than the laconic journal he had kept in the 1890s, the diary is a vital resource for understanding many of Sibelius's moods, opinions, and attitudes towards himself and his music (as well as more run-of-the-mill daily information, along with bloodcurdling data relating to his many debts). Sibelius's diary is no memoir, still less an autobiography, but it is a precious document of European culture and an intimate, if incomplete, portrait of a great artist.

On the day he concluded his *Voces intimae* Quartet, 15 April 1909, perhaps still getting accustomed to writing in a diary again, Sibelius penned an extravagant, melodramatic entry: 'Quartet finished. I – my heart bleeds! – why this tragedy in life. Oh! Oh! Oh! That I exist! My God!' Given a statement like this, it is hard to tell exactly how pleased he was now that he had completed his quartet: doubtless the relief was mixed in with his habitual anxiety and sense of professional insufficiency. Satisfaction and despair were never far from each other in Sibelius's head, a head that had been all too often jumbled by alcohol into oscillations of exuberance, apathy and desolation.

Those last two adjectives, if not the first, might well describe – in some measure – the Fourth Symphony, an even deeper journey into the mind than the *Voces intimae* Quartet. But before the stirring excursion that would help generate his next, and bleakest, essay in symphonic form, Sibelius focused on a pair of smaller projects: first, in Berlin during April and May, a set of eight songs, op.57; then, at Ainola between late May and late August, a set of ten piano pieces, op.58.[106]

Setting texts by Swedish poet Ernst Josephson (1851–1906),[107] whose verses Sibelius had also used for 'Jubal' in 1908, op.57 are a typically Romantic blend of landscapes and fairy tales, full of irony, love and loss, daydreaming, death and despair (though they are not a song cycle as such). The first, 'The River

---

106 There was also the first throb of a larger enterprise: in Berlin's Bar Riche, he sketched out eight bars for a strange new tone poem for voice and orchestra, *Luonnotar*.

107 Josephson was a painter as well as a poet, who lived most of his life in France and studied under Manet, though his paintings have tended to eclipse his accomplishments in verse.

and the Snail' ('Älven och snigeln'), features a poor battered gastropod who clings for life to a mossy stone as the waters course by (via offbeat piano motifs). But things get even worse when a 'barefoot boy' comes to pick mussels along the shore: he spies the snail's house and cracks it open to reveal a radiant pearl that will endure the tough autumn and winter upon the breast of a beautiful queen.

The second, 'A Flower Stood by the Wayside' ('En blomma stod vid vägen'), is simpler, a poignant folk song about a butterfly and a bird sharing a cage, while the third, 'The Mill Wheel' ('Kvarnhjulet'), has the piano follow the rhythms of the first song's water, but by reducing some of the syncopations, Sibelius makes it suggest the mechanical sound of the turning mill. The fourth song, 'May' ('Maj'), has a Schubertian quality to it, a peaceful pastoral with an unpretentious communication of joy at the return of spring.

Song five, 'I Am a Tree' ('Jag är ett träd'), is a more distinctive and exceptional work, portraying a despondent tree yearning for death. Exploring the inner life of an ancient tree, it features a bold sense of line, opening with intense fanfare flourishes on the piano and a rising vocal motif at the beginning of each verse. It is a tempestuous masterpiece of existential torment and personal determination, perhaps associated with its composer's own struggles with alcohol and abstention at the time: stripped bare by a summer storm, the tree longs for the cold embrace of snowy death rather than be compelled to stand naked and undecorated amid the joyous green foliage of its neighbours. In its stark audacity, 'I Am a Tree' anticipates the Fourth Symphony as well as *Luonnotar* and is one of Sibelius's greatest songs, poignant and deeply moving.

Shifting direction, the sixth song, 'Duke Magnus' ('Hertig Magnus'), tells of a duke who thinks he hears a mermaid calling to him from a lake – with predictably soggy results (though a happy ending). The seventh song, 'The Flower of Friendship' ('Vänskapens blomma'), is a venerable, self-possessed study of friendship in nature, while the final song, 'The Watersprite' ('Näcken'), concerns a mythical creature who lures the unsuspecting to a damp demise. It is a capricious song about madness, with frequent shifts in tonality and a weird, volatile piano role, ending in a sombre realm of doubt and despair that, again, foresees the world of Sibelius's Fourth Symphony.

Completed on 18 May 1909, the op.57 songs are an astonishing set, revealing Sibelius's increasing use of spare, frugal textures and less luxurious harmonies, as well as a combination of tense restraint and agonizing theatrical gestures. Still in Berlin, in his diary three days later, Sibelius wrote, 'Must return home. It is no longer possible to work here. A change of style?!' Arguably, with the *Voces intimae* Quartet and op.57 songs, Sibelius had already inaugurated that 'change of style', but it is valuable to have his thoughts confirmed in text from his own hand.

Back home at Ainola, endless invoices had been piling up in Sibelius's absence, and Aino frequently wrote to Jean in letters of misery and extreme unease. Lest we forget, she had a big house and four daughters to care for, as well as enduring worries about her husband's health, especially in terms of those twin maladies relating to his throat: the drinking and the tumour. In reply to this understandable fiscal agony, Sibelius's epistolary counsel was a curious assortment of self-involved statements about his busy work life, lyrical exhortations that the dark night would soon end, and an anomalous slew of practical/heartless advice ('Eat porridge!').

After returning home to face his bills and commitments, Sibelius shortly set about composing a set of ten piano pieces, collected as op.58. Sibelius's piano music has come in for unwarranted scorn – not least from the composer himself, who often claimed not to understand the instrument, feeling it foreign to him. And while his numerous diminutive piano works rarely attain the degree of subtlety or reach as his larger-scale orchestral works, they are not devoid of interest, both in themselves and as markers of his development. To those who are prepared to look and listen, there are innumerable wonders within.

Op.58 was Sibelius's first significant work for the instrument in nearly half a decade (which is readily apparent since the ten pieces showcase the important advances in his musical style). Gone are the Finnish folk elements, along with the grand Romantic/national mould that characterized his earlier works (especially in the First and Second symphonies). Instead, there is a mixture of classical control (Nos.3, 4 and 7), which reflects the developments of the Third Symphony, and more impressionistic textures (Nos.1 and 5) which anticipates those ahead in the Fourth, where taut, dramatic moods are skilfully fashioned and sustained. Sibelius himself confided to his diary that he was pleased with these pieces, and although they do not attain the variety and importance of his Norwegian colleague Edvard Grieg's Lyric Pieces – probably the Finn's overall model – they remain distinguished miniatures.[108]

No.1 ('Rêverie') opens the set compellingly with a dramatic modern work which offers sparse textures, the right hand generating a range of equivocal rhythms and elusive tonalities to disturb the left's melodic line. The piece begins to thicken as it

---

108 Written between 1867 and 1901, Grieg's ten-volume, sixty-six-part Lyric Pieces are a marvel of diversity, management and musical imagination.

develops, perhaps even sounding more traditional, with occasional grandiose gestures, before ending in the gentler atmosphere with which it began. No.2 ('Scherzino'), by far the shortest of the set, begins in fanciful, capricious, almost Berliozian fashion, before reaching a theatrical climax that then subsides into the A major sphere of the opening. No.3 ('Air varié') is an uncommon instance of variation form in mature Sibelius and is full of tonal escapades and ornate figurations that recall the imagination of Bach. No.4 ('Der Hirt') maintains the more classical ambience of No.3, developing it into a pastoral realm of shepherds and jovial diversion, with some delightful metrical conflicts between melody and accompaniment as the countryfolk make merry, the piano almost transformed into a mandolin or guitar.

No.5 ('Des Abends') is a powerful impressionistic tone poem in miniature, a nostalgic portrait of the landscape at dusk, while No.6 ('Dialogue') features a strange, progressively more lively, conversation between the two parts. No.7 ('Tempo di minuetto') returns to the more classical, regimented disposition and is almost a mechanical toy, with curt pauses and enigmatic figurations that seem to yearn for a simpler past. No.8 ('Fischerlied') is a fisherman's song which begins with sparing textures that develop more Romantic notions before thinning out again at the close. No.9 ('Ständchen') is a disconcerting serenade that whisks us down to the dramatic melodies and demonstrative rhythms of Spain, before the E-flat largo of No.10 ('Sommerlied') decrees a return home via a series of grand, solemn gestures, with textures and harmonies that are both more identifiably 'Finnish' and, for perhaps the only time in op.58, more akin to Sibelius's usual medium: the orchestra.

As so often in Sibelius's piano output, the ten pieces of op.58 were – contractual obligations and the need to put food on the table aside – a moment to rest and take stock after the labours of an important work (in this case, the *Voces intimae* Quartet). Nonetheless, whatever op.58's undoubted merits, their clarity and ingenuity, they cannot compete with the sense of structure, unity, compression, and laser-like attention to fundamentals that his greatest works were now able to achieve, not least in the looming Fourth Symphony.

The summer of 1909 was mainly occupied with song and piano writing – and, in consequence, by the occasional paying of a bill. However, two other projects – one reptilian, the other avian; one completed, one unfinished – were also to engage him, and both had important implications, musically and thematically, for his next symphony.

First was the composition of some incidental music for Mikael Lybeck's *Ödlan* (*The Lizard*), a symbolist love triangle drama. The music is not unlike Sibelius's work for Maeterlinck's *Pelléas* or Strindberg's *Swanwhite*, though written for only a small string orchestra (usually three violins, viola, cello and double bass), of which Sibelius makes vivid imaginative and expressive use. *Ödlan* is a brilliantly sly and evasive score, creeping and slithering like the creature of its title: fluctuating and psychologically astute, it follows on from the *Voces intimae* Quartet and unmistakeably anticipates Sibelius's Fourth (as well as some sections of *Tapiola*).[109]

---

109 Sibelius completed the *Ödlan* score on 15 October 1909, and it received its premiere, along with that of the play, at the Swedish Theatre in Helsinki on 6 April 1910.

Second, an orchestral song – with a German text – based on Edgar Allan Poe's menacing gothic poem 'The Raven' (1845), an intensely atmospheric work with a highly stylized language brimming with musicality. Making rich and wide-ranging use of a variety of folk, mythological, classical and religious allusions, Poe's poem tells of a troubled lover visited by a mysterious corvid who antagonizes the protagonist with its relentless repetition of the word 'nevermore'.[110]

Clad in their symbolic black, unfussy devourers of carrion, ravens were often thought in Sweden to be the ghosts of murder victims, and in Germany the souls of the damned – so, given Sibelius's penchant for rendezvous between the natural and the supernatural, as well as his relatively pessimistic disposition at the time, it is easy to see what it was about Poe's poem which appealed. Its shadowy evocation of the raven doubtless also reminded him of the bird's fearsome mythical reputation, especially in northern lands, as a trickster, a sinister creative force, as well as the portent of ominous fate and unhappy surprises – dark veins which continued to plague Sibelius, the memory of his throat tumour still as raw and unwelcome as the night-black bird.

When, on 28 August 1909, he logged in his diary the completion of his op.58 piano pieces, he cites Poe's poem: 'Quoth the raven: "Nevermore"', in part perhaps a wry indication of his continued displeasure at writing for the piano but also an opaque foreshadowing of the ending of the Fourth Symphony. In the following year he sketched an orchestral setting of Poe's 'Raven', but the project developed little further in itself; instead some of its music, and much of its melancholic atmosphere,

---

110 The poem made Poe (1809–1849) almost instantly a household name and national celebrity, though the text has been mercilessly parodied ever since.

were to be reabsorbed into the greater, grander project of the new symphonic work.

By the autumn of 1909 Sibelius was ready for another trip, this time not to the metropolitan jungles of London, Paris or Berlin – to urban work, play and temptation – but to the open expanses and harsh attractions of his homeland: to North Karelia, in the far east of Finland. Here would come the catalytic inspiration for the symphony that had been gloomily fermenting inside him.

Hardly a *Kalevala* Disneyland, North Karelia was nonetheless by now a popular, even fashionable, location for writers, artists and composers keen to immerse themselves in the landscape, folklore and mythology of the region – Sibelius himself had visited it nearly two decades earlier for his honeymoon. Keeping things in the family, this time he travelled with his wife's brother, the painter Eero Järnefelt. They journeyed to the Koli mountain, one of the most prominent elevations in the area, just over the lake from where Sibelius had honeymooned, and such was the popularity of the region there was now a hotel there to accommodate them (though it was not, perhaps, up to the lofty standards of the composer's beloved Langham).

Immersing himself in the sun, wind and rain – all varieties of weather were of interest to Sibelius – the composer revelled in the changing (and changeable) conditions of autumn in a landscape he adored: the birch and larch trees just coming into their autumn colours, the light shifting, the air ever freshening, biting shrewdly, nipping and eager. He was, quite literally, in his element, and during this trip he wrote in his diary, 'On Koli! One of the great experiences of my life! Planning "La Montagne".'

The exact identity of 'La Montagne' is unclear, but it seems certain that it is related to the initial ideas for the Fourth Symphony, a work Sibelius closely related to this trip and the extraordinary environments and impressions he experienced there, as autumn began to encroach further upon the landscape. As we saw at the beginning of this chapter, the strange, smooth round ridge of Koli itself is split into several main summits, not high in themselves, but relatively speaking very prominent and affording outstanding panoramic views of the surrounding lakes and forests, with limitless skies and extraordinary sunsets. With this natural vantage point for an artist to set up their easel, Järnefelt was compelled – both on this trip and on several later ones – to create a variety of Koli paintings that perhaps capture its mystery and moods, and links to the Fourth Symphony, far better than any modern photograph.

One (1928) shows the mountain and its landscape in sun and summer: the lake a piercing arctic blue, the sky full of burgeoning clouds, the bare rock covered by occasional green trees that, while a little sparse and bedraggled, offer life and expectation. Another (1917), with a haphazard lonely pine that is a familiar sight in Koli art, depicts distant storm clouds either in advance or retreat, spraying two rainbows onto a thick, fertile carpet of trees beneath the mountain (which itself takes on a riot of colours – blue, green, orange, white – far beyond the habitual grey).

One painting, however, stands out as a moody masterpiece. Dating from 1935, it shows Koli at its bleakest and most unforgiving, with the exposed rounded rock a site of fear and trepidation: sheer falls intimidate, while the brown-grey surface seems like a maze, disorientating and exacting. Two stark trees seem to face off across the stone, glaring at one another, their bare branches tentative arms sparring for the first strike of a fight. Beside them, another tree, with bright dead orange leaves, seems to referee their bout, while also offering a caution – or a threat – from the centre of the canvas. Far below the trees and rock, the healthier pines stretch away in a green blanket that seems to offer little by way of comfort or protection. But the lake and sky beyond the trees are more elusive still, the grey white of water and air merging together in a frightening expanse that becomes an abyss, the watery sun trying to break through but only confusing the elements into a miasma of distortion and whirling uncertainty.

Static, torpid, morose, but full of tense energy, the painting seems to capture much of the ambience of the Fourth Symphony (which Sibelius dedicated to Järnefelt), its low-mood vibes and anxieties, its mixture of inertia and circular woe. One early critic, Elmer Diktonius, referred to Sibelius's work as the '*Barkbröd* Symphony', its bleakness apparently reminiscent of a nineteenth-century famine, when the populace were forced to eat bark bread or starve. Looking at Järnefelt's desolate, lonely painting and comparing it to the symphony, one can see why.

In 1910, the year after his Karelia trip with Eero Järnefelt, Sibelius returned to the region, specifically to Vyborg and Imatra, this time as a local guide for his English friend and supporter Rosa Newmarch, who was pleased with Sibelius's current teetotalism and generally healthier mien. She reported how, during their excursions into the landscape, the composer would stand perilously near the edge of some rapids, desperate to listen to and transcribe the sounds of the water gushing below, with a view to orchestrating their effect. (Later in the year, a powerful storm also seemed to further stimulate the composer's creative mind as he laboured on the symphony.)

Work on the Fourth had begun in earnest during the spring of 1910, Sibelius's increasing preference for isolation and solitude both facilitating its composition and expediting its mood. Advantageously, his own music no longer required his presence to travel the world: increasingly other musicians were promoting and conducting his symphonies and tone poems to progressive acclaim across the continent. To bring in additional money, he still needed to devote time to composing piano miniatures and songs, but his greater focus and concentration after relinquishing alcohol helped immeasurably when it came to switching projects hither and thither: 'one has to combine things great and small: symphonies and songs', he wrote in his diary on 16 May.[111]

The Fourth's composition was far from plain sailing, however. As spring turned to summer, he found the symphony was gaining in focus and clarity, but it was a struggle, too, and his diary is full of doubt and delay, positive reports and frustrating setbacks. Some of the entries take us straight into the mind of a composer, as Sibelius tells himself (and us) what he wants to do: 'Crossed out all the development. Needs more beauty and genuine music! Not sequences and dynamic crescendos, with stereotyped figures ...' (17 August 1910).

A trip to Oslo in the autumn interrupted work, though it saw celebrated performances of his Second Symphony and also included the premieres of the impressionistic tone poem *The Dryad* (see chapter 6) and the lugubrious funeral march *In memoriam* (part of which was played at Sibelius's own funeral in 1957). From Oslo, Sibelius travelled to Berlin, where he was able to reconnect with several friends while forging ahead with

---

111 Three days before, on 13 May, there had been a famous entry to the diary: 'Do not let all these "novelties", triads without thirds, etc. lead you from your work. Anyone can be a "pioneering genius".' Sibelius was clear about the directions his music was – and was not – going to take.

difficult work on the symphony, especially its complex third movement.

By November he was back at Ainola, trying to fathom exactly how he wanted the finale to proceed. By his own admission he wasted several weeks with the Poe 'Raven' project, which he eventually abandoned on 11 December. On Christmas Eve, he noted excitedly in his diary that an elk had crossed Ainola's grounds 'three times!' – a favourable, even providential, sign – and good progress on the symphony continued into the new year.

The Fourth was largely complete by the start of 1911, though a concert tour to Gothenburg and Riga disrupted the (for Sibelius) always difficult final stages of concluding a work, and it was barely finished in time for its first performance, which it received in Helsinki on 3 April 1911, on a programme which included, in its first half, *Nightride and Sunrise*, *In memoriam* and *The Dryad*.

Audience and commentators alike, for all their polite public cries of 'bravo', were respectfully dumbfounded by the extraordinary new work Sibelius had presented them.[112] 'Everything is strange; curious transparent figures float about, speaking a language whose meaning we cannot grasp', wrote one critic. Another, Karl Wasenius, tried to attach a highly Romantic 'Koli Journey' programme to the work (all moonlight and 'the shadows of a

---

112 Aino was a little heartbroken, noting the 'evasive glances, shakes of the head, embarrassed or ironic smiles' around the hall, along with a lack of post-performance visits to the dressing room. Sibelius, however, was positive, knowing the work's inherent strength and originality, and he immediately prepared the symphony for publication (though with some minor changes to the score).

snowstorm'), which Sibelius understandably denied, though it can still prove useful in probing the symphony's persistent and enduring mysteries (even if Wasenius's elucidations seem – as we will see – a little misjudged). Oskar Merikanto was one of only a few who seemed to positively appreciate the new sound world Sibelius was opening up, recognizing the Fourth's highly developed sense of colour and melody.

The Fourth was a risk that, for now at least, did not seem to have paid off. (Though a repeat concert two days later was a sell-out, still the work confused most of its auditors.) It was a stubborn sky of a symphony, an obdurate beast that refused to surrender to popular sensitivities or fashionable expectations. Given the ongoing struggle against the might of Russian oppression, the work seemed to offer little by way of hope or triumph for the subjugated Finns (as the Second had). Despite some diffident messages of courage and optimism, the Fourth was for the most part bleak and uncompromising, a work that would take time to digest and interpret, perhaps still longer to love.

We can hardly be surprised. Shorn of embellishment or concession, Sibelius's Fourth was a challenge and an enigma, presenting a confrontation between classicism and modernism. It had signs of expressionism, avoiding orthodox forms of beauty by distorting the image of reality in order to convey complex inner thoughts and feelings. But it could occasionally evolve into *im*pressionism, evoking the mood and atmosphere of the landscape, while also retaining many classical impetuses, albeit refracted through the Finn's idiosyncratic lenses.

Sonata form exists here but is now of an exclusively Sibelian type, paying only false tribute to its broad principles (in the first movement, a canonical development section becomes dislocated, indistinct; the scherzo has the usual scherzo-trio-scherzo segmenting but with a cold-blooded compression of its last part). The work is scored for a full ensemble, but the orchestra is used in an economical, reallocated fashion more reminiscent of eighteenth- or nineteenth-century chamber music than the swathes of contemporary orchestras with their sheen and clout.[113] It is a work that offers new viewpoints on the classical, reworking its language, forms and idioms within this composer's own methods and perspectives. The Fourth takes us, and conventional tonality, through a dark night of the soul, but it does survive, the inherent interconnectedness of Sibelius's style creating strength out of punishing uncertainty (even if that endurance is one bound to repeated pain).

Although a work of modernism, and a symphony that screamed early twentieth-century angst, Sibelius was clear about the Fourth's isolation within contemporary modes: '[it is] a protest against present-day music', he wrote to Rosa Newmarch. This tension between heritage, progress and modernity is a key feature of the Fourth, written as Arnold Schoenberg was exploding music via his trademark expressionism and atonality,[114] and Sibelius's symphony, for all its own austere alienation and up-to-date innovation, is also a quiet statement of defiance against prevailing threats – from both inside and outside the symphony. Sibelius was never afraid either to shadow tradition

---

113 Something Gustav Mahler also articulated in his later works, and most especially in his great song-cycle symphony *Das Lied von der Erde* (1909), which uses a vast orchestra in a chamber fashion to create some scintillating, and disturbing, effects.

114 In 1909, as Sibelius was developing his first thoughts on the symphony, his Austrian colleague produced three of his most world-shattering monuments to modernism: *Erwartung*, a one-act monodrama of devastating psychological power; the Three Piano Pieces, op.11, in which Schoenberg abandons the last remnants of traditional tonality; and the Five Pieces for Orchestra, op.16, with their bravura display of total chromaticism and overwhelming explorations of violence, the subconscious and burgeoning insanity.

or to modernize, engaging more startling stratagems, but he did so on his own terms, breaking or following rules only if they corresponded to the inner requirements of his subjects.

Many of the frictions in the Fourth are generated by its inventive deployment of an old musical device: the tritone. An awkward, restless musical interval, the tritone (or 'augmented fourth') is a harmonic and melodic dissonance that has a long history, having even been christened 'the devil in music' for its disturbing, agitated qualities. The Middle Ages used, feared and outlawed it; in the Baroque and Classical periods, it became more accepted, but in a specific, controlled way, often as part of a tension-release mechanism. The Romantics and beyond loved to employ its devilish disturbance – Franz Liszt doing so literally as a suggestion of hell in his *Dante* Sonata (1849). Later Richard Wagner used it to signal the brooding tensions at the outset of *Siegfried* (1871), while tritones are a recurring motif in Benjamin Britten's *War Requiem* (1962), with obvious gestures towards the stress and misery of global conflict and the wretched personal struggles within.[115]

For Sibelius, the tritone forms a kind of anxious motto across the whole of the Fourth Symphony, returning to create tension in each movement. It is easy to see what appealed. The human brain is intrinsically equipped to locate harmony and symmetry in music: any dissonance is abnormal and unanticipated, generating a spiritual tremor, a jolt and a shock akin to missing the last step on a staircase. Endow your entire symphony with such tension and surprises and it becomes an emotional maelstrom, a traumatic minefield. As we saw with the Third Symphony, Sibelius was deliberately cautious about how he used certain musical devices,

---

115 And the tritone's perilous dominion didn't end there: Leonard Bernstein (*West Side Story*), the Beatles ('Within You Without You') and Jimi Hendrix ('Purple Haze') all employed it to various effect.

especially those associated with more groundbreaking strands in contemporary music. But this restraint was also a strength, since it allowed such measures to carry even greater power within more ostensibly conservative contexts, and the Fourth Symphony is an exceptional example of this technique.

For all the shock and confusion when the symphony first appeared, which still persists in pockets of bewilderment or fear, the Fourth stands today respected and revered. It is one of the masterworks of the twentieth century, lying at the centre of Sibelius's achievements as a composer of symphonies – as the creator, too, of moods and atmospheres of unmatched grim beauty and unyielding strength, of vast dignity and honest fragility. Moreover, it is a work of colossal mental and emotional insight, a Freud or Jung for orchestra, a symphonic William James, exploring with great penetration the ins and outs of the human soul and psyche, the varieties of its experience, the conscious and unconscious phenomena that make it up and tear it apart. As a symphony it has an exceptional reach, traversing the boundaries between the natural and social sciences, examining the complex and ever-changing relationship between thoughts, feelings, humanity and geography.

Drawing direct correspondences between life and art is always fraught with danger. But, by its composer's own admission, the Fourth is a psychological symphony born of 'solitude and pain'. It is a work of intense introspection that is also a deep immersion into the landscape of the mind and the mind of the landscape.

Loneliness is something far more than an absence, a negative space. It is potentially and debilitatingly stressful and tyrannical. Like a malevolent dictator, it can twist and distort truth, transforming the ordinary into something troubling, spiteful, malicious. Isolation torments the mind, prowling, skulking, ready to pounce and tease, pulling the nerves almost to breaking point before twanging them like a vindictive violin. And loneliness is infinitely patient, biding its time with all the malign resources of Satan's eternity.

This is true for involuntary isolation, but beyond unwilling seclusion and its opposite, deliberate camaraderie, lie many shades of solitude and gregariousness, pleasure and creativity. Enjoying one's own company, as well as needing peace and quiet in order to work (at various stages of the artistic process), can easily turn out of hand, fostering more treacherous opportunities for gloomy periods and depressive episodes. Sibelius needed isolation – it was part of his character and compositional environment – but it could often snowball into something alarming, even dangerous.

Not least as an outsider amid the current trends in music, Sibelius relished his position apart, alone, nurturing and encouraging his role as an 'apparition from the woods'. In his music generally, but especially in the Fourth, we see this remoteness, this detachment, most clearly, and icily, distilled. Sibelius is a skilled, subtle symphonic dramatist, but the overt theatre of Mahler is absent; so too are the sensual evocations of Debussy, the radiant colours of Scriabin, the opulent excesses of Strauss. This is lonely music from a man who, while given to extreme bouts of gregariousness and festive, convivial fun – i.e., municipal drinking – especially in his youth, had become more inward, more pensive, more brooding.

Much of this was, of course, already present in his character, and in the atmosphere and landscapes in which he surrounded himself. Finland, after all, is a northern country given to extremities of light and dark that have, to an extent, mapped themselves on the national psyche, so it is only natural that this almost archetypal modern Finn should present both aspects of the nation's soul. It is also normal that he should become gloomier and more introspective as he reached middle age – it is a common experience. Our consciousness of our own transience, however present in our youth, becomes more vital, more acute, more pressing, in both physical and metaphysical terms, and Sibelius's brush with death via his throat tumour was a sharp reminder of his own mortality.

The separation and seclusion that Sibelius acknowledged had forged the Fourth Symphony account for its profoundly searching nature, its quest for answers that it knows are unlikely to come. The music seems to mutiny against intention, against direction, against predictability. The first movement is like a vast prologue to nothingness, wary (as well it might be) of A minor, allowing only glimpses of A major; the second loosens into F major, that pastoral key, before plummeting into languorous brooding; the third, too, ends in desolate evaporation. The finale tries to summon a conventional cadence with which to close, but it can only manage an anxious armistice with its own agony. The cycle of pain is set to continue, an orbiting obituary.

It is this sense of vacuum, oblivion, paradox and circularity that informs much of the Fourth's structure, tension and meaning. Its concepts are cosmic, gigantic, contemporary, expanded to almost limitless realms, yet it all occurs within a comparatively constricted frame, almost classical in its spatio-temporal dimensions. The Fourth exploits and engineers the passage of time, confusing our sense of past, present and future, eliminating the steady progress of the Newtonian clock into a much more frightening and disorientating relativity. The Fourth manipulates our comprehension of space too. At times it is immense and open, a huge landscape that can oppress in its limitlessness. But then it can suddenly crush and suffocate, trapping us in a prison of our own making.

Here we can witness the intimate connection between psychology and landscape that the Fourth explores. Landscape, and the weather or climate associated with it, is not merely the visible physical features of the terrain – its trees, lakes, rocks, hills, rivers, clouds – but our relationship with it. However wild or unspoiled the landscape, it is a cultural product. It is far more than the ecological and meteorological setting; it is our experience of it, our contact with the wind and rain, soil and stone, as well as the gods and monsters we have associated with the world that surrounds us, in both its belligerent and benign states.

Ted Hughes's *Crow* (1970), a devastating cycle of stylistically experimental poems written in the aftermath of his wife Sylvia Plath's suicide, explores closely integrated cultural narratives that demonstrate the complexity of our relationship to landscape and environment, one bound up in a dense mythical and psychological past. Guru, scavenger, demon, misfit, survivor – the poet's charlatan crow often echoes the trickster raven that haunted much of the hinterland of Sibelius's Fourth Symphony: sinister energies of nature that point towards and expose our own inner turbulence and capacity to endure. In some sense, too, Sibelius's music, like Hughes's verse, seeks to break down, to dissolve, the frontiers between nature and humanity, and in so doing to reveal the possibilities of their intimate interaction, to show how the tensions between art, intellect, legend and landscape can act as a creative, positive, force.

Eero Järnefelt's paintings, and Sibelius's music, show how Koli and Karelia were becoming firmly established as part of a nascent Finnish iconography with deep political aims. Yet, more personally, their art demonstrates how the original landscape can be transformed into expressions of our own innermost thoughts and emotions. Just as Lear's mental agony and aggression are mirrored by the desolate panoramas and tempestuous weather of his environment,[116] so too this symphony exhibits a complex interface between landscape, mind and music. And it is one without definable boundaries: it is all liminal space, peripheral time.

Sibelius's Fourth is more than, as Karl Wasenius had it, a programmatic description of a journey to Koli, depicting its topography and climatological conditions. It is an intense and abstract sonic expression of being within, or contemplating, such a place. As such, much of the symphony's tension is accordingly generated through its exploration of the battle between internal and external landscapes, of exterior and interior stimuli. Sibelius's Fourth is a conceptual manifestation of thoughts, feelings, emotions closely linked to and aligned with the outside world, existing in a dense, fraught, multifaceted relationship.

The warmer passages of the work – the start of the second and fourth movements, say – offer an escape; a brightening; extroversion, not introspection; perhaps coming close to pleasant feelings of travelling through the landscape (or at least happy memories of it). But for the most part, Sibelius's Fourth Symphony is a frenetic exhibition of static emotional turmoil.

---

116 'Blow winds and crack your cheeks! Rage, blow! / You cataracts and hurricanoes, spout / Till you have drenched our steeples, drowned the cocks!' (*King Lear*, III.iii.1–3)

Yet its harshness and austerity, its agonized sense of despair and brooding contemplation, is also a curious consolation, a reminder of pain that both encourages our empathy and acknowledges our own psyche's private suffering. We are not alone, even at our most lonely.

Like Ted Hughes's *Crow*, Sibelius's Fourth, which has its own corvid links, moves us to love by connecting us to anguish, the great arch of grief in the third movement a bond to frigid and unsettling discomfort. Listening to the music, we feel closer to Sibelius, to art, to ourselves, to the earth and to those around us. We share the composer's pain, visiting a communal well of woe that paradoxically makes us feel better, dispersing the torment and triggering feelings of security, reassurance and belonging.

Just as the Fourth Symphony is itself a confrontation between classicism and modernism, between the now and the then, the melancholy mood of the music also helps spark our memories into modes of nostalgia, activating positive recollections of the past that can provide further solace and serenity in the present.

For all its notorious bleakness, Sibelius's Fourth is actually a psychological comfort blanket.

Symphony No.4 in A minor, op.63

1. Tempo molto moderato, quasi adagio.

Whatever the differences between the Third and Fourth Symphonies – clarity versus opacity; linearity versus circularity

– concision and concentration remain Sibelius's guiding lights: this is a work with a brusque application of its musical material, its compressions frequently removing transitions altogether in the symphony's intrepid quest for inner unity. The huge range of orchestral detachments, the score shifting in chamber-like subdivisions of instrumental groups, plus the variety of speeds the symphony presents, could make for a highly fragmented work were it not for the intimate, even disturbing, affiliation between so many of the harmonies and motifs.

Written in a sonata form that toys with notions of custom and conventionality, the first movement constantly threatens to sway from the traditional path only to maintain a shrewdly recognizable adherence to formal orthodoxy. Nonetheless, for all its sly loyalty, the condensing of material as well as the general hazy ambience make the changes between sections often very difficult to distinguish.

The lower strings snarl the opening notes: C–D–F sharp–E (which should sound 'as harsh as fate', claimed their composer). This initial motif is, at once, an instance of the tritone, that anxious interval and *diabolus in musica* that will dominate the movement (and the entire work) in various malignant guises, its disquieting influence so crucial to the symphony's tense atmosphere but also operating as a crucial binding idea. By beginning the work this way, Sibelius plays with our sense of symphonic time and space: the uneasy interval, followed by the introduction of gradually lengthening notes, distorts our perspectives, like a black hole exerting gravitational time dilation on a neighbouring body.

Bassoons offer their own primeval growls, and in this elemental environment arises the forlorn main theme from a solo cello, offering the words of a spell (or appeals for help), which are slowly enveloped by a grim, equivocating texture that refuses to locate any fixed harmonic status. This is a drifting landscape of indeterminate horizons and puzzling movement. It is bleak and barren, gaunt and grey. Even the main theme itself hardly feels like the principal subject, its attempts to establish A minor vague, indistinct, helpless. If we feel we are going forward, we know not where: it is a journey into nothingness.

The mist and fog are occasionally (once in the exposition and again in the recapitulation) penetrated by dazzling beams on the horns, Brucknerian beacons from a brass lighthouse, though offered less for navigational aid than mere hope. But their signals are interrupted, undermined by great tracks of dissonance towards F sharp. This is the fateful subsidiary theme which proceeds to rugged slabs of sound from the heavy brass reverberating like the heft and weight of mountains, their groans and cries eventually dwindling away into nebulous space. In the development, trembling strings shiver and quiver, their translucent notes wandering like Samuel Beckett's itinerant vagrants, and with spectral weeping rising up from the woodwind.

Slowly, as a contracted reprise emerges on high violins, we realize we have returned to the initial musical terrain: we have been moving in circles in the mist (was ever a sonata-form recapitulation as sombre as this?). The brass again try to offer courage with impressions of idyllic nature, but they seem now only an enigmatic provocation, and indeed the music develops into ominous proclamations of expressionistic despair. Unable to continue, the double basses offer gloomy grumbles as the movement's coda floats nervously into the void.

2. *Allegro molto vivace.*

After the slow, ambiguous, suffocating first movement, the scherzo initially offers life-giving oxygen, a playful F–B tritone from the oboe supported by F major violins. The symphony has, it seems, not only begun to thaw, but to warm up. We are breathing a pastoral air, though for all the difference in colour and mood, we should not be too self-assured, since the material is intimately derived from that which ended the first movement. This is a new harmonic context, but the motifs are enduring.

The consequences of this soon become apparent as the scherzo's trio section (the symphony again avowing its faith in many features of the classical tradition) begins to darken the atmosphere, fretful storm clouds forming in the sky or mind. Like a sneering phantom, the symphony's distinctive tritone figure begins to stress again its anxious curse, now with a ferocious coercion. What had started almost as a good-humoured waltz tableau, bustling through its scenes, is suddenly uncovered as a scam, the tempo ruthlessly halved to present a brutal panorama akin to Bruegel's *Triumph of Death* (c.1562), with its pitiless army of skeletons and blackened, desolate landscape.

Sibelius's leafless trees and mental shipwrecks are ambiguous, bewildering, a betrayal of the opening material, which has been savagely recontextualized in a brutal new light, the tritone exerting its malevolent power to transform. The scherzo is now unable to properly return, and we are offered only a fleeting, almost inadvertent, glimpse on the first violins of the dancing pastoral opening before three soft taps on the timpani cut it dead.

The compression of the material is vindictively jubilant, a distorted echo crushed out of shape by an inscrutable, depressive force – Sibelius's ever-growing powers of symphonic contraction on glorious, dynamic display.

3. Il tempo largo.

The third movement is not only the emotional centre of the Fourth Symphony, it is the soul of Sibelius.

It is a highly original movement which presents its theme in a gradual, quasi-improvisatory fashion, not so much coy as evasive, never looking us squarely in the face. A severe ritual in C-sharp minor (a key which is also only slowly divulged), the movement is intense, sparsely textured, a slow tread of gloomy meditation: indeterminate, questing, probing for answers – a secret? – that never seem to come. Trying to examine exactly how the material interacts becomes immensely difficult, since everything is ambiguously (but logically) controlled by the innermost spirit of the themes. It is a magnificent Sibelian paradox.

Fragments in the woodwind usher us into this lonely, frightening world, transient motifs drifting in hesitant isolation. Amid these eerie threads, the horns seek the main thematic idea, as do the strings, but it will not reveal itself. Everything is detached, too, from any tonal hub, directionless, navigating zones of opaque appeal.

The three main arcs of the movement become gradually more integrated and characterized by that familiar Sibelian pulse of forward momentum which in due course allows a vehement escalating theme to sing out on the strings, proclaiming mournfully ecstatic music reminiscent of Wagner's *Parsifal* (another lonely spiritual journey). Amid all the mental anguish, this seems a wretched, heartbreaking cry for help in the darkness. The secret is out, but is it one we want to hear?

Fortissimo trombones proclaim the tritone motif we heard at the very start of the work in a devastating climax from which the symphony can only subside into a desolate return to the fragments and emptiness that began the movement. A lugubrious coda, it is full of anaesthetized alienation and trauma trapped in that most funereal of keys, C-sharp minor (and, indeed, the Fourth Symphony's largo was one of the pieces played during Sibelius's funeral in September 1957). The seismic struggle has ended in defeat.

4. Allegro.

In formal terms, the finale is a sonata-rondo, and its classical heritage indicates some sense of deliverance – but it is a temporary peace, and a truce of this world, not any broader eschatological victory.

C-sharp minor, which ended the slow movement in such forsaken fashion, now launches the finale, too, but in a frenetic, almost euphoric manner, a perilous wide arc on the strings creating an atmosphere of superficial anticipation and enthusiasm (the haunting tritone motif now seemingly diminished to a mere ornament). Busy motifs twinkle on a glockenspiel, and invigorating gestures sound from the solo cello. Everything seems as light-hearted and fancy-free as the opening of the scherzo, but have we learned our lessons from the corrosive developments that movement underwent? Is this the dangerous manic upswing after a period of horrific depression?

The movement tries to convince us otherwise. The strings gather a sober resilience: the tempo increases, the motifs stretch, and the symphony tries to persuade us that it will acquire a resolution to its problematic persona. But, bit by bit, the finale becomes more harmonically ambiguous, the mists of earlier movements regrouping. These vapours begin to infiltrate the engine of the symphony, generating an underlying strain that it seems initially able to shake off by returning to the movement's opening material, but which then becomes even more destabilizing, indeed threatening to rip the machine asunder.

The movement, and the symphony, have become a fierce clash between the two key centres of A and E-flat (a tritone apart, of course), each of which, within a mesmerizingly tense construction, tries to gain tonal (and therefore ultimate) power. A horn chorale, with a swaying ostinato accompaniment beneath (hyperventilating for strings) is followed by a strange passage of syncopated chromaticism – all of which originate in Sibelius's abandoned sketches for an orchestral song, 'The Raven', setting Edgar Allan Poe in German.

And the all-black bird, *Corvus corax*, the trickster of countless myths and legends, will indeed try to have the last malevolent laugh, for it plays a crucial role not only in the decisive climax of the symphony but in its astonishing coda. The anguished strings are disrupted by a sequence of woodwind bird calls: a remonstrating sing-song solo flute is interrupted three times by a frightening repeated pattern from an oboe, its three-note figuration matching Poe's raven's mocking, incessant cries of 'nevermore!'[117] (It was the same rhythm to be found in both the Swedish word *förbi* – in Viktor Rydberg's translation, where Sibelius encountered Poe's poem – and the German that he was to employ for his song: 'nie du Tor'.)

The strings feebly endure these avian taunts and hostilities for a time before sinking into stoic resignation. It is less despair

---

117 Of all the fine recordings of this great symphony, none seem to realize the protest and terror of this flute/oboe progression quite like that from Sakari Oramo and the CBSO (on the Erato label).

than a kind of depressive exhaustion, the strings alone repeating inscrutable chords. Marked 'mezzo forte dolce', the work ends in a pitiless, unpretentious A minor cadence. Both tender and severe, it is one of the most perplexing, unsettling, but ultimately courageous conclusions to any symphony.

A minor – and perhaps the whole notion of the tonal system – have won through in the end, but at a devastating cost.

Sibelius's Fourth is an immensely personal symphony, charting mental anguish and existential torment in a remarkable way, while also considerably enriching and expanding its composer's aesthetics. It is gloomy, wintry, an unadorned and inhospitable landscape, its skies covered by endless forbidding clouds. Its chill goes right down through the bone and into the soul. Slowly, we discover how psychology and philosophy (of various hues), mingling among the musical notes as private afflictions, are then expanded into planetary and galactic terms, as the individual considers its standing within a vast, unfriendly cosmos, a place of callous indifference.

But this is not the symphony's totality – a caliginous realm of permanent night and hopelessness. We have to probe a little further. For all its darkness and despair, this symphony has a discreet dignity and understated courage, a lilting self-confidence, to go with its audacity and austerity. By allowing its darkness to work on us, we gain in empathy, understanding better our own unique and energetic status in the endless immensity of time and space.

The quiet cadence of A minor, the work's final gesture, signals the affirmative consequence of a long and unpredictable symphonic argument which stretched the recognized hierarchies of attraction, stability and direction in sound to the very limit. Ultimately, Sibelius's Fourth Symphony celebrates and confirms the miraculously organized and interlinked nature of classical tonality, whatever parochial or ephemeral disruptions try to overthrow it. By the same token, listening to this enormously powerful symphony – which is perhaps Sibelius's finest single achievement – we too can appreciate our own positive and meaningful position in an equivocal, unstable universe that is nonetheless organic and interconnected, a circle of eternity.

Sibelius once claimed there was 'nothing of the circus' about his Fourth – and he was right. It is reality and truth, grim and exquisite.

Chapter Nine

Metamorphosis:
The Bard, Luonnotar & *The Oceanides*

As a sensitive boy growing up in an age of rapid industrialization and urbanization, Sibelius was deeply attached to and impressed by the natural world around him. According to childhood friends, he could often be found wandering alone, grasping a butterfly net or holding a tin for flowers and stones: nature was what he wanted to capture, to encapsulate, to take home with him to the usually much less appealing town- and cityscapes. He was in thrall to the sights and sounds the living world presented to him: the dance of light on water, the particular texture of a tree's green, the iridescence of a damselfly's wing, the buzzing of bees, the sonorous calls of large migratory birds. As he matured and turned to music as his means of personal expression, nature continued to inform and inspire him, providing a rich source to feed his imagination – not least in his tone poems, where forests, sunrises, swans, snow and ice pervade the scores.

Between his Fourth and Fifth Symphonies Sibelius wrote, along with numerous other works, a triptych of tone poems, unintended as such but now forming a three-part meditation on art, identity and our relationship with the natural world. They explore the value and importance of the creative imagination in a situation of flux and change, as a means to penetrate and explore the mystical, the spiritual, even the potentially supernatural, in nature. Of immense evocative power, these tone poems investigate the complexion and character of the self, especially the inventive self, within the shifting contexts of the cosmos (both local and universal), forming a nexus of art, environment and religion.

The Bard, *Luonnotar* and *The Oceanides* transcend the engagement with nature Sibelius surveyed in *Pohjola's Daughter* and *Nightride and Sunrise*. These new works are more primarily concerned with the mustering, the sonic congregation, of fundamental forces of nature, exploring a concept of nature not simply as a symbol but as a mesmeric, hypnotic, enveloping state of being (something they all share with the Fourth Symphony).

And such metamorphoses, surpassing the merely figurative, have implications. As humans, when we place nature on the pages of art, we are not commanding or even managing nature; we are a part of it, a feature of its constant and provisional state of fluidity and instability – conditional on, and answerable to, the oscillating dramas of forces greater than ourselves. In our own age of climate change and ecological pressure, Sibelius's music should surely serve to inspire our nobler actions with regard to the landscapes and phenomena that meant so much to him.

The summer of 1911 saw domestic expansions for Sibelius. His eldest daughter, Eva, left school and became affianced to Arvi Henrik Paloheimo, and Sibelius composed a short étude for piano as an engagement present.[118] Meanwhile, another daughter, Heidi, their sixth and last, arrived on 20 June, while renovations to Ainola were taking place – both to accommodate the growing family and to give Sibelius more privacy in which to compose. The house's original architect, Lars Sonck, had been consulted about adding a second floor, and by September Sibelius had a new upstairs study, where he began work on developing his earlier *Press Celebration Music* (1899) into the first *Scènes historiques* (another set would follow in the coming months), along with a number of vocal works.

As ever, however, he was restless to travel. A brief trip to Berlin in the autumn led to Paris, where extravagant living (though *sans vin*) meant he frequently had to downgrade his accommodation, eventually ending up at the Hôtel Danube (which he felt a fire trap staffed by waiters that looked like delinquents from a Zola novel). Musically, he worked on arranging his early choral piece *Rakastava* for string orchestra, timpani and triangle, while also attending concerts of pieces by Stravinsky and Dukas. There was also the small matter of a performance of Strauss's *Salome* (1905), which simultaneously enthralled and appalled him: he wrote to Aino protesting that, although he hoped he was not old-fashioned, he was nonetheless

---

118 Op.76/2. A minute of furious delight and charm, it is an unassuming little marvel. Eva and Arvi would marry two years later, on 10 June 1913, Jean and Aino's twenty-first wedding anniversary, and dozens of guests would descend on Ainola for the festivities.

fairly aghast at the fruity stage action (but still fascinated by his German colleague's masterly orchestration).

Back home on his birthday, Sibelius's work on *Rakastava* and the second *Scènes historiques* continued into 1912 and, soon after, a flattering invitation to become professor of composition in Vienna arrived. He mulled it over for a few weeks, but on 1 March turned it down with a telegram to the conservatoire citing his need for independence and time to compose as well as his own perceived pedagogic shortcomings. The offer was a welcome recognition of his status and ability (even if Richard Strauss and Max Reger had already declined the position), and the day after he rejected heading to Vienna, Sibelius noted his true direction in his diary: 'forged new ideas. A symphony V [5]. A symphony VI [6]: Luonnotar! Remains to be seen if these enterprises will occur. Orchestral difficulties worse than ever.' The immediate future, however uncertain, was tentatively charted.

'A new symphonic mission plays in my thoughts', he noted in mid-April, while simultaneously doubting the success and achievements of his earlier essays in the medium. Again and again he sought solace in his vocation as a composer of symphonic fantasies, explicitly *not* symphonies: in part to free himself from the burden of expectation but also as an indication of the new kind of symphonies he was creating (which would find their ultimate expression in the Seventh). Encouragement, inspiration and self-criticism always collaborated in Sibelius's head, tense artistic forces in anxious creative partnership. He knew the deeper, wider value and importance of what he was doing, along with the difficulty many composers had in having their work understood in their own lifetime, but he was crippled by misgivings, seeing himself at times as an 'unimportant talent', but nevertheless knowing the strength of his overwhelming, uncontrollable vocation.

Sibelius also knew that the balance between tradition and innovation was a precarious one, not least for someone of his psychological constitution. He recognized he didn't have the audacity of a Schoenberg (who, of course, had his own set of self-doubts) and never felt he could construct a drastic new formal theory of composition himself. He admired Schoenberg and was often very intrigued by his works, even if he always remained reluctant to practice such comprehensive revolutions in musical language and style himself.

Nonetheless, the Fourth Symphony had shown just how radical he could be, and, during a creative flash in the summer of 1912, he wrote the Three Sonatinas, op.67, for piano. Apparently innocuous, they contain some of his finest and most challenging work for the instrument. Hovering between major and minor keys, the first of them, in F-sharp minor, has an elusive opacity with a curious modernist employment of register and sonic spacing. Wanting extra harmonic support, it is a strange realm of aphorism and terse truths. The second, in E, is thematically stouter and more down to earth, with lush melodies reminiscent of the national-Romantic Sibelius of the 1890s, but with his more recent thinner textures in place to indicate this is no regression. The third, in B-flat minor, is shorter, self-conscious and more serious, exploring the clutches of darkness and death while also yearning to escape into frivolity and freedom.

In September, he visited Britain for a fourth time, renewing old acquaintances – though he was unable to stay at his favourite luxury hotel, the Langham, since it was fully booked, and he had to slum it at the Richelieu down the road. At the Birmingham Festival on 1 October, he conducted his Fourth on a programme with Delius's *Sea Drift* (1906), in its composer's presence, which also saw Elgar give the premiere of his cantata *The Music Makers* (1912). Delius found the Elgar dull and noisy but was captivated by the new directions Sibelius was taking his music, even if he also felt some of the symphony a little sketchy. Many of the critics, and the audience, were as hostile and perplexed as their peers had been in Finland and would be in America – though a good number were entranced. Ernest Newman astutely recognized the extraordinary interplay of memory and vision in the Fourth, along with the beauties of its strange orchestral colours and harmonies, while also noting it would take time for the work to become comprehensible to most audiences.

While in the English Midlands, Sibelius's old friend Rosa Newmarch gave him a guided tour of Stratford-upon-Avon: he lodged on Chapel Street, in a quaint half-timbered hotel right next door to the site of Shakespeare's house, New Place, and also visited the playwright's grave in Holy Trinity Church. This was a sacred space for Sibelius, the final resting place of a writer who meant so much to him and to whom he would return for one of his last and greatest works, *The Tempest*. He kept the entry ticket to the church in his desk drawer at Ainola as a cherished memento of the occasion.

As he stood over Shakespeare's grave in Stratford, Sibelius's thoughts might have drifted towards his next major orchestral project, a tone poem fittingly called *Barden* (*The Bard*), a work with its origins in the 'Duke Magnus' song from the op.57 set seen in the previous chapter.[119] That number was set to an Ernst Josephson text, but early on during his work on *The Bard*, Sibelius's literary inspiration shifted back to his old favourite, Johan Ludvig Runeberg, and his lyric poem 'The Bard', which tells of a Nordic singing hero whose music captivates all until one day winter ages him. It is a poem consumed by art, nature, mysticism and a benign resignation at the fleeting wonders of the earth: in short, pure Sibelius. (Oddly, though characteristically, the composer would later deny any association with the Runeberg text which appears to have inspired the tone poem, suggesting instead that *The Bard* had links with the world of the *Edda*, Ossianic poems, and ancient Scandinavian ballads from the age of the Vikings. For modern listeners, surely, they can all help inform the various meanings of the work.)

Written over the winter of 1912/13, a first, single-movement, version was premiered on 27 March, but not long after this performance Sibelius reconceived the work as a two-part fantasy, 'intrada and allegro', then as an orchestral triptych,[120] before eventually returning – after *Luonnotar* – to redevelop the highly compressed single-movement definitive form which premiered on 9 January 1916. Whether business or aesthetic pressure led him to expand – and then tighten – the piece is unclear: certainly it might have been commercially impracticable in its shorter form, and his publisher Breitkopf wrote to suggest it might be better as the introduction to a larger work, such as a suite. Sibelius, too, might have spotted further potential in the score, leading to its enlargement, before a hasty retreat into

---

119 At another time, *The Bard* seems to have had the working title 'Der Ritter und die Najade' – 'The Knight and the Naiads', referring to mystical aquatic elves that evoke the Oceanides, nymph daughters of the marine Titans Oceanus and Tethys, and which would form the basis of another, imminent, Sibelian tone poem.

120 '1. *The Bard*. 2. *The Knight and Elf*. 3. *Rondo*.'

concision and economy, embracing his original vision. Alas, the multi-movement version no longer survives, and we are left to imagine what it might have sounded like.

In its final form, *The Bard* is one of Sibelius's shortest tone poems, economical and epigrammatic, suggestive of Webern, with a refined, reserved character, an inward nobility, elegiac and poetic. The scoring is sublime and irresistible, and although it bears no direct connection to the Runeberg poem, the presence of a quasi-obbligato harp carries associations with Orpheus and other musical bards, as does the generally reflective musical atmosphere, which mirrors in sound the poet's text.

Although perhaps less well known than its colleagues, *The Bard* is a precious addition to the rostrum of Sibelius's tone poems, a thoughtful and poignant work full of subtle colours and a glorious architecture: despite being assembled and taken apart several times, the final version bears no trace of its fickle construction. It is a haunting, whispered sphere, with perspectives near and far, implied, then denied, its references muttered, mouthed, suggested, suddenly revealed before being swiftly hidden.

The Bard hovers in a strange space, neither of this world nor the one beyond, outside the grip of time's flow.

After the first version of *The Bard* premiered in March 1913, Sibelius's attention turned irritably to a Danish ballet commission: *Scaramouche*, a project which vexed him. Not only did he feel the scenario inferior, a barefaced replication of better works, but the text was repeatedly changed even after he had begun composition. He came to regret agreeing to the project – at one point (on 21 June) smashing the Ainola telephone in anger against a wall after an argument concerning its progress – and by the end of September he would tell his diary that the work was deeply tormenting him. It was eventually completed by Christmas.

Scaramouche has never gained common approval or support – which is a shame. Not only does it contain some fascinating music, with links to both the aborted 'Raven' orchestral song and Fourth Symphony, but it offers an insight into how an operatic Sibelius might have evolved (the score makes extensive use of neo-Wagnerian leitmotifs). Written for a pantomime with a fairly dreadful plot (involving a ball and the seduction of a wife by a deformed dwarf), the music for *Scaramouche* is nonetheless distinctly Sibelian: there are turbulent, alluring dances, sinister brass, and tender, haunting woodwinds – all of which cohere brilliantly across the score's hour-long span, but which might have been better used in a more worthwhile or profound work.

It was during the arduous, frustrating work on *Scaramouche* in 1913, however, that Sibelius began his next two tone poems: in the summer, *Luonnotar*; in the autumn and following winter/spring, *The Oceanides*. *The Bard* had been, in part, a rumination on the lonely personage of the creative artist, its introspection a reflection of the (as Sibelius saw it) inevitable isolation a composer faced. This sense of creativity as a desolate, secluded activity was to be straightaway considered again in *Luonnotar*, which depicts the nature spirit from the opening of the *Kalevala*. Sibelius had earlier contemplated exploring this in musical terms when working on *Pohjola's Daughter* a few years before, as well as in other, even earlier, projects, such as the Väinämöinen opera. Luonnotar was a figure who had long fascinated him.

This time, however, a suitable invitation allowed Luonnotar to, at last, have wings: the Three Choirs Festival, in Gloucester, England, requested a new piece for the great Finnish soprano Aino Ackté – a legendary singer Sibelius had somewhat forsaken when he abandoned the setting of 'The Raven' which he had promised her. It was the right bait at the right time (though he didn't need much of an excuse to put off work for *Scaramouche*).

Whatever the earlier unsuccessful/reconsidered Luonnotar plans, or the Three Choirs commission, *Luonnotar*'s key musical origins lie in an embryonic eight-bar sketch made at a bar in Berlin in May 1909, and given to a friend as a keepsake, but which he recalled as the figure and its tale continued to haunt his imagination. We can be glad that it did, for this is one of Sibelius's greatest works: part orchestral song, part tone poem, 'a strange eagle from primeval space', as Aino put it, it is an entirely original masterpiece of intrigue and devastating beauty, with a synthesis of ingenious orchestral sonorities and an audacious, tremendously severe vocal line. This latter feature, with the voice occupying a very wide range, is what makes the work so fiendishly demanding, so merciless, despite its relative brevity (around nine or ten minutes): sometimes within a single word, the singer is required to make jumps and drops of over an octave.

Luonnotar was provisionally finished on 24 August, and its world premiere took place in Gloucester's Shire Hall on 10 September 1913. The composer wasn't present for a vast programme which included Hans Sachs's act-three 'Wahn' Monologue from Wagner's *Die Meistersinger* (forming an intriguing parallel to *Luonnotar*'s discussions of creativity and suffering); a Mozart piano concerto (with no less than the seventy-seven-year-old Camille Saint-Saëns as soloist); and the final scene from Richard Strauss's *Salome*, along with works by Debussy, Dvořák, Arthur Sullivan and Herbert Brewer.

Ackté – who was enthusiastic to Sibelius in commending the brilliance of his work – obtained six curtain calls after *Luonnotar*, which was generally well received, *The Times* in particular praising Sibelius's imagination and clarity of line. Nonetheless, the oddity and difficulty of its stark vocal part perplexed many – the *Musical Times*, for one, disliked the indecipherable text but were more intrigued by the orchestral textures, which are indeed splendid, conceding that, as with so many of the Finn's works, repeated listening of the piece would bear much fruit.

The text itself is Sibelius's own adaptation of the allegorical creation myth from the first runo of the *Kalevala*. Luonnotar is the Spirit of Nature or Daughter of the Air, living a lonely existence in the heavens before coming down to earth and roving the seas as the Mother of Waters for seven centuries. A great storm unexpectedly develops, and a distraught Luonnotar calls to Ukko, the Father of the Heavens and Chief of the Gods, for his assistance, which he sends in the form of a seabird. Luonnotar lifts her knee out of the water to create a nest for the bird among the waves, but her leg becomes hot and trembles, pitching the eggs into the water, where their shells shatter. It is from the fragments of one egg, however, that come the celestial bodies: the upper fragment becomes the sky; the white, the moon with its lustrous light; the yolk, the sun, which brightens the frozen terrain beneath; the mottled specks of the shell, the stars in heaven.

To a degree, *Luonnotar* is typical of Sibelius's tone poems: exploring myth and nature, it is cast in a single, organically cohesive movement, evocatively scored. Yet there is something exceptionally, distinctively, powerful about *Luonnotar*, perhaps matched only by *Tapiola* in its peculiar intensity. Sibelius's music is profoundly original, using only standard symphonic instrumentation but with it conjuring up a unique sound world that is supplemented by a disturbing, demanding use of the soprano voice: it is an immensely difficult work to sing, a challenge for even the finest artists.

By giving his titular character – unlike, say, in *Lemminkäinen* or *The Bard* – a literal voice, the Sibelius of *Luonnotar* risked undermining the fruitful ambiguity so much of his music enjoyed. There was a danger that words would restrict the meaning, scope and potential of the tone poem's philosophical and thematic landscapes. And yet, of course, Sibelius's songs and choral works – not least *Kullervo* – had been only enriched by their texts. Like them, *Luonnotar* triumphs in its dark evocation of mystery, creation and despair, with the added frisson of a voice deepening both the drama and obscurity. In part this is due to the inscrutability Sibelius gave the sung text: he had twisted the *Kalevala* phrases to fit music to such an extent that much of the text is unintelligible when heard performed, even for Finnish speakers, the words becoming mere sounds that are features of the overall sonic fabric.

Luonnotar continues to invite analysis. Beyond the more obvious literary-mythic narrative, the work also suggests metaphorical connections with gender, birth, identity, nature, purpose, pain (the ominous, enigmatic ending perhaps a premonition of the First World War, which began the following year), and the whole strenuous business of human creativity and artistic activity. As with *Orfeo*, *Capriccio*, *Ein Heldenleben*, the *Hammerklavier* Sonata and the *Well-Tempered Clavier*, one of the key subjects of *Luonnotar* is musical creation itself, and this unusual tone poem for voice and orchestra is an intricate, unfixed allegory for inspiration, composition and the laborious forging of art from and in the world.

In late August 1913, only a few days after finishing *Luonnotar*, Sibelius received a new commission, via Horatio Parker, an American composer and music professor, from affluent New England patrons Carl Stoeckel and Ellen Battell Stoeckel. For $1,000, they desired from the Finn a new tone poem, not more than fifteen minutes in length, to be premiered at the summer musical festival held on the Stoeckels' estate in Norfolk, Connecticut, the following June.

The piece that was to become *The Oceanides* (Oceanides are water spirits in Greek mythology) had its origins in motifs from the third movement of a proposed orchestral suite,[121] but initial work was delayed by continuing protracted progress on the detested *Scaramouche* project. In the New Year 1914, Sibelius set off for Berlin, where he was at last able to undertake significant work on the new tone poem, as well as attend a number of important concerts (though he just missed a performance of his own violin concerto). These included Schoenberg's first chamber symphony and Bruckner's and Mahler's Fifth Symphonies, all of which intrigued him but which frequently destabilized his own vision for the possibilities of the symphony (his next, *his* Fifth, would accordingly take some time to achieve its definitive state).

Realizing he needed to be at home in his 'cell', as he called it, at Ainola in order to properly concentrate, in February Sibelius returned to Finland. There, *Oceanides* progressed, and a preliminary score was sent to America in early April

---

121 We have the second and third movements, which were premiered by Osmo Vänskä and the Lahti Symphony in September 2002, but the first's location is a mystery. It might have been lost; it might have ended up on the fire; it might exist as an entirely different piece (possibly even *The Bard*). Perhaps one day it will resurface.

(later in the month, Stoeckel's offer was expanded to invite Sibelius to conduct the premiere himself, for which he would be handsomely compensated). Now known as the Yale version, since it eventually found its way into that university's library, the preliminary score refines and expands the length, harmony and overall orchestral coloration of the ur-suite, bringing in motifs for strings and woodwind that resemble the waves of an ocean, as well as reordering many of the musical ideas.

Nonetheless, there remained a considerable space for this aquatic music to voyage through before it reached its final, much more spacious and oceanic, form. This was because, almost immediately after he had sent the score to America, Sibelian doubt and reservation set in, and significant revisions were made. Very significant revisions: he almost entirely recomposed the piece, discarding much new material, frequently reverting the ideas to their original suite order and expanding them, as well as integrating these concepts more closely to one another, toning down the vibrancy of the percussion and changing the main key from a hesitant D flat to a much more beaming and assertive D major.[122]

After weeks of compositional bustle and domestic mayhem, vividly described by Aino in her diary, as Sibelius struggled to complete the score in time, in mid-May he set off for the New World aboard the great ocean liner *Kaiser Wilhelm II* (the same boat that had taken Gustav Mahler back to America for the final

---

122 As well as the overall effect, there were more practical reasons too: in D major it is much easier and more rewarding for string instrumentalists to play fast and with open strings; D flat is tighter, more closed, and as such it is much harder to achieve a clear tone. For some, such as Sibelius's great compatriot and fellow symphonist, Kalevi Aho (1949–), although the change from D flat made the work easier to play, it also removed some of the inherent mystery and veiled dignity from *The Oceanides* (though, of course, we are fortunate today to be able to hear the D-flat Yale version as well and make our own comparisons).

time, in October 1910). He fiddled with the music onboard ship, no doubt inspired by such proximity to the subject of his work, but it was essentially finished, and he wrote to Aino flagrantly delighted with the result: 'I have found myself, and more besides ... There are passages that make me wild. Such poetry!'

In Manhattan, Sibelius was greeted with the level of luxury to which he aspired but could rarely afford: Stoeckel put him up at the Hotel Essex on Fifty-Sixth and Madison, took him to the best restaurants and showed him the growing forest of skyscrapers that were the city's great phenomenon. The new tone poem was rehearsed in Carnegie Hall before Sibelius travelled up to Connecticut on 29 May, where he was treated to yet more indulgence and adoration from Stoeckel and other influential members of the American musical elite. Sibelius recognized the potential of his work in America (in both artistic and financial terms), and he wrote excitedly to his brother of plans for a lucrative forty- or fifty-date concert tour (which, alas, never took place).

Norfolk's concert hall was known as the Shed, a homely wood-and-brick construction that could house an audience of two thousand and was decorated for the auspicious occasion in the national colours of America and Finland. Making use of the best East Coast musicians, especially members of the Boston Symphony, New York Philharmonic and Metropolitan Opera, the orchestra impressed Sibelius, and on 4 June 1914, *The Oceanides* received its world premiere, on a programme which included a wealth of the composer's music: *Pohjola's Daughter*, the *King Christian II* Suite, *The Swan of Tuonela*, *Valse triste* and – of course – *Finlandia*.[123]

---

[123] The second half of the concert included Dvořák's Ninth Symphony, Coleridge-Taylor's *From the Prairie* Rhapsody, the overture to Wagner's *Die Feen*, and, as a special tribute, the Finnish national anthem.

It was a triumph, probably his greatest sensation as a conductor and perhaps as a composer. For most of the audience, too, it was likely the musical event of their lives. The more accessible – certainly compared to the Fourth Symphony – music drew wild praise from the American critics, with Henry Krehbiel and Olin Downes claiming the new work the finest ever evocation of the sea ('closer', the latter said, 'to the coastline of tonality' than Debussy in *La mer* and as such making the suggestion of the sea's power more vital).

To celebrate, Stoeckel took Sibelius to see Niagara Falls.[124] Unsurprisingly, the falls greatly impressed this celebrant of nature in all its forms – though Sibelius declined, when asked by his host, to compose them in music, saying although he had considered it, upon finally seeing them in all their glory, they were simply too solemn, gigantic and majestic to be symbolized in sound by any individual human.[125] From here it was on to New Haven, Connecticut, where the composer was toasted with an honorary doctorate at Yale University to commemorate both his musical achievements and the trip to America.

On the way back home to Finland at the end of June, he heard the ominous news from Sarajevo: Archduke Franz Ferdinand had been assassinated.

---

124 Thus completing two of the three things Sibelius wished to see on his American adventure. Tall buildings he also saw, but the third, a whale, eluded him, despite hours on deck spent searching for one.

125 When working in America, Gustav Mahler had also seen Niagara Falls. Upon seeing them, he exclaimed, 'Fortissimo at last!'

The Oceanides are daughters, numbering some three thousand, of the pre-Olympian Greek gods Oceanus and Tethys – brother and sister, husband and wife, father and mother of the river gods, and themselves offspring of their primordial parents Uranus (Sky) and Gaia (Earth).[126]

All children of the immense world-encircling river, their brothers – the Potamoi – were personifications of the great rivers of the world, while the Oceanides tended to represent more diminutive but often crucial aquatic features that could bring life amid death: springs, streams, brooks or rain (the Argonauts, stranded in the Libyan desert, begged the nymphs to produce a sacred flow of water from the earth to save them). Artemis, goddess of the hunt, childcare, chastity and wildernesses, sought a sixty-strong choir of Oceanides as part of her personal entourage, while sailors habitually venerated and beseeched them, seeking the Oceanides' protection from storms and other nautical hazards through a maze of prayers, libations and sacrifices. Yet the Oceanides' function and characterization often went beyond the overtly hydrological: Metis was the embodiment of intelligence, Europa and Asia associated with great land masses; another, Electra, was mother of Iris, goddess of rainbows and a messenger of the gods.

Sibelius knew his Greek myths well. From this rich, extensive background, he constructed a work he referred to in his diary as 'Aallottaret', from the Finnish word for 'Nymphs of the Waves', which represented both the playful activity of the spirits on the water and the majesty of the ocean itself.[127] We witness the sea

---

126 Such was the life-giving fertility of Oceanus and Tethys, they were eventually ordered to divorce by Zeus.

127 Sibelius's friend, the painter Akseli Gallen-Kallela, had produced a startling canvas, *Aallottaret* (c.1909), with lithe purple nymphs lying on the beach and frolicking in the sunlit waves by the shore, though it is not clear whether Sibelius knew the painting prior to working on his tone poem.

in its placid state; then a gathering storm begins to change its nature, the tempest itself producing great crashes of wind and waves, subsiding as the work ends with a sonic illustration of the monumental power and boundless breadth of the ocean.

Like its neighbouring tone poems *The Bard* and *Luonnotar*, *The Oceanides* is about the essential forces of nature, and watching the Atlantic rise and fall from his cabin, Sibelius must have quietly congratulated himself on capturing these energies so well in music. The score is – as so many have pointed out – a marvellous evocation of the sea, a mirror of its moods and movement, as well as being a portrayal of a state of mind, even a state of being, since Sibelius by now (if ever) was not merely content with painting mere pictures in sound. He wanted to go further, deeper, exploring nature and humanity with the probing pen of the poet, allowing the tides of his art to act as elemental dynamisms upon the listener. Where Sibelius's usual practice of revision involved the condensing of material, in *The Oceanides* he also expanded it, making it more spacious, capacious and vast, turning his tone poem into a vehicle that could both frighten and appease.

Although there are impressionistic elements to *The Oceanides* (1914) that invite endless comparisons with Debussy's *La mer* (1905), along with the basic subject matter, Sibelius had employed such aspects in his musical language several times before, not least in his earlier symphonic works *Kullervo* (1892) and *Lemminkäinen* (1896). To an extent Sibelius's sonic seascape is less progressive than the work of his French colleague of a decade before – yet the Finn's employment of daring tonality, and the way in which he is able to reorganize it within the shifting contexts of his larger structure, is extremely proficient.

The Oceanides is not music that develops towards a superficially remote position; it is concerned, as one might expect, given its subject matter, with a steady broadening and intensifying towards a full permeation, a sonic saturation, of its textural and tonal material. The work is orientated less by a goal or destination than by achieving a state of musico-philosophical being, almost a metaphysical condition. By the tone poem's end, we are left with a sense of abundance and limitlessness, of both fixity and flux – of eternal yet ever-changing oceanic waters that even the diminutive eponymous nymphs themselves dare not hazard. In this sense, *The Oceanides* is a warning of human limitation, of awe and respect in the face of nature's strength.

Sibelius's three tone poems *The Bard*, *Luonnotar* and *The Oceanides* carry some of his most powerful and emotionally demanding music, yet it is music which is also exquisite, sublime, even pacifying. When he had completed the last of them, war hung in the air, an imminent global catastrophe that would also have dire implications for Sibelius's livelihood. The tone poems had spoken of nature's vehemence, Luonnotar singing of 'a sudden mighty tempest', but it was human violence that would dictate the years to come, as Sibelius's homeland gradually achieved its long-awaited independence amid the turmoil of the First World War, and as the composer slowly fought and forged his way towards a new symphony.

The Bard, op.64

The two-part scheme that Sibelius at one time desired for *The Bard* remains manifest in the overall design of the piece, which has two distinct sections (though they are carefully connected in both tone and musical substance). First there is an inert, pensive dialogue between harp and orchestra, lento assai, followed by a more energetic *largamente* that closes with a momentary reappearance of the opening.

The Bard begins with an ambiguous cadence, a musical miscarriage not unlike another recent two-part tone poem from Sibelius's pen: *Nightride and Sunrise*. A strange rising figure on the woodwind is met by the harp, whose first sounds are like the opening of a theatre curtain, or a filmic dissolve into a magical fairy tale. There come rolling, rippling figures on the violas and then a descending fragment (again on the harp). As musical material goes, it is all very slender, but it is advanced with extraordinary delicacy, utilizing the refinement and transparent textures apparent in not only chamber music but the Fourth Symphony. In a miracle of metamorphosis, the ideas advance and merge into tender, measured quasi-themes, some of which echo those of the great *Voces intimae* Quartet of a few years before.

The harp sings, while the orchestra – especially its strings – offer discussion, negotiation and commentary. With scarcely perceptible transferrals of sonic stress, the undulating strings evolve to ascending progressive ideas and iridescent tremolos, patterns that are extended and reiterated so that, by the second section, the material has become more restless and tense. A theme rises like dawn on trumpets and trombones, shining through the orchestral web and towards a huge climax – a twinkling of disclosure – before the brass fade and the strings return the music to the atmosphere of resignation and reflection with which the work began, a series of choral cadences drifting dreamily back into a mystical, nostalgic realm.

Luonnotar, op.70

A pulse of quiet strings inaugurates an atmosphere of anticipation and dread suspense. This ostinato is characteristic of Sibelius's technique in establishing mood while simultaneously urging the music forward into engagement along with a potential resolution: here, the kernels of the work's climax are held within the outlines of the palpitating pulse that opens *Luonnotar*. It is a humming pause in F-sharp minor, the world prior to the moment of its creation.

Against this determining throb, the voice enters (initially alone, then to wind accompaniment). Harsh and austere, it is a truly primordial sound, inert like a declamation, but also dynamic and differentiated, the rising melody gradually expanding to C major, as far from F-sharp minor as possible, before tumbling down to earth. The trade and negotiation between ostinato strings and vocal recitative are repeated, generating the mood of propagative processes that are formed from the variations of circular musical techniques.

It is this practice which largely drives *Luonnotar* ahead before an opposing section, a commotion of wind in B-flat minor, sucks the ostinato's pulsing energy away into a creepy, uncanny realm of dissonant figurations. It is part dream, part nightmare, above which the soprano climbs in a series of long stressed and short unstressed steps, groaning in ecstasy and pain. An unexpectedly impish flute announces the arrival of a seabird before the atmosphere turns intense as it flies around desperately seeking a location to position its egg: 'The wave is taking away my nesting place!' cries the voice before it falls away, inundated by the full mass of the orchestra's aquatic sonority.

The vigour of the storm diminishes, the Mother of Waters raises her knee to offer assistance, and there the nest is built, with a return of the slow rocking ostinato from the beginning. A new world is forming.

There follows an unforgettable concluding section, part recitative, part coda: the narration of the world's creation, one of the most haunting and evocative passages in all Sibelius. Ghostly, ethereal and deeply mysterious (yet as strangely comforting as the slow movement of the Fourth Symphony can be), there is an otherworldly glow to *Luonnotar*'s rising vocal description of the creation of the stars and its glistening final violin chord.

Despite this, however, the underlying dissonance of the work remains unresolved, and its jarring reverberations linger in the cold night sky. It is a new world, but an unfriendly and impersonal one, desolate and uneasy, with an enigmatic, undecided future lying ahead. The stars, it seems, are both warm points of reassurance and indifferent icy diamonds in the blackness of eternity.

The Oceanides, op.73

The Oceanides is constructed, as one might expect, from a series of orchestral cycles, arches and waves: diminutive vacillating currents swell and grow through a trio of imposing sequences that gradually accumulate before eventually bursting forth with incredible vitality and strength at the close.

It opens in the morning, at dawn, with gently swaying strings that broaden, diverge and then begin to overlay one another.

Muted timpani and paired flutes in high register play like the sun sparkling across the surface of the orchestral waves, the woodwind's music undergoing a continual metamorphosis, while violins sing a sprightly, syncopated tune that will recur throughout the work and is as near to a main theme as we will find. All is carefree, amiable, engaging – the very essence of the calm sea.

With the kind of measured, subtle, slow power Sibelius makes his speciality, the grandeur, supremacy and ferocity of the ocean are brought into the score. A second thematic group starts to evolve from the melodies of the cor anglais and oboe, as we begin to move from the shimmering, glimmering surface of the sea to its murkier depths and more alarming possibilities. The two groups begin to alternate, though with an unbroken interdependence to their fluctuations.

In a quasi-symphonic development section, the storm advances: cellos toss and churn, trombones and horns blare and burst, timpani shudder and roll, divided violins quiver and tremble as the waves mount higher and higher. There comes a mysterious, dramatic climax to match that of *Luonnotar*, the ocean swelling and surging, suggestive of the obscure, unrelenting forces at work above and beneath the (literal and symbolic) surfaces of human existence.

From this revelation of immense oceanic power, the music subsides, allargando un poco, into its ending, the waves diminishing in the work's gentle conclusive bars.

Chapter Ten

The Noontide Sun: The Fifth Symphony

The elegant, somewhat sinister, beauty of swans has long led them to be a fixture in global art, religion, myth and culture. They swoop and glide across countless coats of arms and other armorial bearings; their size, long necks and white (or black) plumage have made them ideal for dramatic pictorial representation; folklore, legends and other traditional stories have often employed the motif of swans as emblems of love, fidelity and endurance, as does a swathe of more contemporary literature, from Hans Christian Andersen to W. B. Yeats.

Musicians, too, have been attracted to the sight and sound of these distinctive birds: Orlando Gibbons wrote a five-part madrigal, *The Silver Swan*, exploring the idea that though silent in life, swans sing exquisitely at their own death;[128] Saint-Saëns

---

128 At the gory climax of *Othello*, Emilia says, 'I will play the swan, / And die in music.'

uses a lyrical cello to characterize the creature in his suite *Le Carnaval des animaux*; Orff's cantata *Carmina Burana* has a swan roasted alive; Tchaikovsky wrote his immensely popular ballet about a princess turned into a swan, while Wagner engages them as key symbols and plot points in both *Lohengrin* and *Parsifal*, in the latter crucially triggering the eponymous hero's moral and spiritual development.

Sibelius had already explored the grace and mythological status of the bird in his tone poem *The Swan of Tuonela*, part of his *Lemminkäinen* Suite of 1896 (see chapter 3), and the genus *Cygnus* would come to play an important role in the unsteady progress of his Fifth Symphony.[129] Increasingly cut off (physically, professionally and financially) by the First World War, one day in the spring of 1915, as he worked on the piece up in isolated Ainola, Sibelius made a famous note in his diary:

> Today at ten to eleven I saw sixteen swans. One of my greatest experiences! Oh my God, such beauty! They circled overhead for a long time before disappearing into the solar haze like a silver ribbon.[130]

This overwhelming occurrence was intimately connected with, though not an absolutely direct inspiration for, the iconic 'Swan' theme, whose apotheosis forms the victorious, jubilant climax of the Fifth's last movement, the final piece of the divine mosaic

---

(V.ii.245–6)

[129] The English and German words 'swan'/'*schwan*' derive from an Indo-European root meaning 'to sound or sing'; the Finnish word for the bird, *joutsen*, originates in the term for an arrow, *jousi* – referring to not only the swan's distinctive neck but also the folk belief that they were divine communicators between the living and the dead.

[130] 21 April 1915.

that Sibelius often felt the Almighty threw down at him from the floor of heaven, as he remorselessly tasked the composer with deciphering the patterns of symphonic logic.

The Fifth Symphony evokes the magical spell of celestial lucidity and nature's own blissful sense of reason, recurrence and renewal: it moves through continuous, unbroken progress, eloquent and articulate, as well as also conveying a sense of perpetual stability and equilibrium. Spinning cells journey everywhere and nowhere, echoing the cycles of Finnish folk music and giving the symphony a deep connection to its local landscape, seasons and culture. And yet, for all its eventual clarity and grandeur, this was a work that needed colossal labour and revision, as Sibelius grappled with his own standing as a modern musician, and as he sought to find his own future direction as a composer.

Written and revised at a time when his nation finally found its long-awaited independence, with this work Sibelius made an unambiguous decision: from a point of near crisis, he chose to remain within the traditional, if malleable, borders of Romantic harmonic language. He would find innovation not in the dissonant tonal experiments of Schoenberg or Stravinsky – with which he himself had flirted in his Fourth – but elsewhere, in the sphere of large-scale symphonic structure and in the subtle colours of his orchestra.

When it came, the final version of symphony No. 5 would be one of Sibelius's most glowing and humane constructions, a sonic representation of those sixteen swans vanishing into the glare of the sun.

World War I, raging farther south, did not directly endanger the personal safety of Sibelius or his family, but it nonetheless plunged the composer into an acute pecuniary disadvantage. The payment of royalties from his German publishers was interrupted, then discontinued, as were the social and professional contacts on which he relied – even if he had become more austere and withdrawn in recent years. Consequently, the complex and arduous work needed for a symphony would be continually disturbed so he could dash off dozens of relatively minor pieces for domestic publishers just to ward off hunger and insolvency.[131]

Nevertheless, despite the dire straits of his bank balance and the catastrophe unfolding on the battlefields of Europe, there were reasons for cautious private optimism, even elation: the throat tumour that had threatened his life was now in the past, and the crushing, haunting fear of death had begun to recede. He was gradually becoming a little more companionable and convivial again, while also re-finding his appetite for both tobacco and, to Aino's understandable consternation, alcohol (though both in moderation – at first).

---

131 Although he occasionally felt humiliated by the need to write such pieces, they are by no means insignificant: there were three important groups of six songs (opp.86, 88 and 90), more intimate sets than his previous ones, and several creations for piano, including the Four Lyric Pieces, op.74. A set of five miniatures, op.75, have come to be known collectively as *The Trees*, since each is a portrait of a particular woody perennial: 'Rowan Blossoms', 'The Lonely Fir', 'The Aspen', 'The Birch', 'The Spruce'. It would be easy to reject these pieces as unimportant works written to order to keep the wolf from the door, but they are full of inherent charm and fascination, hinted-at symbols and vivid impressions, and an occasionally orchestral sonority to match their mighty subjects. The last piece, 'The Spruce', is a gorgeous and enticing farewell, a noble waltz with spectral harmonies and broken chords that ends the set exquisitely and carries a particular poignancy, given the dire circumstances of its composition. (*The Trees* have a companion set, another quintet of works known as *The Flowers*, op.85, which, though charming, are not as characteristically engaging as their sturdier counterparts.)

Invited to compose his Fifth at the invitation of the Finnish government in celebration of his own fiftieth birthday (8 December 1915), a day which was to be declared a national holiday, Sibelius would complete it just in time for its commemorative premiere, but would want a second attempt a year later, and then a third three years after that, in order to fully realize what had become a prickly, complex project for him. It was a work distracted and protracted not only by the intricate internal demands of its own complex musical logic, as Sibelius moved the pieces of his symphonic jigsaw about, but by the consequences of a worldwide war as well as by the domestic politics of both Finland and his family.

At home, as he started the symphony, Sibelius's family continued to swell. In the spring of 1915, their daughter Ruth was twenty, Katarina thirteen, Margareta almost seven and little Heidi nearly four. At the other end of the scale, the eldest, Eva, was now twenty-two and, in May, gave birth to the Sibeliuses' first grandchild, a girl they christened Marjatta, a name closely associated with the *Pohjola's Daughter* tone poem (see chapter 6). Over the next few years, as the Fifth Symphony underwent its multiple revisions and as his girls gradually left Ainola to launch families of their own, Sibelius could become a bit miserable, even self-pitying. His heart 'bled' at their departure, but he was buoyed on by his 'little snow buntings', Heidi and Margareta.

Even closer to home, by the time he at long last completed the definitive version of the Fifth Symphony, in the spring of 1919, Sibelius finally shaved off the few remaining wisps of hair that remained to him, and the characteristic imposing, majestic cupola of his head was born. However striking the pictures of him as a blazing moustachioed youth, it is surely the domed giant hewn from stone that prevails as our most abiding image of Sibelius.[132]

By now, booze had begun to dominate his life once again: binges reappeared, not only putting immense strain on his marriage (even prompting ideas of divorce) but blackening the composer's mood to the point where he sometimes seriously considered self-extermination. It is an instructive illustration of the complexities of artistic creation that as Sibelius's personal outlook darkened, his symphony became more congenial. Its first version – though full of the agreeable sonorities and rich melodic expansion/contraction that typified his orchestral style – had incorporated some of the more challenging, modernist elements of the Fourth Symphony. By 1919, however, the Fifth had become smoother, simpler, more obviously classical in approach – yet this was by no means a regression. In fact, this process was continuing to push forward his ideas of symphonic structure and instrumental pigmentation with a heightened sense of subtlety and variation.

Many dissonances and passages of shadowy introspection – in both his symphony and his life – would persist, but they serve to make the final triumph all the more convincing. The Fifth, and Sibelius's existence, could be a struggle, but this only amplifies the achievement, while deepening emotional connections with our own lives and exertions.

---

132 Though he kept the tache for a while, and occasionally grew back his hair for photographs.

Ironically, initial work on the Fifth had progressed well, and the composer was frequently filled with ecstasy and an almost hysterical self-importance (the perpetual flip side to his bouts of self-loathing, doubt and despair). As he put it grandly, but perhaps rather endearingly, too, in a letter to his friend Axel Carpelan, just as work was getting underway on the symphony in the autumn of 1914:

> Another depth of misery. But I am beginning to find the mountain I shall climb. ... God is opening his doors for a moment, and his orchestra is playing the Fifth Symphony.

The fall colours, the increasing shadows and lower sun, which usually would worry him about the onset of another long, grinding winter, were this year only filling Sibelius with delight and inspiration: 'my melodies are divine!' he would tell his diary. Themes for a (later abandoned) new violin concerto arose, as did ideas for another symphony, and these mingled and exchanged with those for the Fifth. It was a period of wild, abundant stimulation and manic cross-fertilization: first drafts of the Sixth ended up in the Fifth, while the second theme in the finished Sixth's finale first appears in a draft for the Fifth. Alas, such fecundity would not last.

By the summer of 1915 Sibelius was fraught with and harassed by the drafts of his Fifth. He complained that he could never focus on the symphony's composition since he was forced – 'at the age of nearly fifty!' – to write what he often regarded as slighter works merely in order to survive – though, as we have seen, many of them (especially opp.74, 75, 86, 88 and 90) are noteworthy, captivating works. As the light and warmth began to fade, however, and as autumn encroached, he made significant progress in what became a race against time to complete the work for its premiere on his fiftieth birthday – a date that, unlike his other deadlines, could not be moved.

In mid-October he worried that although he had the entire outline, he could not hope to realize all the details ready for the concert on 8 December, let alone get them written out and reproduced for the players. As a result, some of the finished elements were sent ahead for the copyists, but it is true that even the completed first version of this work was no more than a jigsaw puzzle, pieces yet to be properly put in place. Had the premiere not been a fixed moment in time, and for such a conspicuous festivity, Sibelius would doubtless – as with other works – have merely postponed it, though it is also true that he could not yet quite see the final vision of the Fifth, so he was hardly presenting a consciously second-rate symphony in 1915. To an extent, it didn't matter. Whatever the flaws in its design and detailing, the first-version Fifth was a much more celebratory and triumphant work than the Fourth, and this alone guaranteed it a jubilant reception.

In the lead-up to the concert, a chamber event celebrated Sibelius's earlier periods – the heroic piano suite *Kyllikki*; the introspective *Voce intimae* Quartet – while his portrait hung in shop windows, and newspaper articles catalogued his life and achievements. He was presented with paintings from leading artists of the nation – for this fiftieth birthday party was also a keenly focused exhibition of Finnishness – as well as a Steinway grand.

On the day itself, Sibelius undertook a rehearsal of the symphony in the morning before he was whisked away to a series of gala proceedings and innumerable messages of congratulations. Then came the concert itself, a significant event in the nation's social calendar: the Finnish premiere of *The Oceanides*, followed by the world premiere of the Two Serenades for violin and orchestra, op.69. After an interval where he was presented with a civic address exhibiting fifteen thousand signatures, the Fifth received its first performance.

The symphony was rapturously received and was followed by a soirée banquet in the hall of the Helsinki Stock Exchange (which, given Sibelius's relative penury at the time, must have grated a little). Robert Kajanus gave a speech that would become a famous element of Finnish history and identity, maintaining that in this work Sibelius had created an idiosyncratic manifestation of Finland in sound. What had gone before, Kajanus claimed, including in his own work, had been only an offshoot of Germanic traditions. This was something distinctively, proudly Finnish. Although there are, and were, obvious problems to that argument – as this book has explored in its earlier chapters, Sibelius had already created something not only markedly Finnish but noticeably his own – it was nevertheless a well-earned recognition of Sibelius's attainments, both in music and for his country's standing in the world.

Flattered but tired of the attention his fiftieth had received, he longed for his work and solitude again, for it was composition that gave life dignity – not gala feasts while young men were massacred in the mud of Belgium and France. He need not have long to wait: after the (admittedly quite artificial) high of his birthday, reality bit soon after. First, the bailiffs came almost immediately for the Steinway (though Sibelius's favourite singer, Ida Ekman, stepped in to safeguard it for him, as well as settling a number of his outstanding debts), and then doubts about the Fifth grew. As we have seen, it was perfectly normal practice for Sibelius to make revisions – some major, some minor – to a new symphony after its first performances. But he felt the Fifth needed something far more drastic.

Although Sibelius was unable to travel to Berlin, as had been his regular habit in recent years, because of the war, early in 1916 there were several important musical opportunities in Helsinki that he did not want to miss: his pupil Leevi Madetoja's thrilling First Symphony, with its gorgeous slow movement (which left the teacher 'spellbound'), as well as Brahms's *Variations on a Theme by Haydn*,[133] Beethoven's Fourth Piano Concerto, Tchaikovsky's Fifth Symphony and Verdi's *Aida* ('entirely marvellous').

In April he once again saw beloved large birds flying overhead – cranes this time, circling the house several times. An excitable diary entry from the time shows just how much such creatures meant to the composer: 'Twelve swans on the lake, on the ice. Seen with my binoculars!! Saw six wild geese ... plus an eagle. A sumptuous day!!'

Throughout 1916 Sibelius laboured away on his symphony, and its second version was presented exactly a year after the first, on 8 December, in Turku. Only a double bass part survives, so it is hard to judge the exact efficacy of the new edition; however, we do know that the first two movements had been superbly fused into one, though other changes (such as cutting the finale's famous succession of six concluding strokes to just two) were not so successful. Further considerable revision would be required, as Sibelius began to acknowledge its initial composition had been too rushed.

---

133 Now also known as the *Variations on the Saint Anthony Chorale*.

By now, Sibelius was back on the bottle in a significant way, causing much heartache for Aino and the rest of his family, as well as numerous quarrels and more serious arguments. At one point early in 1917, Aino visited her daughter Eva, who was now living in the recently rechristened Petrograd – formerly Saint Petersburg – while Jean got drunk in Helsinki. To his diary he confessed the immense damage he was doing to himself and his marriage, simultaneously unburdening his woes and hating himself for his inability to refrain from drink and the poisonous rounds of ecstasy, guilt and depression it caused him.

Despite the pain in his life, sparkling compositions – such as the Six Humoresques for violin and orchestra – flowed from his pen, once again undermining any close correlation between life and art (though the otherworldly nature of the Humoresques seem to indicate a desire to escape into a different realm, far from conflict, shame and despair). Composition of new works, and revisions to the Fifth, continued until another international event refocused his attention elsewhere: the February Revolution of Finland's Russian overlords. (Fortunately, Aino – later followed by Eva and her family – was able to return home before events in Petrograd became too dangerous.)

On 15 March Tsar Nicholas II was forced to abdicate, ending the Romanovs' 304-year rule of Russia.[134] The news was met with wild celebrations in Helsinki, along with some meaningful changes: a new governor overturned all the procedures since 1899 that had sought to restrict Finnish autonomy; the Finnish parliament could also meet again. In his diary, Sibelius guardedly welcomed the prospects. He was right to be cautious, since it was a strange and dangerous time for Finland: Russian soldiers

---

134 The tsar, his wife, and their five children would be murdered a little over a year later, on 17 July 1918.

on the streets were moody, rebellious; Finnish strikes and riots were frequent. Although Ainola was relatively safe, food was often in short supply, the provision chains disrupted, though on 10 June 1917 Jean and Aino celebrated their silver wedding anniversary with a modest party that was somewhat subdued not only by the Russian situation but by the current strains in their own relationship.[135]

Amid these domestic tensions, however, some encouraging musical blossoms were developing: the six so-called 'Flower Songs', op.88. Completed by the early summer, they were written for Sibelius's friend Ida Ekman's farewell concerts, and as such the songs are not especially demanding but consciously offer great opportunities for a vocalist's intelligence and sensitivity to shine.[136] By the autumn, combined external and internal pressures – including desperate inflation – had stalled work on the Fifth Symphony's revisions, so miniatures continued to provide a meagre source of income as well as an escape into some form of work, a welcome distraction even if Sibelius all too often lamented their wider musical worth.

---

135 Only Sibelius's brother, Christian, and sister, Linda, joined them. It was a very rare chance for the three siblings to be together, not least because of Linda's long-term mental health struggles, which meant she was all too frequently incarcerated – though as an eminent psychiatrist, Christian was able to secure better care for her than might have been expected at the time. It was doubtless a poignant reunion for these three, who had played piano trios together as children. And Sibelius was terrified of going mad himself.

136 Sibelius called op.88 a song cycle, though it employs the texts of two poets: Frans Michael Franzén and old favourite Johan Ludvig Runeberg. The latter's work made for more interesting and emotionally varied songs, with 'Törnet' ('The Thorn') a quiet hymn to the endurance of the stark lonely stems who bide their time during winter in order to produce the lovely flowers of spring. Given the political situation in Finland at the time, and the pressures in the Sibeliuses' marriage, it is hard not to see some metaphors at work here.

In October, the Bolsheviks rose up in Russia, while in Helsinki further walkouts and disturbances suggested significant political change was imminent. Indeed it was. On 15 November parliament expressed its explicit desire for autonomy, and on 6 December 1917 Finland declared itself an independent nation. Look at Sibelius's diary on this date, however, and there is no mention of the historic fact. During the coming weeks in the journal, hardly any mention is made of an event that for many people Sibelius's music had always been driving towards. It seems clear that the composer's relative shrug of indifference shows not only how much he saw his own music as both far broader and more personal than any mere nationalist soundtrack, but also how he was further isolating himself from wider affairs. He recognized his 'unhappy country' but did not see himself as part of making its future brighter – he had his own freedoms to fight for and (musical; alcoholic) demons to exorcise.[137]

The year 1917 had not seen any major works, and Sibelius had not heard an orchestra for nearly a year. He was depressed; his wife was depressed; the world remained at war. Finland had gained its independence, but such liberty had come – as so often in these situations – at a heavy price: the country was bitterly divided. 'Red' socialists and 'White' conservatives (Sibelius tended to sympathize with the latter) battled for supremacy, both sides committing shameful acts of barbarism in a civil war that lasted over three months, between 27 January and 15 May 1918.

---

137 On 18 December 1917 the diary mentions two details. Aino went 'into town to buy Christmas presents' while music swirled: 'I have Symphonies VI and VII "in my head". And the revision of Symph V.' This is the first explicit mention of the Seventh, and thus the momentous totality of Sibelius's final completed symphonic work sits splendidly together in a diary entry beside the most mundane and charming domestic detail – though it would be some time before all three musical works were ready.

The south of Finland was generally under Red control, and when a curfew was imposed, Ainola was not exempt – indeed, Sibelius was placed under house arrest, forbidden even to go for one of his beloved walks. Intermittent graft continued on the Fifth (as well as some embryonic work on the Sixth), but times were increasingly hard. The Reds made aggressive searches of properties, including Ainola, while checkpoints were set up throughout the district. Eventually even the stubborn Sibelius was persuaded to leave with his family and seek refuge elsewhere: they stayed for several months at the home of Sibelius's brother, Christian, medical superintendent of a Helsinki psychiatric hospital. Here, too, food was hopelessly scarce, and Sibelius lost a considerable amount of weight (subsisting, it seems, largely on a diet of Cuban cigars).

By mid-March 1918, the Red cause was faltering, and a month later the Whites were triumphant in Helsinki, and soon life began to return to some kind of normality. Before leaving the capital to return to Ainola, Sibelius was fascinated by the 'strange but magnificent' sound of German guns (which had arrived to join the Whites in expelling the Reds). A few weeks later, on 9 May, he was even able to resume conducting in a concert of his Second Symphony and *The Oceanides*, while work on 'recomposing' (as he put it) the Fifth could also take on greater resolve: 'All in all,' he wrote to Axel Carpelan, 'a vigorous intensification right to the end. Triumphal.'[138]

---

138 20 May 1918. In this same letter are also revealed glimpses of the two symphonies to come: the 'wild and passionate' Sixth, a somewhat misleading description of its final form, 'with pastoral contrasts. Probably in four movements, with the end rising to a dark orchestral roar that consumes the theme,' and the Seventh, 'joy of life and vitality.' The composer admits to caution, however, and the strong potential for change, aware that – as ever – he is a slave to his themes and their incessant demands.

As ever, of course, this optimism was immediately beset by misgivings – would the Fifth still be relevant or of interest, so many years after its first appearance? Was its 'Wagnerian pathos' in step with 'today's taste'? Naturally, Sibelius's music was as alien to current trends then as it is now, existing in a far more timeless realm, but it was a reasonable concern to have for music over which he had struggled for so long and under such trying circumstances. These tough times persisted as the Finnish Civil War ended and the World War drew to its bloody, beleaguered close: in October 1918, a few weeks before the armistice, the Sibeliuses were forced to sell the family horse (less of an extravagant novelty than it might seem now), and food remained scarce.

Early in the new year he saw Axel Carpelan – his friend and advocate for so long, whatever the occasional strains and strangeness to their relationship – for the last time. On 22 March 1919, Carpelan wrote Sibelius a postcard, telling of his terrible pain but immense gratitude for their attachment: 'Thanks for *everything, everything.*' Two days later, he died, aged sixty-one, plunging Sibelius into mourning for the man who had supported him in both financial and musical terms for two decades. 'Immeasurably sad. For whom shall I compose now?' he wept in his diary.

A month later, however, the definitive version of the Fifth was finally complete (despite continued dithering and doubts at the end), and the symphony could stand as a lasting memorial to Carpelan and their friendship. It was premiered, in the presence of the recently installed first Finnish president, Kaarlo Ståhlberg, at a sold-out University Hall in Helsinki on 24 November, to euphoric acclaim, the work's true colours and dazzling architecture now revealed at last.

As Cosima Wagner once wrote about her husband's *Die Meistersinger*: Would future generations who sought solace in this music know the pain and tears of its creation?

The exact changes wrought to the Fifth are complex, and it would be out of place in a book of this kind to discuss them in any detail – not least because the first version is hardly ever performed – though significant alterations will be discussed here (and as they arise in the movement-by-movement guide that follows this essay) because they are useful in seeing how the symphony evolved in Sibelius's mind. In many ways it was simply one very long, very complex compositional process like any other, the 1915 and 1916 performances merely ephemeral displays of the ongoing work in progress (albeit very public ones).

Probably the most conspicuous difference between the 1915 and 1919 versions is the change from four to three movements, combining the first two of the earlier edition into a long telescoped opening movement, which wonderfully demonstrates the connections between the ideas. In its original version, the symphony was initially separated into a tender pastoral introduction movement that concluded brusquely, inconclusively, and was then followed by a distinct and quick-paced scherzo. Yet Sibelius did not merely splice the two movements together in the later versions: they are exquisitely linked, showcasing this composer's unique relationship with tempo modulation and organic genesis.[139] Moreover, the coda at the end of the scherzo

---

139 Indications of tempo frequently differ between the 1915 and 1919 editions, either for the sake of clarity or suggesting a change of mind.

section is extended, heightening the overall sense of subtle acceleration (that the conjoined movements had beautifully brought in) as we race towards the final bars.

The andante middle movement underwent less obvious changes in its revisions, generally condensing and reordering some material (and increasing the overall length), subtly varying the rhythm and tone colours a little more, removing some of the strings' pizzicato, as well as generally giving a darker hue to the overall orchestral complexion. The andante's opening in 1919 is less provocative, while its ending is now less contemplative too – though its more sumptuous scoring allows for a finer transition to the new finale but with the loss of some exquisitely poignant music.

It is in the much shortened last movement that many of the most noticeable changes occur, not least with the celebrated 'Swan' theme, where in 1915 the woodwind support is less emotionally effective – and in the famous closing bars. Originally buttressed by a sustained string tremolo and dynamic timpani, in 1919 the mighty and theatrical final chords are interspersed only by silence.

Listening to the original version of the Fifth is a strangely disorientating experience.[140] It is as if – to re-employ our earlier jigsaw motif – the pieces of the puzzle have been nudged slightly out of place, a knee knocking against the table the tiling mosaic lies on. It is recognizably, obviously, the same work, but things aren't quite in the correct position, and their changes/distortions are often confounding, confusing.

---

140 Available in an excellent recording on BIS from Osmo Vänskä and the Lahti Symphony Orchestra, coupled with the 1919 revision – though it has to be said Sibelius would probably be appalled that this early, discarded and superseded version is available for public consumption.

What we gain most, perhaps, from hearing the original version of the Fifth is the illumination it gives to Sibelius's considerable ability to clarify and condense his material, which we have seen several times before in this book. It is so significant a part of his music that it is not simply a feature of his compositional processes but an indication of how his symphonies (and tone poems) function; it also provides evocations of their deeper meanings. And yet so complete is the sovereign control of the final Fifth that it – wonderfully – gives no real hint of the labours beneath the surface, as Sibelius worked and reworked his ideas until he found them to exist in a truly satisfactory form.

In the winter of 1916/17, when Sibelius was working on further revisions to the Fifth, Irish writer William Butler Yeats (1865–1939) was in Galway, west of Ireland, working on his great lyric poem 'The Wild Swans at Coole'. In it, the ageing speaker watches swans return to a lake seemingly unchanged year after year, while he has altered out of all recognition. He fears that they will one day never return, and the swans seem to stand for our yearning for a more stable world, a more enduring beauty.

For Sibelius, too, swans (and other large migratory birds) were important symbols, beyond their intrinsic majesty and attractiveness, and like so much in his life they held dual, often paradoxical (or at least juxtaposed), meanings for him. On the one hand, they had a permanence, a resolution, a strength and stamina: honourable qualities that combined with the beauty of their appearance and complexity of their musical calls; yet they were also enigmatic, fragile, even occasionally given to solitary behaviour despite tending to live in social groups. Much about them spoke closely to Sibelius's own character and sense of self, particularly in his vocation as a composer.

As an artist, especially a Finnish artist, he saw it as vital to recognize and explore the powerful role of fundamental natural energies in human existence – of elements, flora and fauna that were not distinct from humanity but a dynamic, interwoven part of it. As such Sibelius is a significant exponent of a complex interdisciplinary field examining the relationship between nature and its cultural construction. He might even be seen as an ur-champion of the Gaia hypothesis[141] – or at least a metaphorical interpretation of it – where living organisms closely interact with their inorganic surroundings, creating a vast, synergistic system: rivers and stones were as important to him as trees and swans. A strictly scientific homeostatic system at work in the world might not be something Sibelius could know of, or accept, but the Finnish composer certainly knew about the self-regulating and mutually informative procedures at work between nature, his mind and his music.

Although he was profoundly fascinated by birds and was frequently to be found in Ainola's garden or on a walk with his binoculars in hand, ready for a closer inspection of anything that flew by, Sibelius was hardly an ornithologist, or even an especially dedicated twitcher, amateur or otherwise. His enthralment with swans especially was more emotional, coupled to his understanding of the land and landscape, climate and environment – and all their intricate, multifaceted associations with sound, place, music and mood. Swans were a means by which he could articulate his experience of and feelings for the

---

141 Formulated by British scientist, environmentalist and futurist James Lovelock (1919–2022) in the 1970s.

world around him, especially the natural world, which meant so much, along with its relationship to his inner being. For Sibelius there was a key correlation, an unbroken link, between his moods and humours, the particular timbre of a specific bird's call, and then the instrumental or orchestral tone colours that he could derive from them.[142]

The exact connection and/or separation of these associations (and their manifestation in music) is not always easy (or desirable) to distinguish, since they are necessarily both blurred and intersecting, but some more definite connections are possible – and the Fifth Symphony is probably the leading, and most celebrated, example. We saw in the introduction to this chapter Sibelius's excited diary entry of 21 April 1915, where he saw sixteen swans circle overhead before flying into the haze of the sun. The passage goes on to directly link their sounds with music, remarking that the swans' call is similar to the woodwind sound of cranes, though 'without the tremolo'. For Sibelius, swans were closer to trumpets, or even the sarrusophone, a rare woodwind instrument that was intended for military bands to replace oboes and bassoons – which lacked the significant carrying power needed for outdoor marching music – while still retaining much of their distinctive sound.[143]

---

[142] In August 1940, he would tell his colleague Jussi Jalas that a hundred thousand years ago he must have been related to swans and geese, 'because I feel so drawn towards them.'

[143] They have very rarely been employed by classical composers, though they did see some popularity among French musicians around the turn of the twentieth century: Ravel's *Shéhérazade* Overture (1898), *Rapsodie espagnole* (1907) and *L'heure espagnole* (1909), and Debussy's *Jeux* (1913) all make use of the sarrusophone, though its most well-known engagement is probably the creepy effect it has in Paul Dukas's sinister symphonic poem *The Sorcerer's Apprentice* (1897).

We can see Sibelius's precise musical mind homing in on just what a swan sounded like, and a precise, passionate rendezvous between these birds as ciphers and aural muses. He continued: 'A low refrain, like a small child's cries. Nature mysticism and life's sorrow! Symphony V's finale-theme. The slurs in the trumpets!!' For Sibelius, this theme for the Fifth's finale, the great indelible swinging horn tune (which had percolated since at the least the previous autumn and exists in several 1914–15 sketchbook drafts), now had its true, celestial, realization in its connection to the swans in flight above Ainola. The same swan vision doubtless helped to fundamentally develop and give meaning to this theme, even if it did not directly inspire it as such – though this is not to say that other, earlier, avian spectacles had not quietly stimulated the music.[144]

Just a few days after this famous diary entry comes another, on 24 April, where Sibelius professes that swans are constantly in his thoughts, that they give our existence its shine and glow. He claims, with some power and not a little justification, that nothing in all the world, not art nor literature, not even music, had such a formidable effect on him as the swans, cranes and wild geese in the skyscapes around him. They were beyond the world, revelations and expressions of the divine on earth – all ideas intimately connected with his symphony.

---

144 Sibelius's diary from the second half of 1914 mentions several times the 'splendid theme' which can surely only be the great melody from the Fifth's finale. Moreover, 'Symphony V's finale-theme. The slurs in the trumpets' is clearly referring to a pre-existing motivic creation – which he then re-jotted down in the diary – rather than a theme which had directly come to him on 21 April 1915 when seeing the sixteen magnificent swans. It was an association, not an inspiration (which should only heighten its power, not diminish it).

For all the Fifth Symphony's solar radiance, heavenly grandeur and celebration of glory in nature, it is work that also explores the darkness of life, its sadness and transience. Think of the mournful, elegiac bassoon solo in the first movement and the eerie murmuring strings that introduce it, or the wistful alchemy and pensive reveries of the slow movement. Indeed, the Fifth is actually a considerably less sunny work than many people might imagine: amid, and because of, the symphony's radiant light, we can witness umbral networks pervading the score.

A diary entry on 10 October 1914, as Sibelius made initial, fertile progress on the symphony, speaks of his heart's singing sadness, of the bright autumn sun, of nature in its gorgeous colours of departure. He writes about how the lengthening shadows of the fall create a mixture of pleasure and melancholy in him, creating moments of great richness – and suggesting to the composer the atmosphere of the 'adagio' (as it then was) of the Fifth. A few weeks later, in November, the feelings had become even deeper, as he claimed to have found a theme for the 'adagio': 'earth, worms and misery ... lots of sordinos [muted passages]'.

All this exhibits the complex sentiments Sibelius held for the changing seasons, how they were related to his own moods in a much more multifaceted fashion than simply *light = happy, dark = sad*. For all the very real and alarming depressions that could infiltrate and overwhelm Sibelius, especially during the interminable Järvenpää winter, when the sun barely stayed above the horizon for more than a few short hours, he often experienced a kind of syrupy sadness, a warm, tender nostalgic glow in the colder months that enveloped his soul and charged his mind with ideas. He enjoyed yielding to, and indulging in, melancholy, using it as a catalyst for thought and inspiration. The bright, varied but sorrowful colours of autumn were the ideal exhibition of his own ambivalence and complexity, which are so wonderfully on display in the Fifth Symphony.

Near the end of the work, the close association between 'nature's mysticism and life's sorrow' (as he put it in the diary entry when he witnessed the sixteen swans) is made clear. The 'Swan' theme offers hope in the finale, but this movement is permeated by the angst, as well as the ecstasy, of existence, showing how they are often closely related, or at least commonly experienced. The crushing dissonances and frequently quite coarse orchestration of the finale display the struggles of life alongside its wonder.

Sibelius's work in general, and the Fifth Symphony in particular, is music of immense scope and power. It carries a peculiar craggy strength – something often achieved by some deliberately uneven and irregular contrapuntal writing, giving a jagged edge to the score – as well as an imposing grandeur (often produced by not only the molten lava of the Finn's impressive melodies but his habitual long pedals and repeating ostinato textures). His tempos, too, are a fundamental, intricate aspect of the magic of his creations: the balanced way the first half of the Fifth accelerates, while the second slows down into dignity and greatness, is a miracle of subtle patience and intimate musical dexterity.

If the Fourth Symphony, for all its variety of texture and mood, had largely evoked the bleakness and austerity of the northern landscape, in addition to a penetrating psychology, the Fifth is that same region in all its picture-postcard splendour. It has room for the more melancholy moods of autumn and the intermittent despondency of winter, but it is fundamentally a celebration of the north as a landscape, as a culture, as an idea, as a dream or a memory. It is the north in sun and ice, the light sparkling upon the snow, the trees regal and tall, the circling swans magnificent.

Sibelius's Fifth Symphony is the divine majesty of the world, at its zenith and in the noontide sun.

Symphony No.5 in E-flat major, op.82

1. Tempo molto moderato – Allegro moderato.

Sibelius's Fifth Symphony begins with a serene but pregnant and primordial E-flat horn call, gently radiant, with a tremolo from the timpani, all conjuring the mystical monarchy of nature familiar from *Lemminkäinen*. It is a musical kernel, a seed, a door, a briefly rising and falling motif which is then followed by exquisitely augmenting woodwind cadenzas, singing and warbling like birds. They take the theme and rupture it, before turning and developing it with a sense of glorious self-sculpting irrevocability. From here, the (deferred) first appearance of the strings takes us to G major and a feeling of agitated insistence, surging and urging the music forward, while the woodwind offer a rocking subsidiary theme.

The whole sequence is mesmerizing, like a butterfly unfolding its wings, or the golden rays of the sun spreading across a landscape. It is a spectacular specimen of Sibelius's astounding ability to take a nebulous, tenuous idea that then develops organically, imperceptibly, taking on a dynamic journey that constructs a symphonic movement – and, indeed, a whole symphony. The basic themes and form in the 1915 and 1919 versions are not especially different – what is new is the extraordinary manner by which the later rendering integrates and enhances its material, refining it to weapons grade. Cautious and hesitant becomes assertive and vibrant.

Evolving as an incorrigible, uncontainable acceleration in time and space, the movement briefly returns to its origins as mediative horn calls recapture the opening before a shadowy transitional sequence takes us to a dark new realm. Here muttering, whispering, alien sounds come from the strings, chromatic and strange – a winter storm – and there emerges an even weirder lugubrious bassoon solo, perhaps a dying animal's cry, which continues for a long time. The movement almost seems to have lost its way, its swelling energy evaporated.

It was at this point that, in the 1915 version, the movement soon dwindled and inconclusively melted away, before being followed by the faster material of the scherzo. But Sibelius instinctively knew it didn't work and that something rather more bravura and impressive was needed. What he hit upon was ingenious: chopping off the end of one movement and the start of the next, he made the scherzo materialize, like a ghostly apparition, from the tempo molto moderato. From here this phantom could develop with unrelenting force, ignoring any musical handbrakes, simply streaming on to a decisive, electric conclusion.

After the development, with its mournful bassoon, the music expands in anticipation, evolving towards an inevitable climax and – eventually – a shift to a beaming B major (the return to E-flat major takes a little time, heightening both the expectation and the delight when it does emerge). The brass gleefully repeat the rising motifs from the movement's opening, followed by replies from the woodwind, and without our knowing it, the accelerating scherzo is underway.

The scherzo comes complete with a traditional trio section, starting in E flat with a seemingly new trumpet tune, its rhythm bolstered beneath by the timpani, which swiftly shifts to B major on the horns and bassoons. Only apparently original, this melody has clear links not only to the opening horn motif and the subsidiary rocking subject but to the swinging 'Swan' theme to come in the finale. All have a creative, generative, life-giving quality to them that both initiates and nurtures the symphony. Increasingly the inner connections between the themes are revealed, as they are fused together via an incessantly quickening tempo, and the movement pulses confidently forward, to be crowned by a carefree coda as it passes the sound barrier.[145]

To an extent, whatever bending and deformation to symphonic design Sibelius achieved in this extraordinary movement, we might regard the scherzo section as operating like a sonata-form recapitulation. Yet trying to categorize and label Sibelian movements and parts of movements in this way, as scholars have through endless, if frequently fascinating, arguments, sometimes seems to miss the point about just what the Finn was trying to achieve. He was seeking something innovative and new, something deliberately ambiguous, something which developed and, to a degree, did away with traditional notions of form. Their remnants and traces – exposition, development,

---

[145] In 1919, right at the end of the long journey of composing the Fifth, panicking once again, Sibelius briefly considered cutting the second and third movements entirely, and having the symphony end here.

recapitulation and so forth – can be detected, of course, but often it is a case of hunting the wrong thing, since Sibelius has evolved the symphony beyond them, progressing as ever in exceptional self-determination from pre-existing symphonic templates.

The whole effect of the Fifth's first movement, with its nuances of tonality and tempo, its merging of two distinct components into one, as we have seen, took a long time to get just right, but eventually the rotations, disintegrations and reforging of the material emerged into a seamless sequence of incremental acceleration. The language of cinema has often been evoked, Sibelius 'splicing' his two cuts together or creating a 'cinematic dissolve' between the two movements now become one. These are all useful, engaging images, but in truth the subtlety and refinement with which Sibelius joined his movements goes beyond metaphor, existing as a miraculous reworking of symphonic form that was a natural continuation (and fine-tuning) of approaches in the Second and Third Symphonies and which would find its ultimate apotheosis in the one-movement Seventh.

2. Andante mosso, quasi allegretto.

After the gathering energy and momentum of the first movement, the second offers repose and composure, along with some darker reflections conjuring memories of the Fourth Symphony, as well as restrained indications under the exterior of the grand theme to come in the finale.

Significantly reordered by the 1919 version, the movement offers half a dozen sequential reaffirmations, endorsements and textural/rhythmical embellishments of an innocent folk-like G major tune, heard at the outset on flutes and pizzicato strings. In some sense the andante is a set of classical 'theme and variations', but Sibelius was not content to merely repackage the past: in reality this movement circles around itself, surrounding and enclosing its propagative material with what might be a loving embrace – or a noose. The movement's procedure calls to mind the continuous variations ancient Finnish singers gave their melodies, but it has, too, a Beethovenian charm and ambiguity to it – the Beethoven who relished the rural places around Vienna, the sunny peasant dances and the mysterious woods.

Finding where the theme starts and ends is a (calculatingly) tricky task, its meticulous threads woven into such a seamless tapestry that the whole notion of 'theme and variations' really vaporizes in this movement. The decoration and elaboration Sibelius gives to his material is spellbinding, not least as it develops a more unsettled air on uneasy tremolandos in the strings or via ominous climbing brass figures.

Amid these tensions towards the end of the movement, and beneath all this surface adornment, the delicate, understated way in which the double bass line alludes to the 'Swan' theme is a marvel of unobtrusive grace and discreet hope (an effect heightened in the 1919 revision by the increasingly rich orchestration Sibelius gave to the end of the movement).

3. *Allegro molto.*

Tension, coiled in the spring of the andante, immediately finds its release in the astonishingly galvanized start to the finale, a bracing beat of animation and invigoration that takes us to the vivacious entrance of the long-awaited 'Swan' theme, swinging in like bells on the horns and chanted by the woodwind.

Sibelius's counterpoint here is supreme – and is a crucial factor in creating the culminative emotional power of the music.

Simultaneously, the horns, violins, double basses and bassoons play the same basic raw material, but they do so at different tempos, like differently coloured speedboats passing, falling behind and then overtaking one another in a race. It is an inspired employment of musical metre to craft a poignant and deeply affecting impression on the listener, as our hearts and ears swell to the great theme hauling and overhauling itself in the different sections of the orchestra. A sudden shift from E flat to C major is one of the greatest moments in all Sibelius, a forthright, even brazen, mini climax that gives a breathtaking further pulse of energy to the movement, like the first-stage separation of a Saturn V rocket as it surges through the heavens.

From here a brief development takes us back to an enormous, extended reaffirmation of the opening progression. As it is progressing, this affluence becomes first more expansive, then increasingly lethargic, the tempo plummeting as it runs into a range of chromatic complications along the way, which darken the overall mood.

Amid these melancholic and sometimes agitated reflections there re-emerges – what else? – the 'Swan' theme, reborn at a slower speed on the trumpets, which begins an agonizingly beautiful crescendo, full of colossal grandeur and immense nobility. As it grows towards hope and exaltation, the torment of life continually seems to intervene, to slash at the elevation of the music. The 'Swan' theme is split, torn, but try as it might, the pain of existence cannot deny the movement's triumphant reforged rise towards a flawless affirmation in E flat with all the orchestral brilliance of those sixteen swans soaring into the solar haze.

And then the symphony's final, phenomenal coda: a series of sledgehammer blows or imposing explosions played by the whole orchestra at their full strength and punctuated by what can seem like eternal haunting silences. During this immensely powerful chord sequence, Sibelius's Fifth is holding its breath, biding its time, lingering in glorious expectation, before a two-note cadence of gruff magnificence curtly ends the work.

It has landed with several knocks and shocks to its fuselage, and it might not fly again, but the mighty jet plane of the Fifth, after a long and arduous flight, has arrived safely.

Donald Tovey notoriously referred to the 'Swan' theme as 'Thor swinging his hammer' – but does the Norse god of thunder and strength achieve the ultimate victory? How triumphant is the ending of Sibelius's Fifth Symphony? For some, it repositions the universe in an act of moral and cosmic certainty. Yet in other respects, the brusque final jolt is a shrug at the fundamental impossibility of any unequivocal happiness, the preceding hammer knocks a correspondingly bemused, and even slightly amused, indication of life's ambivalence and uncertainty.

The triumph, such as it is, seems necessarily conditional, impermanent, all too aware of the sacrifices of human victories and their ultimately unsettled nature. Although they might be shrugs, the hammer blows are also questions, enquiries, interrogations, their allied silences spaces for contingent answers, all leading to potential but retrospective resolution.

Nonetheless, for all the mystery and ambiguity of the Fifth Symphony's dramatic coda, the expectant radiance of the 'Swan' theme endures as an echo throughout the final hammers and hushes, to offer confidence amid insecurity, freedom among limitation, light in darkness. It is a symphony of unforgettable power and magic.[146]

---

[146] A personal footnote: I know the exact moment I fell in love with Jean Sibelius (in contrast with every other composer). As an undergraduate, I spent a summer travelling around China and Southeast Asia. After a long hot train journey down through Laos and Thailand, I crossed the border from Malaysia to Singapore at midnight on 1 August 2000, listening to the finale of Herbert von Karajan's famous Berlin Philharmonic recording of the Fifth, on Deutsche Grammophon. The mounting, culminative power of the music overwhelmed me: it was love at first listen and the start of my long affair with the great Finn's extraordinary music.

PART THREE

TRANSFIGURATION

Chapter Eleven

Snow Country: The Sixth Symphony

Caught between the solar intensity of the Fifth and the stellar eternity of the Seventh, the Sixth Symphony – all moonshine on a dark lake – has been subject to a little neglect, even derision. In fact, Sibelius's 'pure spring water' (as he once called it) is one of his finest works. A strange poem in the guise of a symphony, the Sixth unfolds with the sense of internal logic and heavenly inescapability we have come to expect with this composer, as if we were witnessing a dream that has inexplicably become our own, surreptitiously turning into our own imagination. A floating and enigmatic masterpiece, this is a symphony that shimmers, subtle and mysterious, offering a soundscape which is neither gloomy nor heroic but something more elusive.

Reserved brass, timpani hymns, gleaming woodwind and strings; esoteric polyphonies, ancient modes, puzzling scales; moderate, almost impassive and expressionless dynamics – Sibelius Six is an often peculiar world, not least when its constituent parts are inspected. But the overall effect is magical, a lunar ambiguity with a generally serene countenance that avoids trauma, drama and the tedium of rhetoric. It is plain yet original, shunning contemporary fashions to embrace a shy innovation that would influence generations of local (and global) composers.

The Sixth reminded its maker of 'the scent of the first snow': a trace of something in the air, a hint of coldness – both a comfort and a fear – familiarity and expectation mingling beneath the quiet undercurrents. Spoken of in this way, the Sixth gives the impression of defining outright the Sibelian symphony, indeed the whole Sibelian method. Understated, rational, it seems entirely representative of what we look for and cherish in this composer. Of course, as this book has tried to show, there are many Sibeliuses; yet it is odd, too, that this most apparently characteristic work seems to remain so overlooked, even by those who applaud his symphonic cosmos.

In the Sixth, voices emerge and dissolve; from time to time, musical majesty and sonic tensions tumble and rise, anxieties disrupting the surface of the work's mostly placid waters. Landscapes, skyscapes, shift and evolve free of overt sonic striving – goals seem not only indefinable but irrelevant, since everything develops with the purity of sublime inevitability. Yet this very clarity and concentration give the work its strength, its focus and energy, a vitality which enlivens and enriches with all the power of an ice-cold shower or naked plunge into a frozen fjord. A darker and more formidable work than is often supposed, it is symphonic immersion therapy, an intense musical exercise where 'pure spring water' not only cleanses and refines but enhances and invigorates.

With the Sixth, hovering between autumn and winter, between beauty and austerity, we head inexorably towards the snow country – as well, perhaps, as the valley of the shadow of death.

Towards the end of the 1910s, Sibelius began to suffer from tremors in his hands – an apparently hereditary disorder that he solved by imbibing whisky and wine that he could not afford (in either financial, medical or marital terms). More than simply a means to steady his hands for composition, however, drinking was once again a negative and manipulative force in his life after several years of abstinence following his throat tumour scare. Back on the booze and with hostilities in Europe at an end, Sibelius rejoined many of his Helsinki social circles before retreating to the isolation of Ainola to compose. This was the set pattern: intense periods of conducting and drinking, followed by remorse and prolonged periods of writing. His diary is full of lamentations about the curse of his alcoholism, his agony at needing to drink, his guilt and shame at its consequences, and his oft-repeated 'pious hope' to give it up for good.

One opportunity to break this cycle of sustained work and extreme drinking (whether publicly during urban hijinks or privately in the study) was offered in the autumn of 1920: a professorship in composition from the recently founded Eastman School of Music in Rochester, New York. It seemed a wonderful prospect as well as a change of scenery – he had enjoyed his trip to America in 1914, and had been well received, plus the department promised that he would be given sufficient time for conducting as well as composition. Despite this, Sibelius wasn't sure. The war had shaken him, and even if the Eastman job presented a way out of some of the pecuniary woes he faced, he was still reluctant not only to be far from his family and homeland, but also feared (whatever the school's assurances) not having adequate time, space and freedom to work on his music. He didn't reject the offer outright but elected to keep it 'in reserve': one never knew when it might be needed.[147]

Two other factors doubtless played their part. First, the offer of several concerts to promote his music again in England, as well as a series of performances in Norway. Second, the gift of 63,000 marks (around €25,000 today) donated by a group of Finnish businessmen and presented to Sibelius at Ainola by the tenor Wäinö Sola on the composer's fifty-fifth birthday (8 December 1920). Welcome as this bequest was, a good deal of it immediately disappeared into the tills of Helsinki's bars and restaurants, Sibelius going on a magnificently imprudent week-long splurge in the capital.

Having arrived in England on 6 February 1921, Sibelius would spend a hectic month in the country, meeting Ralph Vaughan Williams[148] during a drinks reception at Claridge's Hotel in Mayfair and giving several concerts in London,

---

147 He vacillated here and there: on 3 January 1921 he sent a telegram accepting the position, but by April – at the end of a gruelling conducting tour – he withdrew his agreement. In May he was nearly persuaded to change his mind yet again but, as it turned out, stayed with his decision to remain in Finland. His old English friend and advocate Rosa Newmarch might have been a decisive influence: she urged him not to waste his significant genius and valuable time as a composer on teaching apathetic students how to write harmony.

148 The Englishman would dedicate his Fifth Symphony (1943), 'without permission', to his Finnish colleague.

Manchester, Birmingham and Bournemouth.[149] The latter, with the Bournemouth Symphony Orchestra, presented the punters on the English south coast with *Finlandia*, *Valse triste* and the Third Symphony, and was an auspicious beginning for an ensemble that – via Sibelius's compatriot Paavo Berglund – would become one of the leading interpreters of the Finn's music in the later decades of the twentieth century.

One of many London concerts saw the Fourth Symphony paired with Mozart's twenty-third piano concerto, with Sibelius's old friend Ferruccio Busoni on the keyboard. It proved to be the last time they would meet (Busoni would die just three years later, from overwork and heart failure), but they made the most of it: Henry Wood claimed the duo behaved like a couple of irresponsible schoolboys whenever they were together.[150] The Fourth itself was widely praised, regarded by *The Times* as Sibelius's finest achievement in the form: its simplicity of line both puzzling and intriguing, its relentlessly direct sense of movement an incomparable wonder. Sibelius's strong reputation in Britain was now assured – and endures to this day.

From London, Sibelius took a train up the east coast to Newcastle, where he sailed across the North Sea – leaving England for the last time – to Bergen for the first of several Norwegian concerts of his music, all of which were sold out. Paying homage, he visited the home of Bergen's most famous son, Edvard Grieg, and was hosted by the king of Norway, Haakon VII,[151] further evidence to Sibelius of his status and

---

149 He also spent a night in Oxford, seeing the city's sights, dining at New College, and accepting an honorary doctorate from the university.

150 A wonderful photo shows them standing in their fur coats outside Queen's Hall, a grin on each of their faces as they doubtless shared a ribald joke or planned some new hijinks.

151 1872–1957. Intriguingly, he died the day after Sibelius.

accomplishments (and a vital shot in the arm for this terminally insecure composer).

He returned home to Finland in early April, and that summer (10 August) saw Aino celebrate her fiftieth birthday. Sibelius gave a remarkably candid speech to the assembled family and guests, praising her boundless patience and endurance, commending her for enabling him to not only survive but thrive as a musician. He acknowledged the paucity of light amid the hard work he undertook, as well as the dark nights and terrible storms that they had suffered together but ultimately won through. For all his (very human) deficiencies, Sibelius was never unaware of his regretful behaviour and its detrimental effect on those he loved, nor was he oblivious to the importance of Aino in his life. She was the rock to which he could bind himself amid the tempests of an artist's existence.

Composition had been relatively frugal in the new decade. Certainly he had not had satisfactory time and space to concentrate on the Sixth Symphony – sketches and ideas for which had existed by now for several years. Numerous smaller works flowed from his trembling hands, most notably the two cantatas *Song of the Earth* (op.93) and *Hymn to the Earth* (op.95),[152] the Six Bagatelles for piano (op.97), the *Suite mignonne*

---

152 A deeply poignant evocation of nature's reawakening and regeneration, *Hymn to the Earth* (*Maan virsi*) was a balm to the soul and a tonic for the senses after the privations and horrors of war. Only six minutes long, it is an anthem to revival, to the wondrous powers of renewal in the natural world, its colours, scents and sounds. The forsaken and shattered landscape, however bleak, will always come back to life – after winter, after war.

for orchestra (op.98a), and the absolutely enchanting *Andante festivo*.[153]

In January 1922 he completed a strange work for orchestra, *Valse chevaleresque*, which – for Aino – represented little more than an instrumental depiction of Sibelius's carousing and very worst alcoholic dissipations. It was a piece she openly loathed, in a lifetime of devotion to her husband's music: where others heard only merriment and the sparkling wit of an inebriated waltz, she knew the darker side of the demon drink which lurked behind it. Although hardly among the composer's greatest works, it has a certain infectious charm and murky fascination – each listener will have to judge for themselves how far it is a boozy biographical tone poem or something more detached.

In the spring German pianist Wilhelm Kempff (1895–1991), then twenty-six and soon to become one of the leading interpreters of Beethoven, Schubert and Schumann, visited Sibelius at Ainola, playing Bach and promising to add the Finn's own piano music to his growing repertoire (a pledge which he duly honoured). As the year developed, bleaker news arrived: Sibelius's dear brother Christian was critically ill. Since their days playing chamber music together as children, Sibelius had always been very fond of his younger sibling, greatly respecting his work as a doctor and psychiatrist (even if he could not always follow his advice). Christian died on 2 July 1922, and Jean unburdened himself in his diary that grief was far 'too small a word' for how he felt and paid tribute to the 'wonderful brother and human

---

153 Originally for string quartet, in 1938 Sibelius arranged it for timpani and string orchestra. A live worldwide broadcast of the work with the Finnish Radio Symphony Orchestra on 1 January 1939 is the only sound recording we have of Sibelius conducting his own music (and would turn out to be his last performance as a conductor). The *Andante festivo* was one of the pieces played at the composer's funeral in 1957.

being' he had lost. One by one, Sibelius would begin to outlast all those who had led healthier lives than he ever did, an irony of fate that left him increasingly isolated but which helped create the atmosphere for the liberating, redemptive music of his final phase.

Indeed, Christian's untimely death at fifty-three seems to have been a partial spur to revitalize more sustained work on the Sixth Symphony that had begun in fits and starts in the spring, the self-imposed deadline for which was hovering in the hazy future of January 1923. By the end of September he was toiling hard, forging his sorrow into art, recognizing – as he put it in his diary – 'life's perfection and my art's greatness'. It was immodest, but accurate, as Sibelius began to shape perhaps his most subtle, refined and confidential symphony, an autumnal masterpiece that spoke of reflection and rumination but quiet hope too. This was not a time for the grand heroics of the Fifth – the wars, world and civil, had shown the futility of such principles – but muted introspection (though not short of animation), the eloquence of art prevailing over the vacuum of death.

During the autumn and early winter, work on the Sixth was interrupted by both financial worries and his persistent grief at his brother's passing, bereavement intruding on the creative processes where previously it had stimulated them. By 14 January 1923, however, Sibelius could note in his diary the completion of the first three movements of the symphony, which was then finished in time for its premiere in Helsinki on 19 February, conducted by the composer. Critics noted its delicacy, its subtlety, remarking on the steadfast serenity of its mood (oddly also inquiring whether it occasionally needed more spectacle and variety). Where the Fifth was an 'imposing drama', the Sixth was 'an idyll', an unobtrusively innovative marvel that showcased the enthralling range of Sibelius's symphonic art.

The symphony complete and aired, the Sibeliuses headed abroad, partly for a concert tour to further promote the Sixth along with some of Jean's earlier works, but mainly for a holiday in Italy. They headed first for Rome, where the Second Symphony and some tone poems were presented in a matinée concert. Sibelius also granted an interview to *La tribuna* in which he reasserted not only the inspirational quality of the *Kalevala* but that his music, although often closely related to Finnish folk idioms, did not actually make use of them directly, preferring to rely on his own imagination.

After Rome, they headed down to Capri for a real break before retracing their journey north and then travelling on to Berlin and Gothenburg. In the Swedish city on 10 April, Sibelius gave an immensely successful performance of an immensely captivating programme – his Fifth and Sixth Symphonies – followed by a drinks reception where the composer's relief at the concert's triumph led to the ingestion of endless glasses of wine. The following morning's rehearsal for the next day's concert (the Second Symphony) went well enough, the confidence-giving vino still floating about Sibelius's system, but a liquid lunch soon turned into a dangerous afternoon binge (oysters and champagne).

Ushered by colleagues to the performance that evening, in his drunkenness he bizarrely thought he was actually at another rehearsal, stopping the orchestra after only a few bars to correct them before realizing his mistake and then letting things progress relatively smoothly. Afterwards, he was consumed by shame at his error and this very public demonstration of his habitual intoxication. Searching his pockets, he found a small half-drunk bottle of whisky and smashed it on the steps of the concert hall, his disgrace giving way to anger and a rare show of violence, worlds away from the exquisite equanimity of the Sixth Symphony.

For all the essential/apparent tranquillity of the Sixth, it contains both underlying and more explicit stresses, anxieties often generated by the unusual (though not unique) tonality of the work. Much of the musical tension of the symphony originates in the contact between recognizable major/minor – everyday diatonic material – with something more unfamiliar and old-fashioned: modal music, specifically the Dorian mode (corresponding to the white notes of a D minor scale on the piano).[154] For this symphony is only theoretically in D minor; in reality it is constantly shifting between modes and keys, an ambiguous pattern to some extent reconciled only at the very end of the work – though this symphony ends in relative vagueness, a nebulous conclusion far from the orotund decree of the Fifth.

By juxtaposing an old church mode with more contemporary tonality, Sibelius was not only creating a subtle but stirring musical interaction, he was paying homage to the past as well as his detachment from present-day continental procedures in composition (the 'cocktails' of Stravinsky, Ravel or Poulenc to his 'pure spring water'). It was a tribute to both Finnish folk music, which frequently employs modal writing, and the musical traditions of Tudor England (especially William Byrd),

---

154 Though the Dorian mode is quite rare in classical music – Bach's Toccata and Fugue, BWV 538, and parts of the Credo in Beethoven's *Missa solemnis* use it – it has achieved something of a (hidden) utility in pop music, most notably in the Beatles' 'Eleanor Rigby', Jimi Hendrix's 'Purple Haze', Michael Jackson's 'Billie Jean' and Radiohead's 'Karma Police'.

where, just as in the Sixth, modes produce some particularly tart harmonies on the ear. The weird half major / half minor atmosphere of the symphony is perhaps also a reflection of Sibelius's fascination with the Renaissance choral music of Giovanni Pierluigi da Palestrina, whose meditative polyphonies can be detected in the quiet opening of the Sixth. In this strange symphony, the musical past catches up with the musical present, offering something innovative but wearing the cloak of tradition.

This employment of older traditions and techniques to drive music forward was something Beethoven had employed a century earlier in his late piano sonatas and string quartets, in particular using a range of fairly archaic fugal systems to produce some startling new structures and sounds. Famously, Beethoven had also engaged another old church mode – the Lydian – for the slow movement of his string quartet No.15 in A minor (op.132). There, just as in Sibelius's Sixth, a sense of intensified unworldliness and nature mysticism is evoked, the symphony conjuring a pantheistic world of the Finnish forest rather than any specifically religious concepts: the spirituality is indirect, implied, elusive, suggestive. It is, after all, *modern*.

This elusiveness, this ambiguity, is thoroughly contemporary, part of the anxious and fretful twentieth century, but it is also a reflection of Sibelius's own inner angst, and as much a manifestation of his spiritual-emotional turmoil as the more frequently cited Fourth. It is only that its apprehension and unease are more subtly conveyed to us. His earlier works, especially the symphonic *Kullervo* and *Lemminkäinen*, as well as the first two symphonies, are disturbing, death-filled works, music haunted by symbolist obsessions with mortality, lust and despair. By the time of the Sixth, human transience was no longer a lyrical or expressive idea, a distant concern that could be toyed with in the luxury of youth. It was real; it was close by. Sibelius was in his mid-fifties, his healthy younger brother had died, various friends and family were also disappearing fast, and the horrors of the First World War, as well as the Finnish Civil War, were recent memories. The Grim Reaper was now not an aloof Romantic figure, a poetic personified force, but a reality, a forbidding certainty, forming an existential anxiety that permeates the Sixth Symphony's calm exterior.

Just as Gustav Mahler's earlier work had treated death as an idealistic and artistic conception, then transformed it into cold actuality in his final trilogy of symphonies (*Das Lied von der Erde*, the Ninth and the Tenth), so the vigorous bravura in early Sibelius becomes in the Sixth something more elusive yet surprisingly also more proximate and sincere. Fear of death, fear of departure and annihilation, is itself a paradoxical fear but none the weaker for that. In Sibelius's life, alcohol anesthetized the nerves and anxiety but also generated further stresses, augmenting the spiritual and psychological angst; in his art, the Sixth represents a sustained attempt at musical sobriety, albeit one persistently disturbed by tonal/modal and rhythmical tension.

This symphony is therefore more varied and dramatic than its 'serenity' label suggests, even if it is not as blatantly turbulent as other works in the Sibelian set. Yet one of the most fascinating things about the Sixth is how malleable it is, its many mysteries lending themselves to various interpretations for whoever listens. It is one of the great musical puzzles, an elusive jewel marrying luminosity with obscurity, dread with composure.

The work's first critics were very alive to this enigmatic tension and elusiveness, observing its strange construction and unusual methods. In an interview, Sibelius himself also noted that the Sixth had four movements, like most other symphonies, but that formally speaking they were entirely free, none of them respecting the usual sonata scheme. Recognizable formal frameworks are there, just about apparent, but like many of Sibelius's earlier symphonies, they pay only lip service to tradition, existing in a far more fluid fashion than classical custom tended to expect. Indeed, trying to examine and solemnize this work in such terms achieves little, even threatening to undermine its unique and unsettling character. Anticipating the one-movement Seventh, which would follow fast after the Sixth, symphonic and structural boundaries are elided, omitted or merged in this subtle masterpiece, this Cinderella of the seven canonical symphonies covering its tracks and leaving few traces of its meaning or purpose, nor its great impact on Finnish composers who came after Sibelius.[155]

Bar lines, too, are tenuous beasts in his work: they were apparently only added to the manuscript score after the notes had been written. The latter are there in grey pencil, but the bar lines exist as thick wavy red pencil marks, curly intuitions rather than the more familiar stiff perpendicular strokes that divide and create musical time. (It is possible, of course, that Sibelius wrote

---

155 Kaija Saariaho (1952–2023) and Magnus Lindberg (1958–) in particular have been closely influenced by the tempos and textures of Sibelius Six. Saariaho's *Orion* (2002) for large orchestra is a musical voyage into a nebulous, formless interstellar space which maintains the Sixth's sense of myth and dream, along with its mysterious upshots of distancing, of subtle tonal and rhythmical shifts. Lindberg's vast, opulently textured orchestral scores – especially symphonic works like *Aura* (1994) – are propelled forward by a self-sustaining momentum similar to Sibelius's.

the wavy bar lines before the notes, but this seems contradicted by the fluid fluency of the music.)

By operating within this more liquid, sinuous arrangement, Sibelius generated a symphony of suspended animation, time floating amid a freedom that also produces tension. The very opening of the work is a disquieting manipulation of time, the strings and woodwind emanating in a pensive haze – an airy, eerie polyphony – before the harp begins to offer more sustained energy in its rhythms to push the symphony forward. There is an unfurling inevitability to this music that offers assurance, but there is also something peculiarly alarming about its flexible, fluctuating character, shifting among distinctive, dissimilar categories of time and experience.

The attempts of the Sixth Symphony to maintain a voice and direction – the aforementioned harp, or the first movement's conspicuous and climactic discord in the trumpets and trombones – tend to die away inconclusively, activity giving way not so much to passivity but mystery and a sense of inscrutability. The slow movement begins with the whispered triple tap of muted timpani before exploring a spectral realm that ebbs and flows in concentration and intensity. The scherzo establishes expectations of convention but then shies away from them, becoming rhythmically frozen with repetitions and imitations aplenty before a sudden and somewhat brusque ending. The finale bursts into dynamism and a storm of excitement, with some of the most clear-cut subjects of the entire work and much more consistent phrases, even identifiable 'call and response' dialogues, yet ultimately recedes into an impersonal, uncomfortable stillness – or is it redemptive relief, a coda-hymn of release and alleviation?

There is a Nordic despondency and trembling sense of anonymous impenetrability at work in the Sixth Symphony, but it is also a piece that can shimmer like sunlight through autumn trees (or perhaps, as Sibelius indicated, upon the first snow of the season). Luminous, radiant colours offer surges of pleasure, even frivolity and dizziness. Yet darkness can arise just as suddenly as the brilliance and high spirits, horrific moments of unexpected dissonance and imposing assertions that can seem like shouts in the middle of serenity, thunder within the idyll.

As so often in Sibelius, the brass offer greater certainty or authority, repeatedly settling conflicts between the timpani and strings, but they are much more reticent and detached in this symphony than elsewhere in the Finn's output – the trumpet in the final movement plays strange and sustained notes that seriously disturb the cavorting, almost festive, atmosphere. Eventually, however, the simple, sincere joy and advancing momentum of the symphony dissipate and disintegrate, the work ending where it began, in mystery and oblivion, the bid at a resolving cadence broken, suspended, the notes dissolving into thin air and silence.

Winter is coming.

Symphony No.6 in D minor, op.104

1. Allegro molto moderato.

The Sixth's tempo indication – 'allegro molto moderato' – as well as its dynamic marking – 'mezzo-forte' – from the outset denote the strangeness, the elusiveness, of this extraordinary symphony. Neither fast nor slow. Neither loud nor soft.

We open with a lyrical choral phrase from glistening strings of astonishing economy, some mysterious polyphony ushering the symphony into existence apparently from nowhere. We are in the Dorian mode, floating dreamily and ethereally through the forest, the wind rustling in the trees. Woodwind responses – oboe and flute – provide a dialogue which sets the work in motion, and the work quietly builds into more animated music, though maintaining the same essential pulse. It is a glowing tapestry of sound that eventually bursts into an oppressive chromatic discord on the trumpets and trombones, bringing the movement to a moment of harmonic crisis from which can emerge the main allegro with a series of sprightly woodwind calls and energetic dancing harp and strings, fresh ideas materializing thick and fast. It is playful, exquisite, relaxed, busily thronging forward.

Harmonically and modally established, the symphony develops slowly towards its own destabilization, with a plunge from the cellos into B minor (B Dorian) and the appearance of something approaching a tune amid an informal adjacent figuration. This positions the movement back towards a reappearance of the introduction, now with a richer textural augmentation, actively ascending and trying to recapture its initial sonority – which it cannot do, lacking the appropriate harmonic assistance.

Trembling tremolos on dark shuddering cellos create a threatening atmosphere, shadows lengthening, with menacing and eerie horn chords in the distance. The music dissolves, its energy sapped, the movement fragmenting into puzzling pieces and uncompromising modal cadences: aloof, austere, inconclusive.

2. Allegro moderato.

In order to provide a contrast, the second movement probably needs to be played a little slower than its tempo marking indicates – though one of the features of this symphony is the marvellous interconnectivity between the movements (anticipating the Seventh), so it should not be overemphasized. Indeed, there is a strong sense of rhythmic freedom to this movement, written sans bar lines, able to proceed and flow on its own terms.

The movement is launched with three mysterious taps from the timpani, and a strange waltz slowly appears from elegiac but strangely piquant woodwind chords (flutes and bassoons), music that will resurface at various points, offering anguish and ambiguity. The movement itself is mainly a set of metamorphosing variations on a softly swaying violin theme, delivering phrases that are a mixture of defiance and fragmentation as the music quietly accelerates, seemingly goal-orientated and motivated.

Sibelius surprises us, however, when we expect a return of the opening theme to reappear: the movement glances into an enigmatic, even hallucinogenic, pastoral-nocturnal interlude. It is diaphanous and haunting, the Nordic forest at night, suspended in sleep and eternity – motionless, timeless. Supernatural strings oscillate and whisper; the woodwind offer chirpy bird-like calls. If the opening of the symphony called to mind the luminous prelude to Wagner's *Lohengrin* (1850), this section evokes the Forest Murmurs passage from the same composer's *Siegfried* (1871).

A coda briefly recalls the waltz material – a four-bar scrap – with the music weirdly abridged, and the movement ends in unsettling haste. It is another movement, following the first, which has undergone growth and evolution only to descend into dissolution, even degeneration.

3. *Poco vivace.*

From this troubling atmosphere there comes a compact and chilly scherzo, a burst of trapped cyclical animation that is frozen, locked into place by extended, harmonically stagnant passages. An eccentric and insistent movement, spinning and off balance, the Sixth's scherzo at times seems to sardonically anticipate more mechanical trends (themselves often ironic) of imminent contemporary music – the industrial sonic machines in some of Prokofiev or Shostakovich, even Honegger's *Pacific 231* (1923) or Ravel's *Boléro* (1928) – while constantly teasing our expectations. Stressed and goading brass chords supply more colour, but there is a curious disinclination in this movement for true thematic/melodic material to arise and develop. It is a wild ride to nowhere, a strange folk-like conversation between the harp and woodwind offering some of the most dynamic elements until a boisterous chorus from bellowing brass brings matters to a rude conclusion.

4. *Allegro molto.*

The finale has the aura of a rural church, lost in the forest or isolated on some windswept tundra. It opens with a series of noble folk dialogues among instrumental groups – antiphonal interactions between woodwind and strings – that sound like ecclesiastical responses, the recitations of a sermon, or opposing choirs either side of the nave.

Everything is exquisitely regular and symmetrical, but it soon develops into a more lively, peripatetic style which gradually increases in purpose, urgency and direction. It escalates by building and reaffirming its uncomplicated rising, almost scale-like, tune that derives from the first movement but which is now presented in full for the first time, lending credence to the idea that the whole symphony is in effect a monothematic 'theme and variations' unity – albeit one which is perversely backwards – and strongly anticipating both the one-movement Seventh Symphony and the great final tone poem *Tapiola*.

This intensification eventually becomes harmonically very turbulent (what Sibelius in his sketches called 'the pine tree spirit and the wind'). The orchestral forces darken and then surge forth, but the storm is soon interrupted by a return of the opening dialogue, now augmented by the preceding tempestuous theatre. Questions become more passionate, but the responses act as palliatives, free variations on the material which calm the interrogations with comfort and reassurance.

There is a palpable sense of relief to the music as it reaches its enthralled coda, though the very rapt stillness also has an unsettling, anonymous quality. A pensive hymn, violins, viola and subdued timpani sigh the symphony towards its conclusion. The music appears ready to close on a resolving cadence in sun-drenched F major but instead fades quietly into silence and darkness by returning to the chillier minor-mode Dorian (D) province with which it commenced.

At its close, the Sixth shines with thin pale colours in the soft light of dusk, a cycle completed as the year begins to conclude and with winter approaching. The symphony ends where it began: undemonstrative, graceful, offering a combination of resignation and restraint. It is cool and calm but melancholic, too; serene yet a little forlorn, the passing of time and the expiration of the year reminding us of life's transience.

Winter. Night. Death.

Chapter Twelve

Illuminated by Stars: The Seventh Symphony

In his sonnet 'Bright Star' (1819), John Keats wrote, 'Bright Star! would I were stedfast as thou art'. Unchanging pinpricks of light amid the black blanket of the night sky, for Keats the stars were symbols of infinity: they were exquisite, systematic, fixed. A century later, Edwin Hubble announced confirmation of the first galaxy outside the Milky Way: Andromeda, home of countless stars beyond our own and proof of a much larger and more dynamic cosmos than had hitherto been supposed.[156] These two stellar concepts – one scientific, one poetic – coalesce

---

156 Using the hundred-inch Hooker Telescope on Mount Wilson, California, Hubble identified extragalactic Cepheid variable stars for the first time on astronomical photos of Andromeda. They allowed the distance of what was hitherto known as the Great Andromeda Nebula (M31) to be determined, conclusively demonstrating that this feature in the night sky was not a cluster of stars/gas within the Milky Way but a wholly distinct external galaxy situated a significant distance (2.5 million light years) away.

in Sibelius's Seventh Symphony, completed in 1924, the year of Hubble's revelation, where the music is subject to subtle but significant change yet also yearns for, and perhaps achieves, eternity.

Sibelius's Seventh Symphony plays tricks with our notions of time, speed and space, not simply stretching or shrinking them but turning them upside down or inside out, generating time warps, spatial distortions and aural illusions. Textures and colours, too, emerge and evolve at near-imperceptible degrees. At the enigmatic inception of the work, distant nocturnal timpani summon ominous strings from within the void, shrouded hues which gradually progress from hostile dissonance into dazzling novae and the seemingly unlimited sonic space of this symphony. Against the ever-changing, unstable background of the whole work, a majestic theme for trombone broadcasts three times like an astral foghorn in the darkness, brass markers on our strange voyage.

A strange voyage needed a strange vehicle, and in Sibelius's Seventh the composer's lifelong commitment to structural innovation and organic growth reach their ultimate expression. The separate movements of the orthodox classical symphony are dissolved into just one: adagio, *vivacissimo*, allegro moderato and coda sections blended into a single indivisible unity, bound by the key of C (major and minor). Monumental, and possessed of an irresistible varying momentum, this work is never merely episodic. It is continuous, spontaneous, the spellbinding range of atmospheres all growing exquisitely from one another: at times a frightening, fluctuating abyss; at others a galactic carnival, full of colossal energies and vibrant turns. Yet it is always held together with a magnificent cogency, the musical ideas building their own futures and always existing in a marvellous state of *becoming*.

This fusing of distinct parts into a seamless whole was the culmination of processes that had been at work throughout Sibelius's symphonic career. Think of the bridge to the finale of the Second; the actual melding of the third/fourth movements of the Third into one (something similarly realized in the Fifth, where the first movement and scherzo merge). So the Seventh was not only the natural next step but the ultimate destiny of Sibelius's symphonic advances, its apotheosis and end point.

In a paradox typical of art, the Seventh spoke of eternity yet was also, for Sibelius at least, a symphonic dead end: there was nowhere else for him to go. Generations of composers that followed him – from Dmitri Shostakovich to Leif Segerstam, Allan Pettersson to Alla Pavlova – have found endless novel and imaginative ways to develop and explore the symphonic form. But for Sibelius, the Seventh was to be a final symphonic statement: part scream, part sigh, part submission, soaring up from the snow and ice of earth and into the heavens.

Bonding both the gloomy and luminous sides of Sibelius's character, the Seventh is an awe-inspiring work of sublime fusion and compression that crowned Sibelius's career as one of the most far-reaching symphonists of his century. It is a work that – with the physicists – bends time and glimpses beyond itself, beyond the galaxy and even the cosmos, into distant, strange, unknown and unknowable regions far beyond human comprehension.

Throughout this book we have explored the biographical background to each of the symphonies and tone poems. With the Seventh Symphony, however, that context is – at first glance

– much more limited, since the work was completed only a little over a year after the Sixth. However, the compositional process of the Seventh was actually one of the most tortuous in Sibelius's career. The surviving drafts (for which we have more than any other symphony) reveal an agonizing process, not least in its final stage during the early months of 1924, but also in the preceding few years as ideas and sketches overlapped with the Fifth and Sixth. Sibelius was even sceptical as to whether the highly innovative new work he eventually created as the Seventh was a symphony at all, preferring the more equivocal term 'fantasia sinfonica' for the first performance.

By the late summer and early autumn of 1923, the premiere of the Sixth and subsequent conducting tour undertaken, more serious work on the Seventh had been proceeding for a while. Persistent money worries were alleviated a little by a significant scholarship from Helsinki's Kordelin Foundation, presented not only as a reward for Sibelius's music but as recognition of his achievements in promoting this still recently independent nation around the world. November saw the sixtieth birthdays of his sister, Linda, and Eero Järnefelt, occasions which moved Sibelius deeply. His own sexagennial marker was just around the corner, an event he anticipated with some trepidation, given his status in Finland as a national hero (even under the conditions of war, his fiftieth had not been a quiet affair).

Alcohol was still a problem, and this winter's attachment to it one of the worst of all for Sibelius. A few years before, in 1919, a prohibition law[157] had been passed in Finland, outlawing intoxicants. But because of the problem of his hand tremors and the need for alcohol to steady them in order that he could

---

157 A referendum in 1931 overturned the ban as thirsty Finns backed bringing back legal booze by 70.54 percent.

compose, Sibelius had been granted a special exemption: he received alcohol as a prescription drug via pharmacies and various doctors he knew. Medicinal brandy, medicinal whisky, medicinal wine – whatever their remedial value for his hands, they were also vitally needed (as Sibelius saw it) for his soul. His diaries at this time are a harrowing document, as the composer laments his need to drink as a means of staving off professional insecurity and as an insulation against personal loneliness – both of which naturally only increased once the initial boost of booze had been provided.

At times, he confesses, he feels his life has become derailed, overturned, dislocated. He misses his darling girls being at home (even if, like all parents, he is overjoyed by their happiness with their own families).[158] He agonizes over Aino's ill health – much of which he, correctly, attributes to his own behaviour. (Aino herself had been deeply shaken by the embarrassment of the Gothenburg concert – when Sibelius's drunkenness led him to believe he was conducting a rehearsal – and worried constantly about her husband's health.) He realizes, and to an extent is not wrong, that his composing days are probably coming to an end. He hopes now just to complete the new symphony: 'an urgent *necessity*', he calls it (his emphasis). Alcohol deadens his 'nerves and spirit', and he laments the tragic fate of the 'ageing composer', where progress on a piece never proceeds with the same speed as before and 'self-criticism becomes impossible'.

Given the often convoluted, circuitous directions some of his larger earlier works undertook during composition, and the always present presence of self-reproach in Sibelius, we need to take this (as with so much of his diary) with a pinch or two

---

158 The youngest, Heidi, was twelve at the end of 1923, and had started school in Helsinki, so that by now none of his daughters was living at Ainola during the week.

of salt, but it is nonetheless a dreadful indication of Sibelius's suffering at this time. *Nihilism* might be the pervading watchword, the whisky and wine dragging a melancholically minded artist down even further into a kind of compulsive despair.

Yet for all the doom and gloom, he was never subject to bouts of constant depression and self-pity for long, and even amid these catastrophic entries, the diary offers magical glimpses of his indefatigable ability to be happy – with diminutive domestic details, reflections on his music and, as ever, gasps at the natural world. There is also a certain ironic affectation to much of Sibelius's moods as presented in the diaries. At times he almost seems to be wearing a mask, playing a part for posterity, perhaps the role outsiders or the public wanted and which he frequently cultivated for himself: the gloomy genius, isolated and alone in the woods. But it was a mask that screened real fears.

Nineteen twenty-four dawned with the completion of ten new piano works, opp.101 and 103, written amid now heighted labour on the Seventh: and they were probably connected, so that potentially many of the rejected ideas for the symphony were upcycled into the smaller pieces, giving them a second life and function. Certainly the emotional sphere the piano works inhabit is very similar to the extraordinary fusion of austerity and radiance we find elsewhere in late Sibelius – the first of the op.101 set, 'Romance', in particular has a resonance and gracious majesty which would not be out of place in the Seventh Symphony.

Once again dependent on alcohol, and with fraught and anxious work on the Seventh continuing towards its completion, early in the new year Sibelius received a letter from within his own house. It was from his wife. In no uncertain terms – and with the psychological acuity that a letter to sit down and ponder would be far more effective than a simple discussion (or more likely row) – Aino expresses her deep love for her Janne, and the attendant sorrow at his drinking, the ceaseless anguish at its dangers, the damage it did to his mind, her health, and their relationship.

It is a touching and beautiful letter, painful to read but full of Aino's remarkable intelligence and quiet optimism. Its final words, 'Your life companion', were profoundly true: they were the closest of friends despite everything, and each of their lives was to some extent defined by the other. The communication had a significant, if not immediate, effect on Sibelius: even if he could not straightaway curb his drinking, he did learn to meaningfully moderate his intake and to now be very careful about any public displays of inebriation.

At home, efforts on the symphony continued apace. Sibelius tended to work in his study at night: though the house was no longer filled with rowdy children, it was both a habit he enjoyed and an atmosphere conducive to the kind of piece he was creating. It was also a more favourable time to absorb the alcohol he needed in order to steady his nerves, spirits and tremors. This is not to suggest that Sibelius necessarily composed when drunk/drinking: composition is a complex, multipart process, and we would be doing Sibelius, and his music, a disservice if we imagine him permanently under the influence. The actual brainwork required for something as intricate as a symphony – let alone one like his Seventh – could not be properly undertaken when intoxicated. Rather, a good deal of the fine-tuning, orchestration and other details, including getting the thing physically onto paper, tended to occur during these sessions of nocturnal rapport with the whisky bottle.

On 2 March 1924 Sibelius completed what would be his final symphony.

Aino, as she had said in her letter, could not risk a repeat of the Gothenburg incident so did not accompany her husband to the premiere. Despite nearly being scuppered by ice on the Baltic, which delayed the composer/conductor, this took place in Stockholm on 24 March – making the Seventh the only one of Sibelius's symphonies not to be premiered in the Finnish capital. But was it even a symphony?

The manuscript reveals to us the agonies Sibelius went through, even as he had completed his new work, as his self-doubt and self-criticism constantly told him that the extraordinary innovations of his symphony actually debarred it from holding that status. We witness various attempts to conceal the originality of the piece behind equivocal, verbose titles: 'fantasia sinfonica No.1', 'sinfonia 7 continua' and 'fantasia sinfonica' – the last of which did make it onto the concert programme (though erroneously printed as 'fantasia sinfonico'). When the work was first published, by Hansen in 1925, it was designated Sibelius's official 'Symphony No.7 (in one movement)'.

The premiere was well received: Sibelius behaved himself, for the most part avoiding the watering holes of Stockholm (no easy task) and conducting his new work in a manner which he himself approved, despite the very limited rehearsal time. The programme also carried the First Symphony, giving the concert, at least to us, a pleasing circularity and a sense of closure that Sibelius – if no one else in the hall – was beginning to feel. A pair of subsequent concerts in Stockholm maintained this feeling of reflection and finality, of past, present and future linking up. Two days after the premiere of the Seventh, the Fifth Symphony was presented with *Snöfrid*, while at a third concert, on the thirtieth – a matinée that was packed to the rafters – the Seventh received its second performance, alongside some old favourites: three movements from *King Christian II*, *The Swan of Tuonela*, *Valse triste* and, of course, *Finlandia*.

After returning home to Ainola, in early April 1924 Sibelius fell into another black depression. In part, it was caused by his sense that the reviews of the Seventh, though positive, were not as glowing as he had hoped: 'How little they realize what I have put into my work', he grumbled, a little petulantly, to his diary. But there were also the usual forces at work. He writes of the dark spectres from which he cannot escape. Life is full of death and without wonder. He ponders acquiring a place in town so that Aino can live separately, away from his moods and booze, and so that he can drink and sink silently away at 'some out-of-the-way spot here in the country'.

Coming just a few days after the successful premiere of, bar the Fourth, perhaps his finest symphony, it is an extraordinary, even perverse, prospect (and Aino was unlikely to be happy knowing her husband was all alone, drinking himself to death in the forest). Again, part of the diary writing here is fantasy, self-importance, posturing, a state of ironic pretence possible in these private pages. Quite how far Sibelius also thought he was writing for posterity, knowing the diaries would one day become public, is unclear. At times he certainly seems to be playing a bit of a game with future readers. But there is no denying the ability of Sibelius's moods to shift with alarming frequency and apparent ease, from magnanimous joy to narcissistic ostentation or a pitiable self-disgust. We might also recognize that it is common for artists (and others) to sink to low places following an intense and adrenaline-inducing period of work and creativity.

There were also more complex factors at work. To some extent, the drinking (and its resultant problems) was of his own making; so, too, were his self-loathing and self-criticism, though they were clearly also part of his psychological makeup as well as closely linked to his alcoholic intake. The booze itself ate into the household budget, creating not only domestic tension but self-reproach: Sibelius felt humiliated that there were times when he couldn't pay simple bills ('My economic circumstances are now appalling', he wrote on 14 May 1924). Hanging over all this – and making it worse – was his status as a national icon and increasingly global figure. The public persona, the public image, was often deeply at odds with the man behind the mask.

By November, his mood was again bleak. The diary confesses not only that life is little more than waiting for death but that alcohol is 'the only friend, who never fails', and that perhaps it is time to 'descend from the mountain', end composing and retire. Come down from his considerable peak Sibelius would not, could not, however, just yet. Two more key, not to say astonishing, works lay within him, even if a third – an eighth symphony – would lie tantalizingly out of reach.

The Seventh's genesis is intimately entangled with those of the Fifth and Sixth Symphonies: many of Sibelius's final symphony's subjects can be traced back to the early months of the First World War, when the composer was forging ideas for several new large-scale orchestral works, cut off from the rest of the continent and many of his social circles. An apparently insignificant adagio motif appears in a notebook for the Fifth Symphony and later expanded and took root, eventually growing to become the basis for the Seventh, while the origins of the grand, even hallmark, trombone theme that recurs three times in the symphony can be located in sketches the composer made in the late 1910s for a proposed tone poem known as *Kuutar* (*The Moon Goddess*).

A letter to Axel Carpelan in May 1918, when the Fifth was being revised and ideas for a Sixth explored, reveals further early plans for another symphony. It will be, he wrote, a work distinguished by 'joy of life and vitality with *appassionato* sections. In three movements, the last a "Hellenic rondo"'. But the work did not stay with these specific features for long, and by the early 1920s we can see from the manuscripts that Sibelius had expanded his vision for the symphony into the more familiar four movements, with a G minor finale, the key that would, at this stage, apparently dominate key areas of the work.

We can determine with conviction only a small amount about the music for the Seventh at this stage, save for its second movement, a C major adagio, which forms the bulk of the musical material for the work in its final form, with much of the swifter moments deriving from the G minor finale. Work on the Sixth seems to have convinced Sibelius to turn this three- or four-movement symphony into a highly innovative one-movement work. The Sixth, as we saw in the previous chapter, yearned to be united. Its overall symphonic and structural boundaries are much more elided or merged than in his earlier symphonies, even if no movements are actually combined as in the Third and Fifth. Total unity was clearly the destination of the Sibelian symphony – and the Seventh was the chance to achieve it.

It is in the summer of 1923, long after the Sixth's premiere in February, that we first see the Seventh envisioned as a one-movement piece, with significant fluctuations to the tempo, and a symphony with its conclusion uncertain at this stage. Drafts developed at Ainola during the summer and into the autumn, with several endings sketched and re-sketched as time wore on, before the work was finally complete at the beginning of March 1924.[159]

Whatever the compulsive self-criticism that was partly Sibelius's character, partly the result of alcoholic moods, and partly an extraordinary artist's desire for perfection, it is true that the Seventh was something truly groundbreaking – and might well have tried the nerves and composure of the most blasé musical mind. Nothing like this symphony, with its one-movement span, had been attempted before. Alexander Scriabin often called his single-movement *Poem of Ecstasy* (1908) his Fourth Symphony, though it was never officially designated as such and across its twenty-minute span operates more with the freedom of a symphonic poem than the tighter demands of a

---

[159] It is certainly now possible to perform these earlier versions – and indeed they subsist as appendices in the BIS Sibelius Edition (on disc 5 in the volume 12 box, 'Symphonies'). Nonetheless, these alternatives should not be thought of as 'original' versions, such as might exist with the Fifth Symphony, but as conclusions to the symphony that, though achievable in performance, were resolutely discarded by their creator. In the first alternative, the music wanders into a trance after the third and final appearance of the great trombone theme, momentarily recollecting former themes, before escalating to a succinct climax. The second version is potentially more feasible in concert since it not only maintains closer links to the foregoing material but carries an air of dignity more in keeping with the atmosphere of the whole work.

symphony. Richard Strauss's *Alpine Symphony* (1915) might be regarded as a one-movement symphony – though there remain considerable questions as to whether it is in one movement or if it is a symphony. We have to go back a little further to find hints or precursors of what Sibelius achieved in his Seventh.

When he had completed *Parsifal* (1882), his final musikdrama (or *Bühnenweihfestspiel*,[160] as he called it), Richard Wagner intended to shift his attention from the opera house to the concert hall, composing symphonies: specifically, one-movement symphonies. Wagner had always been the master of orchestral transition in his stage works – think of the Descent to Nibelheim in *Rheingold*, the dawns of *Götterdämmerung* or the Good Friday music of *Parsifal* – so this kind of symphonic work would seem to be the next logical step for a composer who had achieved everything he could in musikdrama.

Across his career, Wagner gave greater and greater independence to the orchestra, so that in later works such as *Siegfried*, *Götterdämmerung* and *Parsifal*, the players in the pit are creating most of the drama – before, during and after what is sung up on the stage. From here, Wagner wanted to create works where the orchestra existed on its own terms, without allusion to anything beyond itself – out of the theatre and into independent, self-governing orchestral music. We have little evidence of exactly how Wagner sought to achieve these new kinds of symphonies, however, because he died in 1883 before he was able to realize any of them. It seems that they would have been fixed orchestral

---

160 'Sacred festival stage play'.

improvisations, four-movement symphonies shrunk into a single arc, likely eschewing sonata form and existing as uninhibited and spontaneously constructed works, motifs freely evolving, and probably of quite a significant duration.

This is the form of work to which Sibelius's own symphonic career had been progressing, and it is clear that the dramatic and emotionally expressive consequences gained from fusing movements or eliding recognizable organizational divisions were something that engaged the frustrated Wagnerian in this Finn. Whatever his frequent vexations with Wagner's work, he had always been fascinated by the German's capacity in his musikdramas to broaden, contract and otherwise evolve his musical material with astonishing fluidity and power (and had Wagner actually composed one-movement symphonies, they would likely have been a bit of a stumbling block to Sibelius's own musical vision, even from the outset). Sibelius had made the technique within purely orchestral works his own, however. Formal compression and concision are dominant features of both his symphonies and tone poems, something we have seen throughout this book, especially when Sibelius came to revise works, taking the opportunity to refine and condense the musical ideas further as his abilities grew.

Those talents had explored several ways to advance symphonic form beyond the familiar boundaries of four movements and sonata form (with its progression of exposition, development and recapitulation). Other composers had done this too, of course – indeed, from the very outset of the form, symphonists were constantly toying with ways in which the form could be exploited, manipulated, twisted into new shapes. But Sibelius seems almost obsessively to be investigating ways in which his comprehension of flexibility and organic development in music could be applied to the symphony, that supreme expression of orchestral technique.

The Seventh comes, then, as the reasonable consequence of a maturing personal and historical situation. Whatever the logical goals of musical progression, however, Sibelius's Seventh Symphony does not necessarily exist with any degree of clarity or certainty: its innovation and originality defy many of the usual methods and labels. Is the work several movements exquisitely spliced together like a film reel, or one movement split into divergent episodes, or a set of variations, or a distended sonata-form design, or a form more akin to song, where verses are repeated?

To an extent, aspects of each of these possibilities enlighten us to the identity and form of Sibelius's Seventh, though many of them can prove misleading, undermining the very particular and refined techniques employed. *Episodes*, for example, is too clumsy a term for the sophisticated way Sibelius contrasts his material and subtly moves his score forward, making it virtually impossible for the listener to distinguish precisely where one section ends and another begins.

This basic formal obscurity/originality of itself generates a significant innate tension in the symphony, since it works dramatically (and paradoxically) against the fairly clear and simple layout of the work as a whole. It proceeds with devastating effortlessness, Sibelius's immensely gifted ability to develop, compress and fuse his material giving us supreme confidence in the direction he is taking us, and so allowing the ambiguity of overall form to ruffle, even jar, our perception of the music as we hear it.

Since Haydn had first given the symphony its Cambrian explosion (if not its parturition), each individual movement (typically four) would usually be unified by proceeding in a basically steady tempo, finding musical diversity through the employment of contrasting themes in a range of different keys. In his Seventh, Sibelius turned this principle upside down: the variety of the symphony is achieved through its constantly changing tempo, along with changes in colour, texture and overall articulation. Unity is provided by the key of C, since every noteworthy passage in the work occurs either in C major or C minor.

It was a courageous statement to make, in 1924. The underpinning of centuries of Western classical music, C was by now old hat for many, a tired institution, the fuddy-duddy expression of a world now left behind in the exciting tonal developments of Schoenberg et al. But even the radical princes of the Second Viennese School themselves would hardly have agreed with that. C was just as valuable, as flexible, as radical as it had ever been – if one had the imagination to make use of it.

In Sibelius's hands, C, and especially C major, attains a new freshness, surpassing even his use of the key in his own Third Symphony, and the Seventh is one of the most majestic and outstanding celebrations of the key ever made, a triumph turning the New Testament parable on its head: new wine *could* be poured into old wineskins.[161] Yet while it realizes cleanliness and originality, Sibelius's C major also acquires a darkness to some degree hitherto unexplored. At times the Seventh can

---

161 Cf. Matthew 9:14–17; Mark 2:18–22; Luke 5:33–39.

feel like a scream of pain, a vision of an apocalyptic ending to tonality and the symphony. Sibelius's orchestration is subtle and meticulous enough not to simply pronounce a familiar old key but to exploit its murkier edge, taking us to its margins and hinterlands, its death zones.

It takes the Seventh Symphony sixty bars to properly locate C major, to assert it fully for the first time; at the end it re-embraces C major only after a struggle (of opulent scoring), and even then its accomplishment is harassed by sustained dissonances which only grudgingly resolve. So often in this work, especially at its conclusion, we can feel a sigh of relief that it is over, the striving completed, the release into death and/or infinity achieved. How far this is a positive or a negative thing is up to both individual performers and listeners – which is to say it is a problem for us, not the symphony.

So while the Seventh salvages the potential of tonality – the extraordinary affirmative power of C major – it does so with at the very least a wry smile, and perhaps something far more forlorn than that. The symphony achieves C major, but only with the last gasp of its journey. Given what we know about Sibelius's life at the time, and our hindsight about the position of the Seventh as the last in line of his symphonies, it is hard not to take this as a semi-biographical statement of resignation and release. Nonetheless, Sibelius is extremely careful to leave his ego at the door, and for all the darkness and opacity of the Seventh, it remains a grand statement about the redemptive, transcendent possibilities of tonal music.

The Seventh's engagement with the key of C is one of its defining characteristics. Yet what makes it perhaps most distinctive, and so innovative, is its use of constantly varying tempo (within a seamless single movement) as an elaborate, and profoundly moving, form of symphonic expression.

As a means of understanding how the technique works in practice, one of Sibelius's familiar analogies from nature is a helpful guide. The procedure of symphonic form, he argues, is like the formation of a riverbed: a river is made up of countless tributaries – brooks, creeks, streams, rivulets and so on – all of which eventually extend outwards in a majestic manner into the sea. But it is the transfer and traffic of the water itself which influences, and ultimately shapes, the character and contours of the riverbed. Likewise, in the Seventh the organizational groundwork of the symphony, its overall structure, is determined by the current of musical concepts – they are not bound by superficial or apparent customs of symphonic/sonata form but are liberated into the realm of their own fashioning. And it is the subtle shifts in tempo which largely operate as this symphonic hydraulic action, though minute changes in tonality and texture, corrosive or abrasive action, are also quietly at work.

In the Seventh, Sibelius has the music speed up and slow down with phenomenal delicacy, restraint and expressive power, accelerating from an adagio to an allegro and slackening from presto material back to an adagio. The way in which Sibelius is able to effect the continual, unbroken transition between tempos is the result of decades of refinement in technique and ideas about the evolution of symphonic movements – it is far more than simply increasing the speed like a racing driver pushing their foot to the floor or easing off the gas.

Sibelius is able to twist and bend time, both disorientating us and making us feel infinitely secure. At certain points in the symphony, the music accelerates so much that the general effect is actually of time appearing to slow down, or even operating in reverse. To return to our racing car image, when vehicles travel fast enough, their wheels sometimes seem to travel backwards – something especially apparent on television, where the illusion of movement is created via a series of frames. Each frame catches the wheel at a particular point in its rotation, so that when the wheel's speed is such that it travels through less than one whole revolution before the next frame is captured, the resultant effect is the look of the wheel either slowing down or revolving backwards.

Just as our brain-eye system has a limit on what it can process, so too the brain-ear one is subject to illusions in its perception of sounds. Sibelius has sped up the music of the Seventh so much that time gives the strange appearance of suddenly slowing down: the frenetic, accelerated music becomes the gently rippling current of sound out of which the majestic trombone theme can emerge for the third and final time. It is a musical trick, a sonic deception – and one of the most exhilarating moments in all Sibelius.

IRCAM[162] is a French institute dedicated to the research of music and sound, especially in the fields of the avant-garde and electro-acoustical music. It was founded by that great *enfant terrible* of modernism Pierre Boulez and finds itself at No.1 Place

---

162 Institut de recherche et coordination acoustique/musique ('Institute for Research and Coordination in Acoustics/Music').

Igor Stravinsky, Paris, next to the cathedral of artistic modernity, the Pompidou Centre. Few organizations can claim to be more in the service of pervasive musical progress than this. It was here, in the 1980s, that Sibelius's Seventh was revered as a cult piece by the writers of so-called spectral music – works where compositional decisions are based on sonographic representations and mathematical analysis of sound spectra. The vanguards of modernism were especially in awe of how Sibelius, so often regarded as a conservative bore, was able to conjure up such astonishing luminosity in his string writing. In the same decade, another legendary pioneer of extreme experimentation in music, Morton Feldman, reminded his students at the pugnaciously contemporary Darmstadt Summer School that 'the people who you think are conservative might really be radical' – before mischievously humming a tune from Sibelius's Fifth.

And Sibelius's Seventh is even more radical than his Fifth. It departs from conventional formal paradigms, offering something fresh, self-determining and supremely fluid. But, for all the divergences and innovations, it nonetheless remains an abstract symphony of considerable architectonic quality, dramatic tension and expressive profundity to match any of his – or anyone else's – earlier essays in the medium. It is a construction that seems to simultaneously extend and defy a tradition. Sibelius was a radical, but a quiet one, never a rowdy extremist or a tedious militant in his case for musical progression.

In the Seventh, Sibelius married both the reasoning and interdependence of classical convention with a more extemporizing technique where the music is in a constant state of becoming, arising from within itself. Sibelius showed how traditional forms could be extended, even challenged, with something more modern and self-liberating, but without the need for many of the musical disintegrations of his contemporaries. Accordingly, the Seventh aims to augment classical ideals even as it also unobtrusively seeks to destabilize them – it is what we might call a 'Trojan Norse'.

In both emotional and architectural terms, the Seventh is in many ways the inverse of the Fourth, Sibelius's other supreme symphonic triumph. But where the Fourth, whatever its superb inner logic, can so often chase turmoil, uncertainty, a breakdown into anarchy, oblivion and despair, the Seventh constantly yearns for clarity and inevitability, music elucidated with thoroughgoing logic and lucidity. That the Seventh's progress frequently threatens and undermines its own desire for translucence is a mark of not its failure but its success. It is an enrichment of both its musical language and its sonic journey, a journey as concentrated as the finest single malt whisky – or hydrochloric acid, for it can burn as much as it soothes, the symphony screaming for cogency and coherence.

So much of the conception and execution of the Seventh have a flawless, crystalline quality to them. But the more we listen to the symphony, the less perfect and more human it can become, displaying vulnerability, isolation and all that flesh is heir to. It is not, in truth, the enemy opposite to the Fourth, but is its major-key twin: lonely, exposed, fatalistic. And just as how in the Fourth that work's fabled bleakness functions as a strange comfort blanket, so the major-key resolution of the Seventh is not quite the victory it seems but something more mystical and uncertain.

At its close the Seventh moves towards catastrophe and collapse but is saved, at its last moment, by an abrupt transition into transcendence, benediction and the most ambivalent C major chord in history. It has found liberation through letting go, surrendering itself to the cosmos.

Symphony No.7 in C major, op.105

Given the innovative status of Sibelius 7 as a one-movement symphony, it might seem unwarranted to divide it up here. However, for the purposes of analysis, such dissection – isolating four key areas – will be beneficial, even if we should always recognize the ceaselessly seamless quality of this masterpiece.

1. Adagio.

The Seventh Symphony opens with a drum's subpoena – a triple tap in G from the timpani far away in the night. It rouses a slow ascending C major scale, rising up from the darkness like magma on the lower strings: cellos and basses come first and are soon joined by the violas, then the violins. It is strange, shapeless, threatening, but a remarkably simple and effective means to begin the work. Striking, solemn, it is a series of steps to a place we know not yet where.

These measures, as the symphony bleeds into our consciousness, take us to an unforeseen chord in remote A-flat minor, and the ominous gloom of Wagner's *Tristan und Isolde* seems hazily reminiscent in our ears. Tonal tensions between A flat and other keys will generate much of the symphony's inner drama, and it is important, not to say portentous, that this stress is announced early on. A crucial embryonic theme – dating from some of the earliest sketches for the symphony – comes from the flutes, pensively falling and rising, and is echoed by the clarinets.

This ends the prelude section of the Seventh, and the music is able to develop from here into a noble chorale of polyphonic enchantment with the strings in full voice, the violas and cellos singing an exquisite contemplative hymn. This builds with gathering intensity in sublime anticipation towards the first climax of the symphony when, with inexorable magic, a magnificent trombone theme in C major emerges organically from within the strings. It is an instantly memorable subject, reminiscent of those which govern the finales of Beethoven's Ninth and Brahms's First. One of the architectural mainstays of the symphony, this trombone theme will recur twice more, though in different moods, during the Seventh, three structural-emotional pillars around which the whole work is built. Labelled 'Aino' in the sketches, the theme's three appearances – first awed, second turbulent, third reflective – might be cautiously said to mirror in the symphony features and phases of the composer's relationship with his wife.

2. *Vivacissimo.*

An Olympian apex, from here the music abates into a slower section with a theme which will later reappear under a 'farewell' guise: everything in this weblike work is exquisitely interconnected. The string theme, plus the opening rising scale, along with figures from the trombone theme, are developed together as the first major variation of pulse in the symphony occurs: with infinite subtlety, the music invisibly hastens into its *vivacissimo* section, bucolic in character, like a pastoral interlude, lively, pirouetting, with just a hint of blithe scherzo.

The tempo begins to increase further – along with the tension – and a number of tonal possibilities are explored before C minor is arrived at amid some fast disjointed chords angrily exchanged between the strings and woodwind. The music becomes tremendously tempestuous and much more chromatically agitated, with worrying ascending and descending scales whirling in the strings as the trombone theme reappears, now ferociously turned to the minor, like celestial thunder unable to contain itself. It is a moment of crisis at the centre of the symphony, coming – like many an argument – seemingly out of nowhere, but also as logical and inevitable as a mathematical QED.

3. *Allegro moderato.*

From this cataclysmic summit, the symphony varies and reiterates its themes, manoeuvring stealthily and symmetrically back into its pastoral mode and a section often termed a 'Hellenic rondo' after Sibelius's own use of the phrase. It is truly the calm after the storm, and filled with a wondrously fresh light and air as we find our way back to the topography of C major.

The music once again becomes a gradual accelerando ultimately attaining presto strength, with pieces from the *vivacissimo* section resurfacing in darker colours as the strings restate some of the 'scherzo' material in a vortex of frenzied tension. Everything is surging forward with an unstoppable momentum and logical coherence: it is pure Sibelius.

From here the music broadens via a repeat of the ascending scale motif, which rises up magnificently to become the third and final appearance of the trombone theme. It is luxuriously orchestrated, now in its most majestic formulation, an extraordinary sonic mixture of elation and acceptance, an almost dangerously manic high hovering near disarray. Much of this effect is generated beneath the brass, with funereal rumblings on the lower strings that begin to rise and rise, leading to a catastrophic, overwhelming climax.

4. Coda.

Soon the coda/epilogue (to balance the opening prelude) begins, and the strings recall the 'farewell' motif first heard after the initial appearance of the trombone theme, to be joined by a range of poignant ideas from the woodwind, recollecting the distant past of the symphony.

A melancholic mood emerges amid the strings, but one blessed by a sense of divine sanction, and against a curtain of tremolo in the strings, the symphony briefly glances one last time at the trombone theme – a heartrending valediction to Aino – before the remarkable ending, which was redrafted on not less than three occasions.

The conclusion is a defiant abridged crescendo, contingent but cogent, a straightforward ascendent resolution of dissonance: at the very end, the music aches up from B to the long-expected C. It is a brusque gesture, utterly Sibelian in its concision and emotional power, as well as, perhaps, in its equivocation: for the C major chord which closes the work is surely the most ambiguous ever expounded, transcending into neither darkness nor light but a dignified serenity. After battling through the hostile environment of existence, the symphony rises into the firmament to mingle with eternity and the stars.

One sequence on the double basses very near the close seems to evoke Sibelius's own *Valse triste* (originally part of the incidental music for Arvid Järnefelt's 1903 stage drama *Kuolema*, 'Death', but now better known as an independent concert item). If it is not an actual quotation – this composer tended to abhor such practices – then it is perhaps an unconscious connection of the symphony to the original play's concern with the liminal zones between life and death.

Certainly this appears to offer a more tangible means to comprehend the famous opacity of the symphony's ending, which presents neither triumph nor despair but something more numinous, an almost Buddhist sense of renewal and rebirth, a return to a different state of being. Here death is not solely to be regarded as an annihilation, an eradication of the self into everlasting nothingness, but as an opportunity for inner peace, poise and acceptance of one's unassuming place in the cosmos.

In hindsight, we can see the ending of the Seventh as the perfect, entirely logical, way for Sibelius to conclude his symphonic career. But his restless creative mind would seek one more opportunity to express itself in this ultimate medium of orchestral mastery. It was only natural that he should try to go even further – in the Eighth Symphony – though he did not need to (and, as it turned out, could not).

Chapter Thirteen

A Swarm of Symphonies: *The Tempest*

Just as the Seventh turned out to be an aptly majestic conclusion to Sibelius's great cycle of symphonies and *Tapiola* would come to magnificently close his sequence of tone poems, so too *The Tempest* was to be a remarkable, mercurial way for the Finn to bid farewell to writing music for the stage, an activity that had preoccupied him throughout his career. The subject, too, was entirely appropriate for this composer to conjure up in musical terms: the ageing magus, nature mysticism, supernatural forces, the relationship between freedom and constraint, the tensions linking humanity and its environment – sometimes creative, sometimes destructive – along with the redemptive, epiphanic power of forgiveness.

Although this haunting, enigmatic score, which also exists as two concert suites, is neither tone poem nor symphony, there are several reasons for including it in this book. First, it forms a vital expressive component of Sibelius's final phase, further illuminating the works which surround it. Second, the enchanting and evocative power of the music, as well as its range and refinement, make it nearly a collection of miniature tone poems, a series of highly illustrative pieces categorically tied to narrative, landscape, character and mood. It constantly suggests ideas and images, scenes and situations, and accordingly warrants a place as part of Sibelius's broad command of suggestive and descriptive composition.

Third, the musical kernels of the score operate almost as nano-symphonies, sonic seeds that yearn to be propagated and explored in large-scale structures with Sibelius's supreme gift for organic musical growth and cogent interconnection. Indeed, this was something their composer himself felt keenly, longing to return to his themes in more detail: 'Due to the stage action I have only been able to sketch them', he wrote. Yet for all this thwarted promise, this slight sense of unfulfilled facility, listening to the music, we never feel frustrated that the motifs are in some way stunted symphonies. We revel in their potential and vibrating possibility, admiring their capacity for greatness combined with their absolutely flawless function as – ultimately – supportive or background elements for a stage drama.

That said, of course, the music Sibelius created is background to nothing, for it commands our attention from the first moment it strikes our ears. Through its thirty-six numbers, in a sparkling score that lasts over an hour (one of his longest, and comparable to *Kullervo* or *Lemminkäinen*), it contains a remarkable range of colour, character, atmosphere and mood. This is all conveyed via a huge assortment of musical idioms and styles – evocations of composers ranging from Purcell and Prokofiev to Corelli and Stravinsky – in order to suit the diverse personalities and incidents the Bard packs into what is, after all, one of his shortest plays.

Shakespeare's *Tempest* is a verbal vortex of quirk and caprice, as well as a fascinating study of the human heart, soul and spirit, and an immense challenge to interpret or explain – whichever medium is chosen to do so. Sibelius rose to that challenge with his richest and most ambitious score for the theatre. For all its kaleidoscope of iridescent idiosyncrasies, however, what most especially moves us about Sibelius's music for *The Tempest* is perhaps what it has in common with its predecessors, the Sixth and Seventh Symphonies, and its successor, *Tapiola*. All four of these definitively late works have an ethereal beauty and are written in an elliptical quasi-mystical dialect imbued with a sense of engagement with and immersion into nature, something brought about through compassion and reconciliation – with life, with others, with the cosmos and with oneself.

After the various premieres and performances of the Seventh Symphony in 1924, Sibelius settled back down to life at Ainola. He spent some time with, by his own sad admission, his only true friend – the bottle – and frequented the restaurants of Helsinki (though Sibelius's drinking did not nearly match the industrial quantities imbibed by his neighbour, the poet Eino Leino, who drank himself to death aged forty-seven by January 1926). Sibelius did compose some relatively minor pieces at this time, including the five sparkling *Danses champêtres* for violin and piano, an exuberant, often virtuosic, series of mood and character pieces, not unlike those explored in Sibelius's piano works – and those which we will meet in the music for *The Tempest*.

The *Danses*' ebullience, however, masked a sense of creative inhibition and directionlessness, even apathy – they were diverting compositions which filled the lull and void (and coffers) before bigger projects materialized. The preceding years had seen the major enterprises of the Fifth, Sixth and Seventh Symphonies overlap to a considerable degree both in Sibelius's head and on paper, and the next step wasn't immediately clear, or even desirable, whatever it might turn out to be. Fortunately, he didn't have long to wait. The Seventh Symphony had proved especially popular in Denmark, and in the spring of 1925 Sibelius's Danish publisher Wilhelm Hansen wrote to his most famous client: 'Have you composed music for *The Tempest*? Det Kongelige Teater in Copenhagen will be performing the play and would like to use your music.'

Although Sibelius had not, in fact, written anything for *The Tempest*, Hansen and the Royal Danish Theatre were not the only ones who thought it a match made in artistic heaven. As far back as February 1901, before their friendship, Axel Carpelan – then writing in an anonymous, eccentric but inspirational capacity – contacted Sibelius suggesting musical projects:

> Now look here Mr. S., shouldn't you someday direct your interest to Shakespeare's dramas? … *The Tempest* would be very apt for you: Prospero (magician), Miranda, spirits of the earth and air, etc.

Since Sibelius would, in the year after receiving the Copenhagen commission, 1926, compose another work that Carpelan had earlier proposed – a 'Waldsymphonie' (or 'Forest Symphony', fulfilled as *Tapiola*) – we might hazard that in some capacity *The Tempest* had been quietly percolating in the composer's mind for a significant number of years: and after all, with *Timon of Athens*, *The Tempest* was Sibelius's favourite Shakespeare play.[163] Perhaps only now, as a self-confessed ageing artist, did Sibelius feel properly able to identify and engage with some of the play's subject matter. Hansen and Copenhagen were the right bait at the right time.

Now that he had a project he could get his teeth into, Sibelius's artistic flair was reignited like a bonfire, and he worked extraordinarily quickly – in part because the theatre had set an impossibly tight deadline of the end of the summer, but it was a swiftness given further impetus by the freedom incidental music had always afforded him. No longer bound by the strict laws of his own innovative but astringent symphonic logic, Sibelius's musical imagination could run riot, and this relative autonomy helped create his finest work for the stage. He began composing feverishly and had most of the vast score ready by the end of September – an astonishing feat, not least given the quality of the result. However, despite all the haste and Sibelius's delivery of the manuscript in mid-October, the production's premiere in Copenhagen was postponed until the following March, the theatre not reckoning on the difficulties involved in staging Debussy's *Pelléas* and Stravinsky's *Petrushka* in the same season.

On 8 December 1925, Sibelius turned sixty: a national occasion but one he, perhaps wisely, chose to spend quietly with his daughter Eva and her family at their home in Helsinki, shunning the attention, declining to appear in public, refusing to be the municipal monument he knew he had become for so

---

163 '*Timon of Athens* is dearest to me because of its humanity; *The Tempest* because of its musicality', wrote Sibelius in a letter of 7 January 1926 to Gunnar Hauch, a Danish journalist and ardent advocate for the Finn's music.

many.[164] Birthday gifts in the form of large civic donations and a countrywide collection he did accept, however, money which finally freed him from most of his financial obligations and other assorted economic woes. His pension was also raised, and the mixed-voice choirs of Finland, long dear to his heart, grouped together to purchase for this Finnish icon a hectare of land around the Ainola estate.[165]

The first performances of *The Tempest*, directed by Johannes Poulsen, took place in Copenhagen in March 1926, and although the production itself received mixed notices, the music was deemed an unqualified success: 'Shakespeare and Sibelius, these two geniuses, have found each other', commented one critic. The composer of the music chose not to attend the performances: the constant delays and postponements had, understandably and justifiably, not given him confidence in the theatre. Instead, travelling south from Finland in late March 1926, Sibelius avoided dropping in on the production in Copenhagen and carried straight on to Berlin and thence Rome and Capri, where he continued work on an exciting new commission he had received from New York.

---

164 The president of Finland, no less, Lauri Relander, did track him down, however, presenting the Order of the White Rose of Finland to the composer in his daughter's house. It is not known if His Excellency stayed for tea.

165 Robert Kajanus, himself now nearing seventy, conducted an all-Sibelius concert on 9 December with the First Symphony at the centre of the programme, while several other countries marked the birthday with performances of their own: such was Sibelius's global standing by now.

Shakespeare's expressive power, rich characterization, endless psychological insights – and to be sure, his fame – mean that his plays have proved a happy hunting ground for composers keen to exploit and explore his work in musical terms. Operas, ballets, overtures, tone poems: the collaboration between composers and the Bard has been an immensely prosperous one across the centuries and from a vast range of aesthetic places and perspectives, music transporting the dramas into new arenas of comprehension and debate.

Opera has been the most obvious medium through which composers have responded to Shakespeare, not least because the librettos are – in one form or another – simply there for the taking. The nineteenth century was fertile territory for Shakespearean opera as the Romantic craze for the Bard inspired numerous adaptations: Bellini (1837)[166] and Gounod (1867) tackled *Romeo and Juliet*, Rossini a Roderigo-centred *Othello* (1816), Wagner *Measure for Measure* (*Das Liebesverbot*, 1836), Berlioz *Much Ado About Nothing* (*Béatrice et Bénédict*, 1862), Thomas *Hamlet* (1868), Bruch *The Winter's Tale* (*Hermione*, 1872) and Goetz *The Taming of the Shrew* (*Der Widerspenstigen Zähmung*, 1874). Verdi was obsessed. His *Macbeth* (1847; 1865) was followed by numerous aborted attempts at a *Re Lear*, before he was persuaded to conclude his opera career with two wholly different Shakespearean masterpieces: *Otello* (1887), full of grandeur and agony, then the comic brio of *Falstaff* (1893), amalgamating the often overlooked *Merry Wives of Windsor* with elements from the magnificent *Henry IV* plays, especially the darker, more ambiguous characterization of the titular fat knight.

---

166 *I Capuleti e i Montecchi* – though Bellini was working from an Italian source by Luigi Scevola, even if his overall inspiration was likely to have been the wider Shakespeare fashion at the time.

The craze exhibited no signs of abating in the twentieth and twenty-first centuries, with more recent composers and their librettists becoming far more playful and imaginative, showing often radically inventive departures from their source material. Holst's *At the Boar's Head* (1925) and Vaughan Williams's *Sir John in Love* (1929) re-examined Falstaff from the English point of view, while Cole Porter's *Kiss Me, Kate* (1948) and Bernstein's *West Side Story* (1957) explored new ways of reacting to, respectively, *Taming of the Shrew* and *Romeo and Juliet* from an American perspective.

Britten's *A Midsummer Night's Dream* (1960) utilized the libretto-like qualities of Shakespeare's play in an opera of boundless charm and musical resourcefulness, while Reimann's outstanding *Lear* (1978) took a ruthlessly cruel play and made it even darker, with a sonically savage score. Barber's *Antony and Cleopatra* (1966), when it had recovered from its disastrous Manhattan premiere, was revealed to be a sensitive, fascinating musical consideration of a hybrid gem, and in the new century, Brett Dean's stunning *Hamlet* (2017) has shown that with mischief, wit and imagination, even a play as familiar as the prince of Denmark's can be reborn in astonishing new ways.

The Tempest's blend of nature, magic, exile and reconciliation have proved irresistible to opera composers down the centuries: over forty versions have been ventured, though, of course, many have been lost. Poet Laureate Thomas Shadwell got in early with *The Enchanted Isle*, from 1674, with a score created by a team of composers that included Matthew Locke and Pelham Humfrey, and later given a musical setting by John Weldon (in music often falsely attributed to Henry Purcell). This was followed by voluminous others before Michael Tippett's problematic *The Knot Garden* (1970) reconfigured the play to explore humanity's psychosexual anguish. More successful was Thomas Adès's 2004 *Tempest*: a triumph of creativity, presenting a colourful, tonally inventive score that appropriately ranged from the dissonant to the lyrical. Meredith Oakes's dynamic libretto reduced the text to its essence and showed how Shakespeare operas did not need to be contained by the hallowed text and could take on vibrant, self-motivated lives of their own while remaining true to their source's spirit.

Beyond the opera house, *The Tempest* has attracted countless other musical interpretations: Beethoven's piano sonata No.17 in D minor (1802) is said (by a somewhat unreliable witness) to have been inspired by the play; Tchaikovsky wrote a symphonic fantasy (1873), John Knowles Paine a tone poem (1876), Arthur Honegger an orchestral prelude (1923), while there are numerous ballets, overtures, songs and choral settings stimulated by the stormy subject. Dozens of sets of incidental music have been written for the play's performance – among only the more famous names, Arthur Bliss, Arthur Sullivan, Malcolm Arnold, Lennox Berkeley, Engelbert Humperdinck and Ernest Chausson – but one in particular has become more eminent and enduring than all of them: that from Jean Sibelius.

It is perhaps easy, especially from the position of hindsight, to see exactly what appealed to Sibelius about *The Tempest* – throughout his life, but particularly as he approached sixty in 1925. There was the autumnal setting of Shakespeare's play, belying the implied southerly/equatorial locale of the island, with its air of change, melancholy and reflection. There was the harsh environment, again presented as more northerly and austere than one might expect. There was also this tragicomedy's intricate fusion of conspiracy, wit, death, disaster and compassion – its linking of mournful themes with humorous resolutions – that attracted different sides of Sibelius's personality. There was the drama's formal perfection of tight patterns and compression, taking in nine separate scenes that are not only symmetrically balanced but even palindromic in their sequence (principal characters of each scene given):

A. (I.i)		Shipwreck (Chaos)
B. (I.ii)		Prospero / Miranda / Ferdinand
C. (II.i)		Antonio / Alonso / Sebastian
D. (II.ii)		Caliban / Trinculo / Stephano
E. (III.i)		Prospero / Miranda / Ferdinand
D. (III.ii)		Caliban / Trinculo / Stephano
C. (III.iii)		Antonio / Alonso / Sebastian
B. (IV.i)		Prospero / Miranda / Ferdinand
A. (V.i)		Shipwreck (Restoration)

There was also the way the play both adhered to the classical unities[167] and turned them against themselves through an opening out into unbounded time and space, something Sibelius could exploit and explore via music.

Sound and music, of course, were already integral features of the play, part of its many innovations in the early seventeenth-century theatre.[168] A great deal of the atmosphere is generated

---

[167] According to Aristotle's prescriptive theories in his *Poetics*, drama – especially tragic drama – should maintain one time, place and action.

[168] It was probably written in 1611 for London's new Blackfriars Theatre, which, being an indoor space, could utilize and control sound in a way entirely different to the more usual outdoor Globe.

through sound. Stage directions abound in asking for acoustic effects, while several characters are required to sing: most obviously in Ariel's songs,[169] but drunken revels and the more formal music of the masque are also significant auditory markers. The pervasiveness of *The Tempest*'s sound and music is also conveyed by the text itself. There are its constant references to aural phenomena – Caliban tells the newcomers that 'the isle is full of noises, sounds and sweet airs that give delight'[170] – along with the inherent musicality of the play's language, its poetic ambiguity and elliptical charm, which Sibelius enjoyed so much. It was ripe for musical interpretation.

In terms of characters – *The Tempest*'s animated but ambiguous characters – there was the inspirational energy of Ariel, who acts as a binding gel across the drama (something Sibelius realizes in music too), along with the wilder side of the Finn's personality seen through Caliban (who also contained a quiet nobility amid his persecution). There were the drinking diversions of Trinculo and Stephano, who curiously emulate Sibelius's own behaviour, not least that witnessed in Akseli Gallen-Kallela's (in)famous 'Symposium' paintings depicting the youthful composer in his cups.

Most obviously, of course, there was Shakespeare's great magus, the magician Prospero, as authoritative and compelling a portrayal of the complex creative artist as any in literature, and a symbol for Sibelius of his own being. That this figure was also an exile, and on the threshold of retirement, of relinquishing his powers, of achieving an ambivalent closure, was an additional fascination, allowing the fictional character to merge even

---

169 The original music for two of Ariel's songs ('Full fathom five' and 'Where the bee sucks') survives, composed by a lutenist connected with James I's court, Robert Johnson.

170 III.ii.135–6.

further with the composer's own personality. Sibelius had been withdrawing for years, never into total isolation, but both socially and musically in his life there was a sense of growing renunciation, a need for greater and greater solitude, away not only from people but even artistic manufacture. Cryptic, a little aloof – Prospero mirrored Sibelius as he had echoed so many before (he was even occasionally a bit cranky and had a daughter for added veracity).

Just as the isolation, and to a lesser extent misanthropy, of Timon appealed to Sibelius, so too Prospero's creative fury, vision, lonely wandering and turning away from the world ('every third thought shall be my grave', he laments at the play's end) spoke keenly to the composer. There are many different Prosperos, as with most of Shakespeare's greatest creations – everything from benign parent and pioneering scientist to ruthless dictator and callous bully – but it was the lonely artist that resonated with Sibelius, charging his musical interpretation of the character along with his perspectives of the wider drama.

Solitude, separation, retirement – whatever the sense of loss inherent to Prospero, he is always a creative force, dominating and controlling his play's action, a manipulative inventor and cunning dramatic architect. Add the two together and you generate that elusive, indistinct aesthetic phenomenon: 'late style'. Shakespeare had explored it himself, not only in *The Tempest* but in two other late tragicomedies: *Pericles* and *The Winter's Tale*, both of which carry a similarly wistful air along with narrative trajectories from ostracism towards mercy and rebirth (as well as the role of daughters as redemptive energies, something close to Sibelius's heart, even as he mourned his girls' childhood and their successive departures from Ainola).

'Lateness' in art is an opportunity for renewal and resurgence, even and because it must face up to either death or waning powers. Among Sibelius's composer forebears, Beethoven was perhaps the exemplar here, with his three distinctive (if sometimes misleading) creative periods, the last of which, with the *Missa solemnis*, late sonatas and quartets, offered a very clear sense of contemplative revitalization and proffered final statements. In Sibelius too, a closing tetraptych – the Sixth and Seventh Symphonies, *Tapiola* and *The Tempest* – tendered a creative response to mortality, a personal eschatology in the liminal late zone between life and death.

Yet it was *The Tempest* which offered the most extravagant act of uninhibited rejuvenation, a productive emancipation that could also be an enthralling hub of discovery. The symphonies and pseudo-symphony *Tapiola* were bound both by degrees of convention and Sibelius's own strict rules of symphonic logic. Incidental music carried no such weight of expectation, and *The Tempest* provided Sibelius's powers of thematic resourcefulness and stylistic originality the latitude for extraordinary possibility, even if (as we saw earlier) he would sometimes want to then harness this freedom and develop his material along more symphonic lines – old habits die hard.

In their complete configuration, the magical sonorities of Sibelius's *Tempest* last for over an hour, and this is the only version that should really be heard now – given its richness, variety and immense thematic ingenuity. Whatever the merits of (Sibelius's own) two concert suites in promoting this brilliant music further, they simply squeeze and excise far too much that is outstanding as well as truncate the fundamental narrative, confusing the drama that meant so much to the composer.

The full score requires, as well as a large orchestra, five vocal soloists and a mixed-voice choir, along with a harmonium and additional percussion. One of the work's most fascinating, and innovative, features is the way Sibelius toys with spatial dynamics and effects. The harp is positioned very high over the actors' heads, far away from the rest of the orchestra (for reasons that will become clear), while the choir and several key instruments are likewise relocated above and behind the stage. Sibelius, for all his frustrated attempts at composing a full-length opera, was a great man of the theatre, knowing its acoustic possibilities and peculiarities as well as Wagner or Britten.

To confer unity on this huge score, Sibelius divided his material into, as Daniel Grimley has argued, four key musical categories: nature, archaic, pastoral and orientalist (which usually, but do not always, stand for character groupings). They also crucially function as suppliers of the range of settings and moods this tragicomedy demands, along with fundamental roles relating to dramatic continuity and a wider emotional-philosophical commentary on the action.

The orientalist music – featuring percussion, chromaticism and short, repeated rhythmic patterns – is most closely associated with Caliban and tends to reinforce somewhat outdated, conventional and stereotypical attitudes towards non-European music and peoples. Nonetheless, the composer is careful to blend these sounds with other areas of the score, especially the weird banquet of the European villains with its strange spirits and Ariel as a harpy, complicating any one-dimensional or restricted categorization. The pastoral group is fairly wide-ranging, related to the play's spirits as well as its masque and comedy, bringing a rural atmosphere and sense of bucolic mischief to the music. The archaic category is essentially aristocratic, associated with the leading Europeans – Prospero, Miranda, Alonso – and breathing an air of stylized refinement yet antiquated modality (the Dorian mode, familiar from the Sixth Symphony, is frequently employed).

Above and around these three categories lies that of nature, whose turbulent, unrestrained and sinister quality governs and permeates the score, whether in loud or soft mode. It is most prominent, of course, in the great blustery overture that precedes the action (and replaces the opening scene of Shakespeare's play[171]), one of the most authentic, literal and powerful depictions of a storm ever composed – and which must have startled the audience on opening night in Copenhagen.

Sibelius's storm has a lineage in musical history, owing a great deal of its spectacle to earlier musical tempests: Vivaldi's summer storm in the *Four Seasons* (1725), Beethoven's rural squall in his *Pastoral* Symphony (1808), Berlioz's distant thunder in the *Symphonie fantastique* (1830), the high-altitude deluge that disrupts Strauss's day in the mountains in his *Alpine Symphony* (1915), as well, of course, as Wagner's great sonic tornado that sprays wind and surf into our faces as he opens his maritime opera, *The Flying Dutchman* (1843). What all these works, along with Sibelius's *Tempest* overture, share is their combination of straightforward naturalist musical depictions of extreme climatological conditions with more complex psychological weather – for the characters about to come onstage, those implied

---

171 There had been a precedent, of course: Verdi scrapped the entire Venetian first act of *Othello*, opening his *Otello* instead with a very brief agitated musical prelude, before taking us straight to the action in Cyprus.

by the programme music (such as Beethoven's country folk), or the listeners themselves.

Sibelius combines these meteorological and emotional elements superbly: percussion crash and thunder through the air, scales burst with flashes of dark energy, gruesome brass slide in threatening fashion, piercing woodwind fizz and sputter like lightning or gusts of wind. Boundless waves of sound – whether generated by texture, tune or dynamics – surge through the score, vivacious configurations roaring and dovetailing towards a terrible climax before closing with quivering strings and isolated toiling chords from the wind instruments. As with the storm that opens Wagner's *Die Walküre* (1856), this is not merely a portrayal of nature at its most violent but a psycho-dramatic portrait of a character, showing us inner rage and turmoil, as well as the wider tempests of fragile human existence amid a chaotic cosmos.

A magnificent, thrilling way to open proceedings, the overture works superbly in its musico-dramatic function for *The Tempest*, but it is also clearly linked to the anguish of Prospero's Monologue towards the very end of the score, and to the other storms in Sibelius's final major quartet of works. In Shakespeare's play, Prospero's great speech 'Ye elves of hills' (V.i.33–57) expresses his desire to depart the island and retire, ending with the resonant phrase 'I'll drown my book'. For Sibelius, in music, the speech – evoked only by the orchestra – becomes something even more calamitous, a catastrophe, heightening awareness of contingency, of melancholy, of mortality. The dissonance is deafening, scowling and growling in the most alarming music of the whole score, and with an abrupt interruption when Prospero famously snaps his staff in an ultimate gesture of finality. Yet this becomes the opportunity for the solemn music which follows.

The crisis of the abjuration dissolves into a tranquil string hymn in B major, the dissonance disappearing into an inner/outer calm of classical heavenly harmony (allowing Ariel's final song plus the brief cortège proceedings that ensue).

The B major adagio that follows Prospero's crisis is a celestial balm after agony, the beginning of a new life and reclaimed compassion, but it is also a requiem for lost powers, for the life and creative energies that are now coming to an end. It is a wonderful blend of hope and regret, sorrow and submission. Although both Shakespeare's play and Sibelius's score continue after the 'Ye elves ... drown my book' speech, in many ways it represents the true ending of the drama; the rest is postscript.

It is fascinating, if a little superfluous, to speculate on what Sibelius might have done with this music's transition from catastrophe to peace within a larger framework – though in some sense he did: the Sixth and Seventh Symphonies, plus *Tapiola*, all have turbulent passages that are remarkably conspicuous in their musical journeys towards conclusion and/or fulfilment. In particular, the imposing trombone theme of the Seventh Symphony undertakes a series of metamorphoses not unlike those of Prospero, travelling through glorious majesty to thundery despair to redemptive resignation, its central C minor manifestation a tumult not unlike that of Prospero's Monologue but which likewise opens the way towards resolution. The sonic predicaments and transient devastations of late Sibelius are, accordingly, ruptures towards fortune and form an important part of the structural and salvific features of his final creative phase, offering – in the familiar formula – opportunities as well as crises.

However far we wish to identify either Shakespeare or Sibelius with Prospero, and it is certainly tempting, unfortunately it doesn't quite work. The 'Ye elves ... drown my book' speech is habitually taken to autobiographically express Shakespeare's own imminent withdrawal from writing for the stage, and while he was plausibly aware his career was coming to an end, in fact he continued to collaborate on a number of plays, including *Henry VIII*, *The Two Noble Kinsmen*, and the now lost *Cardenio*.

Likewise, as we can see from both his diary and the character of his later music, although Sibelius's thoughts were tending towards retirement and what he considered to be his impending demise, as both composer and human being, he did not stop writing music. He had done so much: with Prospero he had musically 'bedimmed the noontide sun', set 'the green sea and azure vault' at war, even 'given fire' to the dead by rousing Kullervo to reanimation in his early choral symphony. But for all this realized achievement, retire he did not. Not only did he go on in 1926 to compose one last – and perhaps greatest – tone poem, *Tapiola*, but he planned another symphony, the fabled Eighth, continued to write smaller pieces and tinkered with larger ones.

Sibelius had no intention of abjuring his musical magic, of drowning his book of sounds. He was experiencing various forms of crisis, doubt and dissolution, and these are apparent in his work of the 1920s, but he was also pushing his art further forward into new arenas of imagination and logical expansion. He had nearly reached as far as he could impel that art to go, but he wasn't there quite yet.

For now he remained, in Prospero's words, amid the 'cloud-capped towers, the gorgeous palaces, the solemn temples' of his extraordinary music.[172]

The Tempest, op.109

Prospero, duke of Milan and a remarkable magician, was usurped from his throne by his brother Antonio, assisted by Alonso, king of Naples. Escaping by boat with his infant daughter, Miranda, Prospero fled to a remote island where they have lived ever since. On the island he uses his magic to coerce the monstrous figure of Caliban to protect them, while Ariel, a spirit of the air, serves him. Twelve years later, a ship carrying Antonio, Alonso, his son Ferdinand, and various other passengers passes by, and, exploiting his powers, Prospero conjures a storm to wreck the vessel and bring his adversaries to the island.

Act 1

1. Overture – The Storm and the Sinking of the Ship: *Largamente molto*. [Nature]

Replacing the first scene of Shakespeare's play, Sibelius conjures the storm of the title with an orchestral overture of extraordinary power and imaginative sonority. This staple of musical theatre

---

[172] IV.i.152–3.

might have sounded hackneyed or trite, but not in Sibelius's hands. He had included stormy sections in his symphonies and tone poems, but these had specific tonal/architectural contexts: here he could let his fancy run riot with the storm and its oceanic environment, unfettered by overtly logical restrictions.

Employing a screeching, screaming 'white noise' – hunks of sound generated from whole-tone chords, i.e., without intervening tones/semitones – the effect is marvellously successful: an adrenaline-charged, white-knuckle ride, invigorating and not a little disorientating. Waves smash and winds howl, percussion crashing all over the place, brass and woodwind working especially well against the impatient, agitated and whirling strings to conjure complex upsurges of sound.

This is all underpinned by slow bass pedal notes below the surface texture, a relentless marine undercurrent that eventually dwindles into a sequence of angst-ridden horn calls as the mariners are delivered to the island.

2. Miranda Falls Asleep: *Andante*. [Archaic]

Calming Miranda's fears about the fate of the seafarers, Prospero tells his Mélisandean daughter of his brother's treachery and how they came to live on the island, before placing her in a mysterious sleep with a mesmerizing gilded lullaby for harp and harmonium.

3. Ariel Flies In: *Allegro*. [Nature]

Prospero summons Ariel, and we hear the first of a series of very short recurrent passages depicting Ariel's flight (which reappear in Nos.5, 21 and 28–30). It is typical of this score's strange mercurial magic: a blast of Straussian noise and colour on the brass followed by capricious gestures from the woodwind and strings.

4. Chorus of the Winds: *Molto moderato*. [Nature]

Intoxicating, exhilarating, hallucinogenic, a restful choral song without words, attended by the harp and harmonium, conjures a pacifying atmosphere as Ariel reports on how he[173] raised the storm and wrecked the ship.

5. Ariel Hastens Away: *Allegro*. [Nature]

Commanded to assume the guise of an invisible mermaid ('nymph o' th' sea'), Ariel departs again to a now familiar symphonic burst, and Prospero orders his slave Caliban to assemble firewood.

6. Ariel's First Song, with Introduction and Choir, 'Come unto these yellow sands': *Poco con moto – Poco tranquillo – Poco a poco stretto*. [Pastoral]

Invisible, Ariel sings with the other spirits (mezzo and chorus), making the dogs bark and the cocks crow, and confusing Ferdinand, who has landed on the island apart from the others (and consequently mourns the apparent loss of his father). 'Where should this music be?' he asks, 'I' th' air, or th' earth?'

Ariel's song is a pastoral delight in D major, full of the breezy summer air on the coast, and reminiscent of the sunnier passages of the Second Symphony and *The Oceanides* (which share its key). Nevertheless, the song's beaming D major sunlight is

---

[173] Although Ariel is essentially genderless, Shakespeare's text refers to the character twice using the male pronoun *his* (I.ii.193 and III.iii.52).

progressively obscured by incursions from B flat. Not only does the tempestuous overture's dark influence linger in the memory, but we are reminded of Ariel's own association with the storm: he did, after all, raise it at Prospero's bidding. Ariel is a crucial element of nature, and his wild force is sometimes overlooked while we appreciate his airy charms and capricious evasions.

An orchestral introduction of luscious sweeping strings begins the song, followed by a choral passage from behind the stage with the harmonium high above it: together they make a radiant, encircling aura of sound. Ariel, when he first enters, is almost incidental, casual, by the by, but with a dark tide in the lower strings. His cheery charm is then further undercut by disquieting dissonant intrusions from the brass/percussion (as the dog spirits) recalling the moody reverberations of the storm overture.

7. Ariel's Second Song, 'Full fathom five thy father lies': *Largamente.* [Pastoral]

Refusing to disabuse Ferdinand about the dark fate of his father in the sea, Ariel sings another song. It is a mysterious and unforgettable refrain which employs the infamous tritone, that disreputable devil in music which pervades the Fourth Symphony, to haunting effect. One of the great highlights of the score, the song tolls as a funeral bell, an A minor chord twisted and deformed, drifting like a body down into the ocean depths.

In part a bleak evocation of nature, this is also a mournful lament, the trombones in particular giving the song a solemn dignity that is unmistakeably that of a committal, here a burial at sea (and a death which is twice fabricated – a double layer of imaginary deception – from both Ariel and Shakespeare/

Sibelius). The chorus of sea nymphs is especially effective, their oscillating drone a signal of bereavement and loss, hypnotizing Ferdinand (and us). It is a disorientation deepened by broadening the higher rhythmic patterns while maintaining the fundamental tempo beneath – toying with time, space and perspective much as the Seventh Symphony had done.

Seeing Ferdinand, Miranda immediately falls in love with him, for which Prospero straightaway imprisons the Neapolitan prince for treason.

Act 2

8. Interlude – Prospero: *Adagio – Poco meno adagio – Tempo primo*. [Archaic]

The entr'acte between the first and second acts is a magnificent character portrait of Prospero, as well as a means to transport the action to the other side of the island, where the rest of the shipwrecked but saved nobles have landed. The portrayal itself is a stately hymn, a robust baroque anthem, Purcellian in its dignified magic. Its outer parts are typical late Sibelius, while its more animated internal section recalls the younger composer of the first two symphonies, and even has flashes of *Kullervo*.

9. The Oak Tree (Ariel): *Molto moderato*. [Pastoral]

As per Poulsen's direction in the original Copenhagen production, Ariel is now disguised as a young oak tree. He snaps off a branch and plays a poignant, hypnotic tune, given by the flute, wandering dolefully through its melody and accompanied by harp arpeggios. Although an energetic and lively force in the play – and in Sibelius's music – there is something infinitely forlorn about Ariel: for all his fizzing movement about the island, he remains an imprisoned creature under Prospero's bondage, dreaming of self-determination.

10. Ariel's Third Song, 'While you here do snoring lie': *Moderato – Stringendo*. [Pastoral]

Alonso and Gonzalo (an honest old councillor who assisted Prospero in his original escape, not least by giving the magus his book of magic) have fallen into a deep sleep. As they slumber, Alonso's deceitful brother Sebastian and Prospero's treacherous brother Antonio plot to murder them. They are saved in the nick of time when Ariel's frosty song wakes them (ending with some snappish partings from the chorus).

11. Interlude – Caliban: *Allegretto – Più moderato – Poco a poco stretto*. [Orientalist]

Like Shakespeare's, Sibelius's portrayal of Caliban, the half-man, half-monster native of the island, is a problematic caricature, a somewhat crude stereotype of brutish otherness and exoticism. The music moves with an opaque, vulgar tread, cock-eyed strings and a weird countermelody in the wind – and is further characterized by percussive and tonal effects intended to convey 'oriental' vibes (triangle, xylophone, cymbals, bass drum) but now sounding at best like a childish *Arabian Nights* or, at worst, dangerously racist. For all that, it has a catchy rhythm and enticing charisma that is very effective. Sibelius probably saw a great deal of himself in Caliban: a figure given to wildness, imprisoned by a suffocating society, and with a quiet nobility.

12. Stephano's Song, 'I shall no more to sea, to sea': *Moderato – Commodo*. [Pastoral]

Encountering the marooned jester Trinculo and drunken butler Stephano – who, in his intoxication, sings a merry Scandinavian song of great durability and sturdiness – Caliban mistakes the crooning visitor, with his 'celestial liquor', to be some form of god. (And indeed his alcohol forms an interesting counterpart to Prospero's magic, sharing its mysterious ability to transform people or impart enchanting visions.)

13. Caliban's Song, 'Farewell, master': *Moderato – Allegro*. [Orientalist]

In awe, Caliban transfers his allegiance from Prospero to this new deity, marking the juncture with a rough song accompanied by gorgeous swirling strings and some lively percussion, which is a magnificent occasion for a great Finnish baritone.

Act 3

14. Interlude – Miranda: *Allegretto*. [Archaic]

The act 2/3 entr'acte is another character portrait. In this musical treasure box we re-encounter the dreamy wide-eyed world of Prospero's daughter Miranda. Short-long-short syncopations, musical devices so familiar from earlier Sibelius, are combined with an eloquent melody of wonderful lilting charm. She talks to the imprisoned Ferdinand, who has been ordered to carry wood (the chief penal work on the island, it seems). In this, the central scene (5/9) of the play, they decide to marry.

15. Humoresque: *Allegro commodo*. [Pastoral]

With delightful symmetry the action returns to the antics of Caliban, Trinculo and Stephano, who enter in a surreal merry procession led by Ariel. The three by now very tipsy stooges have dreamed up their own murderous plot to match that of Sebastian's and Antonio's: in their well-oiled state, they intend to kill Prospero. Two clarinets and a tambourine behind the stage, along with the harp high above, offer a magnificently grotesque pageant.

16. Canon, 'Flout 'em and scout 'em': *Allegretto con moto*. [Pastoral]

Together they sing a weird ugly canon, accompanied by the extravagant colours and rhythms of the piccolo, side drum, glockenspiel, harp and harmonium.

17. Antonio; Dance of the Shapes: *Moderato assai – Allegro molto moderato – Poco tranquillo – Allegro e poco a poco stretto*. [Orientalist]

Meanwhile, Antonio and Sebastian are still intending to do away with Gonzalo and Alonso, in order to take the throne of Naples, and Antonio's character portrait forms the next number, a blustering, bombastic 'dance of the devils' in a Spanish style. This prolonged music eventually succumbs to a peculiar, spinning dance of piquant charm as Prospero conjures enigmatic spirits – known as the Shapes – to create a bizarre banquet for the castaways, inviting the nobles to sit and eat before departing.

18. Melodrama – Ariel as Harpy: *Grave*. [Orientalist]

The pleasures of the feast are cut short by Ariel, now manifest as a harpy – a vengeful winged goddess and personification of storm winds. A melodrama, the music is alive with the alarming, enticing sounds of the side drum, harp and harmonium.

19. The Shapes Dance Out: *Allegro*. [Pastoral]

Reminding both Antonio and Alonso of the reprehensible way they behaved towards Prospero, Ariel calls the Shapes back to take away their table and all its gastronomic delights. Although forward-sounding and part of Sibelius's 'brave new world',[174] there is something unmistakably nostalgic and Karelian about the gaiety and flair in this number.

Act 4

20. Intermezzo – Alonso Mourns: *Andante con moto*. [Archaic]

The act 3/4 entr'acte is a sombre, deeply moving intermezzo in E-flat minor depicting Alonso's grief for the son (Ferdinand), whom he believes drowned, just as Ferdinand imagines his father has died. All is muted, whispered, forlorn – an exquisite

---

174 V.i.183.

exhibition of Sibelius's powers and reminiscent of the slow movement of the Third Symphony.

21. Ariel Flies In: *Allegro*. [Nature]

At Prospero's command, Ariel once again flies in (in a reappearance of the brief sonic fancy from numbers 3 and 5) and is directed to conjure up a harvest festival from antiquity to honour Ferdinand and Miranda. This is to take the form of a masque, with the spirits assuming the shapes of Ceres, Juno and Iris – the ancient goddesses of agriculture, marriage and rainbows.

22. Ariel's Fourth Song, 'Before you can say "come" and "go"': *Allegretto moderato*. [Pastoral]

Ariel performs a short but agreeably resounding song lamenting his impending departure from Prospero's service.

23. The Rainbow: *Poco Adagio*. [Nature]

A lugubrious delight, recalling the gloomy world of the Fourth Symphony, this gorgeous but quietly threatening interlude has a rainbow sonically illuminate the celebrations of the masque (something visually staged in dramatic fashion in Poulsen's original Copenhagen production). It is a sublime orchestral picture, an elusive pause, a strange warning, an exalted arch into time and memory.

Serving as an overture to the next sequence of numbers, 'The Rainbow' begins with a deep drone on the horns, bassoons and basses, which are later joined by the cellos and higher strings before, at its centre, the music begins to let some light in, partly due to the introduction of timpani, trumpets, trombones and upper wind before at the close the violins rise up and the bass descends.

This exquisite music is full of elemental sonorities, of primal mystery and magic, a return to the fundamental sounds and intuitive feelings of a pre-rational world (though with an entirely modern design). Sibelius's dark rainbow carries the colours of the mythic past and as such opens a door for the proceedings which follow it. And yet, as ever with this composer, but especially in *The Tempest*, we are given the feeling that nature has greater power than human agency, disrupting, dislocating or intimidating their plans and even their identities.

24. Melodrama – Iris's Recitation: *Moderato assai.* [Pastoral]

To a waltz rhythm, the rainbow goddess recites a melodrama.

25. Juno's Song, 'Honour, riches, marriage blessing': *Commodo.* [Pastoral]

Juno, supreme goddess of marriage, is given a charming song – derived from the same musical material as Iris's waltz – that sounds like it has wandered lost from Vienna. In it she praises the young couples and wishes them a long life of happiness, kindness and love.

26. Minuet: Dance of the Naiads: *Allegretto grazioso.* [Pastoral]

Next to come at the festival are the naiads, or mermaids, who are given a charming minuet which is derived from Ariel's First

Song (No.6, 'Come unto these yellow sands'), when the spirit was disguised as an invisible mermaid and we first encountered Ferdinand.

27. Polka: Dance of the Harvesters: *Commodo*. [Pastoral]

The reapers take their turn and perform a bucolic polka dance, with quick steps and hops.

28. Ariel Flies In: *Allegro*. [Nature]
29. Ariel Hastens Away: *Allegro*. [Nature]
30. Ariel Flies In: *Allegro*. [Nature]

In three very swift, sprightly movements, we hear again the vivid recurrence of Ariel's flight music, with its capricious energy, noise and colour. Ariel flies in (28), and Prospero commands him create a distraction for the blundering, bungling schemers Caliban, Trinculo and Stephano in the form of gaudy trinkets. Ariel departs (29) and then reappears (30) laden with 'glistening apparel', which, as expected, diverts the hapless trio from their murderous plot.

31. The Dogs: *Poco con moto*. [Pastoral]

With Caliban, Trinculo and Stephano suitably distracted and trying on the fine garments, Prospero sets the spirits – in the form of dogs – on them. After some splendid brass, a comic scuffle ensues with nimble pointillistic woodwind and diaphanous strings as the villains are, literally, hounded away.

Act 5

32. bis. Overture – Ariel: *Poco con moto*. [Pastoral]

A brief overture/interlude/entr'acte with a leading oboe solo and vibrant strings introduces the fifth and final act. A submission to happiness and enchantment, it is musically the same as Ariel's approaching fifth and final song (33).

33. Prospero's Monologue, 'Ye elves of hills' (Orchestral): *Largo – Un Pochettino affrettando – Adagio*. [Nature]

Towards the end of the vast score of *The Tempest*, there now comes its key section, with music of immense power, strength and beauty, forming the complex climax of the entire work. Wearing his magician's robes, for the last time Prospero instructs Ariel to marshal all the aristocratic castaways together: their senses are to be restored, their sins forgiven, and Prospero himself will abjure his magical arts. Here the music becomes more dissonant and startling than at any other point in the score: at times, it is truly frightening, and more than fulfils the Copenhagen producer's desire for 'lunatic music'.

First comes an extraordinary largo of terrifying tonality and uneven sonic shifts: it is never merely theatrical or wildly histrionic, but a genuine musical portrayal of suffering and transition. Then there is a sudden moment of dramatic silence as Prospero breaks his staff and casts his book of magic into the sea. From here comes an exquisite, solemn, celestial adagio in B major, the very definition of 'heavenly music' and a magnificent hymn to renewal.

34. Ariel's Fifth Song, 'Where the bee sucks, there suck I': *Poco con moto*. [Pastoral]

Once again dressed in the robes of the duke of Milan, Prospero sets Ariel free from his service, and to celebrate, the spirit sings a delightful quasi-Spanish song using the same tune with which the act began (31 bis).

35. Cortège: *Tempo giusto – P.a.p. stretto*. [Pastoral]

With all the arguments resolved, Prospero invites the shipwrecked nobles to his island cabin, and they set off in procession to the sound of an imposing but elegant polonaise. For this music, Sibelius delved into his ancient back catalogue and reworked a theme originally written as an occasional piece: a cortège composed for theatre director Kaarlo Bergbom's retirement festivities in 1905. Given the nature of the play's discussions concerning Prospero's abjuration of his powers and Sibelius's own impending withdrawal, the music – for all its generous sense of triumphant resolution – has an especially moving air.

36. bis. Epilogue: *Poco adagio – Allargando*. [Archaic]

For performances in Helsinki in 1927, Sibelius composed an additional epilogue: a sombre regal movement in honour of Prospero, who has renounced his magic, his charms now 'o'erthrown'. It can be played as an alternative to No.34, but both pieces are usually performed, a twofold ending befitting this extraordinary work.

As with the cortège, Sibelius sifted through his earlier music for something suitable, this time digging up an old piano sketch in B-flat minor (*c*.1895–97) – which he had already pilfered for his orchestral work *Cassazione* in 1904. Can we begrudge poor Sibelius this double self-theft? He was after all, on the verge of his retirement.

We should be glad of it, for it is a noble, majestic portrait of Prospero's resignation, a spellbinding, dignified way to conclude one of the Finn's finest achievements.

Chapter Fourteen

Weaving Magic Secrets:
Tapiola

In a famous photograph, an elderly Sibelius ambles through some light forest near his home in Järvenpää. Even though the picture is clearly posed, he looks a little startled, as if a paparazzo has just leaped out of the bushes, hoping to snap the great composer for this week's tabloid music mag. Beyond the slightly surprised appearance, however, as usual Sibelius cuts a noble, dashing figure, strolling through the woods with his thick coat, grand hat and walking cane.

While he was also happy on mountains and by lakes, in restaurants and at concerts, spending time in forests was a source of particular joy to Sibelius. It had been since his childhood, when he would often roam in thickets near (and sometimes too far from) home in order to collect insects and rocks, to read and dream, to marvel at the freedom and strangeness these places offered. They seemed to house perils and secrets yet were more appealing than the convoluted weirdness and strife of urban life. They were also time warps, the shifting rays of the sun filtering through the trees and altering one's spatio-temporal perceptions, making the day flow both rapidly and sluggishly, a cosmic arboreal trap mixing movement and stagnation (or was this just a boy's best excuse for being late home for tea?).

It is therefore appropriate that this multifaceted, inherently fascinating space which had preoccupied Sibelius all his life should be the subject of not only his final tone poem but his final major work – and in the ears of many, his greatest work of all. Turning to the forest for inspiration and expression, Sibelius conjured a sonic world that was both familiar and deeply alien, just like its subject matter. With this brooding utterance of intense monotonality and monothematicism, he found a means to extend everything that he had learned in writing symphonies and tone poems – their structure, logic and texture – into one final communication of his personal vision of both orchestral music and the place of our species on the earth.

Although it was a radical piece, it maintained a tradition, since humans have long had a complex, intricate relationship with forests, summoning various expressions and interpretations over countless generations. From the steamy jungles of Java to the boreal taiga that encircles our planet like a northerly halo, forests have helped define us, offering inspiration for some of our richest metaphors and noblest ideals as well as providing regions for our deepest fears and basest behaviour. They are realms of both danger and security, panic and peace – forbidden zones that can also be sublime and silent sanctuaries.

An elaborate network of psychosocial anxieties, cultural manifestations and commercial misuses is fertile testimony to the way forests have functioned within the collective consciousness of our species: as locations of great aesthetic beauty, as sites of economic resource and exploitation, as places endowed with vast sacred worth, as areas of inherent diversity and uniformity, as spaces for mythmaking and storytelling.

Tapiola explores them all.[175]

On 4 January 1926 Sibelius took delivery of a telegram from America. Specifically, a telegram from Walter Damrosch, director of the New York Symphony Orchestra,[176] commissioning a new tone poem from his Finnish colleague, ideally to last between fifteen and twenty minutes, and to be on a subject entirely at the composer's discretion.[177]

---

175 In Finnish, *Tapiola* means 'the realm of Tapio' – the god and animating spirit of the forest in Finnish mythology. Like many 'green man' archetypes across the world, he has a beard of lichen and eyebrows made from moss.

176 The orchestra went through various names, including the New York Symphonic Society. In 1928, it merged with the Philharmonic Society of New York to become the Philharmonic-Symphony Society of New York, later sensibly rebranding as the rather less verbose New York Philharmonic. It now plays at David Geffen Hall, Lincoln Center.

177 A prominent member of the American music scene, Damrosch had been born in Breslau, Silesia, in 1862, and emigrated to the USA in 1871. There he became a key educator and conductor, directing the first stateside performances of works like Tchaikovsky's Fourth and Sixth, Mahler's Fourth and Elgar's *In the South*, as well as founding the Damrosch Opera Company in order to promote the works of Richard Wagner. He was also a pioneer of music on the radio, hosting a series of programmes aimed at children and students, as well as a composer – of which his best-known works are probably his literary operas: the neo-Wagnerian *The Scarlet Letter* (1896) and the no less grand *Cyrano* (1913), exploring the life of the great French author, duellist and libertine.

A few weeks prior to this proposition, as we saw in the previous chapter, Sibelius had received a number of sixtieth birthday gifts in the form of generous pecuniary donations; there had also been recent improvements to the copyright system, meaning he now collected appropriate royalties from his German publishers. Moreover, inflation, while in most respects horrendous, had whittled away considerably at his old debts. All this meant that Sibelius's financial standing was now as stable as it had ever been, and he was in a good position to warmly accept Damrosch's proposal rather than needing to dedicate his energy to the smaller, more reliable money-spinning projects that he had leaned on before.

His new economic status was so satisfactory, in fact, that Sibelius decided a little holiday was in order (not that a vacant piggy bank had ever really discouraged him from such undertakings, especially in his youth). So, in March, wishing to avoid the fuss over the premiere of his score for the new production of *The Tempest* in Copenhagen (which had been a protracted disorganized mess on the theatre's part and source of much irritation to him), he headed south.

Money was in his purse, and the sketches for his new commission were in his suitcase: he had eagerly begun work on the piece not long after receiving the telegram. He went first to Berlin, then to Rome, where he checked into the Hotel Grande Albergo Minerva, then as now one of the most imposing and impressive hotels in a city not known for its modesty. But the creature comforts were for work: he incarcerated himself in a luxurious suite and laboured furiously on his new symphonic poem, which was gathering pace both in his mind and on the page.

Writing to Aino back home, at one point he refers to his working title, which was in English since it was an American commission: 'The Wood'. His wife rather sweetly corrected the slight misstep of his English – it should be 'The Forest'. *Wood*, of course, doesn't quite carry the majesty, size, terror and baggage that *forest* does, yet Sibelius was probably right to settle on the final designation *Tapiola*, given the importance of the mythical and other cultural elements of the work's content. To some extent, however, we can perhaps lament the non-appearance of such a simple, direct and wonderfully atmospheric title for Sibelius's final tone poem: *The Forest*.

On 27 March, Sibelius's childhood friend Walter von Konow joined him in Rome to celebrate the latter's sixtieth birthday, an occasion which we might imagine unlikely to consist solely of tea and cake. Hangovers notwithstanding, from Rome they travelled south down to the Tyrrhenian Sea and the island of Capri just off the Sorrento Peninsula at the southern end of the Gulf of Naples. One day, Sibelius and von Konow visited the Grotta Azzurra, the Blue Grotto, a cave along the Caprese coast known for the thrilling effects when sunlight is reflected through the seawater. Sibelius wrote to Aino that although only painters could capture its true magic, he found it a deeply musical experience.

They returned to Rome on 19 April, and von Konow headed up to Finland the next morning, but Sibelius stayed on a few more days as the compositional urge was strong within. Eventually he packed up and proceeded back north to Berlin, arriving home at Ainola in the middle of May.

It had been an invigorating and extremely productive trip. That a good deal of the labour for a work which is widely regarded as the quintessence of Nordic gloom and darkness should have been undertaken in the light, sun and warmth of both the Eternal City and a Mediterranean island may seem an anomaly. In fact, of course, it is no contradiction. Not only did Sibelius have countless gigabytes of data concerning the mood and topography of the Finnish forest in his head after decades of exposure to it, but he also had an imagination – and arguably that imagination could work far more effectively away from its subject matter, conjuring up the forest and its spirits in his mind and then in the score.

Back home, work on *Tapiola* continued, as it did on Ainola herself: the sauna was taken apart and rebuilt, in addition to being given a new gate on the boundary of the recently enlarged estate. Indeed, the recent expansion had increased the price of the property so that its value now exceeded Sibelius's debts, and accordingly, the couple drew up a mutual will in the summer.

Alongside his tone poem commission, Sibelius had been working on a choral piece for the Sortavala Song Festival: *Väinön virsi* (*Väinämöinen's Song*), for mixed choir and orchestra. Inspired by the *Kalevala*, it could not be further from the melodic unity and intense concentration of *Tapiola*. It is a ceremonial work, and although it has a brief orchestral introduction, the homophonic choir dominates. Premiered on 26 June, it was to be the last of Sibelius's cantatas – an often overlooked part of his output that merits much investigation, for it is a magnificently life-enhancing series. We, understandably, focus on the side of Sibelius expressed in the symphonies and tone poems, but there was a warm national pride to him as well, a quiet satisfaction in his role as a public figure, even if the attention could sometimes be irksome.

By the end of the summer, *Tapiola* was complete and sent off to the publishers Breitkopf & Härtel. Come mid-September, however, Sibelius was writing back to them with cuts he wished to make. Alas, they had already begun to engrave the music. *Tapiola* had placed Sibelius in a rather unusual situation: not only had the premiere been entrusted to another conductor, but it was taking place on another continent across a vast ocean. Normally he could make last-minute changes to the score, fretting and fiddling, and then make further prepublication adjustments in light of hearing the piece in final performance. Here the thing needed to be properly finished and on its way across the Atlantic in good time for rehearsals. Breitkopf & Härtel were kind: in September back went the music to Sibelius and then, on 5 November, the publishers were able to deliver to Ainola the printed score of what was, although he didn't know it at the time, his final major work.[178]

Off to America went the music, and on 26 December 1926, the world premiere of *Tapiola* took place, conducted by Damrosch and alongside Beethoven's Fifth Symphony and George Gershwin's piano concerto in F, with the composer at the keyboard.[179] The venue for the premiere – New York's Mecca Temple – was a domed building in the Moorish Revival style on West Fifty-Fifth Street between Sixth and Seventh Avenues (it is now the New York City Center). It incorporates a range of striking motifs inspired by Islamic architecture and was perhaps an unlikely setting for this tone poem of boreal tensions and northern gloom. Ultimately, of course, it was simply a magnificent building for a magnificent piece of music to enter the world – which it did to only mixed and somewhat muted approval. Damrosch, as we will see, revered it, writing after the

---

178 What would become, and then cease to be, the Eighth Symphony is likely to have begun on 12 September, according to a diary entry mentioning the "new one".

179 The Finnish premiere took place a few months later on 25 April 1927, with Sibelius's old friend and colleague Robert Kajanus conducting. On the programme, and making their own Finnish debuts, were the Seventh Symphony and the prelude to *The Tempest*. It was a fitting collection of final Sibelian pieces.

concert to congratulate its composer, yet even Sibelius's great American champion Olin Downes was a little bemused (though he admired aspects of its style and manner).

It is probably to be expected that a work of such startling innovation, originality and power – nothing else in music *sounds* like *Tapiola* – would not be immediately understood, especially by an audience who were not as familiar with Sibelius's trajectory as a composer as many in Europe were. Nonetheless, it would not be long before the praise became near universal: Scottish critic Cecil Gray, as soon as 1931, claimed that had Sibelius written nothing but *Tapiola*, he would remain one of the greatest of all composers.

Even a casual listening to this astonishing score can surely only invite agreement.

Forests have long played a crucial role in human history and culture: shaping it, defining it, challenging it. They have provided – and continue to provide – homes and shelters, livelihoods and resources: food, fuel and medicine. They offer spaces for recreation, reflection and spiritual sustenance, functioning as sites of worship, meditation, sport, play and reconnection. They are places of identity and inspiration, inspiring a significant amount of myth and folklore, as well as an immensely varied range of art, music and literature.

When Aztec artists portrayed the universe, they painted consecrated trees at the four corners supporting the sky, while two Aztec deities – Quetzalcoatl and Tezcatlipoca – turned themselves into trees to ascend into the heavens. Priests organized elaborate rituals around the cutting of forest trees, since they were the sources of incense, sacred documents and holy instruments. On the other side of the world, one of the metaphors most frequently employed by Chinese poet Tao Qian (365–427 AD) is the forest pine: symbol of strength, longevity, endurance and constancy, as well as a friend in both the cold of winter and the heat of summer.

In Greek mythology, Pan was god of not only the forest but wildness in general, along with shepherds and rustic music (he is usually to be seen with his pan pipes). Half-man, half-goat, he was deity of groves and woodlands, too, and was usually associated with sex and fertility as well as the more debauched possibilities that the concealment of the trees afforded. Disturbed in his afternoon naps, Pan's angry shout stimulated 'panic' in secluded places, not least for those alone in the forest – a dread terror familiar to many across the centuries, and something captured in the static trepidations of *Tapiola*.

Forests abound in Shakespeare. Lear mentions the 'shadowy forests' that form part of his kingdom as he divides it up, with cataclysmic consequences, in the opening scene of his play. There are Timon's sad, inadequate woods outside Athens, which prove an insubstantial place for him to leave humanity behind: a real forest would have been much better. *A Midsummer Night's Dream* shares those Athenian woods for its setting but charges them with woodland magic. There is the purging power of the forest as fat Jack Falstaff is taught a lesson in *The Merry Wives of Windsor*. There is the perilous, deceptive and locomotive forest in *Macbeth*, as Birnam forest threatens to come to Dunsinane.

And then there is *As You Like It*. Set in the Forest of Arden – which might be in England or Flanders[180] – the play explores

---

180 The point is, of course, that it could really be anywhere, however much the play also toys with local references to the Ardennes, and its literary and chivalric

a huge range of people, ideas and situations involving forests. It is a natural forest: at times an astonishingly beautiful forest, rich in colour and life, as well as a site of work, filled with shepherds and woodsmen. But it is also a fictional utopia, a zone of liberty, a place of independence away from the pressures and constraints of court. The key is the way in which Shakespeare mixes the real and the imagined, just as the play toys with ideas of town/country, masculine/feminine, hetero/homosexual, each deflecting and dissolving into the other. Like *Tapiola*'s, the forest of *As You Like It* is a myth, but it is also a reality. In Sibelius's tone poem, it is the interaction between these two aspects that generates much of the tension and drama.

Few writers have damaged the reputation of the forest, cultivating its darkness and horror in our imaginations, like the Brothers Grimm. Their hundreds of folk and fairy tales habitually employ and exploit the forest as a setting to spawn and develop macabre plots, so that many of these stories – which are now deeply embedded into popular culture – are unthinkable in any other context: 'Little Red Riding Hood', 'Hansel and Gretel', 'Rumpelstiltskin'. The Brothers Grimm appear to have had a particular effect on the forest world of *Tapiola*: Finnish culture, especially folk culture, is full of the forest as a place of murky secrets and events, but it is much more a place of freedom and peace, so that Sibelius seems to have taken on a particularly Germanic darkness that was slightly alien to Finland.

Both the Grimms and Sibelius, like most artists who engage with the forest in their work, are keenly alert to its place as an abode of mystery, fear and menace, and to the interplay between psychological as well as arboreal thickets. A forest is not just

---

significances, along with allusions to Shakespeare's own home county of Warwickshire (and the fact that his mother's maiden name was Arden).

a convenient place for girls in crimson capes to encounter loquacious lupine threats but a symbol for a range of human terrors and anxieties – be they sexual, spiritual or economic.

The ambiguous, equivocal character of forests – their mixture of light and dark, life and death – have also made them ideal subjects for music. William Byrd wrote a set of variations of the popular song 'Woods So Wild' (1590), now a favourite with lutenists. Beethoven's *Pastoral* Symphony (1808) seems to evoke the modern-day Japanese concept of shinrin-yoku,[181] the practice of therapeutic relaxation and engagement with forests and nature ('Awakening of cheerful feelings on arrival in the countryside', as the title of the first movement of Beethoven's symphony goes). Forests pervade Schubert's lieder in a darker fashion, most significantly in the gloomy glories of *Winterreise* (1828), where the poet hopes trees will provide solace, but in fact they offer only deeper despair.

Composers who depicted forests in the piano literature abound: Sibelius himself;[182] Schumann in his *Waldszenen* (*Forest Scenes*, 1851), with its rich Romantic evocations of hunters, lonely flowers, haunted places, prophet birds, friendly landscapes and wayside inns. In the first of his Two Concert Études, 'Forest Sounds' (1863), Liszt paints both the light and shade of the trees in sound and imagines the noise of wind rustling through those trees. Channelling Ovid and Euripides, at the end of his enchanting Greek-myth opera *Daphne* (1938), Strauss has his heroine transform into a tree for a magical reunion with her beloved nature, while Ottorino Respighi celebrated the Eternal City's trees in his orchestral masterpiece *The Pines of Rome* (1924), a work which also mourns the ancient forests which had to disappear in order for the great urban landscape to arise.

---

181   Literally 'forest bathing', something wonderfully depicted in the kanji script: 森林浴.
182   *The Trees*, op.75.

Towering above other musical depictions of forests and trees, and an enormous influence on Sibelius in one way or the other, is act two of Wagner's *Siegfried* (1871), the third part of his vast tetralogy, *Der Ring des Nibelungen* (1848–1874). The whole of *Siegfried* (and the *Ring*) is an engagement with nature, an interrogation of myths and fairy tales, an exploration of how they all interact within the human heart, mind and culture. But it is in *Siegfried*'s central act that the subtle, ambiguous forest comes into its own (after the darkness of the cave and before the light of the mountain, in the outer acts), both as a dramatic setting and as a nexus of psychology, philosophy and ecological enquiry. It is here, in this liminal space, this realm of doubt and negotiation, that the eponymous hero is to find his true destiny and purpose, resting amid the noontime delights of the trees before killing a dragon and seizing the objects that will both make and break him.

Wagner's huge score is an unmatched sonic representation of the light and shade of the forest, of its mystery and magic, exhibiting a vast palette of natural greys, greens, blacks and browns in the orchestral colours, and using his extraordinary leitmotif technique to restlessly cross-examine the relationship between past and present, fear and safety, romance and realism. As a student in Vienna in the spring of 1891, a performance of *Siegfried* hit Sibelius for six, its strange power leaving him in a daze and deeply influencing work on *Kullervo*, even if the Finn – like so many – also instinctively lashed back against the power of the Wagnerian musikdrama.

But decades later, the influence of Wagner's sonic forest would find its way into *Tapiola*.

Sibelius's music in its final phase mixes revelation and disguise, concealing as much as it discloses, offering both discord and harmony, the glow of peace and the jagged fright of crisis. Where his late works point forward at their conclusion, it is to either unknowable or disbanded realms, not to upbeat, confident futures. The music is still a forest or a lake, but one ruffled by harsh winds, just as the sun has its black spots. Sibelius's final works travel much of the same topography several times, searching for ultimate meaning but always unstable, part of the mutability and peril of the world.

For Sibelius, nature was sacrosanct, but his engagement with it was never to make it an inert monument. Nature was vital, immanent, dynamic, mythic, and his art reflects this fluid instability along with his experience of the world as a dangerous, often hostile, but ultimately blessed space. His art was part of nature, just as nature was part of him. In *Tapiola*, however, he explores that energy via a chilling paradox: extreme stasis.

The haunting inner presence of this tone poem, an internal aching of acoustic pain, is based on its single core motif, heard on the strings at the start, then perpetually reduplicated, and on its troubled tonal placement within a deep dissonance that plays with our mind more than our ears. At times Sibelius is wallowing in pure sound, the tonal centre evaporating entirely. Tonality is there, but the connection seems fragile, unsubstantiated, frankly Wagnerian, a musical maze of anxiety and disorientation that is also the lost labyrinth of the human psyche, a thicket of tears and fears. There are ferocious thoughts, violent imaginings, and we yearn to escape this forest of the mind but find we are going round in circles.

When, in its closing bars, *Tapiola* finally escapes the minor and finds the major, it is a tonal embrace, a musical hug – yet there is something strangely vacant, even aimless, about it. The exit to *Tapiola* is there, but it is an exodus back into silence, back into the void from which the music, like all music, materialized. For some this is a cause for further terror, an abysmal return to the equal and opposite eternity of darkness that existed before our birth; for others, this same return is a homecoming, a source of reconciliation and inner harmony.

Away from the raw centre – the stagnant tonality and motivic repetition – the surface textures and explorations of *Tapiola* are no less frightening, even if they are to some extent more tangible. We are within a tone poem, after all, and Sibelius gives us what we might expect from a vast northern forest: there are whispering winds and scraping branches, the groans of heavy trees and the gossip of unconcerned gusts. It is neither night nor day but an appalling half light, with a creeping, malignant darkness that oppresses the soul (after it has terrorized the mind). Through the mud and murk and shadows we catch voices muttering like the abject inmates of psychiatric wards or think we glimpse an animal scurrying between the trees. All is invisible, indefinite, but absolutely present: everything lurks with terrible inaction and pregnant possibility. Tapio, spectral divinity of the forest, is at once everywhere and nowhere.

The single core theme of *Tapiola*, a monothematic menace, is arguably not even a theme at all. It is perhaps merely a preliminary tune needed to inaugurate matters but never becoming anything like a regular subject, simply an initial melodic *thing* that can be endlessly spun through itself. It generates a few fundamental and highly interrelated elementary motifs, which in turn produce multiple very distinctive, inventive musical ideas – not unlike how the handful of basic, embryonic motifs in Wagner's *Ring* spawn everything else in the dramas as they are expanded, compressed, broken and reassembled according to need, function and context. More than the *Ring*, however, the thematic variations of *Tapiola*, however original, are severely restricted in their development and are tightly interconnected by Sibelius's merciless command of musical logic to an unprecedented degree.

Ambiguous in communicating the fact though it is, *Tapiola* is both an expression of sonata form and a severe symphonic argument: in many ways its brutal symphonic inferences, and extension of Sibelian principles to their limit, extinguished the possibility of an Eighth Symphony even more than the Seventh did. Sonata form, along with variation form and its associated symphonic logic, give *Tapiola* the vital mixture of direction and stasis, allowing us to feel trapped in its abstract rotations while actually edging forward via imperceptible shrugs and glances.

In *Tapiola*, to locate primitive utterances (and find similar responses in listeners), Sibelius appealed to some of his most sophisticated musical techniques, for this is an immensely distinguished score, written for – by Sibelius's standards – a large orchestra. The way he is able to generate such a range of subtle shades, of relentlessly unstable instrumental hues, from within such a narrow band of one theme is testimony to a lifetime of honing and refinement and of both conception and execution. It is the work of a composer able to identify differences in the aural spectrum with the awe-inspiring precision of a space telescope, isolating decisive moments of fresh enunciation in the variations or minute modulations of the tonality.

The tempos, too, are deeply impressive: the ebb and flow, the twists and turns, of the score are handled with such subtlety that time is dual speed. Listening to the score, we assume the underlying tempo is slow. In fact, almost the entire work alternates between allegro moderato and allegro – again a vital ingredient to produce the fusion of movement and motionlessness and accordingly the fundamental bewilderment of the music for Tapio's domain.

In *Tapiola* we witness Sibelius's techniques reduced to their absolute essentials: the tonal scheme is baldly straightforward; the 'themes', such as they might be evaluated, are closely related to the point of incest; the transitions between sections are so seamless they disappear entirely, allowing for only approximate indication. *Tapiola* is the ultimate logical outcome of Sibelius's lifelong obsession with two musical forms: it is at once a deeply evocative tone poem that is also an aggressively compressed symphony. Yet *Tapiola* has, in reality, developed beyond its parent forms into something uniquely its own, a weird and impressive hybrid (but, it has to be said, one unable to produce any offspring of its own).

Tapiola is a very strange beast – but then, of course, genius often is.

After he conducted the premiere of *Tapiola* in 1926, Walter Damrosch wrote in glowing terms to its composer about what he saw as the work's wonders. Its originality and fascination deeply moved him, not least the way Sibelius was able to give such variety of expression to just one theme, within such a close-knit structure and via such inventive orchestration – all of which, of course, worked together. Yet beyond all this technical praise, Damrosch seemed to have been most intrigued and delighted with the overall poetic imagery of *Tapiola*, the enthralling image of the, as he put it, 'dark pine forests, shadowy gods and wood-nymphs' which Sibelius had conjured up for the audience in Yuletide Manhattan – who, the conductor said, all shivered at the icy winds of the coda.

Tapiola can be regarded as Sibelius's last major engagement with the *Kalevala*, the great Finnish epic that had fascinated him for decades and which pervades his music, whether directly or not. For all that, *Tapiola* does not relate to any specific story concerning Tapio, the animating spirit of the Finnish forest. Rather, it captures his elusive essence, his mysterious power and hold on the imagination – haunting the tone poem just as he haunts the *Kalevala*. Sibelius's works, especially his tone poems, often have only tenuous associations with the tales of the *Kalevala*, whatever their titles may be. As we saw earlier, much of the music for both *Lemminkäinen* and *Pohjola's Daughter* was not originally written with their subjects in mind but was later modified to correspond to them. For Sibelius, the mighty epic formed a vast atmosphere of poetico-musical inspiration, a rich resource that did not need to be directly chomped from, merely breathed and imbibed.

The true inspiration behind *Tapiola*, taking into account the abundant global history of human engagement with forests we discussed above, was simply the Finnish forest itself, whether regarded as Tapio's territory or not. The vast ubiquitous Finnish forests, covering 75 percent of the country's land, are, along with the countless lakes, one of the defining features of Finland – both in terms of its geography and cultural identity in addition to broader social, economic and political activities, a source not only of commercial assets but of leisure pursuits, artistic inspiration and global renown. Touch a Finn, one might say, and you touch a forest.

Sibelius's career, however rich and varied, would feel slightly empty and incomplete without this final, majestic, arboreal commemoration, which – as Damrosch knew – captures the northern forest so well, its sombre lonely moods and fluctuating obscurities. Yet for all the darkness we hear in *Tapiola*, its ominous shifting shades and foreboding minor-key gloom, there is a quiet sense of light and life, of the pleasure and pride to be located in the Finnish forest which it evokes.

Perhaps the darkness and light are interconnected: Are the very things that have allowed Finnish wonder, happiness and success in its forests also the seeds of its own damage and destruction? Maybe this takes things too far, but in wider international and contemporary terms, we must surely see any celebration of nature – which *Tapiola* most defiantly is – as a simultaneously implied alarm at its ruination. Just as it shares a number of musical techniques with the *Ring*, *Tapiola* – and Sibelius in general – also seems inherently to share Wagner's concern for the obliteration of our planet's beauty and variety for personal or short-term gain, the greedy desire for capital and profit at any cost.

Tapiola is both a salutation and an admonition, a warning for us not to take Tapio's kingdom away but to give the forest spirit a place to thrive – in all his moody magnificence.

Tapiola, op.112

Asked by his publisher to clarify the programme of *Tapiola* for audiences likely to be unfamiliar with Finnish mythology, Sibelius responded with a prose clarification of his work's unusual title. With the composer's approval, Breitkopf & Härtel then adapted this material into an evocative quatrain that then appeared at the head of the printed score in English, German and French:

> Wide-spread they stand, the Northland's dusky forests,
> Ancient, mysterious, brooding savage dreams;
> Within them dwells the Forest's mighty God,
> And wood-sprites in the gloom weave magic secrets.

We begin in silence, out of which grumble angry timpani to breathe life into Tapio, the forest and the score.

From here the strings launch the single core motif that will dominate the music. It is an arresting opening cadence that is a premonition of the closing, and which will haunt and obsess *Tapiola* as the quasi-theme constantly seeks to reassert itself with a brutal application and perseverance that borders on the limits of sanity and sense. The dogged nature of the reaffirmation, and the unprecedented interconnection within the motif's progeny, should not allow us to miss the extraordinary variety Sibelius is able to give amid this simultaneously severe unity. That severity at once hides and reveals the vivid detail of the *Tapiola* score, the minute changes (in theme, mood and tone) that subtly infuse the music. The monothematic and monotonal nature of *Tapiola* is not a licence for monotony – quite the reverse, it has an astonishing diversity based on a stark simplicity of material.

The opening motion of the strings is met by an immediate response from cool winds, blowing in further the desolate atmosphere of the bleak northern forest. Forming a prelude, these early gesticulations in fact anticipate the way in which the whole work will end, giving a sense of grand symmetry to *Tapiola* that might be missed if we focus too strongly on its static, repetitive nature at the micro level. The introductory material from timpani, strings and wind ends by means of an impulsive discharge from the brass, which inaugurates an allegro moderato section. The sound is uncertain, obstruse, wavering, lingering, brooding between the governance of B minor and unconvincing gestures towards G-sharp minor.

One of the key overall features of this first cycle of music has been its layers, and the way these sonic strata are able to progress independently: a static revolving bass; a slow wave from cellos and bassoons; restrained melodic avowals from the violas. To move the music forward towards another cycle, with great dexterity Sibelius slowly illuminates the timbre via violins and trumpets. In the texture of sound, as it rises in both pitch and dynamics, the accompaniment of the cellos and basses imperceptibly moves closer to the foreground, while the hypnotic violas and rotating bass fade into the fabric of the forest.

New musical assertions in the upper woodwind and an incandescent oscillation from the violins pull the character of the sound towards an episode Sibelius would, near the end of his life, refer to as the appearance of animals and wood goblins. The music becomes more playful, even dangerously cheery amid the gloom of the forest and in the guise of a wispy scherzo. Much of the effect is achieved through subtle tempo changes, tightening the music from a broad and expansive rhythm to a much tauter, more urgent beat.

But as time wears on, shadows begin to form and reform through the forest. Fragments of sound begin to coalesce into a hymn-like sequence full of peculiar radiance and a strange Nordic light filtering through the pines. It is generated through some glowing writing for divided strings, with a typically Sibelian grandeur and nobility every so often reminding us of the Seventh Symphony.

Out of this imposing tranquillity comes an eerie atmosphere that is often close to silence. Then fury erupts into a reprise of material that leads eventually to the great storm section of *Tapiola*, an orchestral tumult to match those in Sibelius's other late works, the Sixth and Seventh Symphonies – and *The Tempest* itself. A growl in the brass grabs us by the ears, a sonic uproar that swiftly changes the atmosphere into a blaze of instrumental thunder and lightning, crashing and clashing through the trees. A vigorous allegro section is launched, which gives way to the gentler, deeper, pulse of allegro moderato as a final enormous accrual of sound begins. String tremolos and boisterous brass show us Sibelius the music dramatist at full pelt.

Such a devastating orchestral storm seems to have been the logical destination of the music, the violent vortex into which all of *Tapiola* seems to have been irritably and irresistibly dragged. A storm in the forest, as well as in the life and mind, it is an extremely powerful expressive force. Tonal harmony is destroyed, disintegrating into almost complete chromatism with flurries of notes in patterns that thrash up and down like rain lashing the trees.

The wider tonal and motivic logic and goal of *Tapiola* are not to be disturbed by this storm, however. Just as how in *The Tempest* the deafening dissonance in Prospero's Monologue gives way to a heavenly B major and redemption, in *Tapiola* a resolution – of sorts – is reached, and in the same key.

In the coda, after the great tornado and thickets of sound, the orchestra extends itself, the strings dividing into a huge gesture, sprawling, almost prostrate in humility, conjuring a vast and shining orchestral resonance. The music asserts the major – glorious, celestial B major – for the first (and final) time. The flashes of light and joy hinted at in the scherzo-like episode now appear as true sunbeams, permeating through the trees of the Finnish forest.

It is a fleeting moment of extraordinary power, the forest – and all nature – showing itself to be our friend, not a stranger or an adversary but a companion in hope and beauty before the inevitability of death and silence.

Chapter Fifteen

Phantom and Oblivion: The Eighth Symphony

In 1937 the American music critic Olin Downes, long an advocate for Sibelius's music, wrote to the composer informing the Finn that his mother, Louise, was not so much bothered about hearing the Eighth Symphony – by then many years overdue, its premiere repeatedly postponed – as his *Ninth*, a work which would, she claimed, represent the 'summit and synthesis' of Sibelius's achievements and confirm his place as a true descendant of Beethoven.

It is comforting, in our fraught and complex world, to know that there exist souls – if music critics' mothers have souls – who believe that artistic worth and its confirmation revolve around the numbering of a composer's works and the caprice of the catalogue. That Sibelius's Seventh was apparently neither summit nor synthesis, that Sibelius himself often considered *Kullervo* and *Lemminkäinen* to be symphonies – making his Seventh arguably his Ninth anyway – does not seem to have occurred to the impatient, implacable Mrs. Downes.

What transpires to *us*, from the uneasy benefit of a few decades' hindsight, is that not only would there be no ninth symphony, but there would not be an eighth symphony, either, save for inside Sibelius's head. After years and years of delay, deferral and procrastination, the score to the Eighth likely ended up in flames, the composer unsatisfied with what he had achieved, unable to finish it and unwilling to publish what he had completed. It would remain one of the great unknowns and lost possibilities in music, the vanished symphony becoming a fable and a myth, a lost Atlantis of wealth and beauty.

But what were the precise circumstances of Sibelius's last years, those final three decades from the completion of *Tapiola* in 1926 to his death in 1957, years which saw affluence, semi-retirement and bonfires at Ainola?

Following the premiere of *Tapiola* in Manhattan at Christmas 1926, Sibelius did not, as many would have us believe, put down his quill and stop composing. Production slowed, it is true, but work on he did. During the early months of 1927, Sibelius was occupied with several projects, the first of which was completing his *Masonic Ritual Music* (op.113) for its premiere performance on 12 January. As we might expect given its destination – the secretive Finnish lodges – this is one of Sibelius's most inscrutable and puzzling, if often deeply moving, compositions, revolving around charming songs for tenor and harmonium, which he would come to revise and add to in the 1940s, adding some elements for male voice choir.

Money, at least, was no longer a problem – he had paid off his debts and was receiving more and more income from his music as German and Finnish copyright law moved belatedly into the twentieth century. This meant his life, and Aino's, was free of financial concern. However, not only was more cash available for whisky and wine, it also took a slight edge off the need to compose – especially the myriad smaller works for piano, chamber group or voice which had helped provide an income, and which are a bounteous harvest for us. (The larger pieces, like the tone poems or symphonies, had never been written primarily for money.) This is not, of course, the principal explanation for the slowing of musical production in the years to come, but it was likely an initial factor: quite simply, the pressure was off.

And the gifts were on: in early 1927, Aino received an alarmingly expensive leather coat from her husband and he also whisked her away to Paris for several weeks, where they stayed at the Hôtel du Quai Voltaire – an absolute palace overlooking the Seine, equidistant from the Musée du Louvre and Musée d'Orsay – and attended concerts of contemporary French music. Unfortunately, following the holiday, in the spring loneliness, isolation and drinking took over again: 'I must have alcohol in order to survive', he laments to his diary. The only solution, for now, was work, and he was soon labouring on a somewhat vexing project: creating the two concert suites from the incidental music to *The Tempest*, an enterprise its composer likened to having to repeat one's own homework.

The suites were finally done, but the summer of 1927 was an immense struggle against losing himself in the comfort and cosiness of the bottle. Again and again his diary provides stark, horrific details of what was a daily battle against becoming a full-blown alcoholic. Neat notes mention rare days 'sine alcohol' when no booze was taken; more habitually it was a case of at best 'one whisky', but too often a frightening day's drinking is observed. The confrontation he would, eventually, win – to an extent. He did moderate his drinking, even if he never became entirely teetotal.

In September, Olin Downes visited Ainola – thankfully without his mother – and the man who had been christened 'Sibelius's apostle' by the American wags was now at the home of his master. Earlier in 1927 Downes had tried to lure Sibelius back across the Atlantic for a lucrative concert tour, but Sibelius claimed he was too busy with new works. Now, in person, Downes could quiz the Finn on precisely what those works were. Sibelius's response was sketchy, evasive, and perhaps untruthful, but we do apparently learn that he was – as Downes had supposed – at work on a new symphony, that two movements had been set down on paper and that the others were still in his head. It must have been a hard struggle for Downes not to slip away from his hosts at some point, steal into Sibelius's study, and sneak a peek at the manuscript. At that point, of course, the Eighth was not the legend it now is, it was simply the (highly likely) next symphony, but it must have been tempting.

In February 1928 Sibelius travelled to Berlin. Aino observed that the trip would probably do him good: he had become something of a hermit and recluse, staying at home listening to the radio and gramophone records, rarely venturing out to socialize (often claiming, against reality, that all his friends were dead). It must have been a bind for Aino: on the one hand, pleased he wasn't tearing it up at the Hotel Kämp, but sad to see him so withdrawn and alone.

The German capital offered some old friends and plenty of concerts – including the mouthwatering prospect of his violin concerto with Ferenc von Vecsey as soloist and Wilhelm Furtwängler conducting – but it was mainly for work. Writing home, Sibelius declared to his wife that the Eighth was going to be 'wonderful', though progress was a little slower than he might have hoped – but then of course, he also observed, he wasn't in any hurry.

He returned to Ainola in March and set about composing some minor pieces, but it was generally a quiet year. In the autumn Serge Koussevitzky, increasingly one of Sibelius's greatest international advocates, conducted the Third Symphony with the Boston Symphony and wrote to its composer politely inquiring whether the Finn had a new work in the pipeline that he might offer for performance – a none too subtle appeal for the premiere of the Eighth Symphony. Alas, said Sibelius, he had nothing yet, but he promised to keep Koussevitzky informed, flattered to be asked by such a distinguished conductor of such an illustrious orchestra. It was a start of a frustrating back and forth that would irritate both men for years.

In early 1929, some delightful chamber works were written, and listening to these compositions – the Five Esquisses for solo piano, op.114, and two works for violin and piano, opp.115 and 116 – we sense that Sibelius was moving into a new sound world, away from the thematic assimilations of *Tapiola* and the Seventh and into something altogether sharper, more piquant, with more impudent and fearless harmonies. Hearing these abstract pieces – their naturalistic titles are often rather redundant – is perhaps as near as we can get to actually eavesdropping on the Eighth Symphony. It is only the potential sound, not the structure, but it is a tantalizing hint, the flashed menu card of a delectable final feast.

To some extent, of course, Sibelius worked on opp.114–16, and the other music he composed at this time, to dodge the pressures of the Eighth – though there is no reason why he should not have been permitted this easier work, just because the world was impatient for another symphony. And, as we have said, if he was on or over the threshold of a new stylistic period, he would need to try out these advances on smaller pieces.

By the dawn of 1930, it had been nearly six years since a last Sibelius symphony. Voices in Finland and from America were starting to appeal in more direct terms for the Eighth. Sibelius's fame in his own lifetime was reaching its zenith. In the second half of May, his old colleague and champion Robert Kajanus made the first recordings of the first two symphonies, at Central Hall Westminster, with the Royal Philharmonic Society – recordings available today and a hint, but naturally only a hint, at what Sibelius himself might have sounded like performing his own symphonies.[183]

Hard, glacial, work on the Eighth continued, and 1930 produced only one completed work – a strophic song, 'Karelia's Fate' – written in the summer for a political rally aimed at showing support for an anti-Communist faction. On 7 March the following year, 1931, the painter Akseli Gallen-Kallela – creator of one of the most infamous images of Sibelius from

---

[183] Available in an excellent seven-CD set from Warner Classics: *Jean Sibelius: Historical Recordings and Rarities, 1928–1945*.

his youth, *Symposium* – died, and Sibelius was invited to write music for the funeral. He prevaricated endlessly but eventually composed *Surusoitto* (*Funeral Music*) for organ, op.111b, and even attended the funeral himself, something he did only on extraordinary occasions (he would have avoided his own, had he had a say).

Surusoitto might have disappeared into Sibelius's vast catalogue as a slight occasional piece were it not for the loss of the Eighth Symphony. The organ piece is around seven minutes long and seems to have been written in only a few days – perfectly possible, but a speed which many, not least Aino Sibelius herself, have suggested might mean Sibelius borrowed discarded ideas from his Eighth in order to fulfil the funeral commission for his friend Gallen-Kallela. Certainly much of the material for *Surusoitto* was not new – it appears in earlier manuscripts – but if he was taking up rejected material from the Eighth, does this indicate he was either already at such an advanced stage with the symphony that he could comfortably use cast-offs, or that, at the other extreme, he was so disillusioned with it that he cared not where the rejects went?

The latter seems unlikely, not least because it would be well over a decade before Sibelius decided once and for all that the Eighth would not exist. As with opp.114–16, however, listening to *Surusoitto* – which is an enthralling, often alarming piece for organ – we are left wondering, speculating against hope and imagining against sense at what the Eighth might have sounded like, how it might have fitted together, how it might have extended the Sibelian symphony further.

A few weeks after Gallen-Kallela's funeral, Sibelius set off – astonishingly, for he was an inveterate traveller and to live for a further quarter century – on his final trip abroad. With the kind of neat symmetry only real life can throw up, his last destination was the same as his first, way back when he was a student in 1889: Berlin. Again time was spent with friends and working on the Eighth, but on this occasion he fell ill and had to return home after a nasty series of experimental medicines.

At Ainola, towards the end of the summer of 1931, there was a charming sixtieth birthday present for Aino – the piano duet *Rakkaalle Ainolle (For My Dear Aino)*, JS 161 – while there was also the resumption of Sibelius's correspondence with Koussevitzky, which led the composer to rather rashly offer his conductor colleague the premiere of the Eighth the following spring in Boston: doubtless a sincerely made promise, but one the Finn could hardly swear to.[184] Indeed by early 1932 he wired Koussevitzky to postpone until October. It was frustrating for Boston, but an indication, surely, that the Eighth was nearing some sort of completion – Sibelius was infuriating, but he wasn't mad. In mid-July he wrote again to Koussevitzky warning him not to programme the work just yet (the Russian was planning a complete cycle of Sibelius symphonies for the 1932/3 season), as it had experienced several disruptions.

October came and went. December was the new promise. Christmas came, as did the New Year 1933. Still no Eighth Symphony materialized. A brief telegram in mid-January apologized that the work would not be appearing in Boston this season. A diary entry on 4 May ('It is as if I have come home!') indicates Sibelius was hard (and happy) at work on the first movement (which calls into severe question the veracity of his comment to Olin Downes in September 1927 that the first two movements were complete, though of course the statements do

---

[184] Around this time Basil Cameron had been similarly promised the London premiere, and Georg Schnéevoigt the Helsinki one.

not directly contradict one another). Over the summer, Sibelius told the journalist Bob Davis that the Eighth was approaching completion, but that it would be his last: 'Eight symphonies and a hundred songs – it has to be enough!' he exclaimed, with some justification.

At any rate the first movement was now ready enough to be dispatched to a copyist – Paul Voigt – who invoiced Sibelius on 4 September for twenty-three pages' labour on the symphony. Sibelius thanked him and made three crucial points for our detective work: first, that there should be a fermata (a pause) at the end of the movement and, second, this would then lead directly into a largo. Third, that the whole work was to be around eight times the amount Voigt had so far undertaken, so around 180 pages, perhaps as long as the Second Symphony. But this is the last point at which we hear any significant news about the Eighth or can trace with any conviction its shape and scope. From now on, it is mainly speculation and guesswork, with the trail essentially going cold. So what are we to make of his statements to Koussevitzky – and others – about the near complete status of the symphony?

It seems highly unlikely he was lying or in any way intentionally attempting to conceal the truth. The complex reality was that his own intense self-criticism, which we have seen again and again in this book, finally killed off a major work – just as it might have done with many an important piece, not least the Fifth Symphony. The fact that the symphony was at an apparently advanced stage is not that relevant: if it did not meet the exacting standards Sibelius demanded, it did not matter how much work had been spent on it, how close it was to achieving its goal. We – or Koussevitzky, come to that – might not have minded: a second-rate Sibelius symphony, after all, is a lot better than most other symphonies. But, quite rightly, it mattered to Sibelius.

Over the coming years, Sibelius would tinker with what he had, but he also knew it was not what he wanted. He had found no way to go beyond either the Seventh or *Tapiola* to his own satisfaction.

As the father of five girls now producing their own increasingly sizeable broods, there were a lot of Sibelian grandchildren – and soon even great-grandchildren – to occupy Sibelius's time now that he had essentially put the Eighth to bed (if not yet the bonfire). Beyond the growing family, a great number of friends, colleagues and other personalities visited Ainola, and Sibelius was a big-hearted, open-handed and convivial host, willing to converse on any subject that was not his music. Journalists were predisposed to persist in this line of questioning but were politely refused any nuggets of gossip or insight – and anyway, Sibelius tended to prefer the social warmth of musicians, writers and the swarm of diplomats and other dignitaries that made a beeline for Ainola in the 1930s and '40s, and welcomed them generously.

Others could not attend for they had departed. His sister, Linda, and brother-in-law, Arvid Järnefelt, died in 1932, Robert Kajanus in 1933 – the latter's death especially perhaps a factor in killing off any lingering hopes for the Eighth Symphony's delivery. Add to this the lack of Sibelius's conducting experience in recent years – the Gothenburg drinking incident in 1923 had seen to that – the illness on his last trip to Berlin, his shaking hands, and a general feeling that he could not create with the same power as before, and the prospect of more orchestral wonders from the Sibelian pen seemed unlikely. He had financial security and a huge family around him. Art could, at last, take second place.

All his girls were now gone: the nursery had been turned into a library. Days were spent reading books and newspapers, walking or attending art exhibitions with his brother-in-law, the painter Eero Järnefelt.[185] Evenings meant listening to a growing record collection on the gramophone or concerts on the radio – especially of his own music, now a fairly frequent occurrence as his international reputation grew and grew.

His seventieth birthday in 1935 was a significant event, not just nationally in Finland but globally: he was by now a worldwide icon, the most popular living composer, especially in Nordic countries, Britain and America (though even the philistines of Nazi Germany grudgingly awarded him the Goethe Medal). A concert of his music was held in Helsinki and broadcast around the world,[186] and was followed by an extravagant banquet held in his honour and attended by presidents past (the present one had a diary clash). As the dishes were cleared away, large speakers were set up in the hall: a live relay from New York allowed the guests to hear Otto Klemperer conduct the Second Symphony as they sipped their brandy and smoked their postprandial cigars. It would be Sibelius's final major public appearance.

In an interview given to mark his milestone birthday, Sibelius mentioned an orchestral work that had been written and then destroyed. Irritating questions persisted about the existence and status of the Eighth – Sibelius's daughter Katarina would later remark how such interrogations pained and exasperated her

---

185 Eero would die in 1937, leaving Sibelius even more alone, truly the death of one of his few close friends.

186 *Finlandia* and the First Symphony, along with excerpts from *The Tempest* and *The Captive Queen*, a patriotic cantata for mixed choir and orchestra, dating from 1906.

father, who wanted this work to be finer than any of his others but simply couldn't achieve what he desired with it. It became a burden, and it would be up to the generations of composers who followed him to find a new path for the symphony in Finland. They did not let him down.

Such was the bulk of Sibelius's correspondence by now that a secretary was needed: they went through several before finally hiring Santeri Levas, who would stay with the composer until his death. Levas's companionship – as well as competence – meant a great deal to Sibelius in his old age, and the secretary's recollections are also a precious resource. Away from work, many photographs from the Ainola garden at this time show Sibelius as a contented family patriarch: relaxing in a hammock and chinwagging with a diminutive grandchild; quizzing his dashing adolescent grandson Erkki during afternoon tea; sitting quietly in the evening sun with Aino.

Nights still sometimes meant a little composition: fiddling with the Eighth, if he could muster the strength, as well as new versions of old works like *Lemminkäinen*. On 1 January 1939 he was persuaded – to everyone's great surprise – to mount the podium one final time. He conducted his *Andante festivo* with the Finnish Radio Symphony Orchestra in a closed session for the New York World's Fair. It is the only recording we have of him conducting his own work, and it is a priceless, intensely moving, musical document.

When war broke out in 1939, Sibelius and Aino had recently moved into a rented modern flat in Helsinki: this was intended to be a new winter residence that would be easier to manage than Ainola, and with the bonus of being closer to their daughters and grandchildren in the city. Downstairs, a singing student was lodging with an elderly widow and would engage in daily vocal exercises that began to try Sibelius's nerves. The widow was a huge devotee of music, not least her new neighbour's, though she was apparently unaware who the couple now living upstairs were. Her expression on the day when Sibelius finally lost patience and went down to knock on her door and politely ask if the student could limit her practicing must have been quite something to behold.

The eruption of another global conflict led to offers of refuge abroad, but Sibelius refused them all, partly because he was stubborn, partly because he liked his home and family, but also because he was not oblivious to his status as a national icon and symbol for his country. The outbreak of the Winter War on 30 November, when the Soviet Union attacked Finland, meant a retreat back to the isolation of Ainola. When the Moscow Peace Treaty was signed the following March, Finland ceded several eastern territories to the Russians and, to protect herself, forged closer ties with Hitler's Germany.

Returning to their Helsinki flat in September 1940, Jean and Aino stayed for nine months until the late spring, taking in Sibelius's seventy-fifth birthday, before being forced back to Ainola in June 1941 with the outbreak of the so-called Continuation War (the Second Soviet-Finnish War). This would last for three miserable years, plunging Sibelius back into many of the privations of the First World War: loss of income and lack of food.

Midway through the war, Sibelius returned to his diary, which he had discontinued eight years earlier. He laments the primitive and vile antisemitism of the Nazis, notes that the Finnish army admitted Jews, and mentions – somewhat wryly – that a German TV crew had visited Ainola and garnered various empty platitudes about the Germans and German-Finnish unity from him. It was an honest mistake, but a mistake nonetheless, and it damaged Sibelius's reputation for a while, presenting him as a Nazi sympathizer when he was nothing of the sort.

In December 1942 the Sibeliuses gave up the Helsinki flat, deciding to stay permanently at Ainola. Two months later Sibelius told his secretary that he had a major work in progress, one that he wished to see completed before he died: it seemed the Eighth was not yet extinguished, and in September of the same year, his diary records that 'the symphony is in my thoughts', though it would soon be laid aside in favour of other work.

On 30 September 1943, Adolf Paul died in Berlin: a dear old friend whom Sibelius always visited when in the German capital. It was a hard blow, but that very evening a broadcast from Stockholm of Ralph Vaughan Williams's Fifth Symphony, only recently premiered in London, sweetened the bitter pill. RVW had dedicated his Fifth to Sibelius – 'without permission' – and the Finn was deeply moved by the performance, noting in his diary the work's 'culture and rich humanity!' He continued: 'I am so grateful. Williams gives me more than can be imagined.' Vaughan Williams would send Sibelius New Year's greetings at the end of 1946, 'from one who admires and loves your music', adding a well-intentioned postscript which can only have irked its recipient: 'Please give us your Eighth Symphony soon!' But it was likely too late anyway: the Eighth probably no longer existed.

Given the almighty suffering and destruction going on around Europe and the world at this time, artistic losses must be judged relatively, but at some point between January 1944 and

August 1945 there took place at Ainola the domestic bonfire which probably consumed the Eighth Symphony, along with several other works. As Aino later recalled, Sibelius gathered a lot of manuscripts in – of all things – a laundry basket, took them to the great green fireplace in the dining room and set about burning them. We don't know exactly which scores were obliterated – Aino herself could not bear to watch the horror of it all – but she noted how much calmer her husband was afterwards. It seems that the burden had been lifted, the immense weight of the Eighth gone. 'It is wonderful to be appreciated in one's own lifetime', he reflected around this time: he knew the value of what he had achieved already.

Minor compositions continued to come – the so-called Silence of Järvenpää was never entirely Trappist – and after the war, a film crew came to visit Ainola for a couple of days, and we can touchingly observe the Sibeliuses about their daily routines. The composer's eightieth birthday on 8 December 1945 was a muted affair: gifts and flowers overflowed around the house, but Sibelius could receive only a few visitors as he was ill in bed.[187] He often hated this time of year: the relentless darkness in the period up to Christmas depressed him, but his mood always improved with the festivities and the promise of more light every day. (In December 1948 Sibelius remarked in a radio interview that one should live in either the forest or a big city, and that at Ainola the silence spoke exquisitely.)

In the summer of 1949, the legendary Armenian Canadian photographer Yousuf Karsh visited Ainola (laden with gifts of cognac and cigars, plus an inscribed manuscript from Ralph Vaughan Williams). After sharing coffee and Finnish cookies,

---

[187] Though he soon improved and was by and large well for the rest of his life, boasting that few men of his age could eat and drink as he did, though cataracts in both eyes impeded his sight.

Karsh created some of the most famous images of Sibelius: in one his eyes are cast down in noble reflection; in the other he looks up in gallant wonder, with just a hint of sadness. The clarity, lighting and atmosphere of both photographs is extraordinary, and they endure as rare and profound visual documents of a great composer: 'The structure of his face,' Karsh later recalled, 'reminded me of carved granite, yet with infinite warmth and humanity.'

The following decade was spent quietly composing small pieces or adjusting others – such as revisions/additions to the *Masonic Ritual Music* – walking, reading, enjoying time with his cherished family. He became a little less vivacious as he approached his nineties, preferring time alone with nature. In the spring of 1957, he made new orchestral arrangements of two songs, including one – 'Kullervo's Lament' – that took him back to the very work that had established his name all the way back in the early 1890s.

The summer was quiet, Sibelius now spending most of his time indoors, realizing that the end could not be far away. 18 September was a cool, overcast, dull day in Järvenpää, but that morning Sibelius saw something spectacular, and for the last time: a flock of cranes flew low over the house. 'There they come! The birds of my youth!' he cried to his daughter Margareta. Watching from Ainola's terrace, he saw one bird break away from the others and circle over the building before joining up with the main group, which then departed together, migrating for the winter to the paradises of the south.

On the following day, Sibelius had a phone call with conductor Martti Similä, during which they discussed the Third Symphony, followed by another call, with conductor Malcolm

Sargent, who was in Helsinki to conduct a broadcast performance of the Fifth Symphony the very next day.

When he woke on Friday, 20 September 1957, Sibelius said he felt a little dizzy, but he was able to sit up in bed and read the morning papers. Later he rose and dressed himself, as normal, and went down to lunch. At the table he collapsed: a cerebral haemorrhage. A doctor arrived within fifteen minutes, and the composer was carried to his bed. During the afternoon his daughters Eva and Katarina joined Aino by his bedside. 'Father, Eva and Kai are here', said Katarina. 'Eva and Kai', he replied. He never spoke again.

He became unconscious at four o'clock and passed away that evening at around nine, just as the performance of his Fifth Symphony was being broadcast live from Helsinki. Aino wondered whether if they turned the volume up it would stir her husband. But he was gone.

Sibelius's death at ninety-one was a huge national, even international, event. Newspapers marked his passing the following day with significant articles discussing his life and impact on music and the country of Finland. On the twenty-ninth a small private ceremony was held at Ainola before the coffin was driven to Helsinki for what was, in effect, a state funeral, worthy of a monarch or president.

At Helsinki Cathedral on 30 September, the service took place. The high altar was ornamented with seven gigantic candles, one for each of his seven symphonies. Sibelius's own music was played: extracts from *The Tempest*, then *The Swan of Tuonela*, the funeral march *In memoriam* and the slow movement of the Fourth Symphony. Aino and the Finnish president, Urho Kekkonen, laid wreaths, and the coffin was taken to the waiting hearse as musicians played the *Marche funèbre* from the *Masonic Ritual Music*. The streets were lined with mourners as the cortège took Sibelius home, one final time, to Ainola, where he was buried in the garden of his beloved house. As his coffin was lowered into the earth, choirs sang his 'Sydämeni laulu' – 'My Heart's Song' – and his wife laid another wreath.

That winter, the white beauty of snow glistening all around, Aino would visit his resting place every day. At night, before she went to sleep, she would turn on the light of her bedroom and illuminate the grave, which was near the house, and say goodnight to her beloved husband, her best friend, her life's companion.[188]

The story of art is littered with loss. Shakespeare's *Cardenio*, likely based on an episode from Cervantes's *Don Quixote*, exists now only as a title. Dozens of Bach's cantatas are probably gone forever. There are the paintings annihilated in the Second World War, including Van Gogh's *Painter on His Way to Work*; Courbet's *Stone Breakers*; the art of Saint Mary's, Lübeck; and at least thirteen canvases by Klimt. Countless novels, poems and plays have been lost over the millennia, from the decaying parchments of the classical world to the inadvertently deleted computer files of our own age. Hundreds of operas with thousands of haunting arias, witty duets and grand finales will never be heard by human

---

[188] Aino herself would live on at the place named in her honour until 8 June 1969, when she died at the age of ninety-seven.

ears again. To this horrific pile of loss, damage and destruction, whether intentional or as part of the grim workings of time and history, we can sorrowfully add Sibelius's Eighth Symphony.

One day, of course, copies of the score might turn up, in whole or in part. But we should be cautious about hoping for such things. We already have the First and Second Symphonies. We have *Kullervo*. We have *Finlandia*. We have the Third Symphony and *Lemminkäinen*. We have *Pohjola* and the Fourth and Fifth. We have *Luonnotar*. We have the Sixth and Seventh, *The Tempest* and *Tapiola*, plus countless other riches from Sibelius's extraordinary musical mind.

We don't need the Eighth Symphony.

APPENDICES

Table of Sibelius's Major Works

Work	Catalogue	Composed	Premiere
Kullervo	op.7	1891–92	Helsinki, 28 Apr 1892
No.1 in E minor	op.39	1898–99; rev. 1900	Helsinki, 26 Apr 1899
No.2 in D major	op.43	1901–2	Helsinki, 8 Mar 1902
No.3 in C major	op.52	1904–7	Helsinki, 25 Sep 1907
No.4 in A minor	op.63	1909–11	Helsinki, 3 Apr 1911
No.5 in E-flat major	op.82	1914–15; rev. 1916–19	Helsinki, 8 Dec 1915
No.6 in D minor	op.104	1914–23	Helsinki, 19 Feb 1923
No.7 in C major	op.105	1914–1924	Stockholm, 24 Mar 1924
No.8	JS 190	1924–*c.* late 1930s–1945	n/a
En Saga	op.9	1890–92; rev. 1902	Helsinki, 16 Feb 1893

Spring Song	op.16	1894; rev. 1895	Vaasa, 21 Jun 1894
The Wood Nymph	op.15	1894–95	Helsinki, 17 Apr 1895
Lemminkäinen	op.22	1893–95; rev. 1897/1900/1939	Helsinki, 13 Apr 1896
Finlandia	op.26	1899–1900	Helsinki, 2 Jul 1900
Pohjola's Daughter	op.49	1903–96	Saint Petersburg, 29 Dec 1906
Nightride & Sunrise	op.55	1908	Saint Petersburg, 23 Jan 1909
The Dryad	op.45/1	1910	Oslo, 8 Oct 1910
The Bard	op.64	1912–13; rev. 1913	Helsinki, 27 Mar 1913
Luonnotar	op.70	1913	Gloucester, 10 Sep 1913
The Oceanides	op.73	1913–14; rev. 1914	Norfolk, CT, 4 Jun 1914
Tapiola	op.112	1926	New York City, 26 Dec 1926
Violin Concerto	op.47	1903–4; rev. 1905	Helsinki, 8 Feb 1904
Voces intimae	op.56	1908–9	Helsinki, 25 Apr 1910
The Tempest	op.109	1925	Copenhagen, 15 Mar 1926

Further Reading: Books on Sibelius

Sibelius, Volume I: 1865–1905
Sibelius, Volume II: 1904–1914
Sibelius, Volume III: 1914–1957
Erik Tawaststjerna

Thankfully reissued in the Faber Finds series, this classic of Sibelius studies – excellently translated by Robert Layton and abridged from five to three volumes – is now available to a much wider audience. The key biography of the composer, full of essential analyses of his works, Tawaststjerna's is a devoted, magisterial and revelatory guide to this all too enigmatic musician.

Granted access to a swathe of papers, letters and diaries unavailable to earlier researchers, along with numerous conversations with Sibelius's widow and other family members, Tawaststjerna can claim a special authority even in his most basic materials, which he uses to cast fresh light on a colourful, extraordinary life. We witness Sibelius's personal struggles – lack of money and too much booze – and the way they disturbed his psyche and pressurized his marriage. We observe his engagement with, and creation of, a national and idiosyncratic Finnish culture, as well as his extensive global activities. We see the creation of towering symphonies and evocative tone poems as well as the corrosive self-critical streak that all too often threatened to destroy them.

This is a composer biography to match Henry-Louis de La Grange's Mahler or Alan Walker's Liszt, and Layton's fine translation offers an understated, erudite but accessible rendition of Tawaststjerna's prose, succeeding in reproducing both the veracity and the style of the original.

Sibelius
Andrew Barnett

A worthwhile, clear and engaging one-volume biography that takes the reader through Sibelius's life, briefly lingering to discuss the music when it arises before swiftly moving on. Full of rich biographical details, myth-slaying and a notable, admirable desire to positively consider much more of the rarer music – especially the songs, piano and chamber works – than is usually the case, this is a welcome book and useful resource.

Jean Sibelius
Tomi Mäkelä

Powerfully locating Sibelius amid the tumult and turmoil of the late nineteenth and early twentieth centuries, Mäkelä studies the Finn's music within its biographical, social and historical contexts and reaps many rewards through doing so. We witness a more troubled and disturbing series of compositions than they are often claimed to be, works that came from personal and political angst and which we should now hear in a much more nuanced, precarious fashion. Although Mäkelä's arguments are often dense, his language obstruse – and the book's structure hardly ideal – this is a volume which repays close attention, for there are revelations on every page.

Jean Sibelius: Life, Music, Silence
Daniel M. Grimley
An excellent recent addition to the Sibelius bibliography from a very experienced Sibelian, Grimley's new book takes us with passion and aplomb through the composer's life with significant extended passages to discuss the works – especially the theatre music. Rightly keen to lay to rest a few falsehoods, Grimley writes with polish and panache, taking us deep into Sibelius's world, not least the complex, burgeoning society around him, with its shifting trends in art and architecture, literature and lifestyles. Concise, fresh, inventive: warmly recommended.

Sibelius: A Composer's Life and the Awakening of Finland
Glenda Dawn Goss
Beautifully written and full of extensive research, this more historically informed approach to Sibelius's life and art allows absorbing new insights to be made as we see the simultaneous birth of a musical genius and the rebirth of a major European nation. An endlessly intriguing book.

Sibelius
Robert Layton
A bit old-fashioned now, and sadly out of print, but nonetheless a charming little guide to the life and music if you can track a copy down.

The Songs of Jean Sibelius: Poetry, Music, Performance
Gustav Djupsjöbacka
A long-overdue landmark issue, the first to discuss all Sibelius's songs within their musical, literary and artistic context, this is a well-organized, audacious book of continual surprises exploring works that deserve to be heard much more frequently.

The Cambridge Companion to Sibelius
ed. Daniel M. Grimley
Something more for music students and scholars rather than the general reader, this is nonetheless a valuable book, with fascinating essays from a range of Sibelius experts covering a variety of material and perspectives.

The Northern Silence: Journeys in Nordic Music and Culture
Andrew Mellor
Exploring how the five Nordic countries went from being relative cultural backwaters to occupying the forefront of international creativity, in music and the other arts, this unusual book converses with a range of people – writers, composers, performers, designers, administrators – and considers the traditions, attitudes, values, identities and aspirations of a diverse and fascinating region. Mellor refuses to shy away from the darker sides of the success (xenophobia, alcoholism, and so on), inviting us to see their role

in the whole. A wry and wonderful achievement: informative, entertaining and full of insight.

Kalevala: The Epic of the Finnish People
ed. Elias Lönnrot
(Penguin Classics, trans. Eino Friberg)
A clear first choice now among translations in English of the great Finnish epic, this is essential reading for a deeper understanding of Sibelius's musical worlds. Friberg's rendition captures the spirit and magic of the original in all its fire and ice, its poetic violence and lyrical grace. A wonderful issue.

The Kalevala
ed. Elias Lönnrot
(Oxford World's Classics, trans. Keith Bosley)
A very readable version, though seeming to lack some of the soul and flavour of the original. It nonetheless has an excellent introduction and is a useful companion for comparison with the Penguin Classics version.

Further Listening 1: Sibelius on Record

The magnificent **BIS Sibelius Edition**, in thirteen thematically ordered boxes, each containing four to six CDs, is strongly recommended. Showcasing the full range of Sibelius's gifts as a composer, it is an absolute treasure trove of hidden gems and buried surprises, with many world-premiere recordings of obscure wonders alongside superlative renditions of the more famous works and an encyclopedic number of alternate/original versions (it even includes a tiny idea for the Fifth Symphony taken from a letter by Sibelius to Axel Carpelan). Naturally the whole set does not come cheap, but among the individual volumes worth considering are the theatre music (No.5), songs (No.7), works for voice and orchestra (No.3) and the two piano sets (Nos.4 and 10). Each box comes with excellent supplementary material in the form of full sung texts/translations and essays by Sibelian Andrew Barnett (largely adapted from his fine biography).

Sibelius's symphonies and tone poems themselves have proved to be exceptionally lucky on record, with dozens of outstanding recordings that can be daunting to navigate as well as fascinating to explore. This brief overview of some of the best and/or most interesting cycles is hardly exhaustive or conclusive – and it is certainly subjective – but hopefully will prove a useful tool for those wishing to expand their stock of Sibelius on the home library shelves.

(The complete cycles discussed below each include the seven canonical symphonies, often the early vocal symphony *Kullervo*, and sometimes several of the tone poems, the violin concerto and miscellaneous other works too. The contents naturally vary with each individual volume, and readers are advised to check the exact track list, as it may not always be clear from these brief reviews.)

Jean Sibelius: Historical Recordings and Rarities 1928–1945
Robert Kajanus, Thomas Beecham, etc.
(Warner Classics, 7 CDs)

A time machine, a wondrous window on the past, this is an extraordinary survey of Sibelius's music from some of his earliest advocates, pioneers in promoting the Finn's new worlds of sound. We have Sibelius's friend Robert Kajanus conducting, among other works, *Tapiola* and symphonies 1, 2, 3 and 5 – in some respects as near as we are likely to get to hearing the composer himself. Whatever allowances need to be made for recordings from nearly a century ago, the experience is a magical one, with Kajanus's great sense of impetus and drive radiating authority and belief in these masterpieces. Things never feel hurried or hasty, though there is occasionally a sense that the players are, understandably, only just getting to grips with how to perform these tricky and elusive new works.

Beecham's recording of the Fourth with the LPO is another highlight, a justly famous musical document made in consultation with the composer (who sanctioned the use of glockenspiel rather than tubular bells in the finale). The performance is truly Romantic, a world away from the harsh austerity and grim foreboding many conductors impose on music that is far more varied and sunlit than we often imagine.

A generous and essential box set.

Osmo Vänskä / Lahti Symphony Orchestra
(BIS Records, 4 CDs)

One of the great cycles and an authoritative set, part of a wave of smaller regional orchestras bringing their formidable talents and considerable local insight to Sibelius's work. These are musicians living and breathing the sounds and atmospheres generated by the composer, but they also bring exulted, exemplary ability, all shaped by Vänskä's vision.

The Second has innumerable competitors, but here the recording shimmers with authority and eloquence, as does the Third, even if both are sometimes a little self-conscious. The First and Fourth rank as high as any, unfolding with irresistible momentum and control, energy and intelligence working in sublime accord. Vänskä's Lahti Fifth (including both the definitive 1919 and fascinating 1915 versions) has all the grand architecture we expect from this work, while the Sixth and Seventh (coupled with *Tapiola*) are a suitable climax, capturing the character and structure of the works with thrilling persuasiveness. Vänskä's Lahti *Kullervo* is also available separately and is an electrifying, intense and wonderfully atmospheric reading, perhaps surpassed only by Thomas Dausgaard in Glasgow (on Hyperion).

No one cycle can unlock and explore all the alchemy and equivocality in Sibelius, but if forced to pick one set, it might have to be Vänskä at home in Finland. He has an uncanny fidelity to the scores which is never fussy but only revelatory, consistently allowing the music to speak for itself, permitting the arguments to run their course. Challenging, rewarding, deeply spiritual but never too ponderous, Vänskä does what Sibelius asks for, granting the enigmas their mystery and the revelations their magic.

Osmo Vänskä / Minnesota Orchestra
(BIS Records, 4 CDs)

As with Davis and Berglund (see below), we are lucky to have more than one Vänskä cycle, this time in the American Midwest with the brilliant abilities of the Minnesota Orchestra and a superior recorded sound which allows some ravishing details to come through along with the intensity. The tempos are superb, the transitions smooth and well-considered – Vänskä remains wonderfully faithful to Sibelius's complex, subtle demands – while the textures and orchestral colours convey that marvellous Sibelian paradox: sober and severe but opulent and multifaceted too. Included in the set is Vänskä's American *Kullervo* (with a Finnish chorus), and it is just as compelling as his Lahti one, passionate and exhilarating. A splendid cycle – dedicated, majestic, transcendent – and a worthy successor to Vänskä's work in Finland. Not to be overlooked.

Anthony Collins / London Symphony Orchestra
(Beulah, 4 CDs)

The earliest full cycle of Sibelius symphonies undertaken. It can be hard – from our perspective of abundant cycles available at the click of a button – to recognize just how important this series was. In the 1950s, when it was made, Sibelius's achievements were becoming lost amid the riot of anti-melodic modernism and pale neoclassicism, making this an audacious, even foolhardy, project, but one which paid off and with results discernible today. Collins is able to explore the mixture of tension and entertainment Sibelius exudes, showing both the pressures and the respites of his symphonic range. Like his contemporaneous mountaineers tackling the tricky slopes of the Himalayas, Collins brings drama, anxiety, ecstasy and relief – plus rough magic and sweet civility. These are distinguished recordings all serious Sibelius collections require.

Colin Davis / Boston Symphony Orchestra
(Decca, 5 CDs)

No single Davis cycle can claim supremacy, though most listeners will have their favourite: each of the three sets has something to say and often says it very well. The first of them, understandably, has a brisker, fiercer and more youthful feel, a profusion of dynamic muscle and clout. For all the Bostonian swagger, however, tempos are immaculate, shaping the overall architecture with lithe power, naturalness and well-argued charm. The Fifth and Seventh are particular highlights, since their inherent divine grandeur is never allowed to wallow, flounder or sag. A brilliant cycle.

Colin Davis / London Symphony Orchestra
(RCA, 5 CDs)

Oddly derided in some quarters, Sir Colin's first LSO cycle is marked by the distinction of the London players and a fine recorded sound. *En Saga* and the Third are especially magnificent, full of authority and discreet sorcery; the Fifth is a dazzling marvel, while the Sixth slightly improves on Davis's excellent Boston version, the London strings fabulously sonorous. The RCA LSO *Kullervo* ponders a bit too much, however, and is a little lacklustre, even dreary.

Colin Davis / London Symphony Orchestra
(LSO Live, 4 CDs)

For many this cycle captures the right balance of weight and exhilaration Sibelius needs, mixing the thrill of live performance with the thoughtfulness this conductor brought to his earlier London cycle. The new Davis *Kullervo* is light years from the leaden RCA recording, an outstanding reading of great excitement, atmosphere and insight, perhaps matched only by Vänskä/Lahti and Dausgaard/BBCSSO. We feel every sinew of exertion and pain. The canonical symphonies are no less stimulating, with a superb clarity and precision. The Seventh crowns the cycle impressively – melancholic but full of flux and triumph.

Sakari Oramo / City of Birmingham Symphony Orchestra
(Erato, 4 CDs)

Oramo's Sibelius is impulsive but not reckless, spontaneous but not unstructured, and often blazing with concentration. The

Oramo fires, for all their intensity and passion, never smoulder to a cinder, however, always warming and illuminating. Works like the Third and Sixth, which can sound pallid in the wrong hands, are here presented in their full radiant colours. The Fourth stands perhaps peerless among its many competitors: exquisite, stark, consorting conviviality with contemplation. The Seventh is wondrously determined and single-minded, refusing to go gently into the good night, but burning and raving at close of day. Among the tone poems, Oramo's *Tapiola* is supercharged, the woods apparently ablaze with terror, mischief and wonder. Throughout the discs, Erato's recorded sound is absolutely exemplary. An unmissable set.

John Barbirolli / Hallé Orchestra
(Warner Classics, 6 CDs)

Spacious, appealing, full of eloquence, ardour and a lovely warm-heartedness – though with an exquisite chill in the Fourth. The Second and Fifth are great highlights, noble and inevitable, though the Sixth is enchanting too, radiating beauty and elegiac splendour.

Paavo Berglund / Bournemouth Symphony Orchestra
(Warner Classics, 4 CDs)

Of Berglund's three complete cycles, his Bournemouth set is perhaps the most absorbing: the interpretation is weighty and broad, dark and foreboding, full of menace and mystery. Yet despite the slow speeds, there remains a wonderful spontaneity to the playing and some gorgeous textures. Berglund's Bournemouth *Kullervo* was the work's premiere recording, and it has lost none of its magic: a rugged, intense reading that put this astounding choral symphony on the map.

Paavo Berglund / Helsinki Philharmonic Orchestra
(Warner Classics, 5 CDs)

A swifter conception than on the English south coast, Berglund here is a little cool, more impassive and detached – which can on occasion reap benefits, of course. His First, by avoiding overt Romantic thrust and Russian allure, sounds more shrewd, more subtle, more quietly convincing.

Paavo Berglund / Chamber Orchestra of Europe
(Finlandia Records, 4 CDs)

The smaller ensemble size of the Chamber Orchestra of Europe makes for a fascinating, even groundbreaking, reading of exceptional clarity – though the performances don't persuade as powerfully as in Bournemouth or Helsinki.

Herbert von Karajan / Berliner Philharmoniker
(Deutsche Grammophon, 2 CDs)

Containing *Tapiola*, *The Swan of Tuonela* and symphonies 4–7, this is a truncated but absolutely essential Sibelius set from Karajan and the Berliners. All the performances are excellent, but it is the Fourth that lingers longest: one of the most searching and profound recordings of the work that lies at the literal and spiritual centre of Sibelius's art.

Alexander Gibson / Royal Scottish National Orchestra
(Chandos, 3 CDs)

Consistently pleasant, very often impressive, and a great favourite among compulsive Sibelians, for me Gibson is nonetheless more rational and reasonable than compelling or captivating.

Leif Segerstam / Helsinki Philharmonic Orchestra
(Ondine, 4 CDs)

An infamous set that charms and infuriates in equal measure. Romantic and full of a raw energy that sometimes reveals and sometimes distorts, these are recordings that are not to be missed even if they are only brought out for special occasions (1 April; Hallowe'en; Walpurgis Night?). Segerstam's is a brilliant and truly thought-provoking cycle that will make you reconsider many aspects of these often very familiar works. Indispensable.

Vladimir Ashkenazy / Philharmonia Orchestra
(Decca, 4 CDs)

Unswervingly enjoyable, the great pianist-conductor spotlights Sibelius's colour, theatre and exuberance more than his Nordic clarity and logic. A cycle that blazes and rages.

Simon Rattle / City of Birmingham Symphony Orchestra
(Warner Classics, 4 CDs)

You can feel the Nordic crispness in the Midlands air. The cycle is a bit slow to get off the ground – 1 and 2 are a little hesitant – but 4 and 6 are especially mesmerizing, the former a terrifying, brooding, boundless landscape of menacing intensity and ominous presentiment.

Simon Rattle / Berliner Philharmoniker
(Berliner Philharmoniker Recordings, 5 CDs)

After the freshness of Birmingham comes a disappointing, deliberate and often dull revisit in Berlin, the players seeming obstinate in the face of Rattle's demands. The playing, as you might expect, is superb – technically – but it wants for charm, for spontaneity, and it sounds curiously apathetic, sonorous opulence smothering tension and impulsiveness. It's odd because Rattle's accounts of the same works with the same band in London's Barbican around the same time were magical, full of a depth and impetuous authority rarely apparent here. A dreadful shame.

Jukka-Pekka Saraste / Finnish Radio Symphony Orchestra
(RCA, 8 CDs)

One of the pioneers of the wonderful wave of Nordic conductors, Saraste's cycle (in a very generous box) is still compelling decades after it came out, with a great sense of narrative and detail.

Klaus Mäkelä / Oslo Philharmonic
(Decca, 4 CDs)

There is a wonderful warmth and ambience to these recordings, and the playing is consistently gorgeous. The articulation and sense of rhythm can be excellent, though probably too often Mäkelä fails to make the works hold together organically, allowing them to slip into slightly dizzy episodic affairs without their natural evolution, lacking the necessary developing energy. (A 2024 recording of the violin concerto, again with the Oslo Philharmonic and with the carefree, exquisitely expansive Janine Jansen as soloist, is much more successful – and, indeed, will surely take its place as one of the great recordings of this work. Full of colour, vigour, personality and real expressive depth, its architecture and pacing carry immense conviction across the whole span. Not to be missed.)

Maurice Abravanel / Utah Symphony
(Musical Concepts, 3 CDs)

Like Abravanel's Mahler cycle (with the same forces), his Sibelius set is hardly known at all. A great shame, because this is a discreet gem: there is a natural elegance and effortless charm to these records that will merit repeated explorations after more famous accounts have lost their shine. Take the diversion – and revel in the translucent singing, the sophisticated interiority, the unified allure of Abravanel's very fine Sibelian vision.

Neeme Järvi / Gothenburg Symphony Orchestra
(Deutsche Grammophon, 7 CDs)

Another cycle that is beautifully performed but wants for spontaneity, verve and the kind of dynamism these works surely demand.

Okko Kamu / Lahti Symphony Orchestra
(BIS Records, 3 CDs)

In a more forensically analytical, even mechanical, approach than Vänskä with the same band, the lean, rather stoic Kamu speaks plainly, overtly, often removing the sense of mystery inherent to this music. The engineered sound is faultless, but only 3 and 6 convince.

Lorin Maazel / Vienna Philharmonic Orchestra
(Decca, 3 CDs)

Though they are often criticized for attempting to awkwardly fit Sibelius into the grand Austro-German symphonic tradition, there is no denying the power and majestic beauty of these recordings: the brass are magnificent throughout, the strings as silky as we expect from the Vienna Phil. Perhaps lacking a more authentic, energetic sound that we have come to expect these days, these discs are nonetheless worth exploring for their richness, their dignity, their nobility.

Herbert Blomstedt / San Francisco Symphony
(Decca, 4 CDs)

A fine and confident cycle, navigating these works with power and imagination, the transitions evolving with seamless elegance and lovely balance. A worthy companion set to Blomstedt's excellent Nielsen series.

Paavo Järvi / Orchestre de Paris
(RCA, 3 CDs)

A welcome foray into Sibelius from a French ensemble, these recordings are sadly a little unpersuasive, too often sounding conventional and pedestrian – though it has to be said the

Sixth has a lovely intimacy and discreet potency and is one of the finest recent accounts.

John Storgårds / BBC Philharmonic
(Chandos, 3 CDs)

The playing is impressive, and these are thrilling recordings to listen to. There is a danger that the overall approach seems a little rushed, diminishing the careful logic of Sibelius's craft, but there is no denying the excitement Storgårds and the BBC Phil bring.

Petri Sakari / Iceland Symphony Orchestra
(Naxos, 4 CDs)

Especially fine in the later symphonies, from the Fourth on, this cycle should not be overlooked. It has great bark and sparkle, even if the Icelandic orchestra is not as honed or virtuosic as we might want. That said, the occasional roughness adds to the charm – if you see these discs for a bargain in your local charity shop, snap them up without hesitation.

Additional Recommendations

Kullervo
Thomas Dausgaard / BBC Scottish Symphony Orchestra
(Hyperion)

Second Symphony
John Barbirolli / Royal Philharmonic Orchestra
(Testament)

Seventh Symphony – *Tapiola – Oceanides – Pelléas*
Thomas Beecham / Royal Philharmonic Orchestra
(Warner Classics)

The Tempest (Complete)
Osmo Vänskä / Lahti Symphony Orchestra
(BIS)

Incidental Music
Leif Segerstam / Turku Philharmonic Orchestra
(Naxos, 6 CDs)

Violin Concerto
Walter Susskind / Philharmonia Orchestra / Ginette Neveu
(Warner Classics)

Tapiola – En Saga – 8 Songs
Hannu Lintu / Finnish Radio Symphony Orchestra / Anne Sofie von Otter
(Ondine)

Luonnotar – Tapiola – Spring Song – Rakastava
Edward Gardner / Bergen Philharmonic Orchestra / Lise Davidsen
(Chandos)

String Quartet in D minor, *Voces intimae*
Ehnes Quartet
(Onyx)

Sibelius: Songs, Melodies, Lieder
Vladimir Ashkenazy / Tom Krause, Irwin Gage, Elisabeth Söderström
(Decca, 4 CDs)

Further Listening 2: Beyond Sibelius

Sibelius's influence on subsequent generations of composers in Finland has been profound, though his impact has also been felt across the general Scandinavian/Nordic region, as well as in the wider musical world. What follows is a brief consideration of some of the music (especially symphonic music) which followed from Finland and its neighbours in the twentieth and twenty-first centuries – some of which is unambiguously the natural heir to Sibelius, while others represent a reaction against him. It can, of course, only be a limited and personal survey – just twenty composers – but hopefully it will provide a number of useful starting points in addition to prompting further explorations of a region alive to artistic innovation. (All composers Finnish unless stated.)

1. Erkki Melartin (1875–1937)

Melartin is a significant figure – with Sibelius – in the late Romantic and early Modern music movement in Finland, but his six completed (and three unfinished) symphonies have only been patchily performed and recorded. More successful have been his Wagnerian opera *Aino* (1912), based on the *Kalevala*; his impressionistic tone poem *Traumgesicht* (1910); and the magnificent symphonic song *Marjatta* (1914), a work which invites close comparisons with Sibelius's contemporaneous *Luonnotar*. *Traumgesicht* and *Marjatta* have been recently recorded on an excellent CD by Hannu Lintu and soprano Soile Isokoski.

2. Leevi Madetoja (1887–1947)

Leevi Madetoja is, with Toivo Kuula, one of the most significant of Sibelius's pupils, and his three completed symphonies are late Romantic, folk-infused wonders. The First (in F major, 1916) shuns the overblown histrionics of so many first symphonies, opting instead for a work of dreamy, quixotic concision and passionate maturity worthy of his teacher, delighting in vibrant seductive colours and an exquisitely organic organization. The Second (in E-flat major, 1918) bears the scars of the personal and universal tragedy of war and is an intense, extended exploration of conflict, despair and resignation. The Third (in A major, 1926) is a more lyrical and optimistic work, Madejota's *Pastoral* Symphony, and one of the finest post-Sibelian symphonies to emerge from Finland. Several recordings of the Madetoja symphonies now exist, with those from John Storgårds and the Helsinki Philharmonic on Ondine being especially receptive.

Madetoja's two operas are also worth considering: *The Ostrobothnians* (1924) is alternately comic and tragic, a brilliant folk opera that can claim to be the national musical stage work of Finland, while *Juha* (1935) is more theatrically suggestive of Janáček, featuring a rural love triangle and dramatic aquatic demise.

3. Rued Langgaard (Danish, 1893–1952)

A moody and unconventional prodigy, Rued Langgaard was a troubled, poetic soul creating wonderfully strange and powerful works, including his inexplicable but enthralling 'church opera' *Antikrist*. Langgaard was a giant of twentieth-century Danish music, and his symphonies and string quartets are some of the finest ever created for those genres, repaying endless engagement and repeated listening.

Of the sixteen symphonies, the First (1913), written when Langgaard was still a teenager, is the best known – and justly so, for it is a solar-alpine phenomenon. A vast pictorial work taking in the grand visions of Wagner, Bruckner and Strauss, it is full of sumptuous melodies, opulent orchestration and rich harmonic textures, and depicts a journey ascending a mountain, with all its trails, trials and magnificent summit views. An excellent recent recording from Sakari Oramo and the Berlin Philharmonic does great justice to this fanciful but always intriguing work, refusing to let its many passions and pleasures run amok.

The string quartets offer even greater peculiarity, but it is a maverick weirdness always underpinned by a thorough understanding of musical structure and organization. This extraordinary music shifts from poised classical restraint to wild abandon in the blink of an eye, lavish and lush in its emotional vortexes, always experimenting, always testing our patience but expanding our imaginations too. The marvellous Nightingale String Quartet have recorded all Langgaard's works for quartet on the Dacapo label.

4. Uuno Klami (1900–1961)

Like his compatriot Sibelius, Klami turned to the *Kalevala* for many of his works, though he was also influenced by a number of Spanish and French composers, including Ravel, while Stravinsky also impacted him: *The Rite of Spring* (1913) can be detected in the *Kalevala* Suite (1933; revised 1943). His lyrical, optimistic First Symphony (1938) is intimate in scope and mood, reminiscent of Melartin's early symphonies and Madetoja's Third, as well as some of Sibelius's theatre music or even the cheerier passages of Prokofiev's *Romeo and Juliet*. The Second (1945) is much grander and more hard-nosed, a startling work reflecting the privations and suffering of wartime Finland (a conflict which Klami served in), though with atmospheric echoes of the French impressionists, as well as Tchaikovsky and even Bax.

5. Helvi Leiviskä (1902–1982)

Leiviskä was a student under both Melartin and Madetoja, as well as a distinguished concert pianist, and worked mostly as a librarian at the Sibelius Academy. None of her works were published in her lifetime, though her wonderful music is gradually beginning to emerge from its long sleep. The First Symphony (1947), the premiere of which Leiviskä paid for out of her own pocket, is a striking work of organic integration and appeal, enigmatically fusing a range of musical styles – impressionism, expressionism, symbolism and romanticism. The Second (1954) is more austere and tragic, with some startling dissonance helping create a magnificently melancholic air. The Third (1971) explores the dialogue between romanticism and neoclassicism, with deliciously playful woodwind, exquisite muted brass and gorgeous sweeping melodies that cry out to be heard by more ears.

6. Vagn Holmboe (Danish, 1909–1996)

A Danish prince of uncompromising classicism who wrote numerous concertos for almost all the instruments of the orchestra, plus thirteen symphonies and twenty-one string quartets (the last of which was completed by his compatriot Per Nørgård), Vagn Holmboe was a giant of twentieth-century music, creating dynamic, living worlds of logic and clarity that engage – like Béla Bartók – with both landscape and folk music. Of his symphonies, the Eighth (1952), subtitled *Sinfonia boreale*, is perhaps the key work, a stunning essay in sound that is both a confrontation and a comfort, both abstracting and embodying the idea of the north, linking humanity and nature through their mutual creative processes.

The contemporaneous Fourth String Quartet (1954) is one of Holmboe's finest for the medium: most of his quartets take Haydn's as a conscious model, but the form is fitted here with queer Mendelssohnian departures and some devastating fugal writing. The Tenth Quartet (1969) is a probing, tough work, with a heartfelt slow movement and snowstorm finale. The quartets become more complex over time, more concentrated and more personal: No.15 (1978) is acerbic and austere, while No.17 (1983) mixes cries with smiles in a severe arboreal atmosphere.

7. Allan Pettersson (Swedish, 1911–1980)

Sweden's finest composer grew up in poverty with several siblings in a cramp, damp basement apartment under the iron fist of a violent alcoholic blacksmith and wrote seventeen symphonies (though Nos.1 and 17 are incomplete) that reflect this harsh, unforgiving entry into existence. Tending to employ large-scale one-movement works which allow for huge, often very subtle emotional evolutions, Pettersson's music is heavy, intense, full of hurt and anger, anguished voices and spiritual distress, laced with melodies which unravel like unresolved trauma or chorales that shock, destabilize, disturb: background music this is not.

Appreciating the complex interplay between public and private worlds the symphony afforded, for such emotional, intellectual and psychological depth, Pettersson needed the broad, difficult canvas of this medium – a form largely out of fashion by the time he started writing for it (No.1 was begun in 1951, the year the composer turned forty). These post-Sibelian, post-war, post-youth symphonies are restless quests for answers which mirror and explore our own spiritual vacuums and voids, our cruel world with its cancers and criminality, its homelessness, H-bombs and heart attacks.

Yet this is also music which offers quiet support amid the isolation and despair. It is simply too easy, and misleading, to characterize this music as pessimistic or gloomy: for all their captivating expressionism and disturbing bleakness, these works are incredible symphonic constructions, their formidable structures working to generate both the overall emotional depth and their sweeping redemptive power. (Of his seventeen works in the medium, sixteen are purely instrumental. Only the mighty Twelfth, from 1974, has a vocal element: an almost continuous choir sing texts teeming with anguish and brutality, giving this alarming, shattering symphony a quasi-requiem feel.)

Though all Pettersson's symphonies reward close attention – as do other works, such as his vast violin concerto No.2 (1977), the edgy, creative Seven Sonatas for two violins (1951) and the huge song cycle *Barefoot Songs* (1945) – the Seventh (1967), Eighth (1969) and Ninth (1970) form the centre of his considerable symphonic achievement. Threatening, mesmerizing, consoling – and treasured by Petterssonians – No.7 is a mountain range of pain, a Himalaya of destiny and deliverance, using recurrent themes like crampons in the ice to grope a way forward amid searing anguish.

A symphony of great and manipulative contrast, the Seventh opens with a sinister two-note motif – a Scandi-*Jaws* – which generates immense suspense from its strange limping form. All is desolate and foreboding, the outright despair alleviated only by spectral military marches which build in menacing opulence and with some near-atomic orchestral explosions. Pettersson's patience is extraordinary: a stoic allowing his symphony the space to ratchet up its tensions, to release and reconnoitre its considerable expressive depths. Waking from its nightmare, the Seventh enters a period of hazy tranquillity before passages of violence and agitation are intercut with lyrical lament – especially in the great threnody, a three-minute section at the exact centre of the symphony, of chilling emotional power – which eventually give way to a more prolonged peace and grief-laden hope. It is a symphony which, once heard, is not easily forgotten, the screaming, weeping strings and mental anguish of the threnody especially a haunting reminder of just how powerful music can be. A symphonic *Guernica*.

No. 8 is divided into a pair of enormous, closely interrelated movements (the break between them a rare moment of respite in a Pettersson symphony) and is a work of agony and sorrow, though the considerable crisis it probes is able to locate resolution. The extended phrase from the strings which opens the symphony is a classic feature of this composer: though this is music which floats in apparent eternity, the string melody's very limitlessness generates contingent unease. We cannot distinguish its parts, its beginnings and endings. It is a typical, and revealing, Pettersson paradox of anxiety and yearning.

As he worked on No.9, his longest work, Pettersson's health – never good – deteriorated considerably. He somehow completed the symphony just before serious illness confined him to a hospital bed for nearly a year. Wonderfully fusing a range of styles and moods (the opening is disconcertingly quirky), it is a richly ambitious work with a tightening emotional noose that repays repeated listening to probe its almost Beckettian depths and idiosyncrasies.

Symphonies 7–9 form an unholy trinity, three technical and emotional masterpieces that offer immensely rewarding introductions to Allan Pettersson's lonely, remorseless, quietly hopeful – and absolutely extraordinary – symphonic cosmos.

8. Joonas Kokkonen (1921–1996)

Kokkonen's four symphonies were a key conduit to connect Sibelius with contemporary Finnish symphonists, but they reimburse careful attention themselves, as does his wildly successful opera, *The Last Temptations* (1975). The First (1960) and Second (1961) Symphonies combine elements of Sibelian organic structures with the twelve-tone method, resulting in two remarkable works of expressive reticence and restraint, featuring sinewy counterpoint and a forbidding sense of resolution. The Third (1967) is more palpably appealing, with a dazzling emotional ambience that nonetheless retains a (very Sibelian) paradoxical sense of Nordic austerity, while the Fourth (1971) similarly engages our ears with a logical lyricism conveyed in a rainbow of muted monochrome colours. All four feature in spellbinding recordings from Sakari Oramo and the Finnish Radio Symphony Orchestra.

9. Einojuhani Rautavaara (1928–2016)

Eloquent, incisive, Einojuhani Rautavaara wrote several operas, numerous concertos and dozens of other orchestral works, plus copious music for chamber groups and soloists, yet it is probably his eight symphonies that constitute his finest overall achievement. The First (1956) has a Shostakovichian intensity, the Second (1957) echoes of Stravinsky's antagonistic games, and the Third (1961) a Bruckner-like sense of mystery, while the dissonant Fourth (1962) and harmonious Fifth (1985), two decades apart, offer passionate extremes of musical sentiment.

The Sixth (1992), *Vincentiana*, developed themes from Rautavaara's *Vincent* (1990), a heavily symbolic opera written to mark the centenary of Van Gogh's death. Inspired by the paintings themselves, the symphony has movement titles like 'Starry Night' (a delirious nocturnal waltz) or 'The Crows' and is a spectacular interdisciplinary, cross-cultural work featuring electronics alongside and within the orchestral tapestry. (By a strange coincidence, Russian composer Alla Pavlova's own Sixth Symphony, from 2008, was also inspired by and is an exploration of Van Gogh's oil on canvas *Starry Night* of 1889.)

Rautavaara's Seventh (1994), despite its somewhat mawkish celestial subtitle *Angel of Light*, is an intriguing symphony mixing meditation with commotion, serenity with anxiety, ghostly harmonics engaging with monolithic chords. The Eighth (1999) again presents a misleadingly twee subtitle – *The Journey* – for a complex, engrossing work that is by no means sentimental. Rising romantic strings expand in scope and possibility, cultivating colour, vehemence and variety as the symphony travels on its strange voyage towards a victorious, arresting conclusion.

10. Per Nørgård (Danish, 1932–)

Per Nørgård has created an immense, wide-ranging and highly idiosyncratic musical universe in his ten decades on the planet, challenging our notions of classical expectation with – among many other works – eight irresistible, mind-bending symphonies, ten gratifyingly abnormal string quartets, and several demanding operas, especially the mythological masterpieces *Gilgamesh* (1972) and *Siddhartha* (1983). The Third Symphony (1975) is perhaps Nørgård's greatest work of all, a hypnotic sequence of astonishing orchestral colours, with dances and dreams floating, then colliding through the musical landscape. It is a mercurial world: a hallucination, a nightmare, a curious symphonic palace in the sky.

11. Aulis Sallinen (1935–)

Known for his operas *The Horseman* (1974), *The Red Line* (1978), *Kullervo* (1992) and *King Lear* (1999), Aulis Sallinen has also written several concertos and quartets, along with eight symphonies, the first appearing in 1971 and the last in 2001 (all eight are on an excellent five-CD set from CPO, conducted by Ari Rasilainen).

The Fifth (1985), a commission from Mstislav Rostropovich, is a representative work, depicting a forsaken post-Sibelian landscape, with snow flurries and jagged splinters of ice, both of which spin and swirl in the wintry symphonic vortex, a living but severe farewell to the orchestral legacies Sibelius bequeathed upon his fellow Finns.

Symphony No.8, *Autumnal Fragments*, is both an abstract elegy for time's passing and a more concrete requiem for the victims of the September 11 attacks on America, which occurred during the work's composition. As with so much of Sallinen's work, the Eighth is a continuous discourse exploring the dynamic tensions between the natural symphonic desire for organic discipline/unity/continuation and more modernist trends towards fissure and disintegration. Growth and decay (stasis, deterioration and change) dominate both the material and structure of the symphony – it quotes the 'Theme of the Dead' from Sallinen's own opera *Kullervo* – as the music battles the sinister and austere forces of entropy, always seeking to fold and re-enfold itself together into a cohesive unit. (Along with the Rasilainen set mentioned above, the Eighth has received a fine recent recording from Paavo Järvi on a disc entitled *Baltic Portraits*, featuring Sallinen, Salonen, Sumera, Tüür and Pärt.)

12. Paavo Heininen (1938–2022)

Finnish modernist Paavo Heininen's eight symphonies traverse sixty turbulent years – from 1960 to 2021, Kennedy to Covid, *Psycho* to SpaceX – and present a similar span of fracture and rupture, an unyielding, persistent, even obstinate serial cycle that can be hard to love but is impossible to ignore. Disciplined and demanding, his symphonic rigour is often abrasive (in a way Sibelius's own ruthless logic never is), but it also carries a crystalline charm, a sonic purity.

The symphonies, as they progress, often seem to react against one another: the swollen First (1958; rev. 1960) was followed by the slimline Second (1962). The Third (1969; rev. 1977) squeezed its dense material into tight spaces, but such intensity was again upturned by the more straightforward Fourth of 1971. When Heininen returned to the form three decades later, his Fifth (2002) was a hostile and unfriendly retort before another break and the insubordinately playful reply of the Sixth (2015).

Dialogues and responses continued with Heininen's multi-textured Seventh (2020), composed during his last illness. Written for a gigantic orchestra, the work occupies a vast five-movement symphonic arch and devises its own complex internal networks, connections and divergences to complement those wider ones across Heininen's career. (The Eighth Symphony, from 2021, is – at the time of writing – still awaiting its first, posthumous, performance.)

13. Leif Segerstam (1944–)

Blink and Leif Segerstam will have written another symphony or downed another pint. That's the joke, the cliché, the legend. But there is a lot more to this extraordinary composer-conductor than his prodigious output of symphonies (as of 2024, over 350) and ability to consume intoxicants.

Living on a diet mainly consisting of raw fish and grated ginger, the hirsute and inexhaustible Segerstam composes symphonies at an astonishing rate, but there is quality as well as quantity, excellence amid the eccentricity. Most of the 350-plus each occupy a single movement of around twenty minutes – not unlike Sibelius's Seventh, for Segerstam the ultimate gauntlet to be taken up – and are performed by a conductor-less self-governing orchestra. They usually have weird, intriguing titles: *After the Flood* (No.12, 1986), *In a Baggage to Japan* (No.59, 2001), *Some more summery summaries …* (No.131, 2005), *I ate-ate … "188", in RUSKA-clothing for the Autumnal LEAVE …* (No.188, 2007) and *The most famously known car registration number … !* (No.313, 2017). (These are some of the more sensible designations.)

Over a third of the series have never been performed (never mind recorded), but from what we can hear so far, Segerstam's symphonies each create a private cosmos, a unique and subjective universe unto themselves: digressive, anarchic, but improbably coherent. They seem to abide by their own rules and bylaws, mingling chance with precision, allowing musicians autonomy within certain constraints.

Acquire some CDs of Segerstam's work, or better still, search for them on YouTube – the composer himself is keen, impatient even, for a world with free online access to all his music – and prepare to be amused and bemused in equal measure.

14. Kalevi Aho (1949–)

One of the greatest of all symphonists, Kalevi Aho is also a prolific, highly inventive composer of concertos – and for an extraordinary array of instruments: piano (2), violin (2), viola, cello (2), double bass, oboe, recorder, piccolo, flute (2), bassoon (2), clarinet (2), saxophone (2), tuba, trombone, trumpet, horn (2), percussion, timpani, harp, theremin, accordion (2), guitar, and kantele (the traditional Finnish/Karelian zither so beloved by Sibelius). More recently, apparently running out of available single soloist possibilities, he has composed a series of brilliant concertos for combinations of instruments: violin and cello, harp and flute, harp and cor anglais, viola and percussion, two cellos, two bassoons, *four* saxophones …

Opera, chamber music, piano and organ works have also been an important part of Aho's extraordinary output, including five numbered string quartets and multiple quintets which, like his concertos, recruit a range of soloists to take on the fifth part with a quartet, as well as other less orthodox five-part groupings. His exceptional *Chinese Songs* (for soprano and orchestra, 1997) use rich, sensual texts for exquisitely crafted music that grows progressively darker until light and life break out in the final song. It is an enchanting blend of a thoroughly Finnish emotional response to the sounds and sensibilities of more distant lands, evoking, but never merely imitating, the East, preferring inspired orchestral colours to contrived pentatonic clichés.

And yet, for all this copious and varied activity, it is probably in his symphonies that Aho's musical intelligence and imagination are most often on display: he has produced some of the finest works in the genre since Pettersson or Shostakovich (the latest, Aho's Eighteenth, premiered in February 2024). These are strange worlds of sound: moody, acerbic, colourful, dramatic, full of shifting emotional states and a kaleidoscope of styles – but always held together by this composer's stunning musical brain.

Aho's first outright masterpiece is the Fourth (1973), a work of both early summary and pregnant prophecy. The murky Bartókian first movement maintains Aho's feeling for musical shape and form explored in his first three symphonies but now endowed with greater emotional power, spine-chilling fugal writing transmitting infinite dread and despair. Mahlerian passion and ferocity explodes in the second movement with virtuosic orchestral writing before a return to hypnotic isolation in the finale for music that never reaches absolute despair, only a kind of tranquil but detached ambiguity and obscurity.

Elaborating themes from his opera *Insect Life* (1987), the Seventh Symphony (1988) – the *Insect* Symphony – is one of Aho's most moving works, with movements named for various forms of invertebrate existence, including 'The Tramp, the Parasitic Hymenopter and Its Larva', 'The Foxtrot and Tango of the Butterflies', 'The Working Music of the Ants', 'The Dayflies and the Lullaby for the Dead Dayflies'. These movements quiz and question one another, each successive part interrogating its antecedent, with anarchy and disarray sown further as the symphony progresses. Yet it is never complete chaos, for there is a careful plan at work, the oppositions weirdly labouring to support each other, their antagonisms providing a flexible strength, not a fragmentation. In some respects an anti-symphony, Aho's *Insect* is furiously unusual, exploiting a strange subject and a stranger structure to marvellous effect in order to examine the whole notion of what a symphony (or any piece of music, come to that) is. Far more than just an amusing collection of hexapod tone paintings, its complex construction and intricate interactions bestow upon it an intense musical and philosophical depth that far outlasts its colourful set pieces.

Like many of his symphonies, Aho's Thirteenth (2003) is full of concerto-like virtuosity for particular instruments or instrumental groupings – a contemporary Finnish heir to Bartók's great Concerto for Orchestra (1943) – while his Fifteenth (2010) is a self-described 'apotheosis of the dance', developing a range of rhythms and abundant use of exotic percussion, including Egyptian and West African goblet drums, Afro-Cuban bongos and Arabian tambourines.

15. Kaija Saariaho (1952–2023)

Kaija Saariaho was a composer of staggering reach and power, and her scintillating, audacious music often used electronics to fashion new soundscapes, new relationships between music and technology, equipment and emotion – and with some thrilling results. Her *Verblendungen* (1984), for orchestra and tape, and *Lichtbogen* (1986), for ensemble and electronics, were dazzling innovations that explored the textures and gravity of sound, its reflections, refractions and interpolations, manipulating our responses and expectations.

Luminous, dreamy, nightmarish, Saariaho's art refused to fit into convenient categories. A development into opera, however, marked a change in her output, and reception, taking her more mainstream – though naturally with no loss of pioneering flair, adventurous activity and complex, sumptuous sonorities. Modal phrases and emotionally charged repetition continued to develop in her musical language with the astonishing *L'Amour de Loin* (2000), based on the life of a twelfth-century troubadour, the first great opera of the twenty-first century and a shattering exploration of love, art and loneliness.

The ones that followed were no less intriguing, no less imaginative, no less overwhelming: a devastating war opera (*Adriana Mater*, 2005); a monodrama based on an eighteenth-century mathematician (*Émilie*, 2008); a Noh-inspired pair of chamber operas, with a text by Ezra Pound (*Only the Sound Remains*, 2015); and her final stage work, a troubled, exhilarating opera centred around a school shooting (*Innocence*, 2021).

16. Magnus Lindberg (1958–)

With one notable exception, Magnus Lindberg's numerous chamber and orchestral compositions have tended to eschew classical forms, preferring instead looser, more ill-defined arrangements which he fills with energy, colour and intensity. *Feria* (1997) explodes with animated rhythmical ideas, repeating brass fanfares engendering the abstract sense of a vivacious public festival out of which emerge more tangible (and human) sonic images. Similarly, *Fresco* (1997) is alive with colour: textures and motifs shift with dexterous ease and sonic flexibility, bright and blue, soft and loud – orchestral murals.

The classical concerto is one form Lindberg has embraced, though naturally giving the medium his own very modern slant. So far, a clarinet concerto, three piano concertos and two each for violin and cello have been written, of which the most recent – the Third Piano Concerto (2022) – is perhaps the most fascinating. Inspired by and composed for the phenomenal Chinese pianist Yuja Wang, in both architectural and emotional terms, it is one of Lindberg's largest pieces, an agile beast of irony, virtuosity and retrospection, with dazzling orchestral writing and a prodigious piano part.

Glancing back in design to the grand concertos of Chopin, Tchaikovsky and Rachmaninov, but infusing the harmonic and melodic patois with the explosive stresses of Bartók or Prokofiev, Lindberg's Third is a complex, many-headed monster, a fusion of imposing gestures and reprobate spontaneity. By turns savage and tender, this cross-breed concerto is a hybrid creature deliciously, deliriously confused by the wild sound and colour experiments its creator Frankenstein has let loose upon it. This is a new work that pleads for multiple recordings, to tease out and exploit every shade and nuance of its chic colours and ardent energies (though whether anyone else can keep pace with Wang's gifts at the keyboard remains to be seen).

A thrilling and absolutely furious twenty-first-century piano concerto.

17. Lotta Wennäkoski (1970–)

Any composer who has written a concerto for *orchestra and juggler* deserves, to my mind at least, all the attention, respect and record deals they can get. And yet, although this neo-Nabokovian work (*Jong*, 2013) is self-consciously humorous and humorously self-conscious, it also invites deeper questions of form and texture, space and situation – even society and culture at large, breaking down boundaries between entertainment, art and amusement.

Social engagement has long been a vital part of Lotta Wennäkoski's work, music that aims to make more than a mere statement but rather a commitment to dialogue and discussion. Vocal music consequently features significantly in her oeuvre: the song cycle *The Love and Life of a Woman* (2003), which thrusts the traditional Romantic-era lied into modernity; the people trafficking and prostitution monodrama *Lelele* (2010); and the forthcoming opera *Regine*, which will explore the life of philosopher Søren Kierkegaard's fiancée, Regine Olsen.

Wennäkoski is a composer of great originality, connectivity and impact, and her fascinating, often frightening, art employs translucent, gleaming timbres and pensive, dreamy soundscapes that can be suddenly undercut and hijacked by energy or absurdity. She knows that comedy is as deadly serious as tragedy, and just as able to explore the depths and perils of existence.

18. Anna Thorvaldsdottir (Icelandic, 1977–)

As you might expect, the awesome beauty and chastening immensity of Iceland's landscapes inform the vast sound of Anna Thorvaldsdottir's music. Her highly atmospheric orchestral scores moan and groan like shifting glaciers, before erupting like sonic volcanoes: brass lava, percussive tremors, icy string textures. Such metaphors and imagery might seem a wearisome cliché for contemporary (or earlier) Nordic composers, but Thorvaldsdottir is clear that the physical wonders of her homeland inform both the mood and methodology of her music, nature's structures, laws and processes providing both technical and aesthetic impetus when she constructs a work.

Like Sibelius's *Tapiola*, Thorvaldsdottir's compositions are bionetworks, their musical material evolving patiently and unselfconsciously, deepening their textures and complicating their ecosystems, accumulating greater and greater power as well as fragility. Everything is fluid but precise, a carefully controlled arrangement than nevertheless gives the impression of being entirely spontaneous, pure, organic. Her scores can be monoliths or monuments, but within that surface uniformity they exploit and explore every hue of darkness, every shade of colour, every detail of textural possibility.

The extraordinary *Dreaming* (2008) is one such testament: daunting, desolate, threatening, delineated by sinister shifting silences and inconspicuously interwoven orchestral fabrics. Likewise, *Aeriality* (2011) builds its vast textures from obscure single sources, ultimately creating a disturbing musical space that slips effortlessly back and forth between ominous proto-symphony and a sonic installation at MoMA or Tate Modern.

More recent works have continued this creative tension between static shrine and embryonic developing drama, between escalating inertia and instrumental independence. *CATAMORPHOSIS* (2020) is a seven-part single-movement work for large orchestra, exploring the delicate, precarious relationship we have with planet Earth and the urgent impetus we have to metamorphose beyond catastrophe: appropriately, Thorvaldsdottir has described her music as an 'ecosystem of sounds'. Like *CATAMORPHOSIS*, *AIÔN* (2018) and *ARCHORA* (2022) are physical, tactile – and therefore emotional – scores, music which invades your body like an alien life form or the forbidding majesty of sun/sea/sky.

19. Outi Tarkiainen (1985–)

With orchestral titles like *Midnight Sun Variations* (2019), *Songs of the Ice* (2019), *The Ring of Fire and Love* (2020) and *Polar Pearls* (2023), the prize for guessing where Outi Tarkiainen hails from is not a big one. This music lives and breathes Finland. And yet, more than this, like many of her contemporaries Tarkiainen is concerned that her music properly engages with wide audiences while at the same time refusing to remain fixed, recognizing the past but progressing music forward into new and often challenging spheres. Art is a witness, a testimony – and a campaigner.

Born in the Finnish Lapland, Tarkiainen has looked to the surroundings of her upbringing for inspiration without ever letting it define her music or restrict her vision. Local Sámi poets provide the texts for her extraordinary song cycle *The Earth, Spring's Daughter* (2015), a work with echoes of Alban Berg's emotional agony but a poetry and pain all its own. Autonomy and emancipation are features, even persistent themes, of Tarkiainen's work, meditations on childbirth and womanhood explored with uncommon delicacy, perspicacity and insight. Such concerns have culminated in an absorbing opera, *A Room of One's Own* (2022), which dramatizes Virginia Woolf's seminal text and explores why women have remained in men's shadow for too long.

An essay on social injustice might not seem promising material for a musical stage work, but Tarkiainen (and her librettist, the director Francis Hüsers) fashioned a theatrical, passionate, optimistic opera from the range of metaphors, images and individuals Woolf's text discusses – including Shakespeare's sister, Judith. It is centred around three different characters called Mary; each has a distinctive musical profile, though their aural outlines are subtly interlinked, entwined, allowing the score to expose different sides to the same personality as well as suggest the repeated familiarity of women's fate over the centuries.

20. Cecilia Damström (1988–)

Continuing the similar social, political and ecological engagement undertaken by Wagner in *Der Ring des Nibelungen* (1848–1874), Cecilia Damström's music refuses to see art as a separate or special category, aloof and detached from the world in a halo of refined majesty. Instead, it aims to make listeners think, ponder, feel – and ultimately act, in the face of global eco-catastrophe or the numerous interrelated mental health, refugee, economic and environmental crises that plague our planet.

Western materialism is one factor that connects many of the issues, and Damström's recent orchestral work *Wasteland* (2022) explores the needless, mindless squandering of clothes that pervades contemporary culture. Divided into five movements – 'Wear', 'Toss', 'Sort', 'Burn' and 'Flow' – it uses instruments, structures and techniques as potent symbols for debris, abuse and misuse (orchestral glissandos, clinks, clunks, thumps and thuds). Damström's symphony orchestra is full of strong, incensed dynamics, rich, dazzling colours and severe, snappish contrasts: summertime hymns, Bizet's *Carmen*, playfully recognizable *Schlager* music – all are wittily pinched and performed as a means to accentuate the costs of complacency and self-gratification. In *Wasteland*, music draws attention, shames and convicts through a resourceful intelligence which ultimately seeks equality, empathy and compassion as the route to end both suffering and destruction.

This new generation of Finnish music, represented by Damström, is not so far from the fundamental meaning and significance of that of its grandfather figure, Jean Sibelius. Both are music which aims to participate in and cherish our world, to respect it, embrace it, love it, upholding and maintaining earth's diversity and splendour for the future. With creativity and conscious determination, with the added inspiration and coercion of music, humans can repair the damage and forge a finer tomorrow.

But time, like the notes of a score, is running out.

About the Author

Dr David Vernon is a writer and academic. He studied at Trinity College, University of Oxford, before teaching language and literature in China and Japan. After returning to Europe, he completed his doctorate on Shakespeare's tragicomedies in Berlin and taught English literature for many years in London.

He has written extensively on classical music and literature, and his first four books, *Disturbing the Universe: Wagner's Musikdrama*, *Beauty and Sadness: Mahler's 11 Symphonies*, *Ada to Zembla: The Novels of Vladimir Nabokov* and *Beethoven: The String Quartets* were published to critical acclaim. He lives in the Highlands of Scotland.

www.ingramcontent.com/pod-product-compliance
Lightning Source LLC
Chambersburg PA
CBHW030538080526
44585CB00012B/192